For Bill Martinez with
best wishes!

22.4.23

more or fewer members consumed by these powerful prejudices. Most importantly, Zitelmann's book makes it undeniable that irrational hatred and bias against the rich is as real, palpable, and dangerous as racism, religious bigotry, and tribalism. In a world well convinced that religious bigotry, racism, and tribalism exist and deserve repudiation, Zitelmann adds one more nasty '-ism': upward classism, the envy and covetousness directed at the successful and wealthy. Using serious scholarship, he exposes this vice, quantifies it, and makes it impossible for future generations to ignore: *Atlas Shrugged*—with numbers and footnotes."

—Grover Norquist, president, Americans for Tax Reform

"This book is not just another book with a series of ideas, philosophies, and a boring central thesis: it is dynamite! Zitelmann is a bias-breaking machine. He destroys empirically and logically the virtue-signaling arguments that so often attack the rich. Rich people are a minority—a minority that, through risktaking and delayed consumption, allows billions of us to have jobs, to feed our families, and to have more goods and services at our disposal compared to previous generations. Zitelmann does a superb job of revealing the media and public bias against the very people that allowed most of the world to overcome poverty and reach the middle class. An important contribution that sets the record straight!"

—Wolf von Laer, CEO, Students for Liberty

"Rainer Zitelmann's study offers a fascinating insight into a much overlooked yet often criticized minority—rich people. However, this book is more than just a thorough account of the prejudices and stereotypes against affluent individuals in different countries. It also raises the awareness for the general biases of the media against the people who have created value not only for themselves but especially for the society they live in. This makes the book a great read for everyone interested in the intersection of sociology and economics."

—Frank Schäffler, president, Prometheus –
Das Freiheitsinstitut, Berlin

THE RICH IN PUBLIC OPINION

THE
RICH IN
PUBLIC
OPINION

WHAT WE THINK WHEN WE THINK ABOUT WEALTH

RAINER ZITELMANN

The Rich in Public Opinion was originally published in Germany as
DIE GESELLSCHAFT UND IHRE REICHEN: VORURTEILE
ÜBER EINE BENEIDETE MINDERHEIT. © 2017 Rainer Zitelmann.

Translated by Sebastian Taylor, Capital Language Solutions.

Print ISBN: 978-1-948647-67-0
eBook ISBN: 978-1-948647-68-7

Library of Congress Cataloging-in-Publication Data.

Zitelmann, Rainer, author.
  The rich in public opinion : what we think when we think about wealth /
  Rainer Zitelmann.
  Gesellschaft und ihre Reichen. English
    pages   cm
  Includes bibliographical references and index.
  ISBN 9781948647670 (hardback) | ISBN 9781948647687 (ebook)
  1. Rich people—Public opinion. 2. Wealth—Public opinion.
  3. Social classes. 4. Prejudices.
  LCC HT635 .Z5813 2020 (print) | LCC HT635 (ebook)
  305.5/234—dc23   2019051409

Cover design: Lindy Martin, Faceout Studio
Jacket imagery: Shutterstock

Printed in Canada.

CATO INSTITUTE
1000 Massachusetts Avenue NW
Washington, DC 20001
www.cato.org

CONTENTS

PREFACE   ix

PART ONE   1
Prejudice, Classism, and the Rich

CHAPTER 1   3
What Are Prejudices and Stereotypes?

CHAPTER 2   21
What Is Classism?

CHAPTER 3   43
Warmth and Competence: How We Judge Out-Groups

CHAPTER 4   53
Academic Research on Envy

CHAPTER 5   79
Zero-Sum Beliefs: Your Gain Is My Loss

CHAPTER 6   85
The Psychology of Scapegoating

CHAPTER 7   93
Preserving Self-Esteem: Compensation Theory

CHAPTER 8   105
Explaining Success: Individual Ability or External Circumstances?

CHAPTER 9   121
The Rich: An Admired but Mistrusted Minority

PART TWO   147
What the Germans, Americans, French, and British Think of the Rich

CHAPTER 10   149
How Germans View the Rich

CHAPTER 11   191
How Americans View the Rich

CHAPTER 12   215
How the French View the Rich

CHAPTER 13   239
How the British View the Rich

CHAPTER 14   259
Four Nations in Comparison

PART THREE   287
Media Representations of the Rich

CHAPTER 15   289
The Rich in the Media: Executive Pay, Bankers' Bonuses, and the Gap between Rich and Poor

CHAPTER 16   323
"To Hell with the Rich": The Panama and Paradise Papers

CHAPTER 17   345
Online Comments about the Rich

CHAPTER 18   363
The Rich in Hollywood Movies

CONCLUSION   385

ANNEX: THE QUESTIONNAIRE   403

NOTES   411

BIBLIOGRAPHY   439

INDEX   451

ABOUT THE AUTHOR   465

PREFACE

For this book, the polling firms Ipsos MORI and the Allensbach Institute conducted identical surveys in Germany, the United States, France, and Great Britain on attitudes toward the rich. The surveys' first question was used to determine the extent to which society would tolerate critical opinions of various social groups, especially critical opinions related to minorities.

The interviewees were given a list of various minorities: Muslims, immigrants, Jews, blacks, homosexuals, disabled people, people receiving welfare benefits, unemployed people—and people who are rich. Women and Christians were also listed. Which of these groups, the respondents were asked, do you need to be careful not to criticize in public? Respondents in each of the four countries felt that publicly criticizing people who are rich was the least problematic, or nearly so.[1] On the other hand, 67 percent of interviewees in Germany and France, 59 percent in Great Britain, and 56 percent in the United States said that you have to be careful when criticizing Muslims in public.

However, the point here is not about criticism of individuals, but about the extent to which it is socially acceptable to voice sweeping negative statements about certain groups, or even to place them under general suspicion when some of their members violate social norms.

Consider the following example: For years, individuals with Islamic backgrounds have committed terrorist attacks in these and other countries. In the aftermath of such attacks, politicians and journalists regularly and emphatically warn against placing Muslims under a general suspicion, with the media insisting that not every Muslim is a terrorist. The majority of Muslims, the media reiterates, are peaceful, law-abiding citizens.

In contrast, when reporting scandals involving executives who received generous severance packages despite their failures, or bankers who received massive bonuses despite their unchecked risk taking, or some rich people who legally avoided—or illegally evaded—tax payments, the media almost never caution against generalizations or warn that rich people, executives, or bankers should not be placed under general suspicion. On the contrary, such cases are often subject to sweeping generalizations, as the media analysis in Part Three of this book shows.

Even when pronounced hatred of rich people is articulated in public, it rarely has negative consequences for those who express themselves in this way. In Berlin, my hometown, demonstrators were pictured brandishing large placards emblazoned with the words "Kill Your Landlord" on the evening of May 1, 2018. A year later, activists sought to mobilize demonstrators by hanging posters of guillotines all over the city. The image of the guillotine was accompanied by the following text: "Against a City of the Rich." When I saw the posters everywhere, I couldn't help but wonder how people would react if the target of such intense hatred were not the rich or property owners but members of other minorities. The indignation in this case would have been—rightly—great. One of the few counterexamples in which inciting hatred of the rich did actually have negative consequences was the case of Professor Chris Knight, a renowned anthropologist at the University of London. He gave a radio interview in March 2009, in the wake of attacks on the home and car of Sir Fred Goodwin, former director of the Royal Bank of Scotland. One of the groups behind the attack had declared, "We are angry that rich people, like him, are paying themselves a huge amount of money and living in luxury, while ordinary people are made unemployed, destitute and homeless."[2] In the interview, Professor Knight commented on the victim of the attack and a planned demonstration: "We are going to be hanging a lot of people like Fred the Shred

[Sir Fred Goodwin] from lampposts on April Fool's Day and I can only say let's hope they are just effigies." He added: "To be honest, if he winds us up any more I'm afraid there will be real bankers hanging from lampposts. Let's hope that that doesn't actually have to happen." And: "They [bankers] should realise the amount of fury and hatred there is for them and act quickly, because quite honestly if it isn't humour it is going to be anger."[3]

Another newspaper reported, "Knight's garden is awash with homemade props, including bloody effigies of dead bankers to be hung from lampposts when protesters converge on 'the belly of the beast,' the Bank of England, on 1 April."[4] The professor was then suspended. He had crossed a line. Today, however, he is back teaching—at University College London.

The German philosopher Christian Neuhäuser, whose 2018 book *Reichtum als moralisches Problem* (*Wealth as an Ethical Problem*) generated a great deal of attention, including positive reviews in conservative newspapers,[5] may have been less aggressive, but he was still quite radical. According to the philosopher's central thesis, wealth should actually be forbidden. In his words, someone is rich "if they have considerably more money at their disposal than would usually be needed to take care of themselves in an appropriate way and to respect themselves as a person of equal status."[6] Since this formulation is somewhat abstract, Neuhäuser made it clear that he means not only millionaires or billionaires but "really all people who have more than 200 or 300 percent of the average income."[7] In his opinion, everyone who earns so much has far more money than they need for their self-respect.

Neuhäuser says that wealth is morally problematic simply because it potentially gives the rich power over other people. He illustrates this statement with the example of Bill Gates:

> If I bruise the ego of a very wealthy individual, maybe Bill Gates, he can use his money to torment me in the cruelest ways possible without my being able to do anything about it. He can harass me with endless lawsuits. He can simply buy the company I work for and rationalize my job away. He can buy my entire neighborhood and ruin it at will. He can do the same to all the people I love. Whenever I go on holiday somewhere, he can organize a nerve-racking event at exactly that place. There is no limit to the trouble he can cause me.[8]

Of course, Neuhäuser is not actually accusing Bill Gates of doing anything like this, but he is making the point that rich people pose a threat to others simply because of their wealth. After all, they could theoretically use their wealth to do horrible things. If we follow Neuhäuser's logic, wealth is always morally questionable. And it is not only a problem if it can be exploited to hurt the self-respect of other people: "Second, wealth becomes an ethical problem because the excess money could easily be used to help restore the dignity of people who have been deprived of their self-respect, but this does not happen."[9] Neuhäuser adheres to the zero-sum belief that wealth needs to be distributed more equitably so that everyone can be better off. With so much poverty in the world, any wealth would thus appear to be morally problematic, because the rich could give their money to the poor in order to "help them live more dignified lives." If the rich do not do so, then from Neuhäuser's point of view, that equates to a failure to provide help—and it shows that wealth is morally questionable and should therefore be forbidden.

In most cases, feelings of hostility toward the rich are not expressed in such explicitly aggressive language. But prejudices against the rich are widespread in all strata of society, as this book shows.

Today, several thousand academic books and articles have been published on stereotypes and prejudices. The bibliography of just one book, *Psychology of Prejudice and Discrimination*,[10] contains some 2,400 titles of prejudice research. And a bibliography of works on prejudices and cultural and national stereotypes,[11] published back in 1986, contains about 5,500 titles. Most earlier works focused on prejudices directed at minorities, women, and the people of other nations. In recent years, a flurry of studies have also explored prejudices and stereotypes concerning poor people.[12] In contrast, there has only been sporadic research into stereotypes about the rich, for example, in the field of classism, discussed in Chapter 2, or the stereotype content model, discussed in Chapter 3. No comprehensive, scientific study of this topic has yet been published, until now.

This book consists of three parts. Part One presents the methods and findings of research into prejudices and stereotypes and examines how to apply these methods in the present inquiry.

Part Two presents the findings of the abovementioned surveys in Germany, the United States, France, and Great Britain.

Part Three examines the media. Most people do not personally know any millionaires, let alone billionaires, so the media play a particularly important role in forming those people's opinions on them. This section examines the image of the rich in newspapers, magazines, and popular movies.

Readers who are less interested in scientific definitions and research debates will still understand and enjoy the rest of the book, even if they skip Chapter 1.

When I began to delve into the subject, some people questioned whether I was wasting my time. I think the pursuit of knowledge is always worthwhile, especially when it relates to fields that have hardly been researched, and that includes attitudes toward rich people. Skeptics who ask why we should even attempt to understand prejudices against the rich are often expressing the attitude, whether explicitly or implicitly, that even if negative prejudices against the rich do exist, rich people shouldn't be too concerned. After all, the rich are much better off than most other minorities. In a public discussion, a politician from Germany's left-wing party Die Linke told me that, as a rich man, I had made my own bed and should lie in it. Unlike black people, for instance, she pointed out that I had the opportunity to rid myself of the problem by surrendering my wealth. This view seemed to me just as mistaken as to argue that no Muslims need be upset about prejudices, because they could convert to Christianity. As one of the rich, I see the situation differently.

It is most often the case that people who are themselves the target of prejudices are most interested in researching them: Jews have made decisive contributions to research into anti-Semitism, and gender research is dominated by women. In and of itself, that phenomenon is entirely legitimate. But being personally targeted and having a total commitment to one's own cause should not be allowed to influence the scientific standards of objectivity and openness that are so important in academic research. The empirical analyses for this book—surveys, media analyses, and so forth—should speak for themselves.

As a historian and sociologist, I am keenly aware from history that negative prejudices and stereotyping have repeatedly been used to justify the exclusion, expulsion, persecution, and murder of minorities who have been scapegoated at times of social crises. The 20th century is full of examples of rich people, including capitalists, kulaks, and other groups, who were victims of deadly persecution. In Russia's October Revolution, one of the first instructions issued by the head of the Cheka (the Soviet political police) was: "We don't make war against any people in particular. We are exterminating the bourgeoisie as a class. In your investigations don't look for documents and pieces of evidence about what the defendant has done, whether in deed or in speaking or acting against Soviet authority. The first question you should ask him is what class he comes from, what are his roots, his education, his training, and his occupation."[13] At the end of the 1920s, the GPU (the new name for the Cheka) introduced a quota system: each region, each district, had to arrest, deport, or shoot a certain percentage of people from "enemy" social classes. In the 1930s, hundreds of thousands of kulaks were deported or murdered simply because they were wealthy.[14]

Hitler declared in 1933 that if he had turned against communism, "then [it was] not because of the 100,000 bourgeois—it can be of complete indifference whether they go under or not." He admired Stalin for his revolutionary consistency and, according to the reports of a confidant, agreed that "Bolshevism has simply removed these creatures. Because they were worthless for mankind, only burdens for their nation. The bees also sting the drones to death when there is nothing left for them to contribute to the hive. The Bolshevist procedure is therefore something quite natural."[15]

In the 1970s, the Khmer Rouge in Cambodia killed hundreds of thousands of people, perhaps even as many as several million.[16] As a rule in this persecution, "The higher the social class before the revolution, the faster its members were branded as enemies of the revolution."[17] People from higher social strata received such low food rations that many died of malnutrition during the revolution.[18] Those who belonged to the upper economic and educational classes fell victim to the regime at the slightest offense or sign of displeasure at the new order.[19] But persecution—as in the Soviet Union or China—soon spread to numerous other social groups and was by no means limited to the economically better-off. From the outset, however, all of those revolutions aimed to economically or physically destroy the bourgeoisie and anyone deemed rich.

It is only in exceptional situations that prejudice against social groups leads to such dramatic consequences, but even in more moderate forms it also harms society at large, not just the rich. This fact is illustrated by the example of the 2008 financial crisis. When the real, very complex causes of such a dramatic crisis are not properly analyzed, and when politicians and the media resort to pillorying scapegoats (rich people, greedy bankers, and managers), then the real problems will very likely never be solved.[20] Resentment against the rich has often had a negative economic impact in democratic states, as seen in Sweden and Great Britain in the 1970s, where nationalization programs and punitive high-tax policies led to massive declines in prosperity.[21]

However, stereotypes do not always have to be negative, as shown in Chapter 1 of this book. Even people with a positive view of a given social group often base their opinions on stereotypes. For example, many people think that the rich are particularly industrious, which is generally true but is certainly not the decisive factor in becoming rich. Most people, regardless of whether they have positive or negative opinions of the rich, think they know both why people are rich and how the rich live, yet those beliefs are shaped by prejudices and stereotypes. Some are true, but many are not.

The same is true, then, of the rich as of other minorities: negative prejudices and stereotypes are generally more pernicious than positive prejudices and stereotypes. This book aims to examine how we think about a minority that, while undeniably powerful, can still be the subject of negative stereotypes, prejudice, and scapegoating, often with dire effects for us all.

PART ONE

Prejudice, Classism, and the Rich

CHAPTER I

WHAT ARE PREJUDICES AND STEREOTYPES?

One can have prejudices about many things, but today the term is mostly used in connection with opinions about groups of people; it often refers to opinions about minority groups. We rarely use the term when someone has a positive opinion of a group of people. And we also don't use the term colloquially if we share the other person's opinion or regard it as correct. By accusing another person of prejudice, what we really mean to say is, "You have a negative opinion of a group of people, and your opinion is wrong."

This everyday use of the word is problematic; it conveys unspoken assumptions that need to be critically questioned. The first assumption is that a prejudice is an *unfounded and erroneous* opinion. The second assumption is that a prejudice is a *negative opinion.* The third assumption is that if only the person we accuse of prejudice were better informed, that person would have arrived at a different, more positive opinion.

Prejudice, when used this way, is not a scientific term; it is a polemic term. And that is how it is mostly used in everyday language. Researchers who have studied prejudice do not uncritically accept this use of the term. Many researchers deny that a prejudice must necessarily be wrong. Some also deny that it has to be negative. I will come to both points later.

ARE OUR JUDGMENTS REALLY BALANCED AND FACT BASED?

I would like to start with the most complicated question, namely, whether prejudice arises because someone has not dealt intensively, in sufficient detail, with an issue—or with a group of people. The prefix "pre-," coming before the root indicating judgment, suggests that someone has made a judgment before finding out all the facts. *Merriam-Webster's Dictionary* defines "prejudice" as a "preconceived judgment or opinion" and an "adverse opinion or leaning formed without just grounds or before sufficient knowledge."[22]

These definitions leave many questions unanswered, however. Does anyone always use *all* the facts available to them before forming an opinion? Isn't it entirely unrealistic to expect the majority of people to know or consider all the facts about the things they judge and to arrive at their judgments only after a comprehensive investigation? If we take this broader concept of prejudice to its extreme, we would have to accept that all judgments not made by specialists are, by their very nature, prejudices.

An unspoken misconception underpinning many notions of prejudice is that having extensive knowledge of a subject is a cast-iron guarantee against negative prejudices. This is not the case, because value judgments cannot generally be derived from factual findings or considerations. If someone has deep-seated negative feelings toward a group of people, then even developing a deeper factual understanding of that group will not always lead to a more positive attitude. When confronted by information that contradicts their views of an out-group, many people acknowledge the information but interpret it in such a way as to reinforce their prejudice: conflicting data are filed away as the exception that confirms the rule.

Whether people justify their negative attitudes with a barrage of facts and dispassionate language or whether they simply let their negative emotions run their course in the form of derogatory statements has a lot to do with their education and linguistic abilities, but it may have little to do with their degree of prejudice.

There are even researchers who spend their whole lives gathering facts that reinforce their original prejudices about a subject. One can rightly argue that those researchers are not upholding scientific standards at all, because such an approach does not meet the criteria of objectivity that is the hallmark of science properly conducted. Nevertheless, many of these researchers are held in high regard; they may be professors at prestigious universities and may use the methods, arguments, and language of science. They can be criticized for a great deal of things, but they certainly cannot be accused of not having dealt sufficiently with an issue.

The complexity of the matter is illustrated by the fact that the number of definitions of prejudice is almost as great as the number of authors writing about it. Some of those definitions will be presented and discussed below to explain how I use the term in this book.

Gordon Allport's classic treatise *The Nature of Prejudice* contains the shortest definition we will examine: "thinking ill of others without sufficient warrant."[23] Allport also added that this first attempt to define the term was inadequate and proposed the following definition: "an avertive or hostile attitude toward a person who belongs to a group, simply because he belongs to that group, and is therefore presumed to have the objectionable qualities ascribed to the group."[24]

Not every negative generalization is a prejudice in Allport's view, although he considers the term to be justified if a person is not prepared to change his or her judgment in the face of conflicting information. *"Prejudgments become prejudices only if they are not reversible when exposed to new knowledge."*[25]

We have since learned that prejudice is not always irreversible, and that people and even whole societies can change their attitudes toward groups. The latter can sometimes happen within a few decades, as the changing attitudes toward gay and lesbian people in many Western societies show.

The definition Earl E. Davis proposed in 1964 therefore seems somewhat more precise—albeit only with a view to the question of immutability and rigidity. He does not claim that prejudices and stereotypes are irreversible but says that they are difficult to correct, which is more accurate: "[Prejudices] are usually characterized by (a) over-generalization (the traits are attributed to all, or nearly all, members of a race, nation, etc.); (b) over-simplification (one, or at most a few, characteristics are used to

encompass the complexity of a whole race, nation, etc.); and (c) rigidity
(due to selective perception and interpretation, contrary evidence is often
either ignored or seen as confirming the preconceived notion)."[26] However, this definition has other weaknesses, because it generally reduces
prejudices to negative attitudes. That need not be the case.

In early research, prejudices were often regarded as diseases and as
expressions of personality disorders. Thus, prejudices would be excep-
tions rather than the rule. In 1969, Heinz E. Wolf distinguished between
the "exception thesis" and the "equality thesis." According to the equality thesis, the emergence of prejudice is an inevitable process that affects
all human beings. Nobody is therefore free of prejudice; only the inten-
sity and object of the prejudice must be differentiated.[27] The exception
thesis, on the other hand, assumes that prejudice is an individual form
of behavior typical of a specific personality type. The concept of the
"authoritarian personality" developed by Theodor Adorno and others is
a classic example of this line of thought. The problem with this approach
is that those who did not share the researchers' political opinions were
all too quickly dismissed as "prejudiced people with a pathological character structure."[28] These definitions perpetuated the view that prejudice
was inappropriate.

According to sociologist Bernd Estel, an important characteristic of
prejudice in the general consciousness is its "factual inappropriateness, its
falsehood."[29] Prejudice is to be regarded as predominantly false, or at least
as biased or one-sided, if

- the underlying (correct) information basis is too narrow to
  really permit a judgment ("prejudgment"); or
- the person making the judgment bases his judgment
  only on the limited information available to him ("bias,"
  "preconception"); or
- the person refuses to take note of (new) information that
  contradicts his judgment ("rigidity").[30]

These criteria seem questionable. After all, by these standards,
almost all of the judgments we make in everyday situations could be

classified as prejudices. When is the underlying information basis for a judgment too narrow? And what is the benchmark for determining whether a judgment is based on sufficient information? Can it be said that direct, personal exposure to the facts is a sufficient prerequisite, or must that be supplemented by in-depth or even quasi-scientific research? Not everyone is in a position to carry out such research. The claim that most people use only a small selection of the information available to them as a basis for their judgments is also likely to apply to a majority of judgments in the wider sense. And we often take less notice of information that contradicts our judgments; people commonly exhibit selective perception.

In addition, there will not necessarily be a consensus among people with comparable knowledge and information on how to weight and evaluate that information. Otherwise, all equally well-informed persons would share a similar political conviction or ideology, for example. We all know that's not the case, and it seems incorrect to conclude that all disagreements are matters of prejudice. Even after a very extensive and intensive study of a subject, people will arrive at different conclusions. The same conclusion may, from one person's point of view, be a gross prejudice based on a mistaken perception of reality, whereas for the other, it is a factual finding.

Wolf provides the following definition: "*Prejudice* is defined as a *binding statement made on a subject without sufficient, objective knowledge of the empirical factual structure or having taken it into account.* . . . The definition contains one *main* and two *secondary criteria*, the last two being mutually exclusive: a) The *binding nature* of the statement (main criteria), with b) a *lack of sufficient, objective knowledge,* or c) *disregard of this knowledge.* Prejudices are thus defined by criteria a+b or a+c."[31]

The weakness of this definition lies, among other things, in the lack of clarity as to what constitutes the "sufficient, objective knowledge" required to ensure that a judgment is not a prejudice. When is my knowledge sufficient? Many opinions held by people who don't have "sufficient, objective knowledge of the empirical factual structure" are also held by experts who have dealt intensively with the subject. Thus, great expertise does not automatically lead to a correct judgment, and lack of expertise does not necessarily lead to an erroneous judgment.

ARE ALL PREJUDICES WRONG?

Prejudices and stereotypes themselves have been stereotyped by repeatedly ascribing to them characteristics such as "inaccurate," "unjustified," "exaggerated," and "not based on empirical evidence"—without carrying out empirical research on these "characteristics."[32]

Some scientists have tried to find out whether or not a judgment described as a prejudice is factually correct. In one study, they asked subjects to estimate how often black Americans engage in behavior stereotypical of them. For each participant, a "diagnostic ratio" was determined by dividing the estimated prevalence of this behavior among black Americans by the percentage of all Americans who exhibit the same behavior. The result was compared with data from official U.S. population statistics.[33] In another experiment, participants were asked to estimate the grades of Canadian high school students from nine different ethnic groups. The resulting ranking was then compared with the actual ranking. In both cases, the estimates turned out to be relatively accurate.[34]

In his 2012 book *Social Perception and Social Reality*, Lee Jussim lists numerous studies in which scientists have attempted to use statistical comparisons to check whether and to what extent stereotypes are accurate.[35] This approach raises numerous questions, such as when a stereotype applies and when it does not: How different do the presumed and actual findings have to be for a stereotype to be deemed incorrect? Jussim adopts a general guideline and considers a stereotype to be correct if there is a statistical correlation of at least 0.4 between the stereotype and reality.[36]

Other researchers have dismissed all work that focuses on the accuracy of stereotypes, arguing that even where correlations between stereotypes and real-world data have been demonstrated, it is not possible to draw conclusions about individuals from general, stereotyped characteristics. However, this is not a valid objection to such research, as the essence of a stereotype need not necessarily apply to every single person in the group: "It is not possible to evaluate the accuracy of a belief about Asians in general by using as a criterion the characteristics of my friend Hong."[37]

In my opinion, criticism of research into prejudices that uses the kinds of tests described above is both justified and unjustified. The unjustified criticism includes arguments of a pedagogical nature, which claim that, ultimately, research into prejudices can lead to undesirable and even "dangerous" results: "As scientists concerned with improving the social condition, we must be wary of arguments that can be used to justify the use of stereotypes."[38] Knowing what is actually the case is precisely the business of social science, even when what is actually the case proves to be unsettling.

However, legitimate doubts also exist with regard to the procedures for assessing the accuracy of prejudices. In some cases, it will be possible to determine whether or not a stereotype is correct. Yet many prejudices and stereotypes do not relate to verifiable demographic or other characteristics, as in the examples above, but to abstract attributes such as "kind" or "lazy," which are naturally more difficult to verify.[39]

Rupert Brown rightly opposes the assumption, explicitly or implicitly contained in many definitions of prejudice, that a prejudice is false, irrational, or based on an unacceptable generalization. Such definitions are based on the assumption that we can determine whether a judgment is right or wrong. However, this determination is often not possible, because prejudices are frequently formulated in ambiguous or vague ways, which make them difficult to objectively evaluate. If a landlord refuses to rent an apartment to a person of color, claiming that they often "create problems," then this is a statement whose factual content is difficult to verify, Brown argues, in part because of the vague wording the landlord uses.[40]

Many of these statements are indeed difficult to verify, for example whether Italians are better lovers than other people (a positive prejudice) or whether Americans are culturally unsophisticated (a negative prejudice). There are sure to be very different opinions about what makes a good lover and what may be considered culturally unsophisticated. Often no empirical studies will exist to provide reliable indications of the truth of such statements. And even the question of whether a prejudice is positive or negative is not always clear. Some scholars do not regard describing women as "helpful," "warm," or "understanding" as examples of positive prejudice, for example; they detect negative prejudices hidden in such attributions.[41]

What's more, many prejudices contain a kernel of truth, which even people who do not share the prejudice would have to admit. Thus, all those people can object to is the generalized nature of the statement. This point is strongly emphasized by supporters of the "kernel of truth" theory, who believe that the only problem with stereotypes is that they employ overarching generalizations. This theory, in turn, is criticized by "constructivists," who dismiss any discussion of the degree of truth or reality underpinning stereotypes. This dismissal reflects their fundamental view that an objective reality cannot be recognized in any case, and that any statement purporting to describe one is ultimately a social construct.[42] Even if one does not share this constructivist position, it is often difficult, for the reasons described above, to determine whether a prejudice or stereotype is wholly or predominantly false or whether it is based to some extent on reality.

An additional problem arises because everyday language differs from scientific language. When someone says, "Rich people are tax cheats," they probably don't mean "all rich people evade taxes." It would be unfair to try to refute the person who makes such a statement by pointing out that the statement certainly does not apply to *all* the rich. Strictly speaking, it would be possible to refute the statement "rich people are tax cheats" (if "rich people" is understood in the sense of "all rich people") by naming a single rich person who does not evade taxes. But that would be too easy, and unfair, because when someone says that "rich people are tax cheats," what they probably mean is that rich people evade taxes more often than the average population, or than lower earners.

But even this interpretation is difficult to verify. First, it is not clear what is meant by "rich people." Surveys show that the public disagrees about whom they consider to be rich: for some, wealth begins with a net household income as low as $40,000; for others, it means several billions in assets. Even if one could agree on a definition of "rich," the statement would still be difficult to verify. Does it mean that there are more tax cheats among the rich than there are among other population groups? Because of the high number of unreported cases of tax evasion, it is impossible to say whether this is so. Laypersons also do not necessarily make a linguistic distinction between tax evasion, in the legal sense, and elaborate but legal tax structuring.

Naturally, people do not usually formulate their statements like scientists—and this alone makes it difficult to check whether or not statements about another group of people are correct, as demonstrated by the following thought experiment: If a student formulated the prejudicial statements above as hypotheses to be scientifically tested, then a professor would certainly point out that they were far too vague and needed to be reformulated if they were to be scientifically tested. However, we must not place the same demands on everyday language that we place on scientists and researchers. No normal person would say the following in everyday conversation: "The proportion of migrants who violate the law is significantly higher than the corresponding proportion of nonmigrants." This is the kind of statement that is precise enough to be verified, although even here, some scientists would demand that—to avoid comparing apples with oranges—any comparison should only be made between socially identical groups, for example, between young male migrants with no educational qualifications and young male nonmigrants with no educational qualifications.

Some scientists believe that because certain offenses (such as violating residency permits) can only be committed by foreigners, these offenses should be excluded from any such comparison. Other scientists say that it is unnecessary to make such distinctions and adjustments in order to verify the above statement. In the end, two scientists seeking to verify whether the above statement was true or false could arrive at completely different conclusions. The very fact that it is often impossible to reach a consensus on whether a prejudice is right or wrong suggests that the correctness of a statement should not be used as a criterion in determining whether it is a prejudice.

Applying the definitions above, it is clear that prejudices are also not only negative. After all, the assumption that prejudices are firstly false and secondly negative leads logically to the conclusion that the "right" judgment about a group must always be a positive one. This assumption is optimistic, but it is itself a prejudice.

VALUE-FREE DEFINITIONS OF "PREJUDICE" AND "STEREOTYPING"

The philosopher Hans-Georg Gadamer describes prejudice, in contrast to many definitions that have been presented so far, as a value-free precursor to an opinion that exists at the birth of knowledge. He insists that prejudice, in its original and legal meaning *prae judicum*, does not presume a positive *or* a negative judgment. "This fundamental prejudice of the enlightened man is the prejudice against prejudices in general and thus the disempowerment of tradition. Only through enlightenment does the concept of prejudice take on the negative connotation we are accustomed to."[43]

A more recent definition comes closer to this principle of value-free inquiry, according to which prejudice is understood as an association between the collective memories of a social group and a negative (or positive) judgment, which is more or less automatically activated in the presence of the object of judgment.[44]

The distinction between the terms "stereotype" and "prejudice" is not entirely clear. Depending on the definition used, both terms may even refer to the same thing. A standard textbook by Mary E. Kite and Bernard E. Whitley Jr. defines "prejudice" as follows: "Prejudice is an attitude directed toward people because they are members of a specific social group. . . . Attitudes are considered to be evaluations of or emotional responses to an entire social group or individuals who are members of that group."[45] Stereotypes are defined as follows: "Stereotypes are beliefs and opinions about the characteristics, attributes, and behaviors of members of various groups."[46]

From my point of view, the distinction between stereotype and prejudice is not actually all that significant. Both terms have a wide range of definitions, many of which overlap. Although the term "stereotype" often has a negative connotation, from my point of view it at least has the advantage over the term "prejudice" in that, unlike prejudice, it doesn't signify the notion of a premature judgment or a judgment formed before a subject has been sufficiently examined.

According to the principles of nonnormative science, stereotypes can be defined as "perceived correlations between group membership on the one hand and characteristics and behavior on the other."[47] In the branch of social psychology known as self-categorization theory, stereotypes are a consequence of categorization. Thus, they are the result of a normal process of generating meaning in a given social context. According to this understanding, stereotypes are neither cognitive distortions nor irrational, rigid, or formulaic, as suggested by other definitions.[48]

Yet Martina Thiele, among others, has observed a normative tendency in the use of the term "stereotype": "Taking a longer term look at the development of the terminology, a normative tendency emerges, according to which stereotypes have been conceptualized as *misperceptions* and were therefore per se 'bad' and to be combated."[49] Jussim puts forward a series of convincing arguments to challenge the widespread notion that stereotypes are inherently wrong. According to Jussim, when someone using everyday language accuses someone else of stereotyping a group, it is tantamount to a damning indictment of the other person's beliefs. The assertion, whether explicit or implicit, is that *"My beliefs are reasonable, rational, and appropriate; yours, at least when they differ from mine, are mere stereotypes."*[50]

Of the modern definitions, Jussim describes the one from Richard Ashmore and Frances Del Boca as the most convincing: "A stereotype is a set of beliefs about the personal attributes of a social group."[51] This definition is appropriate because it leaves open aspects of stereotypes that are assumed in other definitions. As the authors write:

Stereotypes may or may not:

1. be accurate and rational;
2. be widely shared;
3. be conscious;
4. be rigid;
5. exaggerate group differences;
6. assume group differences are essential or biological;
7. cause or reflect prejudice; and
8. cause biases and self-fulfilling prophecies.[52]

Stereotypes, as Jussim demonstrates, can sometimes be true and rational, sometimes inaccurate and irrational. He criticizes the negative connotations that arise when stereotypes are described as mental short-cuts and generalizations.

> Generalization, however, can be viewed as an extraordinary cogni-tive and intellectual achievement that marks one of the key strengths of human beings, rather than as a reflection of laziness or simplicity. People who cannot reach generalizations and abstractions are seriously cognitively impaired, and scientific theories often require extraordi-nary leaps from specific instances to general principles. . . . Without the power of generalization, it is unlikely that *Homo sapiens* would have reached their current position as the dominant species on Earth.[53]

Maybe we should make it a little easier for ourselves by determining what happens in the mind of a person who harbors prejudices against a group of people. A prejudiced person first identifies the other as a member of a specific group. Spontaneous mental associations are activated, trig-gered by the association of certain characteristics and behaviors with this group of people. These associations are linked to certain judgments ("cold," "lazy," "industrious," "intelligent") and trigger very specific emotions.

In my opinion, it is irrelevant whether a person articulates these associations spontaneously in the form of emotive utterances or wheth-er he tries to rationalize the judgments and emotions associated with them and to articulate them in a more sophisticated way. A prejudiced person projects these associations onto the other person: depending on his prejudice toward the group, his judgment about the other person will be more or less favorable than it would have been without those group-related associations. Even if it is obvious that these associations do not objectively apply to the other person, the prejudiced person's judg-ment of the group as a whole does not change; rather, he sees this person as an exception that confirms the rule. Since a prejudice cannot easily be corrected by knowledge, facts, or experiences that contradict it, the prejudice remains firmly held.

Social prejudices are therefore associations (usually of a judgmental nature) with characteristics of a group that are considered typical of them by another group. However, these associations are never shared by all people, because they do not represent the undisputed characteristics of the group. Rather, they are attributions and generalizations that seem true from the perspective of the person holding the prejudices, but they are often vague, and their justification is necessarily arguable. They may lead to heated discussions, of course, especially when the associations and attributions are extremely negative.

It is characteristic of prejudice, however, that members of the target group are generally judged better or worse on the basis of their membership in, or associations with, the target group. Alice H. Eagly and Amanda B. Diekman write, "It is this lowering of the evaluation of members of the target group because of their group membership that constitutes role-incongruity prejudice." A black dentist, for example, may be evaluated positively (because he is a dentist) by someone who harbors prejudices against blacks, but less positively than a white dentist because of the color of his skin.[54]

As has been shown, it is often difficult or even impossible to determine whether a judgment is right or wrong. In this book, I will only very rarely address the question of whether or not prejudices and stereotypes against rich people are true. In some cases, this determination is difficult to measure. For example, how do you measure whether rich people are "cold hearted"? In principle, it would sometimes be possible to determine whether a prejudice is correct—for example, whether people of a particular income or wealth category are more intelligent than the average population. But in many cases, even where this determination is possible in principle, there are simply no scholarly studies of the prejudice, which makes it impossible to determine the truth of it.

BLATANT AND SUBTLE PREJUDICE—AND WHY THEY ARE SO DIFFICULT TO MEASURE

Thomas F. Pettigrew and Roel W. Meertens distinguish between "blatant prejudice" and "subtle prejudice."[55] This distinction has become ever more important, because prejudices against certain groups (e.g., migrants) are often no longer expressed openly because of a change in values and widespread political correctness. People have the feeling that expressing such prejudices, even to a pollster, is socially unacceptable. For example, very few anti-Semites would openly admit to their prejudices, even when asked anonymously, because they are desperate to present themselves in a positive light. Therefore, in addition to direct questions, researchers have begun to develop other analytical methods that allow more subtle forms of prejudice to be identified. For example, reaction-time methods are used to measure how quickly certain terms are associated with each other.[56]

Subtle prejudices have been characterized as commonly having three components.[57] The first component is the "defense of traditional values," with the critical, perhaps tacit assertion that members of out-groups do not behave in accordance with these values. The second component is the "exaggeration of cultural differences," which strongly emphasizes the differences between an in-group and an out-group. The third component is the "denial of positive emotions" toward members of the out-group.[58]

The problem with the concept of "subtle" prejudices is that it is susceptible to inflationary usage. For example, one essay explaining the difference between blatant and subtle prejudice states that people harboring subtle prejudices said that they did not want to deport all immigrants, they just wanted to deport those for whom "ostensibly nonprejudicial reasons could be found (e.g., deportation of convicted criminals)."[59] People who argue in favor of deporting criminals are thus described as prejudiced, which in my view is an arbitrary attribution.

In the same vein, the following attitude is sometimes described as "symbolic racism" (this term is similar to that of "subtle prejudice"): "a reluctance to take affirmative action to advance black people in employment, education, welfare, and so forth."[60] Thus, everyone who opposes affirmative action is described as prejudiced against black people. Although one can assume that everyone who is prejudiced against black people also opposes affirmative action, this statement by no means justifies classing everyone who opposes affirmative action as being prejudiced against black people.

A third example: In a research paper on Islamophobic stereotypes, obvious prejudices such as "Muslims are liars and hypocrites" or "Islam is cultureless and inferior to the West" are equated with opinions that Islamophobes may share with others, such as "Islam is homophobic."[61]

Controversially, Pettigrew and Meertens see the fact that someone attaches significance to traditional values and adheres to conservative beliefs as one of several components of subtle prejudice.[62] And even stating that illegal or criminal migrants should be deported is cited as an indication of subtle racism.[63] For example, anyone who openly expresses a desire "to deport the outgroup if they have committed serious crimes or do not have their immigration papers"[64] is regarded as having subtle prejudices. Ultimately, according to this view, only extreme egalitarians who advocate a certain type of immigration and refugee policy could be regarded as not prejudiced. Thus, the term "prejudice" becomes a polemic term directed against political dissenters—in this case, against conservatives.

Lars-Eric Petersen distinguishes among persons with no prejudices and those with blatant and subtle prejudices as follows: "Nonjudgmental people internalize the norm, while people with blatant prejudices ignore or reject it. Persons with subtle prejudices behave as far as possible according to the norm . . ., but behave in a xenophobic manner according to their subtle xenophobic attitudes, if they find themselves in an environment that accepts such behavior, or if they are encouraged to discriminate by someone in a superior position and are thus able to absolve themselves."[65]

It seems plausible that people no longer dare to openly articulate attitudes that have been branded as prejudices, but it is also true that attitudes toward gay and lesbian people, for example, have actually (and not only superficially or supposedly) changed fundamentally over the past 50 years. And there is a risk that indirect measurements may classify certain views as racist or sexist and that this classification would erroneously lead to everyone who shares those views being classified as racist or sexist, even when they are not.

Allison Aosved, Patricia Long, and Emily Voller developed a questionnaire to measure intolerance. They found that people who exhibit prejudices and intolerance against one group are often also intolerant toward other groups. Their test consists of questions concerning prejudices against six groups:

1. Prejudices based on sexual orientation (e.g., against lesbian, gay, bisexual, or transgender people)

2. Class-based prejudices (e.g., against the poor)
3. Sexist prejudices (e.g., against women)
4. Racist prejudices (e.g., against black people)
5. Ageist prejudices (e.g., against old[er] people)
6. Religious intolerance

The questionnaire's 54 questions demonstrate just how difficult prejudice is to measure. On the one hand, it is true that prejudices cannot simply be measured on the basis of direct racist or sexist statements, because respondents will not openly admit, for example, that they discriminate against black people or women because such statements are regarded as highly socially undesirable. On the other hand, it is just as problematic when researchers attempt to measure prejudice using legitimate political statements of the kind commonly expressed by people with prejudices *but by no means only by such groups.* Here are some examples from the questionnaire:[66]

- Marriages between two lesbians should be legal. (Reversed)
- I favor laws that permit racial minority persons to rent or purchase houses, even when the person offering the property for sale or rent does not wish to sell or rent to minorities. (Reversed)
- Racial minorities have more influence on school desegregation plans than they ought to have.
- Racial minorities are getting too demanding in their push for equal rights.
- Most old people can be irritating because they tell the same stories over and over again.
- Too many of my tax dollars are spent to take care of those who are unwilling to take care of themselves.
- There are more poor people than wealthy people in prisons because poor people commit more crimes.

We have seen that modern prejudice research increasingly employs implicit measurement methods in order to reduce the problems associated with social desirability bias. The more society outlaws openly racist or sexist attitudes, the greater these problems become. In such cases, direct interviews will not necessarily be able to identify prejudices. Francesca M. Franco and Anne Maass investigated when prejudices should be measured with explicit methods and when they should be measured with implicit methods. Implicit methods include the following:

- The formulation of "soft" statements in surveys so that respondents should not be concerned that their agreement would be interpreted as sexist or racist;
- Physiological measurements taken during interactions with minorities (proximity, eye contact, etc.); and
- Reaction time measures in which subjects are not aware that a category or group label has been activated.[67]

As traditional interviews are easier to conduct than implicit measures of prejudice, and as the latter encourages the problematic broadening of the concept of prejudice described above, it is necessary to decide when direct interviews can be used without fear of major distortions. The authors assume that the weaker the moral normative rules against discrimination toward minorities are, the less problematic explicit measures are.

The researchers determined the extent to which 13 social groups enjoyed normative protection against open discrimination. On a scale from 1 (absolutely unacceptable to express negative judgments) to 9 (absolutely acceptable to express negative judgments), Jews scored 2.1 and Islamic fundamentalists 7.1. In Italy, at the end of the 1990s, when this study was carried out, it was considered highly socially undesirable to openly discriminate against the handicapped, Jews, and black people. The groups at the other end of the scale, which could be talked about negatively without fear of sanction, included Mafiosi, skinheads, and Islamic fundamentalists. Homosexual people, Jehovah's Witnesses, and Hare Krishna followers scored in the midrange.[68]

Franco and Maass hypothesize that explicit and implicit measures would produce different results for groups for whom there was a norm that would encourage the inhibition of prejudiced responses (e.g., Jews) than for groups for whom there was no particular reason why people should be concerned about publicly expressing dislike of them (e.g., Islamic fundamentalists). This hypothesis has been confirmed in several experiments.

My hypothesis before the start of this survey was that people are more willing to articulate negative statements about the rich than they are about other minorities. This hypothesis was tested and confirmed using one of the survey's questions (see page 403). But even if it should turn out to be true that it is more acceptable to be openly negative about the rich than about other minorities, it seemed important in the survey to ensure that the questions were not too direct, because that could trigger a reflex to provide more socially desirable responses ("It's not right to speak so badly about others or to generalize"). This is especially true for questions concerning envy directed at the rich, because the expression of envy in general is considered undesirable.

CHAPTER 2
WHAT IS CLASSISM?

Since Walter Lippmann's classic *Public Opinion* was first published almost 100 years ago (1921), researchers have been examining prejudices and stereotypes. Over the past few decades alone, scholars have published thousands of articles, papers, and books on the topic. In particular, the research has focused on the following prejudices and stereotypes:[69]

- Geographical stereotypes (e.g., those related to other countries and regions)
- Ethnic and racial stereotypes (e.g., those related to black people or the Sinti and Roma)
- Gender and sexual stereotypes (e.g., those related to women or to gay and lesbian people)
- Age-based stereotypes
- Occupation-based stereotypes
- Economic and class-based stereotypes
- Physical stereotypes (e.g., those related to the obese)

Particular attention has been paid to racist and sexist prejudices. However, less research has been done on occupation-based stereotypes. Where studies have been conducted to investigate occupation-based stereotypes, they have tended to focus on journalists, politicians, scientists, and doctors. Preference has been given to occupational groups that require academic training, largely the classical professions.[70]

Bettina Spencer and Emanuele Castano observe that "traditional stereotyping and prejudice literature has focused on issues of race and gender."[71] Much less research has been conducted into prejudices based on class or class affiliation. According to Spencer and Castano, members of the lower class are far less visible as such than members of ethnic minorities or women.[72]

The literature frequently refers to a resolution passed by the American Psychological Association (APA) on August 6, 2000, that called for a rigorous inventory of the differences between the living conditions of the poor and the rich in the United States. In a 17-point catalog, the APA undertook to advocate more effectively for "social justice." The catalog's first point deals explicitly with the importance of research that examines classism.[73]

Prejudices based on ethnicity and class often go hand in hand because people frequently see correlations between the two. "As they say in Latin America, 'money whitens.' A wealthy or highly educated minority person receives higher status. More and more often, class can trump ethnicity."[74] Several studies have confirmed that class-based prejudices are more pronounced than those based on ethnicity or gender. Researchers examined the impressions that participants formed when rating a woman who had applied to become vice president of her children's Parent-Teacher Organization: "The target woman was perceived to be Latina, Jewish or Anglo-Saxon, as well as working-class or middle-class. Across ethnicities, the working-class target was rated as significantly less strident, less perfectionist, more unemotional, meeker, cruder, more irresponsible, and more unsuitable than a middle-class target. The target's ethnicity did not lead to as much stereotyping as her class background."[75]

Spencer and Castano go on to explain that psychological research into stereotypes based on socioeconomic status has been far more limited than research into stereotypes based on gender, ethnicity, or other characteristics. They claim that this disparity may be because psychologists generally belong to the middle class and therefore unconsciously perpetuate such prejudices themselves. "This gap in the psychological literature parallels the invisibility and exclusion that low-SES [socioeconomic status] individuals already face in their interpersonal and institutional relations. The reason may be that psychologists generally base their theories on people who are similar to themselves, that is, middle-class, and thereby add to, and perpetuate classism."[76]

Despite their importance, stereotypes based on class affiliation have been identified and researched far less than other stereotypes. "Once this idea is more widely accepted, perhaps there will be more psychological research focusing on socioeconomic status, and we will next find a way to combat the stereotyping and prejudice of low-SES individuals and the negative impact that these have on their lives," write Spencer and Castano.[77] Yet they do not ask whether the absence of research into prejudices and stereotypes about high-SES individuals can also be traced back to causes similar to those of the lack of research on prejudices toward lower-SES individuals.

DOWNWARD CLASSISM AND UPWARD CLASSISM

The term "classism" is less well known than the term "sexism." In 2016, Andreas Kemper and Heike Weinbach wrote, "In contrast to racism, sexism and anti-Semitism, the history of the scholarly, or even pop scientific, elaboration of classism is only just beginning."[78]

"Analyses of classism address the stereotyping and degradation that go hand in hand with socioeconomic status and are thus legitimized," they observe.[79] However, the term is often reduced to stereotyping and prejudice against the socially disadvantaged alone: "Missing teeth, tattered clothing, watching TV and DVDs all day, no interest in high culture, alcoholism, neglecting their children, promiscuous lifestyles, the inability to operate successfully and a lack of self-control have become the stereotypical stigmatizations of the unemployed, low-SES individuals and low-earners."[80]

In discussing classism, a distinction is made between downward classism and upward classism. "The first form of classism," explains William Ming Liu, "is what is usually considered to be classism: those in power or higher social classes marginalizing and discriminating against those in lower social classes. This is what I would call downward classism or classism prejudice and discrimination targeted against those who are perceived to be in a lower social class position."[81] The second form is upward classism: "Upward classism is the prejudice and discrimination that occurs against those who are perceived to be in a higher social class. For example, perceiving or labeling someone as elitist, a snob, or bougie (slang for bourgeois) is a form of upward classism. Interpersonally, upward classism may also manifest as jealousy or envy."[82] In addition, Liu introduces the terms "lateral classism" and "internalized classism"; however, these terms have not yet established themselves in the research.

Even authors who are fundamentally critical of the concept of upward classism do, however, admit "that prejudices also exist on the part of blue-collar workers, for example against the rich or intellectuals."[83] Stereotyping and degradation by recipients of government income support, for example, "towards the rich or academics are also forms of discrimination, even if the former are not able to make their discrimination hegemonic or normative because of their social disadvantage. However, such discrimination also contributes to a political climate of degradation and devaluation of people."[84]

Much controversy exists as to whether classism should also include prejudices against the rich and against high-SES individuals in general. Opponents of this extended approach define classism restrictively as a "top-down practice" that is based essentially on "structural advantage."[85] Classism, it is argued, is not simply a prejudice but a form of oppression, with oppression understood as a combination of prejudice and social power. This framework is also applied to other forms of oppression, such as racism or sexism. "Members of the dominated and dominant groups have mutual prejudices against each other, but only the dominant group has the power to make its prejudices structurally effective through oppression."[86]

These are the reasons why most analyses of classist prejudices and stereotypes are limited to those directed against blue-collar workers or low-SES individuals. According to this understanding, classism is always directed against the less powerful: "Like sexism, racism, and heterosexism, classism denotes negative attitudes, beliefs, and behaviors directed toward those with less power, who are socially devalued."[87] Ironically, however, in lamenting the lack of research into class-based stereotypes, the same author, Bernice Lott, chooses herself to perpetuate negative prejudices and stereotypes about the rich. She describes the social circumstances of the poor with the greatest empathy, whereas her description of the lifestyles of the rich is limited to repeating particularly extreme individual examples from Robert Frank's book *Richistan*.[88] These include caviar costing $9,800, three months of home flower arrangements for $24,525, and a set of 25 cigars for $730.[89] This is the perfect example of what those who argue for more research into class-based prejudices have long criticized: because the authors themselves obviously do not know any rich people, they repeat the stereotypes that are communicated in the media. Of course, some rich people are willing to spend a lot of money on such luxuries—but there are probably many more who would never engage in such conspicuous consumption. In Lott's article, rich people are stereotypically portrayed as indulging in excessive luxury. They are also shown breaking the law, lying during negotiations, exhibiting unethical behavior, and achieving their wealth primarily through professional relationships rather than through their own efforts. Thus, classism researchers themselves perpetuate classist stereotypes— when they refer to the rich.

Liu cites a newspaper article describing a family with a household income of $300,000 a year struggling to afford their lifestyle. The family's monthly after-tax income is somewhere between $15,000 and $17,000 per month, sums that the author clearly struggles to imagine. He makes this clear when he uses quotation marks to describe the family's "needs" or "necessities," which include $40,000 a year for a nanny.[90] "That is, if internal dispositional attributions of 'laziness' are directed to those who are poor, is it fair to characterize greed and hedonism in the same vein?" he asks.[91]

Psychologists in the United States repeatedly attempt to explain why far less research has been devoted to class-based prejudices than, for example, anti-Semitism, racism, or sexism. One explanation is that psychologists have had their own experiences with racism, sexism, ageism, heterosexism, and ableism. But only a small minority of psychologists trace their social origins to low-SES or working-class families— and even for this small minority, poverty is definitely more of a past concern than a present reality.[92]

In 2002, Lott criticized the fact that "the near invisibility of the poor in psychology as well as psychologists' lack of attention to social class in general continues even when there is a direct focus on multiculturalism and diversity. . . . The glaring omission of social class in considerations of multicultural issues illustrates certain realities about the discipline of psychology. Psychological theories are preoccupied with people who are like those who construct the theories, that is, those in the middle class (and primarily European Americans)."[93]

This argument is plausible, but it is also the reason why researchers deal so little with classism directed upward. It has largely been Jews who have advanced anti-Semitism research, female researchers who have focused on sexism, and gay and lesbian people who have spearheaded research into prejudices against sexual minorities. It is no coincidence that researchers such as Barbara Jensen (see page 37), who researches class-based prejudices against the working class, herself comes from a working-class family. And it is no coincidence that I—as someone who has risen from the middle class to the ranks of the rich—research prejudices and stereotypes against the rich.

Classism researchers have so far had a very one-sided focus on downward classism and, in many cases, prejudices and stereotypes against rich people are not even regarded as such. Liu, one of the leading classism researchers in the United States, denies, for example, that negative behaviors lead to sweeping generalizations that strengthen stereotypes against rich people: "For instance, there is virtually no meaningful identity assault on a person who is White, wealthy, and male. And . . . each White wealthy man is evaluated independently such that one White wealthy man's poor behavior does not necessarily create a group stereotype or declination in power for all White wealthy men."[94] Of course, it is not always the case that one person's negative behavior reinforces the stereotypes directed against that person's in-group as a whole.

Often, however, it is: If a manager or banker behaves unethically or receives a substantial bonus despite questionable behavior, then many people, and the media, regard this as not only an individual problem, but as an underscoring of the stereotype of the "greedy manager" or "greedy banker."

Alexander J. Colbow and colleagues developed a series of instruments to measure downward classism and upward classism. A number of items were used to measure upward classism:

- In most difficult situations, wealthy people take the easy way out.
- Wealthy people are out of touch with average people's experiences.
- Rich people's kids are trouble makers.
- I resent people from higher social classes.
- Many rich people are trying to abuse the system.
- More often than not, wealthy people are selfish.[95]

The strongest negative association found in their study was between upward classism and "life satisfaction,"[96] even when other variables were controlled in the multiple regression analysis.[97] Satisfaction with life was measured using a seven-point scale. Sample items included "So far I have gotten the important things I want in life" and "If I could live my life over, I would change almost nothing."[98] Those who scored highly on this scale were less likely to exhibit upward classism.

The authors advanced the following hypothesis to explain their findings: "Individuals who are unhappy with their life circumstances or prospects for upward mobility may seek to externalize blame, and rationalize that those who are perceived to be economically more well-off are also not worthy of success. . . . Wealthy people may be an easy scapegoat for which to blame one's problems or rationalize one's situation to reduce disequilibrium or dissonance."[99]

Very small, but statistically significant, negative correlations were also found between upward classism and income and gender. Upward classism was more prevalent among low-income groups than it was

among high-income groups. It was also more pronounced among men
than among women.[100]

Classism in American Media

One of the few extensive and in-depth works of classism research that
also deals with stereotypes against the rich is Diana Kendall's *Framing
Class: Media Representations of Wealth and Poverty in America*. It is not a
quantitative media content analysis, but the author has reviewed an
extensive selection of material—including the *New York Times*; numerous popular TV shows, such as *Real Housewives* and *The Bachelorette*; and
special-interest magazines and related TV shows that focus on the rich
and their consumption habits. As a result, Kendall's book is not limited
to purely political or business reporting. The book examines "media
framing," which it defines as follows: "The term *media framing* describes
the process by which the media (newspapers, magazines, radio and television networks and stations, and the Internet) package information and
entertainment before presenting it to an audience."[101] The media feed
off their readers' and viewers' emotions toward the rich, which consist of
simultaneous admiration and rejection: "The most popular media frames
for news accounts and entertainment TV program story lines about the
rich play on the preexisting schema within many people's minds that it
is okay simultaneously to love and hate the rich."[102] The author distinguishes among six different media frames:[103]

- The consensus frame: the wealthy are like everyone else.
- The admiration frame: the wealthy are generous and caring
  people.
- The emulation frame: the wealthy personify the American
  dream.
- The price-tag frame: the wealthy believe in the gospel of
  materialism.
- The sour-grapes frame: the wealthy are unhappy and
  dysfunctional.
- The bad-apple frame: some wealthy people are scoundrels.

The consensus frame. In this frame, the media emphasize that rich people are, in many respects, similar to people in other classes by downplaying important differences between the wealthy and others. Examples of consensus framing in media stories include articles that portray the rich as also suffering from the recession of 2008 and the fall in house prices. Kendall not only describes these frames but also criticizes them—always from a decidedly anti-capitalist standpoint: "If the very wealthy are viewed as down-home people who just have more money than everyone else, the invidious distinctions inherent in the capitalist economy are obscured and class-based oppression is downplayed, or appears to be nonexistent, in news accounts and entertainment programming."[104]

The psychological function of such reports, which stress the similarities between rich people and everyone else, could, however, be interpreted in a completely different way: Media reports on the everyday problems of the wealthy, especially those that highlight the fact that the rich are not all that different from everyone else, offer solace to those who are not rich. "What is the use of being rich if, in the end, rich people have the same problems as everyone else?" one might ask. The message is clear: money alone does not make you happy. Such views serve a psychologically reassuring function, because wealth may no longer seem so desirable—money supposedly does not solve so many problems. If anything, it actually creates new ones. This leads to another frame, the sour-grapes frame (see page 30).

The admiration frame. This frame is all about portraying the rich as generous and caring people who make charitable donations and support good causes. Admiration framing commonly publicizes charity parties and philanthropic activities. Kendall criticizes such framing as follows: "The media may serve as a public relations outlet for the wealthy, helping to smooth the rough edges of their business dealings and (sometimes) unscrupulous acts by letting others know about their good deeds."[105]

The emulation frame. This frame usually refers to articles about people from the lower rungs of the class system who have risen from poverty to wealth. Their inspirational stories are held up as personifying the American dream. Kendall highlights one such tale, the real-life story of Oprah Winfrey.[106] Such media portrayals of people who have achieved outstanding success emphasize the importance of hard work and having the right mindset or personality traits. Kendall criticizes the fact that this portrayal perpetuates the myth of the American dream.[107] "Given the long odds against such an outcome, emulation framing not only creates unrealistic expectations given economic and social realities in the 2000s but provides an excuse for those who are better off financially to deride those who are not."[108] What Kendall neglects to mention is that, compared with the 1980s, the proportion of self-made superrich who have earned their wealth is far higher today than the number who became rich through inheritances.[109] In addition, it is normal for the media to report on unusual events rather than common ones; for example, it is more likely that journalists will report on a plane that crashes than on every plane that lands safely. And it is not a modern phenomenon that "heroes" are admired precisely because they stand apart from the masses—and can thus motivate and inspire other people.

The price-tag frame. This frame deals with the American media's penchant for providing very precise information about the costs of things only the rich can afford. Examples of price-tag framing include descriptions of extravagantly expensive villas, lavish yachts, private planes, luxury cars, and expensive toys for rich children.[110] Kendall's criticism: "Based on media reports of wealthy parents' purchases for their children, some parents with average or lower-than-average incomes feel inadequate because they cannot afford even the far-less-expensive items they would like to buy for their own children."[111] Whether media reports of a Superplexus toy that costs $30,000[112] would really elicit feelings of inadequacy from average parents is pure speculation. Again, there is an alternative interpretation of these depictions of the rich with their conspicuously expensive luxury goods that leads to a point of criticism Kendall fails to make: Price-tag framing creates the impression that the rich, or at least a majority of the rich, are superficial materialists whose sole purpose in life is to buy overpriced luxury goods in order to show off.

The sour-grapes frame. This frame includes depictions of the personal, psychological, and other traumas associated with people who have inherited large sums of money. Many of these stories convey the suffering of the wealthy, including their low self-esteem, lack of self-discipline, boredom, alienation, guilt, and suspiciousness. Articles also often point out the difficulty rich people have in establishing positive relationships with others, because they never know whether someone loves them for themselves or for their money. The foibles of wealthy families, particularly those with members who engage in infidelity and personal disputes, are also often portrayed in TV shows like *Dallas*, which was popular around the world.[113] The author's "sour grapes" interpretation is convincing because, in essence, such depictions give audiences the feeling that it might not be so great to be rich after all. From my point of view, this framing performs a psychologically reassuring function: ordinary people need not ask themselves why they are not financially successful when being rich is not all it is cracked up to be anyway—and this is precisely the conclusion readers and viewers draw when, in the media portrayals mentioned above, the problems of being rich are emphasized rather than the advantages.

The bad-apple frame. This frame describes many negative media portrayals of rich people—for example, when the media shows wealthy people who believe they can buy anything, or bribe other people, or so on. Bad-apple framing is also used in reports of fraudsters and criminals who have become rich through illegal activities. Kendall criticizes this frame for not presenting the problems as being rooted in the capitalist system and social inequality. According to Kendall, such phenomena are wrongly depicted as an "individual pathology, not a structural concern rooted in the larger economic, political, or social inequalities in society."[114] She raises the point that journalists, by choosing to focus on a few bad apples, ignore the possibility that there could be something inherently wrong with the system.[115] It would, however, be possible to criticize such reports from exactly the opposite perspective. These reports, whether explicitly or implicitly, create the impression that top-tier managers and the rich engage in more fraud and more tax evasion and take more liberties with the letter of the law and with morals than do poorer people. Such stereotypes, which by their very nature cannot be substantiated by the individual cases depicted in the media, do not have to apply. Naturally, misconduct by celebrities and the rich is reported more frequently than misconduct by middle-class people, often because the sums involved are far higher than, for example, a smaller instance of tax evasion by an average earner. The laws of the media jungle dictate that an air crash that kills 200 will garner more interest than the one million people who die as a result of car accidents around the world each year—precisely because each of these accidents causes only one or a few fatalities. In many cases, the media create an impression of events that does not correspond to their actual frequency or danger.

Kendall's work embodies the bias of existing classism research. Although she criticizes the allegedly overly positive tenor of media reporting on the rich, her criticism of the portrayals of the poor and of workers exhibits precisely the opposite tendency. Although she does admit that media reports are predominantly accurate and elicit sympathy by putting a human face on poverty, she criticizes news items that view the poor primarily as statistics because they do not portray the personal experiences of the poor—and she criticizes stories about personal experience because the structural causes of poverty are not addressed: "[This type of story] still fails to examine the larger structural issues that perpetuate poverty, such as growing rates of economic inequality, a decline in the number of available jobs, continuing racial and gender discrimination, and other social and technological changes that reduce opportunity."[116]

Kendall also laments that news items sometimes create the impression that the poor are "partly responsible for their plight" because of certain actions, such as taking illegal drugs or not looking for a job.[117] Underpinning Kendall's criticism is a concept of humanity that is based on the idea that people are responsible for neither the positive nor the negative outcomes in their lives. Media reports of rags-to-riches stories and the wealthy are criticized because they sometimes give rise to the impression that success is due to personality traits and individual effort. At the same time, news items on the poor are criticized because they perpetuate the impression that some people are at least partly to blame for their fate.[118] From the perspective of Kendall and other classism researchers, the capitalist system and "structural" injustices are always to blame for making people rich or poor, while reporting on individual causes is branded as an attempt to blame the poor for their fate.

Yet Kendall also criticizes factual articles that use statistics to explore increases and decreases in the poverty rate or in the number of hungry people. "Articles about the numbers debate make hunger seem like a numbers game and of little consequence."[119] She continues, "As we have seen, thematic framing in news reporting emphasizes data and how they are gathered. Although the media may occasionally show audiences the 'human face' of the poor, the larger issues associated with poverty, hunger, and homelessness are easily lost in debates over how government statistics are generated, interpreted, disseminated, and employed in social policy decisions."[120]

According to Kendall, negative framing in stories about individuals' experiences of poverty is "often subtle and thus open to a variety of interpretations by readers."[121] However, Kendall does not go on to ask why the (really or supposedly) negative tenor in news items about the poor is subtle, whereas the rich are very openly and sharply criticized in the media. One obvious explanation is that open and direct criticism of the poor is considered politically incorrect, while such criticism is viewed as absolutely necessary when directed against the rich. Kendall also criticizes media reports on crimes committed by the poor, pointing out that such crimes are far less interesting than those of wealthy elites— such as white-collar offenses.[122]

In particular, Kendall criticizes media stories that focus on people who have lifted themselves out of poverty because these stories emphasize the importance of willpower and positive thinking. Such reports indirectly communicate the message that others might be able to do likewise, if only they set their minds to it.[123] "Individuals . . . who improve their living conditions, overcome hardships and addiction, and find happier lives are clear examples of pulling yourself up by your own bootstraps, but exceptionalism framing ignores the more typical experiences of the poor and homeless, leaving media audiences with an individualistic view of poverty and homelessness that does not focus on the larger 'societal issues' associated with these problems."[124]

Taking this logic to its natural conclusion, the media should refrain from reporting aspirational stories about people who do manage to escape from poverty. Otherwise, readers and viewers could forget that the vast majority of poor people never succeed in lifting themselves out of poverty. According to Kendall, such stories also ignore the larger societal issues associated with poverty. The objection to this is clear—would it be better to communicate a dispiriting and hopeless message to readers and viewers: "The system is to blame. As long as the system is not fundamentally changed, you don't have a chance anyway"? And is it really up to the media to focus their reports only on statistically common occurrences? Is it not in their very nature to report on rare and unusual events?

Kendall's work suggests that classism researchers may feel obliged to take a specific ideological position, advocating for the poor and working class while sharply criticizing the rich and the capitalist system. Factual news items, for example, those dealing with statistics on increases and decreases in poverty rates, are criticized as an expression of cold disinterest in individual destinies. And reports on personal experiences of individuals are criticized because they do not address the "systemic" and "structural" causes of poverty. From this perspective, every single article that does not pose the "systemic question," that is, that fails to criticize purported structural injustices, is itself worthy of criticism. This ideological frame ignores the specific reasons why certain individuals manage to rise above poverty and denounces reports about people who have successfully pulled themselves up by their own bootstraps as merely reinforcing the capitalist system.

A similar trend can be seen in the work of Heather E. Bullock, Karen Fraser Wyche, and Wendy R. Williams, who published their overview of research in an article titled "Media Images of the Poor." Over a three-month period in 1999, Bullock, Wyche, and Williams analyzed the content of 412 articles in leading American newspapers (including USA Today, the Washington Post, and the New York Times) and several regional media outlets.[125] They found that a clear majority of the articles portrayed welfare recipients sympathetically. Overall, 60 percent of the articles depicted the poor and welfare recipients as deserving of support, as hardworking families with children in need. A negative tone prevailed in 17 percent of the articles, which portrayed the poor and welfare recipients as drug addicts or as neglectful parents. And 14 percent of the articles were neutral.[126]

These findings contradict the authors' assertion that the poor are devalued and stereotyped in the media. According to Bullock, Wyche, and Williams, classist representations in the mainstream media in the United States are a result of the fact that major media outlets are controlled by a few powerful corporations and reflect the interests of dominant social groups.[127] Given that the findings of their own empirical research contradict their theory that the media portray the poor in a negative light because the media are controlled by the economically powerful, the authors' explanation for this discrepancy approaches a conspiracy theory. The reason the poor were presented more favorably in the period under study, the authors claim, was because the U.S. government had passed the PRWORA Act (Personal Responsibility and Work Opportunity Reconciliation Act) three years earlier and the media were now endeavoring, on behalf of the government, so to speak, to portray welfare reform as a success and to show that the poor were taking up work in increasing numbers.[128]

Since their empirical findings did not correspond with the expectation of dominant classist stereotypes, Bullock, Wyche, and Williams's main criticism is directed, among other things, at the scarcity of media coverage of the structural causes of poverty: "Although most articles were neutral in tone and portrayed the difficulties facing welfare recipients and the poor sympathetically, they did little to contextualize poverty or illuminate its causes."[129] And "In the strongly individualistic, capitalist United States, reliance on public assistance signifies failure."[130]

The authors also criticize the dominance of "episodic" framing over "thematic" framing. What they mean is depictions of the circumstances of a poor individual or family outnumber news programs that focus on the structural explanations for poverty. An analysis of television news coverage of poverty between 1981 and 1986 found that episodic framings, or stories dealing with personal experiences of poverty, were more common than thematic framings, or stories providing a general analysis of the causes of poverty.[131] However, this result is not surprising, as stories that focus on individuals are better suited for television programs than abstract analyses. The authors complain that episodic coverage was far more likely to focus on the personal responsibility of the poor for their own fates in contrast to thematic, structural analyses. "Framing techniques that present poverty as an individual problem rather than a societal issue rooted in economic and political inequality further reinforce the perceived undeservingness of the poor."[132]

Explicitly or implicitly, most works on classism assume that the poor are almost never responsible for their poverty and that the rich do not deserve their wealth. These researchers take a fundamentally critical view of media reports that attribute poverty to personal failure or wealth to personal effort. From their point of view, people are never actually responsible for their own fate but are always innocent victims (the poor and the working class) or undeserving profiteers (the rich). Therefore, media reports that do not fit this worldview are criticized.

CLASSISM AS A PERPETUATION OF MIDDLE-CLASS VALUES

Liu—like other classism researchers—refuses to explain poverty by lack of personal motivation and effort. He also refuses to recognize the value of hard work and effort as essential factors in the success of the rich. He states that if a company CEO earns a salary 100 or 300 times higher (and sometimes more) than the company's lowest-paid employee, this cannot be tied to the CEO's level of effort or hard work.[133] Classism researchers accuse others of absolutizing middle-class thinking, yet, with such arguments, that is precisely what the researchers themselves are doing. In the case of regular employees, there is normally a direct link between the number of hours they work and how hard they work and the salary they receive. Members of the middle class—including researchers—have clearly internalized that a person's salary should be based exclusively on academic qualifications, effort, and hard work. It is therefore beyond the scope of their imaginations that, based on their understanding of "fair pay," there could be areas of society where these links have less bearing. Areas where, for example, innovative ideas and well-cultivated contacts make a greater contribution to economic success than the number of hours someone works or the level of effort they put in, which is, after all, not really that interesting when the value of someone's work is judged by the value of the *results* they achieve.

Although classism researchers have focused intensively on poverty, their research has normally been directed at examining not how poverty can be overcome but how inequality can be eliminated. When the incomes of the lowest earners increase, Liu and other researchers do not regard this as progress, insofar as the incomes of the rich increase disproportionately.[134] But even if the incomes of the poor and the rich increase proportionally (by 3 percent each, for example), researchers relativize such gains with the argument that 3 percent of $50,000 is much less than 3 percent of $10 million.[135]

Classism researchers' often Marxist view of the world is not shared by the poor or by blue-collar workers, who—from their point of view—do not see the system as something outrageous that it needs to be overturned. This matter poses a challenge for researchers, who repeatedly attempt to explain this discrepancy. For example, the researchers often criticize a worldview they refer to as "naturalistic." Under this rubric, they condemn the belief that rich and poor have always existed in our society—and in other societies throughout history—as an inadmissible justification of the status quo.[136] Or they seek explanations in psychology for why workers and the poor endorse the status quo, suggesting, for example, that this endorsement is a rationalization of their helplessness. "It may be that their internalization of this helplessness becomes self-blame for not being successful, and because others are being successful, it must be the person's deficiency that is causing the nonsuccess."[137]

Without being aware of it, classism researchers criticize the very thing they themselves are all too often guilty of. They, as members of the middle class, set their own value system as a yardstick by which everything else is measured. Barbara Jensen criticized the absolutization of middle-class thinking in her book *Reading Classes: On Culture and Classism in America*. On the one hand, she reports on her own life and demonstrates both how difficult it was for her to advance from the working class to the middle class and, above all, the psychological processes associated with such social mobility. On the other hand, as a psychologist, she also addresses the subject of classism from a scientific standpoint.[138]

Jensen does not define class primarily in economic terms but rather culturally. Classism is regarded as an instrument for maintaining class rule. Jensen defines classism as follows: "Class is an injustice that says some Americans deserve much more time, leisure, control, and far more financial reward than others. Class*ism* is the set of myths and beliefs that keep those class divisions intact, that is, the belief that working-class cultures and people are inherently inferior and that class itself demonstrates who the hardest workers and rightful winners are."[139] Her primary focus is on cultural classism: "By 'culture' I mean a constellation of accepted values, customs, mores, attitudes, styles, behaviors, and, especially, worldview—the shared *unconscious mind* of a community, to put it in psychological terms."[140]

She defines classism as the assumption that the middle-class culture is superior to working-class cultures.[141] "Classism in America is based on the assumption of the superiority of middle (and upper) class styles, tastes, attitudes, and values. Everyone is taught in school which ones are the 'good' manners, 'proper' English, the 'good' schools, the 'best' occupations."[142]

The political direction Jensen takes becomes clear when she complains that classism needlessly divides the vast majority of well-meaning Americans, namely, the working class and the middle class, who actually have more in common (especially economically) with each other than they do with the upper, or capitalist, class.[143] Jensen believes that the working classes and the middle class should act in solidarity and unite against the capitalist class, rather than allowing themselves to be divided.

Jensen concedes that working-class people harbor prejudices against the middle class, as demonstrated by numerous insulting epithets: "Eggheads, sissies, cold fish, pencil pushers, spoiled brats, and bloodsuckers are a few."[144] However, Jensen argues, it is ultimately the middle class that defines what is considered "normal" and "cultivated" in the United States.

According to Jensen, the very act of distinguishing between "high" and "low" culture is itself an expression of classism.[145] As she explains, classism is also evident when the louder, more expressive, and more highly emotional behavior that is more common in working-class cultures is interpreted as a flaw of personal character.[146] "This classism harshly judges people who 'put on a show' or have a 'big mouth,' people who come off 'too strong' in style, opinions, food or behavior."[147] However, Jensen fails to address the fact that these middle-class prejudices are directed not only against working-class people but also against the rich and members of the upper class, who in some ways are even more similar to the working class than are the middle class.

According to Jensen, "socioeconomic classism" is an attitude that regards economic success as proof of one's own superiority and qualifies people who are not financially successful as "losers."[148] In working-class cultures, in contrast, an *"anti*status ethic" dominates, because aspiring to a higher social status threatens solidarity within the group.[149] Jensen tells the story of a woman who was promoted to supervisor from her job on a production line. Within two weeks, the woman was back on the assembly line because she couldn't stand feeling like a "boss" or working in a role that threatened the solidarity and friendships she enjoyed with her previous colleagues.[150]

In Jensen's opinion, a strong emphasis on individualism is an expression of the cultural classism that sets the values of the middle class as the general norm. For working-class women and men, belonging is a far more important value than developing individuality and competitiveness.[151] According to Jensen, differences between class value systems are also evident in the way members of the working and middle classes use language. Whereas middle-class groups use language to display individual abilities and articulate different opinions, working-class groups use language more to find agreement within the group.[152] Jensen is joined by other authors in arguing that working-class language systems should not be judged to be inferior; in fact, she states, they should actually be considered superior in some respects. The working class uses language to deemphasize individualism and promote a sense of community spirit: *"Me* and *mine* are replaced with *us.*"[153]

According to classism theorists, working-class children do not have language deficits that need to be overcome in school; they simply speak a different language that should be regarded as at least equivalent to the language of the middle class, commonly referred to as "proper English." Middle-class workers should therefore learn to understand the language systems of working-class groups. The central thesis is that "U.S. schools are biased against, even punitive toward, working class dialects, styles, attitudes, and values—in effect, against working-class kids."[154] Given the fierce competition at elite universities, Jensen explains, students are often forced to choose between friendship and personal success. This factor makes it especially difficult for working-class students to succeed because they put more store in being loyal than in being "a show-off."[155] The classist system forces working-class groups to abandon their superior values, such as modesty and inclusiveness: "You must leave behind your low-class ways, your 'bad' English, your values of humility and inclusion (don't 'show off' and be a big shot because it might make someone else feel bad) and much more—not least of which are the people you love most deeply."[156]

Proponents of the theory of classism do not believe that children from working-class families should be required to assimilate with the middle class, as this assimilation could cause lifelong, sometimes serious psychological problems.[157] Jensen, who herself rose from the working class to the middle class, reports on countless serious psychological problems that she and others have suffered—and that she understands as being rooted in society and its classism: "My list of working class difficulties in college includes any of the following: (1) serious mental health problems such as major depression (including suicide), dysthymia (a lower level, long-standing depression), post-traumatic stress disorder, and substance abuse; (2) a complicated and confused bereavement, or grief process—of leaving home forever; (3) internalized classism; (4) anomie or a sense of placelessness; (5) imposter syndrome; and (6) survivor guilt."[158]

According to Jensen, working-class families are understandably concerned about their children moving up into the middle class because they worry about being alienated from their children. They also blame members of the classes above them for ultimately making working-class lives so difficult: "Is it any wonder that working class families do not easily surrender their children to the people they know help make their own lives difficult, or worse?"[159] From these and many other statements, it is clear that those authors who speak out most strongly against classism (insofar as it is directed against working-class groups and the poor) actually endorse some key prejudices and stereotypes directed against the middle class and the rich. Assenting to these stereotypes may even make class mobility more difficult.

Although these authors view the world from an extremely ideological perspective and their idealization of the working class goes hand in hand with a massive resentment of the individualism of the middle class and with prejudice against the rich, they nevertheless draw attention to one important point: the middle class absolutizes its specific values and norms. But what has so far been overlooked is that this absolutization is directed against the upper class and the rich as much as it is against the working class. The major difference, however, is as follows: If children from working-class families do manage to learn the language of the middle class and internalize its values, they have the opportunity to climb the social ladder. After all, social advancement is not possible if someone does not speak "proper" English and internalize certain values. The same emphasis and absolutization of middle-class values, however, make it more difficult to elevate oneself to the upper class, because in some cases this shift requires one to adopt completely different attitudes, skills, and values than those taught in schools. This is one reason why education does not automatically allow someone to move up from the working class to the middle class, nor does it guarantee that someone will be able to advance from the middle class to join the ranks of the rich. Each of these groups has different values. Classism researchers, despite their ideological prejudices, have nevertheless succeeded in pointing out the extent to which middle-class values are absolutized.

CHAPTER 3

WARMTH AND COMPETENCE: HOW WE JUDGE OUT-GROUPS

Psychologist Susan T. Fiske and other researchers have developed a model that makes a major contribution to understanding stereotypes about the rich, even though their model only tangentially deals with attitudes toward rich people. In fact, their model is more concerned with demonstrating that prejudices and stereotypes are not necessarily purely negative in nature and that images of out-groups are frequently formed on the basis of mixed combinations of stereotypes.[160]

THE STEREOTYPE CONTENT MODEL

According to their "Model of (Often Mixed) Stereotype Content," two primary dimensions shape affective reactions to social out-groups. The first dimension is *warmth*: an out-group can be stereotyped as warm and friendly or as cold, untrustworthy, and unfriendly. The second dimension is *competence*: an out-group can be stereotyped as confident, hardworking, and ambitious or as lazy and incompetent. Studies show that these two dimensions are responsible for more than 80 percent of the variance in cultural stereotypes and individual impressions.[161]

There are four possible combinations for how out-groups can be perceived:

1. Warm and competent
2. Warm and incompetent
3. Cold and competent
4. Cold and incompetent

Why have the researchers used these terms in particular? When people meet others, as individuals or as group members, they want to know what the others' goals are and whether they mean well or badly vis-à-vis the self or the in-group. Is the other or the other group friendly or unfriendly toward their own group? This is the dimension of "warmth." The second question they ask is to what extent the other individual or group is in a position to pursue their positive or negative goals. In short, how capable or competent is the other or out-group?[162]

Negative attitudes and prejudices toward out-groups are essentially based on two different assessments: either the out-group is seen as lacking competence, such as we find in negative stereotypes about housewives, disabled people, or senior citizens, or the out-group is seen as lacking warmth, such as we find in negative stereotypes about Asians, Jews, or female professionals.[163]

In several studies, individuals were asked to score social out-groups on a scale of 1 to 5 for the dimensions of warmth and competence. To alleviate the problem of socially desirable answers, test participants were informed that the researchers were not interested in the participants' own perceptions and personal beliefs but in the participants' assessment of how these groups were perceived by others.[164] Four important findings emerged:

1. The highest ratings for warmth and competence went to the in-group—the studies' participants were predominantly white and middle class.
2. Disabled people and elderly people were among the groups perceived as warm but not competent.

3. Jews, Asians, and rich people were given very high scores for competence but very low scores for warmth.
4. Welfare recipients and homeless people were regarded as neither competent nor warm.

The highest levels of competence were attributed to rich people, who were also rated low in warmth. Welfare recipients were perceived as low in competence and low in warmth. In contrast, elderly people were viewed as low in competence but high in warmth.[165]

Analyzing the interviews, the researchers determined the variance in scores awarded to the target groups for the two dimensions of competence and warmth. Of 23 groups evaluated by the studies' participants, the greatest difference between scores for competence and warmth was for rich people, followed by Asians. These two groups were perceived as extremely competent but low in warmth. At the other end of the spectrum, housewives and disabled people were rated as low in competence and high in warmth.[166]

The same researchers also examined which emotions the stereotypes of these groups elicited. High-competence and low-warmth groups, including rich people, Jews, and Asians, were met with mixed feelings of admiration and envy. The strongest emotion elicited by groups perceived as high in warmth but low in competence, such as disabled or elderly people, was pity.[167]

When out-groups are regarded as highly competent, this view can heighten negative feelings and attitudes against them.

High status out-groups may elicit an envious mixture of admiration (rather than disrespect) plus intense dislike motivated by a sense of threat (for dangerous competitors). Thus, a person's belief that Asian Americans, Jews, and businesswomen are competent (perhaps even hypercompetent) may only add fuel to the fire of prejudice. Anti-Semites, for instance, often believe outrageous conspiracy theories of Jewish economic and social influence. In this case, positive stereotypes of an out-group's competence (along with correspondingly negative stereotypes of the group's lack of warmth and ill intentions) drive a particularly dangerous form of prejudice that all too often results in extreme forms of violence.[168]

The stereotype content model has been validated in a U.S. representative sample survey and in group studies in more than three dozen countries. "The warmth × competence map apparently captures some human universals," concludes Fiske.[169] According to Fiske, people all over the world see rich people and entrepreneurs as competent but cold.[170]

In 2005, Monica H. Lin and colleagues used the stereotype content model in a number of studies to research stereotypes and prejudices against Asian Americans. In their conclusion, they suggest that when this model is employed, images of Asian Americans closely resemble images of other groups—they explicitly mention Jews and "images of rich people all over the world."[171] Asian Americans are perceived by white Americans as highly competent, but uncomfortable and lacking interpersonal skills. Above all, the 1,296 participants in the Lin study strongly associated the following characteristics with Asian Americans:

- Constantly in pursuit of more power
- Obsessed with competition
- Think they are smarter than everyone else
- Strive to become number one
- Motivated to obtain too much power in society
- Compare own achievements to other people's
- To get ahead of others, can be overly competitive
- Enjoy disproportionate economic success[172]

At the same time, Asian Americans were perceived as devoting little time to socializing and as not functioning like other groups in social situations. It can be supposed that similar characteristics are also ascribed to rich people, a question we will turn to later. The study concluded, "Asians are thus the targets of resentful, envious prejudice: grudgingly respected for their presumed competence but disliked for their alleged lack of sociability."[173]

Prejudices against groups such as Asians, as well as Jews and rich people, therefore differ from prejudices against African Americans and other minorities, who are deemed low in competence. Asian Americans are among the groups that are met with a mixture of "admiration, resentment, and envy."[174] To provide a rationale for rejecting such an out-group—whose competence cannot be denied—images of the out-group are based on allegedly low "sociability" characteristics, for example, that Asian Americans are socially isolated and awkward. "To justify discriminating against a high achieving outgroup, stereotyping them as socially inadequate provides a ready excuse."[175]

The Cold and Calculating Rich on Television

The portrayal of rich people in films and on TV frequently corresponds directly to the stereotype content model. Let us consider two examples from the TV crime series *Derrick*, which was broadcast in Germany from 1974 to 1998. As the series was a major international success (it was sold to over 100 countries), the stereotypes depicted in the show would appear to correspond not only to the attitudes of a German audience but also to those of viewers in many other countries. The following story was told in the episode "Eine eiskalte Nummer" ("An Ice-Cold Number"):[176]

Two men break into a luxury villa. The villa's owner is wealthy; he drives a Jaguar. He surprises the burglars, but he shows neither fear nor any other emotion. He is almost robot-like in his gestures, language, and behavior. He analyzes the situation coldly and makes the burglars the following offer: He will tell his bank to bring 20,000 deutsche marks to the villa. The rich man makes fun of the criminals' highly emotional state: "You have sweat on your forehead . . . a whisky will do you good, that will calm you down." One of the burglars who, unlike the rich man, is wracked with nerves, says to him, "You have ice in your veins."

The burglars leave the house with the 20,000 deutsche marks but forget their gun. Shortly afterward, the rich man's business partner comes to visit him. The partner confronts him with evidence that the rich man has defrauded their customers. During the dispute with his business partner, the rich man confesses: "I have cooked the books. . . . I have found a way that, well, is a little outside the law. . . . But what's life? It's a tightrope walk! It's all about keeping yourself from falling, whatever it takes." The business partner sees things differently and announces that he's going to press charges. The rich man mocks him and laughs: "Let's all celebrate your good character. You have such a good character, show it to the whole world. I'm sure they will admire it."

The rich man seizes the opportunity and shoots his business partner with the burglars' pistol, clearly intending to frame them for the murder. After meeting the rich man, Inspector Derrick says to his colleague, "He's an ice-cold number."

The rich man is depicted as emotionless and yet highly competent, a portrayal that corresponds almost perfectly to the stereotype content model's image of rich people, who are perceived as lacking warmth and emotions but highly intelligent.

Here is a second example, also from the series *Derrick*. The episode "Kein teurer Toter" ("No Costly Corpse")[177] tells the following story:

> An entrepreneur, the owner of a sawmill, is the victim of threaten-ing calls. Someone is calling him, accusing him of exploiting other people. A lawyer, a friend of the entrepreneur's family, calls Inspector Derrick. But the entrepreneur, who isn't taking the calls seriously, throws Derrick out and asks him whether he has nothing better to do. Eventually the mill owner is murdered.

The lawyer describes life at the sawmill: "He runs his business with an iron fist. He enjoys offending other people. If you don't fight back, you are out. He's like a slave driver." The entrepreneur describes himself thus: "I didn't get where I am by making friends. And if someone wants to call me a slave driver, he should. That's exactly what I am!"

His secretary has the following to say about the entrepreneur: "He hated everyone. . . . Whenever he entered the room, my heart stopped. And I couldn't breathe normally for the rest of the day." The foreman echoes what the others have already said, "He was an obstructionist—a real nuisance."

Derrick's assessment was equally negative: "He was an evil man. And I have the feeling he was proud of the fact, too." And "The dead man despised the rest of mankind. He was always looking for someone to hurt."

In his private life, too, the entrepreneur was a tyrant: he beat his daughter, who—like his wife and everyone else he came into contact with—lived in constant fear of him. After the murder, everyone breathed a sigh of relief. His family became cheerful and relaxed, and the secretary also breathed freely again. Here, too, the rich entrepreneur is portrayed as financially successful but cold and inhuman.

HIGH-STATUS GROUPS IN THE CROSS HAIRS

The importance of exploring prejudice, stereotyping, and envy, especially when directed against privileged groups and ruling classes, comes into focus when we consider the role of these factors in history. As Lasana T. Harris, Mina Cikara, and Susan T. Fiske write, "History suggests that high-status groups are often the targets of genocide. During social upheaval and threat, envied social groups often become the targets of the most severe types of harm—attempted elimination en masse. Concurrently, these groups have often been the most respected, even if resentfully, and as such, have been often cooperated and associated with on other occasions. This strange mix of both respect and dislike make this ambivalent emotion very complex and volatile."[178]

Envy is an emotion that arises from the desire to acquire the other group's resources: "You have something that we value, and we would like to take it away from you, if we can," as Harris and colleagues put it.[179] Envy is characterized by an ambivalence of positive and negative feelings; envied persons or social groups experience respect, admiration, and intense rejection all at once.[180] "This complex social emotion is reserved for high-status out-groups in all samples (e.g., businesspeople and rich people); envy can be a volatile affective response. These groups receive passive benefits because other groups associate with them on account of their high status and resources. But these groups also sometimes are attacked on account of being privileged outsiders. So envy elicits resentment and the volatile mix of association under stable conditions and attack under unstable social conditions."[181]

Envied groups, together with those that are admired (without envy), enjoy high status and are perceived as being competent. But the envied groups differ from the admired groups in that the former are also perceived as less warm. A group that is perceived as not warm is seen as "supra-human" or "more like automata."[182] The groups perceived as cold but efficient are the targets of dehumanized perceptions, stripped of characteristics such as warmth and sociability.

Stephen Loughnan and Nick Haslam examined people's perceptions of other social groups. According to their 2007 study, people generally tend to attribute fewer uniquely human emotions to out-groups than to their in-group. However, the researchers distinguish between two different senses of humanness: "human nature" traits, which appear early in development, and "uniquely human" traits, which are late in developing. Although it may not be intuitive, this distinction is quite relevant to our study.

Human nature traits include the following:[183]

- Curious
- Friendly
- Fun loving
- Sociable
- Trusting

- Aggressive
- Distractible
- Impatient
- Jealous
- Nervous

Uniquely human traits include the following:

- Broad-minded
- Humble
- Organized
- Polite
- Thorough

- Cold
- Conservative
- Hardhearted
- Rude
- Shallow

As their research demonstrates, out-groups that are more strongly perceived to have "human nature" traits are more likely to be associated with animals in the process of stereotyping, whereas out-groups that are more strongly perceived as possessing "uniquely human" traits are more closely associated with automata and robots. "In addition, the humanness traits are differentially associated with distinct types of nonhumans," they write. "Uniquely human traits are associated with automata more than with animals, and human-nature traits are associated with animals more than with automata."[184]

Haslam distinguishes between two forms of dehumanization, which correspond to the two distinct senses of humanness and occur when an out-group is denied the senses' respective properties. He terms them "animalistic dehumanization" and "mechanistic dehumanization." These two forms of dehumanization are very different; in mechanistic dehumanization, out-groups are denied emotional responsiveness or interpersonal warmth.[185]

As prejudice research and the stereotype content model show, rich people and businesspeople are indeed dehumanized by associating them with computers and automata. Fiske emphasizes: "These cold but effective out-groups are likened to robots. Perceived as threatening because they seem like automatons, out-groups dehumanized in this way are not so much disgusting as chilling. Think cyborgs. Businesspeople and their paraphernalia, from briefcases to suits, are associated in our mind with automatons, from androids to software. On the downside, we link businesspeople and robots to being cold, conservative, heartless, and shallow, though we acknowledge that they are also organized, polite, and thorough. What both CEOs and computers are *not* is typically human: curious, friendly, sociable, and fun-loving."[186] Perceiving the rich and others as "competent but cold" and less than fully human may explain why they are the victims of extreme active harm in times of social unrest.[187] "In the worst case, such a perception would justify the elimination of a high-status group as a threat to 'us.'"[188]

In general, groups that are perceived as low in warmth are dehumanized, both rich people and groups such as drug addicts and homeless people, who are perceived as low in both competence and warmth. Measurements of human brain activity have shown that such groups are rated significantly lower on a number of traits central to humanized perceptions. Comparisons between different social groups show that envied groups—unlike homeless people and drug addicts—are perceived as very competent. "However, both targets were rated as not typically human, compared with warm groups that elicit pity and pride."[189]

Envied groups are perceived on the one hand as hypercompetent but on the other as devoid of emotionality. Perceptions of envied groups as less warm are also a result of the fact that efficient social groups cannot be denied competence—although they may be said to "deserve attack" for being significantly lower on warmth and morality. "People are likely to harm targets with whom they do not empathize, [as well as] targets who are perceived as not having internal mental states and emotions."[190]

Under stable conditions, envied groups are less at risk, but they are actively attacked under social breakdown. Envy predicts not only a lack of compassion or willingness to help an envied group but also a feeling of spiteful satisfaction when the envied group suffers. This effect creates a vicious circle: the more an envied group is attacked, the more schadenfreude envious people experience. "If in fact active harm is accompanied by the experience of malicious pleasure, it suggests a dangerous reinforcement learning cycle," write Harris and colleagues, "whereby pleasure reinforces enactment of harm and increases the likelihood that aggressive acts will be repeated subsequently. In other words, if it feels good to actively harm an envied group, harmful behavior is that much more likely to persist."[191]

According to Harris and colleagues, in times of social stability, the negative and aggressive tendencies against envied groups are not activated; people work together with these admired groups. But "high-status, competitive out-groups need to remain aware of the very real personal dangers of social unrest,"[192] because, in times of upheaval, they are at risk. The specific form of "mechanistic dehumanization" (Haslam), in which rich people are associated with inhuman automata, is a prerequisite for persecuting or even murdering such groups—especially in exceptional situations such as crises or wars. After all, no one has compassion for heartless machines.

CHAPTER 4

ACADEMIC RESEARCH ON ENVY

Wherever the stereotype content model has been tested, the rich are always among the groups perceived as competent but cold, and they elicit *envy* from others. Psychologists Elizabeth Baily Wolf and Peter Glick reported that in American samples, envied groups include feminists, businesswomen, Asians, Jews, and the rich. In South Korea, employers, the rich, and intellectuals fall into the envied category. And in west Germany, career women, the rich, and feminists are perceived as "high in competence but low in warmth."[193]

Social comparison research has demonstrated that we constantly compare ourselves with other people, consciously or unconsciously, in order to obtain indispensable data for self-evaluation. By the same token, when we evaluate ourselves, we also compare ourselves with other people. This comparison happens automatically. After all, we can only evaluate ourselves when we compare ourselves with relevant others. This is the only way we can get an idea of whether we are tall or short, strong or weak, ugly or beautiful, intelligent or stupid. And since no two people are the same, we always measure ourselves according to our superiority or inferiority. "We all place ourselves and identify ourselves in relation to others. This confronting procedure is, at the same time, unavoidable, for it is founded in the structure of human knowledge."[194]

Envy is aroused when person A compares himself with person B and person B has qualities, possessions, or status that person A would like to have but does not currently have. In the age of the internet, social comparison has expanded considerably; we are now constantly comparing ourselves with people all around the world.[195] Previous generations would only have been able to compare themselves with neighbors and people they knew personally. Opportunities for social comparison have expanded rapidly, increasing the likelihood of envy. Envy is no longer necessarily targeted at a single person, but at abstractions, such as "the rich" or "the elite."[196]

These comparisons often take place below the level of conscious awareness. What people are normally aware of is not the feeling of envy itself, but the results of envy, namely, the negative feelings they experience toward the person they envy. In seeking to explain these negative feelings to themselves, people may exaggerate the faults of the superior target, or even manufacture faults that do not exist.[197] An envious person overlooks what others have done well, choosing instead to find "intellectual mediocrity in athletes, physical weakness in geniuses, aesthetic insensibility in scientists, lack of knowledge in artists, extravagance in innovators, vulgarity in traditionalists, and so on. . . . And when there is no alternative but to admit to some merit then there is still comparison with the ideal, to which it should or could have arrived."[198]

It is therefore important to distinguish between situations in which people are conscious of envy and those in which they are motivated by envy but are unaware of the fact. Sometimes, according to psychologist W. Gerrod Parrott, envious people are the *last* to learn that their actions are motivated by envy.[199] Normally, however, we are far more likely to experience envy only in relation to a domain that is important to us. A philosophy professor living in a forest is unlikely to envy his neighbor's hunting prowess, and the neighbor is unlikely to envy the professor's superior grasp of Hegelian dialectic.[200] Domains that are particularly relevant to a person are most likely to lead to envy. Naturally, these dimensions are different for each person. Domain relevance can also change over the course of a lifetime.[201] Researchers additionally believe that those domains that were evolutionarily relevant to successful reproduction are often the most likely to cause envy, in part because these domains—starting with sex and reproduction—remain important to so many people today. "They [the researchers] propose that domains that were important for reproductive success in humans' ancestral past will be the ones that are most prone to eliciting envy and that there will be some sex differentiation due to men and women having faced 'qualitatively different adaptive problems.'"[202]

According to this theory, it is plausible that the domains that are most relevant for men are also those that played a key role in their evolutionary biology, such as physical and mental superiority, together with success in the appropriation of material resources. Money and material resources are symbols of success and serve to increase men's chances of choosing a partner.

In particular, envy occurs in "zero-sum games," where one person's gain is another's loss. On this point, it is interesting to note that people have different perceptions of what constitutes a zero-sum game.[203] This difference is important when it comes to perceptions of the rich: if I believe that one person's wealth can only be achieved at the expense of another person's poverty (and vice versa), then I perceive economics as a zero-sum game, and this perception will tend to prompt envy. We will consider this in more detail in the next chapter.

Envy researchers resoundingly agree that people tend to envy those who are similar to themselves.[204] On the one hand, this makes sense: it is quite unlikely that I will envy a chess world champion if I myself have no interest whatsoever in chess. The same cannot be said for someone who aspires to win the world chess title and, in contrast, may well be envious. On the other hand, it is not easy to determine what factors contribute most to people's perceptions of similarity. As Christine Harris and Peter Salovey point out, "It remains unclear if, or how, similarity contributes to envy between groups. The stereotype content model proposes that envy is the emotion arising toward high-status out-groups. Yet similarity is a recurring theme within the work that focuses on envy at the individual level (and presumably people feel more similar to in-group than out-group-members). Future research that directly compares envy of out-groups to that of in-groups might help shed light in this issue."[205]

Envy is an "uncomfortable emotional state,"[206] which we therefore
attempt to avoid. For certain domains, it is objectively easy to make
direct comparisons; for others, it is harder. For example, it is difficult to
deny or relativize another person's financial or professional superiority. In
contrast, it is not easy to make objective comparisons in social domains,
such as courtesy or cooperativeness. Here, it is easier to deny the superiority of another, or at least question its magnitude or significance.[207]

Envy is almost always greater when the inferior comparer believes
that he or she has little chance of achieving the superior target's status.[208]
In response, people seek to obviate and minimize their envy. They may
be able to do so by reducing the gap between themselves and the person
they envy. If they are unsuccessful, they can use the following strategies (which Mark Alicke and Ethan Zell refer to as "secondary control
mechanisms"):

1. Envious people can emphasize their advantages in traits or
   characteristics that are unrelated to the domain they are comparing.[209] For example, the envier could say, "I might not be
   as rich as X, but I'm better educated, or a nicer person."

2. Enviers can downplay the importance of the domains in
   which they are inferior and emphasize the domains in which
   they compare favorably.[210] The envier could say, "Life is not
   all about money and material values anyway; other things
   are far more important, such as . . ."

3. Enviers can exaggerate the abilities of the target of their
   envy to such an extent that the inferior comparers' own status appears in a relatively favorable light.[211] When someone
   like Warren Buffet is perceived as a one-of-a-kind financial
   genius, it is easier to accept his superiority. Under these circumstances, the enviers can acknowledge to themselves that
   although they might not be a genius, there's no shame in
   comparing unfavorably with a superstar.

4. Enviers can engage in magical thinking and fantasize about
   future success and ultimately overcoming the target of their
   envy.[212] For example, they may believe that the roles will

be reversed in paradise, where the poor will receive more blessings than the rich.

5. A weaker coping strategy: Enviers can imagine the decline or downfall of their superior target.[213] This strategy appears to have played a role in communism, whose adherents constantly waited and worked toward the day when the rich would be stripped of their wealth.

ENVY AND THE FEELING OF INJUSTICE

According to Charles E. Hoogland, Stephen Thielke, and Richard H. Smith, people experience envy because they feel that "something is not right."[214] This feeling allows the envious person to rationalize the (undeserved) advantage of the person he or she envies. From the envier's point of view, it is therefore not important whether the envied other has gained an unfair advantage as the result of personal wrongdoing.[215] The authors suggest that the envious person blames the fact that the envied other has gained an advantage on the rules of the game, which the envier sees as unfair.

Smith argues that envy is usually characterized by a feeling of injustice: the conviction that the envied person has gained advantage in an unfair way, or that the differences between the envier and the envied are unfair: "Thus, a full explanation of the hostile feelings typical of envy may require that the envying person must also feel a sense of injustice. In other words, a person feeling envy in its typically hostile form may have to believe that the envied person's advantage is, to some degree and on some subjective level, unfair."[216]

It is not easy to distinguish between justified indignation and envy, because in both cases, (real or imagined) injustices are the focus of hostility. Richard H. Smith, Gerrod (Jerry) Parrott, and Sung Hee Kim asked 150 undergraduates to write detailed accounts of an occasion when they had felt strong envy. A distinction was then made between statements in which the feeling of injustice was subjective—for example, "It seemed unfair that the person I envied started out in life with certain superior talents, abilities, or physical attributes"—and those in which the indignation was objectively justified, such as "an objective judge who knew the facts would agree that the person I envied did not deserve his or her good fortune."[217]

In the first case, according to Smith and his colleagues, any feeling of injustice is based on an envious person's subjective perceptions. This means that when the situation is viewed objectively by a third party, no unfairness or injustice would be discernible. In the second case, the feeling of injustice arises from obvious cases of unfair treatment that others would perceive and criticize as such.[218] Smith acknowledges that it is not always easy to distinguish between these two feelings—envy on the one hand and justified indignation on the other. "Although envious hostility may be based on subjective, illegitimate beliefs of unfairness, whereas resentment proper is based on legitimate beliefs of unfairness, the quality of the hostile feelings in both cases is probably more similar than different."[219]

In everyday situations, it may be easy to determine whether a person's emotional hostility is based on actual injustice and unfairness or whether it is merely the result of subjective perceptions. It is easy to picture a situation in the workplace in which one employee believes it is unjust that one of his or her colleagues is being paid more. In fact, after an objective examination, it becomes clear that no evidence of unfair treatment exists, and that the discrepancy in pay actually reflects the envious employee's inferior performance. Of course, the envious person will be unwilling to acknowledge this fact.

It becomes more difficult to make clear distinctions in a larger social context. Anyone who experiences a sense of injustice when CEOs earn more than 100 times as much as some other employees can find plenty of people who share that opinion. And on the political stage, they will also find many voices agreeing that such extreme income differentials are an expression of economic injustice. Many people are thus united by the belief that protesting against excessive manager salaries is by no means an expression of envy, but a justified criticism of social injustice.

Smith is right to note that the hostile component of envy is often rooted in the envious person's subjective feelings of having been wronged and treated unfairly. In politics in particular, envy is almost always masked in outrage at a supposed lack of "social justice." In many cases, the outraged do not even bother to explain precisely what they mean by "social justice." When envious people speak of "justice," what they often mean is "equality."

Envy therefore arises when someone feels unfairly treated or feels inferior to someone else. In a 1994 study, Richard H. Smith and colleagues asked 427 students to think of a situation in which they had experienced envy. Once the students had described the situation in writing, they completed a questionnaire that asked them to rate the feelings they had during their episode of envy.

In particular, the experiment measured two specific sets of beliefs:[220]

1. Subjective injustice beliefs, for example:

   • "Feeling unfairly treated by life."
   • "Resentment over the unfairness of life itself."
   • "It seemed unfair that the person I envied started out life with certain advantages over me."
   • "It seemed unfair that the good fortune of the person I envied came naturally to him/her."

2. Inferiority beliefs, for example:

   • "The person I envied made me feel inferior."
   • "Aware of my inferior qualities."
   • "The discrepancy between the person I envied and me was due to my own inferior qualities."

The researchers found that a subjective feeling of injustice is a central component of envy: "Interestingly, subjective injustice was the only independent variable strongly linked both to depressive feelings and to hostility. As the hostile and depressive components of envy seem so common and central to how the experience of envy is defined, the dual association that subjective injustice beliefs have with those components suggests that such beliefs may be singularly characteristic of envy."[221]

Thus, envy clearly arises from a feeling of inferiority. Inequality exists in every society, which means some people will always feel relatively disadvantaged compared with others. "Any human system in which differences among people have consequences for obtaining resources and for enhancing reproductive fitness creates dilemmas for individuals finding themselves relatively disadvantaged."[222] One consequence of such situations is envy: "envy is an adaptive, frequent response to disadvantage."[223]

According to Susan T. Fiske, envy arises when people who are less successful and have fewer resources seek explanations for what they perceive are the unjustified advantages of their peers who have achieved greater success or have amassed greater resources. "If a peer can succeed, then people feel inadequate for not doing equally well. Envy also makes people angry at the injustice of their low-status positions. Those who succeeded must have had unfair advantages. Envy correlates with depression, unhappiness, and low self-esteem."[224]

The effect of envy depends on the specific constellations in which it arises. In certain situations, it may directly benefit envious people to come to an arrangement with the more successful targets of their envy. In other situations, however, envy can lead to aggression against the envied. This is the inherent danger of envy. "Envy can lead to going along with the higher status and with more powerful others, but also to sabotaging and attacking them. Envy is harm waiting to happen."[225]

WHY PEOPLE DENY THEIR ENVY

"Nowadays we are generally reticent and inhibited when it comes to the imputation of envious motives," observed Helmut Schoeck in his book *Envy: A Theory of Social Behaviour.*[226] Accordingly, envy is the most commonly denied, repressed, and masked emotion. In a 1972 article titled "The Anatomy of Envy: A Study in Symbolic Behavior," George M. Foster stated that, across all cultures, people are highly reluctant to admit to envy. Over a period of several years, Foster asked his undergraduate students about their feelings of envy. About 50 percent said they were virtually without envy, 40 percent said they were moderately envious or only occasionally envious, and only 10 percent described themselves as very envious.[227]

The finding that most people, when asked directly, do not describe themselves as envious is also supported by the only large-scale longitudinal research into envy and its possible repercussions. In 2005, 2009, and 2013, researchers interviewed 18,000 randomly selected Australian adults. One of the survey's questions asked, "How well do the following words describe you?" and included "envious" as one of the possible responses. Respondents rated themselves on a seven-point scale ranging from 1 ("Does not describe me at all") to 7 ("Describes me very well"). Almost 54 percent of respondents awarded themselves the lowest scores for envy, namely, a 1 or a 2. And just over 72 percent rated themselves with a score between 1 and 3. In contrast, just over 3.6 percent gave themselves a 6 or a 7, thereby admitting to being very envious.[228] Nevertheless, it would be a mistake to conclude from this study's findings that envy is a seldom-*experienced* emotion. If it is true that people tend to deny envy more than any other emotion and, as we have seen, many scientists have proposed plausible arguments for this theory, then envy cannot be measured by asking someone directly. As with racial prejudice, more realistic results are obtained from questions whose answers indirectly indicate that the person is envious. Thus, the results of this study need to be treated with caution.[229]

In his book *Egalitarian Envy,* Gonzalo Fernández de la Mora also noted that envy is a widely denied emotion: "One may admit to pride, avarice, lust, anger, gluttony and laziness, and one may even boast of them. There is only one capital sin no one admits to: envy. This is the dark, hidden, eternally masked sin. One tries to hide it from others with multiple disguises; its symbol ought to be a mask. The envious person avoids seeing this emotion as it is and buries it in the subconscious or rationalizes it in order to distort it. People conceal their envy and, furthermore, disown it."[230] One reason for this concealment is that when someone publicly admits to being motivated by envy, any actions they take to remove the cause of their envy would be deemed socially illegitimate. When envy becomes recognizable as such, or is openly communicated, then the envious person automatically disqualifies the intention of satisfying it or eliminating it.[231]

Foster explains that envy is laden with fear. People fear being envied for what they have and want to protect themselves from the consequences of the envy of others. At the same time, people also fear being accused of envying others and are afraid of admitting to themselves that they are envious.[232]

Foster also asks why people can admit to feelings of guilt, shame, pride, greed, and even anger without loss of self-esteem, but find it almost impossible to admit to feelings of envy. He offers this explanation: Anyone who admits to themselves and others that they are envious is also admitting that they feel inferior. This is precisely why it is so difficult to acknowledge and accept one's own envy. As he puts it, "In recognizing envy in himself, a person is acknowledging inferiority *with respect to another*; he measures himself against someone else, and finds himself wanting. It is, I think, this implied admission of inferiority, rather than the admission of envy, that is so difficult for us to accept."[233]

Foster raises an issue that is of key significance in exploring the envy directed at rich people. Envy begins when one person recognizes that another person has something that they would also like to have. This recognition necessarily leads to the question "Why don't I have it? Why have they succeeded in achieving what I could not?" This insight explains why most people do not want to admit that they are envious: "Envy is not pleasant because any formulation of it—any implicit process connected with it—necessarily starts with the point that you need something, some material thing that, unhappily, someone else has. This easily leads to the question, Why don't you have it? And that is itself enough in some cases to provoke insecurity, for apparently the other fellow is better at assembling those material props of security than you are, which makes you even more inferior."[234]

According to Foster, to resolve their feeling of envy, envious people need to shift the blame for their failings to circumstances beyond their control: "Inferiority perceived as due to uncontrollable agents or conditions outside the individual, while unpleasant, may be at least bearable. Inferiority perceived as due to personal inadequacy, lack of competence, or poor judgment is much more difficult to accept, since it is so damaging to the self-image."[235] If the envious person can blame fate, chance, or dishonesty for the success of the envied person, that blame places much less of a burden on the envious person's self-esteem.

This may be one reason why people attribute the success of the rich to factors such as luck, the use of morally deplorable methods, or unfair advantages. Or an envious person may claim that wealth is not worth striving for anyway. After all, the best avoidance strategy is simply to claim that you have very little interest in money. The same effect can be achieved by juxtaposing alternatives that in reality do not exist—as expressed in proverbs such as "It's better to be poor and healthy than rich and sick."

IS THERE SUCH A THING AS BENIGN ENVY?

It is sometimes argued that envy does not necessarily have to be negative, or that there is a benign form of envy. Schoeck explicitly rejects this view. "On rare occasions," he writes, "as in certain poems, envy is invoked as a stimulant, as something sublime or constructive. In such cases the poet has made a poor choice of words; he is really referring to emulation. The really envious person almost never considers entering into fair competition."[236]

Schoeck describes envy as a feeling of aggression that is already conscious of its own impotence, so that from the start some of the aggression and a good measure of anguish and torment are somewhat masochistically turned back upon the subject. "One begrudges others their personal or material assets, being as a rule almost more intent on their destruction than on their acquisition."[237]

The envier, according to Schoeck, has little interest in acquiring anything of any value from the other's possession. "He would like to see the other person robbed, dispossessed, stripped, humiliated or hurt, but he practically never conjures up a detailed mental picture of how a transfer of the other's possessions to himself might occur. The pure type of envier is no thief or swindler in his own cause. In any case, where that which is envied is another man's personal qualities, skill or prestige, there can be no question of theft; he may quite well, however, harbour a wish for the other man to lose his voice, his virtuosity, his good looks or his integrity."[238]

Schoeck's view has not, however, remained unchallenged. Jens Lange and Jan Crusius distinguish between "benign" and "malicious" envy.

Other languages also make semantic distinctions between these two forms of envy, including Russian, which has "white" and "black" envy, and German, which has *Neid* and *Missgunst* (although *Neid* also serves as the superordinate term for both forms of envy).[239] According to Lange and Crusius, benign envy increases the enviers' motivation to move upward, to improve their own positions, whereas malevolent envy increases the motivation to harm another person or damage their status. According to the authors, "Dispositional envy is a comparison-based emotional trait that leads to frustration when people are confronted with an upward standard. . . . In general, envy's functional goal is to level the difference between the self and the envied person. In the case of benign envy, the envier tries to level up whereas in the case of malicious envy, the envier tries to level the envied person down."[240]

The authors developed their own 10-item Benign and Malicious Envy Scale to allow them to differentiate between the two, a distinction that previous scales did not address. Among the items that measured benign envy was the statement, "When I envy others, I focus on how I can become equally successful in the future." Among the items that measured malicious envy was this statement: "I wish that superior people lose their advantage."[241]

Parrott distinguishes between "nonmalicious" and "malicious" envy. Nonmalicious envy is exemplified when someone says, "I wish I had what you have." In contrast, malicious envy is typified by the statement, "I wish you did not have what you do." According to Parrott, malicious envy is purely destructive: "To the person suffering malicious envy, the marvelous car should be stolen or damaged, the virtuous person corrupted or killed, the beautiful face covered or disfigured. In malicious envy it is not necessary to desire what the other has—only to desire that it be taken away from the other."[242]

In their paper "Why Envy Outperforms Admiration," Niels van de Ven, Marcel Zeelenberg, and Rik Pieters propose the hypothesis that benign envy, not malicious envy or the emotions of admiration, is what motivates people to improve themselves. They state that, in contrast to the frustration of (benign) envy, admiration might be a positive feeling, but it is rarely an incentive to improve oneself.[243] The authors do,

however, concede that admiration can sometimes have positive consequences,[244] although they point out that far more frequently, admiration has a negative effect on motivation. The researchers also claim that
admiration, when limited to the recognition of an outstanding performance of another person, likely leads to a decrease in motivation. Of the
three possibilities of upward social comparison (benign envy, malicious
envy, and admiration), they state that benign envy is most likely to motivate self-improvement.

The findings of the longitudinal study on envy in Australia cited
earlier would seem to contradict the thesis proposed by van de Ven,
Zeelenberg, and Pieters. The Australian study demonstrated that envy
has a negative effect on people's well-being and that no empirical evidence suggests that envy acts as a useful motivator—not even, for example, as a motivator for economic success.[245]

Justin D'Arms and Alison Duncan Kerr dismiss any distinction
between benign and malicious envy. They argue that there is actually no
such thing as benign envy. As they observe, Immanuel Kant defined envy
as a propensity to view the well-being of others with distress. Envy aims
to destroy someone else's good fortune.[246] The authors suggest that the
idea that some envy is benign is the result of the use of the word "envy"
in everyday language (e.g., "What a great house you have; I envy you.").
As they point out, however, emotion researchers are well aware of the
fact that natural language is often sloppy about attributing emotions. For
these authors, envy is not just a painful longing for a good that someone
else has, but, far more, the desire for the other to lose that good, advantage, or status.[247] Thus, they conclude, the notion of "benign" envy is a
contradiction in terms.[248]

If an envious person is given a choice between a rival's possessing a
good or neither of them possessing the good, the envier will choose a
situation in which neither of them has it. For example, if my neighbor
has bought a Mercedes and I am envious, my envy will not necessarily
disappear if I buy one myself a week later. But it will disappear immediately if my neighbor loses his Mercedes, for whatever reason.[249]

In contrast to Smith, D'Arms and Kerr believe that envy is not necessarily associated with a sense of injustice. They suggest that an envious

person is disturbed by a rival's advantage, regardless of whether or not this advantage is justified. In fact, they note, those who envy will often find some moral complaint to justify their negative feelings toward their rival, that is, they will morally package their envy.[250]

In my opinion, little is to be gained from making distinctions between deserved or undeserved advantages or judgments about "fair" and "unfair" holdings by others. After all, everyone has a different concept of justice. And to appease any feelings of inferiority, losers are apt simply to convince themselves that the very rules of the domains in which they are competing are unfair. Yet advantages are distributed unequally by nature; nature does not care for a concept of "justice" in the sense of equality, not even in the sense of equal opportunities. Here's just one example: A beautiful woman has the upper hand when choosing a partner. Has she "earned" her advantage? A less attractive woman, who is at a disadvantage when choosing a partner, will bemoan the fact that appearance plays such a key role in finding a partner. Disadvantaged people always wish the rules of the game were different. The less attractive woman wishes that appearance weren't so important, and the less affluent would prefer that money weren't so important.

What others have described as benign envy (i.e., envy without anger, hostility, or ill will), Harris and Salovey also argue, would be more accurately described as "desire or longing."[251] Envy has two aspects: On the one hand, the envious person focuses on taking away what the other person has, perceiving the inherent inequality of the situation as unjust. On the other hand, the envious person interprets the inequality of the situation as the result of his own failure, which threatens his sense of self-worth and self-esteem.[252]

In view of the many frequently contradictory definitions of envy, Yochi Cohen-Charash and Elliott Larson propose a definition to unify all the concepts of envy: "Negative social comparison, feelings of pain, longing for the object of envy, and the goal to eliminate the pain of envy. These elements are seen in all writings about envy, and hence can be the agreed-upon bases of an envy definition."[253] They identify the common denominators of all envy definitions thus: "Therefore, we define envy as a painful emotion that involves the beliefs that (a) one lacks a desired object that another person has, and (b) the desired object is important to the person's self-concept or competitive position. Envy includes the motivation to reduce the pain it entails and to improve one's relative standing."[254]

ENVY AND SCHADENFREUDE

As far back as Aristotle, philosophers realized that malicious joy and envy are closely linked. Baruch Spinoza defined envy as a feeling of sadness about the good fortune of another person and of happiness when something negative happens to the other person.[255] Social science research supports this framework. According to the results of psychological experiments reported by Richard H. Smith and colleagues,[256] an envious person experiences schadenfreude, a malicious feeling of pleasure, when an envied person suffers misfortune. "Our findings suggest that an envious response to someone's superiority will have important implications for how we subsequently feel about a misfortune befalling this person. Rather than feeling sympathy, we are likely to feel *schadenfreude*."[257]

These scientists conducted an experiment to measure the responses of subjects to positive or negative everyday events occurring to different people. In doing so, they employed the stereotype content model presented in the previous chapter. Their experiments involved a series of images in which something happens to someone in everyday life. For example, a wealthy businessman accidentally sits in chewing gum on a park bench or steps in dog excrement. After the test subjects had viewed these images of positive and negative everyday experiences, they rated each image according to how they would feel if they saw this happening in real life. A 10-point scale was used, ranging from 1 ("I would feel extremely bad") to 10 ("I would feel extremely good"). At the sight of negative events befalling envied groups (including rich people), subjects experienced the least negative reactions and, at the sight of good events, they experienced the least positive reactions, when compared with all other unenvied groups. In addition, the researchers used a device to measure the movement of the subjects' smile muscles. For envied out-group members alone, these smile muscles activated more for negative events than for positive ones. As the researchers observe, "People can't help smiling a little when an investment banker 'steps in dog poo.' This is schadenfreude."[258]

In further experiments, Mina Cikara and Susan T. Fiske investigated which groups are most likely to evoke schadenfreude. In addition to direct questions, the researchers also measured changes in facial musculature, because, as they observe, expressions of schadenfreude are likely to be constrained by social desirability effects. Facial electromyography allows even the smallest changes in facial musculature to be measured. Test subjects have much less control over such muscular responses than they do over their verbal utterances.

In another experiment, test subjects were shown photos of various people experiencing positive, neutral, or negative events. One of the people was an investment banker. The result: "Participants felt *least bad* about *negative* events, and *least good* about *positive* events when they happened to envy targets as compared to other targets. . . . Though participants did not want to explicitly report feeling pleasure when envy targets experienced a misfortune, these facial [electromyography] findings provide preliminary evidence for the *presence of positive affect* (i.e., smiling)— not just the absence of negative affect—in response to envied targets' misfortunes."[259]

Cikara and Fiske note that, in many cases, people do not feel compassion toward members of higher-status groups when an accident happens to them; by contrast, they often experience malicious joy. "However, not all outgroups are equivalent; high-status, competitive groups are more likely than other outgroups to be targets of Schadenfreude, as well as active harm. Knowing that perceptions of warmth and competence drive these responses allows us to predict which groups are at greatest risk in times of social instability."[260]

When other people suffer misfortunes, the typical response is to feel sorry for them. Nevertheless, according to Caitlin A. J. Powell, Richard H. Smith, and David Ryan Schurtz, there are a number of contexts in which it is apparently permissible to feel a gloating joy instead. In their view, envy is an unpleasant emotion, and the pain of envy is reduced when the envied person suffers misfortune.[261] The authors observe that when people compare themselves with others and the result of their comparison is unfavorable their self-esteem is threatened. "If people feel envy, they usually feel a threat to self-worth. Thus, scholarly treatments of envy usually emphasize that envy involves some sense of inferiority, one of the main reasons why envy can be such a painful emotion. A misfortune befalling the envied person should lessen or remove the cause of the inferiority, and this should be gratifying."[262]

The envier interprets the rival's superiority as unfair: "The advantage may be construed in a biased way as undeserved, a construal that gives false credence and fuel for the envying person's hostility."[263] In fact, the authors note, the undeserved nature of the envied person's advantage or of the envier's disadvantage is a key component of envy. The envious person subjectively perceives this advantage as unjust. The consequence: when people who enjoy a (supposedly) unfair advantage suffer to some extent, or a misfortune cuts them down to size, schadenfreude seems quite fitting.[264]

The term "tall poppy syndrome" refers to the envy and resentment directed toward successful people. Australian professor Norman T. Feather examined the emotions and attitudes experienced by members of the middle class when a particularly successful person falls from grace. Feather started by observing that Australians (his research involved Australian students) reacted positively when an important politician was caught in a foolish act, when a businessman lost a lot of money in a stock market crash, or when a television celebrity suffered a sudden decline in popularity.[265] He complained that there is relatively sparse psychological literature on attitudes toward people in high positions.[266]

Feather's initial hypothesis was that attitudes toward very successful people are often mixed or ambivalent and that this ambivalence should be reflected in emotions and attitudes toward the fall of such tall poppies.[267] On the one hand, he posited that high achievers or successful people should, at least in some respects, be regarded more positively than average people. "For example, the high achiever will probably be regarded as more competent, hardworking, efficient, confident, and as deserving of more respect and admiration than the average performer in societies that value individualism and achievement."[268] On the other hand, he suggested, it is also possible for people to hold negative attitudes toward high achievers that conflict with positive evaluations. "For example, they may tend to see high achievers generally as distant, unsociable, competitive."[269] Though he was working outside the stereotype content model, his research clearly led to a similar place.

Feather hypothesized that collectivist values are antithetical to respect for tall poppies, though I would refer to such values as *egalitarian*: "Collectivist values within a culture may also underlie feelings of satisfaction when a tall poppy falls, especially when the fall takes the tall poppy to an average position and makes the tall poppy more similar or equal to others. In contrast, the fall of an average achiever would be welcomed less because the fall removes the person from the collectivity that is identified with the middle range of accomplishment."[270] Although Australians value success, Feather noted, they also believe that no one should be *too* successful or *too* far above the average.[271]

Feather's experiments confirmed his hypotheses. His test subjects were more pleased (or at least less unhappy) when a high achiever failed than when an average achiever failed. The subjects were also relatively more pleased when failure took a high achiever to the middle of the performance scale than to the very bottom. "The middle or average position may be taken as the group norm, the position that represents the collectivity."[272]

Strikingly, Feather found no evidence that his test subjects were initially more negative toward high achievers than they were toward average achievers. In this context, Feather cited Foster's observation that people fear the consequences of envy and that envy is therefore often denied. "It may be easier to observe negative feelings towards high achievers when there is a clear pretext for expressing them, as when a high achiever suffers a fall."[273]

In a second study, Feather examined how subjects would react when a high achiever committed a misdemeanor and whether they would report feeling more pleased about the high achiever's subsequent fall. The test subjects reported that, even when committing the same misdemeanor, high achievers deserve to be punished more harshly than average achievers.[274] "Thus, subjects may have reported feeling more pleased about the high achiever's fall in both studies because the fall cut the tall poppy down to size, showed that the tall poppy was fallible, and made the tall poppy more like others."[275]

Feather conducted a third study, this time not an experiment but a survey designed to examine attitudes toward high achievers and whether they correlated with the self-esteem of the survey's respondents. To this end, Feather constructed a scale to measure attitudes toward high achievers and then correlated the scores on this scale with scores on a measure of self-esteem with value priorities.

Here are some of the items from Feather's questionnaire that elicited the strongest responses in favor of the tall poppy's fall:[276]

- It's good to see very successful people fail occasionally.
- Very successful people often get too big for their boots.
- Very successful people who fall from the top usually deserve their fall from grace.
- Those who are very successful ought to come down off their pedestals and be like other people.
- Very successful people sometimes need to be brought back a peg or two, even if they have done nothing wrong.
- People who always do a lot better than others need to learn what it's like to fail.
- People who are very successful get too full of their own importance.
- Very successful people usually succeed at the expense of others.

Such statements received strong support from those who were pleased with the failure or fall of the tall poppy. On the other hand, subjects who believed that high achievers should be rewarded responded strongly to statements such as:[277]

- People who are right at the top usually deserve their high position.
- It's very important for society to support and encourage people who are very successful.

- One ought to be sympathetic to very successful people when they experience failure and fall from their very high positions.
- People who are very successful deserve all the rewards they get for their achievements.

The key findings of Feather's correlation analysis were as follows:[278]

- Subjects with lower self-esteem scores had stronger negative attitudes toward high achievers.
- Subjects with lower self-esteem experienced more satisfaction at the high achiever's fall.
- Subjects with a preference for more left-wing politics were more likely to favor the tall poppy's fall and were less likely to support rewarding the tall poppy when compared with subjects with differing political views.

Envy as a Motive for Advocating Wealth Redistribution

So how do feelings of envy relate to support for the redistribution of wealth? To answer this question, a team of researchers conducted 13 studies with 6,024 participants in the United States, Great Britain, India, and Israel.

Among the examples of items used to measure support for economic redistribution are "Wealth should be taken from the rich and given to the poor" (scale of 1 to 7) and "The government spends too much money on the unemployed" (reversed, scale of 1 to 7).[279] Dispositional compassion was measured using statements such as "I suffer from others' sorrows" and "I tend to dislike soft-hearted people."[280] Envy was measured with items including "I feel envy every day" and "It is so frustrating to see some people succeed so easily."[281]

Expected personal gain from redistribution was measured by the question: "Imagine that a policy of higher taxes on the wealthy is implemented. What overall impact do you think the higher taxes on the wealthy would have on you?" On a scale of 1 to 5, respondents could indicate to what extent their "own economic situation would significantly worsen—[or] improve."[282]

Two alternative fiscal scenarios were also presented to model the results of higher taxes on the rich:

- The top 1 percent wealthiest individuals pay an extra 10 percent of their income in taxes, and as a consequence the poor get an additional $200 million.[283]
- The wealthy pay an extra 50 percent of their income in taxes, and as a consequence the poor get an additional $100 million instead of an additional $200 million. (To make this plausible to the survey's respondents, the researchers explained that the rich earned more when tax rates were lower, so under that scenario more tax revenue would be generated, which could then be redistributed to the poor.)[284]

Fairness is more difficult to measure because everyone has different concepts of fair and unfair. The study's authors therefore decided to use separate instruments to measure support for "procedural fairness" and for "distributional fairness."

- Endorsement for "procedural fairness" was measured with items such as "The law of the land should apply to everybody in the same way" and "It would not bother me much if different groups or people were subject to different rules" (reversed).[285]
- Support for "distributional fairness" was measured with a set of seven decisions about how to allocate a financial windfall. The seven decisions differed in both the amount of the windfall and the options for allocating the money.[286]

In all four countries, the study found that beliefs about both variants of fairness (equal distribution and equal application of laws and standards) had little to no measurable effect on support for redistribution.[287]

However, crucially, the researchers confirmed that the three factors of compassion, envy, and self-interest had measurable effects on support for redistribution and that each factor acted independently of the other. Between 14 percent and 18 percent of the surveys' participants even went so far as to advocate redistribution through very high taxation of the rich (an additional 50 percent in taxes), even if the poor would receive only one-half of the sum hypothetically generated by a moderate tax increase (an additional 10 percent in taxes).[288] In the United States, the United Kingdom, and India, the more envious the participants were, the more likely they were to prefer the "wealthy-harming scenario."[289] The researchers' analysis also reveals that dispositional compassion was the only reliable predictor of giving aid to the poor, whereas envy had no effect on the willingness to personally aid the poor. Conversely, envy— but not compassion—was the reason participants supported high taxa-tion of the rich even when it was detrimental to the poor: "Envy, but not compassion, predicts a desire to tax the wealthy even when that costs the poor."[290]

Envy is as old as mankind; it is an anthropological constant. Thus, envy itself is not the invention of any political forces, although it can be exploited and magnified to political ends. The most important banner for mobilizing envy in recent years has been social justice, understood as a type of radical egalitarianism. As Fernández de la Mora writes, "A fundamental postulate is established that the more just a society is, the more equal its members are in opportunities, position, and wealth; and immediately it is established that the party will fight without rest to achieve such 'justice.' The appeal of this axiom and of such a program is evidently unbeatable for the envious, since it promises to abolish the unassimilated inferiority that causes them so much pain. Equality is a paradisiacal promise for the envious, the definitive incentive."[291]

Yet envy also harms the envious, as observed by Fiske and other researchers.[292] After all, envious people, who tend to blame the pow-erful and rich targets of their envy for all of the evils in the world, undermine their own sense of control over their circumstances, a state that has been proven to cause ill health. Inflicting damage on envied targets prompts even the most envious people to accept disadvantages for themselves. And the very thing that people from lower classes crave the most—namely, respect—is particularly endangered by the dynamics of resentment against "those at the top." As Fiske so succinctly puts it, "Envy eats the envious."[293]

The study from Australia cited above offers empirical proof that envy is harmful to psychological health and well-being. Admittedly, one of the study's weaknesses is that only those who self-reported as envious were deemed to be envious. Nevertheless, among these participants, it was clear that the envious are less satisfied with life and less healthy than those who reported being less envious. The researchers used the SF-36 Mental Health Index to determine which participants should be classified as envious and which as less envious. Participants were also asked about their general satisfaction with life ("All things considered, how satisfied are you with your life?"). The result: "What these sets of fixed-effect equations demonstrate is that contemporaneous changes in reported envy are inversely correlated, both in a substantive and statistically significant sense, with changes in people's satisfaction with life."[294] And "The higher is envy today, therefore, the lower is mental well-being in the future."[295]

DOES MORE EQUALITY LEAD TO LESS ENVY?

Simply put, no: envy cannot be reduced by redistribution and a higher degree of egalitarian social justice. Schoeck repeatedly emphasizes this observation, and there is even an old proverb that says, "The more one tries to gratify an envious man, the more envious he becomes." This observation, stresses Schoeck, is so important because it has been confirmed so many times. According to Schoeck, the more effort you (the envied) make to deprive envious people of their professed reason for their envy, for example, by giving them gifts and doing them favors, the more you demonstrate your superiority and highlight how little you will actually miss your gift.[296] "Once the process of envying has begun, the envious man so distorts the reality he experiences, in his imagination if not actually in the act of perception, that he never lacks reason for envy."[297] For this reason, Schoeck dismisses the concept of a society freed from envy as nothing more than a utopia. In fact, he believes the opposite to be true: "In a hierarchically structured stable society, envy raises fewer problems than in a society with great social mobility."[298]

Hans-Peter Müller takes a similar tack and argues that in earlier, highly hierarchical societies, social comparisons always related exclusively to one's in-group. In the past, it was out of the question "that barbarians would compare themselves with Greek citizens, that women would compare themselves with men, or that slaves would compare themselves with their masters. Any comparison related only to one's own status group, within which it was necessary to assert the better or worse position, the higher or lower position. Other classes lived in a completely different social world. The desire to cross role and class boundaries would have been perceived as arrogance, hubris, even insubordination."[299]

In modern societies, the situation is different. Müller writes:

> Despite the fact that society is initially wide open to all individuals, so in the end only a very small few can rise to the upper echelons of society. There will inevitably be many people who will either end up empty-handed, suffering from unemployment and failure, or who will have to make do with professional positions which remain below their skills and abilities. There are winners and losers in this game, too. In processing the disappointing reality of their "fate," the losers will develop envy and resentment towards the "beati possidentes," however much their success in life and career seems to be justified by the ideal of meritocracy. Yes, perhaps it is only the fact of legitimate inequality that fuels resentment because, in addition to resentment, there is also the perception of one's own powerlessness.[300]

The paradox of this finding is obvious: In a culture of inequality, envy and resentment are kept in check because they relate exclusively to the social differences within an in-group. "In a culture of equality, however, where everything is apparently promised to everyone (as an ideal), but certain career and life paths are only open to a few (as a reality), the scope for envy, malevolence and resentment is also opened wide. Unlimited equality as an (empty) promise liberates poisonous feelings."[301]

Echoing Georg Simmel, Müller postulates that social inequality and the efforts to neutralize it are a perpetual process without climax or endpoint. He observes that it is not only absolute inequalities but also relative inequalities that elicit feelings of envy, malevolence, and resentment. "The greater the external social equality, the more sensitive the population becomes to residual inequalities. More equality sharpens the awareness of inequality."[302] Schoeck pointedly formulated this thought when he wrote that "man's envy is at its most intense where all are almost equal." He went on to observe that calls for redistribution are loudest when virtually nothing is left to redistribute.[303]

According to Müller, modern welfare states are particularly susceptible to feelings of envy: "Societies that have enthroned the welfare state as the central agency for the distribution of opportunities in life pay the price for failure in the form of causal and guilt attribution. In place of 'self-blame,' they experience 'system-blame.' People don't blame themselves for their failures, they turn on 'father state' or 'society' when they measure what they wanted against what they have achieved."[304]

CHAPTER 5

ZERO-SUM BELIEFS: YOUR GAIN IS MY LOSS

George M. Foster's research highlighted the link between envy and the belief that life is a zero-sum game, in which the advantage of one inevitably means the disadvantage of the other. "In zero-sum game societies—or situations—it is the *relative* difference that triggers the latent envy always present, and this difference may be produced by both rising and falling fortunes of people in the same group."[305]

A zero-sum game is a game in which the sum of the payouts to the players is zero. One player's gain is automatically another's loss. Non-zero-sum games, in contrast, are games in which the sum of the payouts to the players is not constant. In such games, both parties can win or lose, or one party can win without the other losing, and so on.

Researchers believe that the tendency to regard life in zero-sum terms has its roots in past forms of society in which situations with limited resources were the norm. "When resources are limited, the allocation of desirable resources means that those resources will soon be depleted," explains psychologist Daniel V. Meegan.[306]

The American economist Paul H. Rubin has shown that folk economics, or popular or amateur ideas of economic life, are entirely focused on the question of the distribution of wealth, not on how that wealth is produced.[307] "The key point is this: folk economics is the economics of wealth allocation, not production. Naive people or those untrained in economics think of prices as allocating wealth but not as influencing allocation of resources or production of goods and services. In folk economics, the amount of a good traded—whether in aggregate or by each individual—is fixed and independent of price. Moreover, each individual is concerned with the distribution of wealth and income . . . , not with any efficiency gains from economic activity. The world of folk economics is a zero-sum world, and the primary economic problem for each individual is to maximize his or her own wealth in this world. One of the goods traded is labor, so the number of jobs is also viewed as fixed. Thus, in folk economics, if one person gets a job someone else must lose a job."[308]

Technical advances are therefore often viewed only as a threat to existing jobs. This was the fear of machine breakers at the beginning of the 19th century. Today, people worry about becoming superfluous when robots take over their work. All these ideas are based on a way of thinking that does not focus on the new jobs created, the efficiency gains, and the economic growth that result from innovation but only on the "fair" distribution of supposedly fixed resources.

Rubin attributes this kind of thinking to conditioning in the human brain, which he explains in terms of evolutionary biology.[309] Over millions of years, there were hardly any improvements in technology or growth. The pace of change in primitive societies was so slow that individuals could hardly perceive it during the course of their lives. Everyone lived in a world with seemingly unchanging technology, and no advantage existed for people who had an understanding of growth—precisely because there was virtually no such growth. There was also hardly any division of labor, apart from the division of labor between children and adults and between men and women. Trade was not an expression of a systematic division of labor, but rather the result of chance—merely by luck, or perhaps by geography, someone had something in abundance that another could use. If people in such societies had advantages or disadvantages, then those stemmed mostly from one person's not treating another fairly, or by his holding a real but serendipitous advantage over the other. Therefore, according to Rubin, people developed a strong sense to recognize and avoid situations in which they could be victimized or cheated by others.

In precapitalist societies, one person's wealth was in fact often based on robbery and the exercise of power. However, the free-market system is not based on robbery and is not a zero-sum game. It is based on the fact that the person who satisfies the needs of as many consumers as possible becomes rich. That is the logic of the market. And the economic growth characteristic of capitalist systems makes it possible for some people to become much richer than others—in most cases, without this happening at the expense of other people.

Recent developments in China provide a notable example of this phenomenon: state influence has been curbed and market elements and private property rights strengthened. China's development shows that rising economic growth—even with rising inequality—benefits most people. Hundreds of millions of Chinese are much better off today, not *despite the fact* that there are so many millionaires and billionaires, but precisely *because* such people exist. As the reformer Deng Xiaoping declared, "Let some people get rich first." Deng was right. If we look at which provinces have seen the greatest reduction in poverty in China in recent decades, it is those with the highest economic growth. And something else is remarkable: the chances for social advancement in China have increased considerably in recent decades.[310] At the same time, inequality between rich and poor in China has increased sharply. This situation contradicts the notion many people have of the distribution of social wealth.

Terms such as "distributive justice" are therefore misleading because they suggest that there is a certain fixed sum of resources to be distributed within society. The economist Ludwig von Mises fundamentally rejected the distinction between production and distribution with the following argument:

> In the market economy this alleged dualism of two independent processes, that of production and that of distribution, does not exist. There is only one process going on. Goods are not first produced and then distributed. There is no such thing as an appropriation of portions of ownerless goods. The products come into existence as somebody's property. If one wants to distribute them, one must first confiscate them.[311]

Economic laypeople are inclined to see life as a series of zero-sum games. For example, they tend to assume that trade must always have winners and losers. They also overlook the fact that any intervention in the distribution of the economic cake will affect its size and that, for example, excessive taxation of companies or entrepreneurs may result in the cake becoming smaller overall. Likewise, tax cuts may lead to an increase in overall tax revenues when such cuts are used to stimulate growth. More importantly, tax cuts for corporations and the wealthy may work to the benefit of all.

Sociologist Patrick Sachweh conducted interviews in Germany for a qualitative study on "interpretative models of social inequality." His findings confirmed that many people really do see economics as a zero-sum game. He found that in the minds of many interviewees, "There is only a limited number of privileged places that can be occupied or a fixed sum that can be distributed, and therefore there must be disadvantaged people when others are better off. Within this interpretation, a relative improvement of a few is only possible at the expense of the disadvantage of many others."[312]

Belief in zero-sum games can be the basis for envy and prejudice against social out-groups. "Applied to inter-group judgments, the zero-sum heuristic would lead to the conclusion that a gain by another group (*outgroup*) means a corresponding loss for one's own group (*ingroup*). . . . Assuming that the CEOs of major corporations can be considered a group, public anger over high executive pay could stem from the feeling that their gain is our loss."[313]

Bertolt Brecht concisely expressed this attitude in his 1934 poem "Alfabet," in which two men—one rich, one poor—come face to face:

Said the poor man with a twitch:
Were I not poor, you wouldn't be rich.[314]

This is how many anti-capitalists understand economic life. Accordingly, rich countries should give some of their wealth to poor countries, and rich people should give aid to the poor. From this point of view, it is only because the rich are so selfish and mean-spirited that so many people are still poor.

Several experiments conducted by Meegan have demonstrated that people can believe they are playing a zero-sum game even if that belief is objectively incorrect: "Zero-sum bias describes intuitively judging a situation to be zero-sum (i.e., resources gained by one party are matched by corresponding losses to another party) when it is actually non-zero-sum."[315]

For my study (see Chapters 10–14), an item was used to measure the extent to which Americans, the British, Germans, and the French believe in a zero-sum game in relation to the distribution of social wealth.[316]

In short, it is obvious that zero-sum beliefs are a crucial basis for envy and resentment against rich people. Logically, if someone believes that any increase in the wealth of the rich is automatically linked to losses for the nonrich, they will perceive the fight against poverty as synonymous with the fight against the rich and in favor of redistribution.

CHAPTER 6

THE PSYCHOLOGY OF SCAPEGOATING

On Yom Kippur, the day of atonement in Judaism, the high priest confessed the sins of the people of Israel and symbolically transferred them to a goat by laying on hands. These sins were dispelled when the goat was driven out into the desert, hence the term "scapegoat," the English translation of the Hebrew word ăzāzêl.[317] Scapegoating describes a mechanism by which other persons or out-groups are blamed for the problems of the in-group. Peter Glick defines "scapegoating" thus: "an extreme form of prejudice in which an outgroup is unfairly blamed for having intentionally caused an ingroup's misfortunes."[318]

Throughout history, certain groups were singled out to blame for negative events that could not otherwise be explained. In many cases, scapegoats were even blamed for natural disasters.[319] Ben Irvine shows that scapegoats were often chosen because they were perceived as strong. As an example, he cites the persecution of witches. In Europe, between 40,000 and 60,000 people, overwhelmingly women, were victims of witch-hunts in the Middle Ages and the early modern period.[320] Witches were blamed for the spread of disease, crop failures, natural disasters, and many other negative events that people at the time could not explain. It was claimed that they had supernatural abilities: "Although they were scapegoats, witches were perceived to be terrifyingly powerful; after all, any person who can raise a tempest, destroy a harvest, cause diseases and infertility, and fly on a broomstick, is hardly a pushover."[321]

Gordon Allport emphasizes the importance of scapegoating in his classic *The Nature of Prejudice*. He describes scapegoating as "probably the most popular theory" of prejudice.[322] According to Allport, one reason for this popularity is that the scapegoat theory is particularly easy to understand, which in turn may also be an argument for its validity. Indeed, the ease of understanding the theory, Allport argues, must be related to the general familiarity of the experience.[323]

Allport observes that infants react to frustration with aggression, whereby they attack not the actual source of their frustration but any person or object that crosses their path.[324] Later in life, children and adults develop a considerable degree of frustration tolerance and learn to deal with frustration in a more differentiated and appropriate way.[325]

According to Allport, the scapegoat theory rests exclusively on this "frustration-aggression" hypothesis. Frustrations arising from the fact that many people in a competitive society are not as successful as they or others expect are particularly important. "The intensely competitive culture of the United States, for example, must be expected to engender irritation in the individual who fails to reach the high level of attainment that is set for him: in school, in popularity, in occupational achievement, in social status."[326] Allport argues that this dissatisfaction could lead to frustration, which could then be displaced onto immigrants, for example.[327]

Allport points out, however, that the scapegoat theory has weaknesses and is by no means sufficient to explain prejudice on its own. First, frustration does not always lead to aggression, and even when it does, aggression is by no means always displaced onto innocent out-groups.[328] In addition, the frustration-aggression theory cannot explain why certain groups are chosen as scapegoats while others are not.[329]

Prejudice research following Allport has offered different interpretations of the scapegoat theory. In some cases, the scapegoat mechanism has been interpreted psychoanalytically, in the sense that negative traits that people did not wish to acknowledge in themselves are repressed or psychologically projected onto others. For example, Glick reports that anti-gay prejudice can be explained by the fact that some people who exhibit this prejudice are themselves latent homosexuals. Researchers have also explained—somewhat more straightforwardly—that people turn their frustration into aggression against other groups, which serve as scapegoats.[330]

Attribution theory emphasizes that people tend to explain complex events that elude simple explanation by assigning explanatory attributes, including simple guilt, to certain persons or groups. Glick argues that only groups perceived as having the power and intent to cause negative events will be scapegoated. However, these groups are *not* defenseless minorities. Glick cites the stereotype content model developed by Susan Fiske and others and concludes:

> High status or powerful (e.g., socioeconomically successful) minorities that are viewed as competing with the dominant group are subjected to *envious* prejudice: they are admired for their success, but also resented for it; stereotyped as highly competent, but as having hostile motives. Because envied minorities are viewed as having the power and intent to harm, they are at risk of being blamed for causing group-level frustrations.[331]

According to Glick, this assessment is the root of conspiracy theories, in which scapegoated groups are portrayed as omnipotent. The consequences for these groups can be fatal: "If a scapegoated group is viewed as both powerful and malevolent, even the most extreme actions against them (e.g., murder) can be rationalized as self-defense."[332]

It is especially in crisis situations, Glick argues, that people seek scapegoats, because most people cannot understand the true complex causes of the crisis at hand:

> Incorrect attributions may occur because information and people's cognitive abilities to process it are limited, especially when coping with large-scale problems in complex, modern societies. For example, even professional economists may be unable adequately to explain an economic crisis. . . . Scapegoat movements attract followers by offering simpler, culturally plausible explanations and solutions for shared negative events.[333]

Glick rejects Allport's thesis that weak, defenseless minorities are always chosen as scapegoats. In fact, he claims, the opposite is often true: "It is precisely the perceived power of a group (not its perceived weakness) that makes it likely to be scapegoated."[334] As examples, Glick cites the Armenians in Turkey, the Jews in Germany, the Tutsi in Rwanda, and the rich and intellectuals in Cambodia. In all these cases, economically successful groups were first scapegoated and then murdered.[335] "Are groups always chosen for their perceived vulnerability? No, precisely the opposite—groups are scapegoated because they are (often falsely) perceived to be powerful and malevolent."[336]

In modern times, Jews were often scapegoated precisely because they were perceived as economically successful. Research on anti-Semitism has shown that anti-Semitism, which was frequently motivated by religion in early Christianity and the Middle Ages, took on an economic character in the modern era. "The content-related areas existing in the Middle Ages have all merged into the modern stereotype, but their proportions have meanwhile shifted completely. The area of religious content has declined sharply. On the other hand, the statements on the economic actions of Jews have multiplied considerably and are so dominant that they have become central in the modern stereotype."[337]

By the mid-19th century, descriptions of Jewish wealth were already common. Even earlier, in 17th-century Hamburg, this description was published as an attack on Sephardic Jews who had been arriving in the city as they fled the Iberian Peninsula: "They parade around, adorned with golden and silver pieces, with exquisite pearls and precious stones; at their weddings they dine from silver vessels and cover the table with so many bowls and confit, and finally they arrive in such splendid carriages with a postilion and large entourage."[338]

The founder of the French Antisemitic League (*Ligue antisémitique*), Édouard Drumont, wrote in 1890, "The Semite is mercantile, covetous, scheming, subtle and cunning. . . . The Semite is earthbound, with scarcely any concern for the life hereafter. . . . The Semite is a businessman by instinct; he's a born trader, dealing in everything imaginable, seizing every opportunity to get the better of the next man."[339] His words fit all too well the stereotype content model that we have been working with, in which Jews are cold and yet highly capable, and therefore dangerous.

Adolf Hitler's anti-Semitism also had a strong anti-capitalist component. This aspect is particularly evident in his early speeches, such as one given on August 13, 1920, on the question "Why are we anti-Semites?" Here, he accused the "(international) stock market and loan capital," which was financed by the Jews:

> Therefore this capital grew and today rules practically the whole world, immeasurable as to the amounts, inconceivable in its gigantic relationships, uncannily growing and—the worst part—completely corrupting all honest work, because that is the horrible part, that the normal human being who today has to bear the burden of the interest on this capital has to stand by and see how despite diligence, industry, thrift, despite real work, hardly anything is left to him with which only to feed himself, and even less to clothe himself, at the same time as this international capital devours billions in interest alone which he has to help pay, at the same time in which a racial class is spreading itself out in the state which does not do any other work than to collect interest for itself and to cut coupons.[340]

The National Socialists and other anti-Semites did not perceive Jews as a weak group. On the contrary, Jews were seen as a particularly strong group, as demonstrated by the (fake) *Protocols of the Elders of Zion*, which are cited by anti-Semites as evidence that the Jews strive for world domination.

The Jews were ideally suited as scapegoats because, according to Hitler's *Mein Kampf* and his early speeches, they were the masterminds behind both capitalism *and* communism. In *Mein Kampf*, he had developed the mass psychological fundamentals of his propaganda and in this context had explained why it was better to unload everything on a single scapegoat:

> The art of leadership, as displayed by really great popular leaders in all ages, consists in consolidating the attention of the people against a single adversary and taking care that nothing will split up that attention into sections. The more the militant energies of the people are directed towards one objective the more will new recruits join the

movement, attracted by the magnetism of its unified action, and thus
the striking power will be all the more enhanced. The leader of genius
must have the ability to make different opponents appear as if they
belonged to the one category; for weak and wavering natures among
a leader's following may easily begin to be dubious about the justice of
their own cause if they have to face different enemies.[341]

Hitler faced a variety of enemies: capitalist democracies and the commu-
nist Soviet Union. Thus, Hitler needed to find a common denominator
and make it appear that both opponents "belonged to the one category"—
and this common denominator was the Jews.

Although anti-Semitism played a major role in Hitler's early speeches and in *Mein Kampf*, it was nowhere near as prominent between 1929
and 1932, when Hitler rose inexorably to power. In his speeches during
these years, which saw the National Socialist Party gain widespread
support, other motives, especially sociopolitical promises, played a far
greater role. Hitler was just as fanatical a Jew-hater in those years as he
was in the early 1920s—we know he remained anti-Semitic throughout
his life—but he had recognized that this hatred alone was not enough
to mobilize the masses in Germany. This observation speaks against an
overly simplified interpretation of the scapegoat theory, which would
attribute the rise of the National Socialists amid the economic crisis
from 1929 onward to their propagandistic scapegoating of the Jews.

In World War II, Hitler advocated the theses of Jewish capitalism
and Jewish Bolshevism, both twin brothers, entirely in accordance with
the propagandistic principles he had developed in *Mein Kampf*. In truth,
as numerous statements he made to his inner circle show, he himself
no longer believed in the thesis of "Jewish Bolshevism"; however, it
appeared useful to him in propaganda.[342]

This example confirms Glick's psychological considerations cited
above, namely, that the minorities most likely to be scapegoated are
those that appear overwhelmingly powerful—in this case, the Jews, who
from the point of view of National Socialist propaganda were depicted as
the omnipotent masterminds behind both capitalism and communism.
According to National Socialist ideology, Jews were not a weak minority
but a particularly strong—and therefore particularly dangerous—group,

because they placed great importance on the "purity of their race." These stereotypes were the basis for the later exclusion and persecution and finally for the mass murder of the European Jews.

Ervin Staub's book *The Roots of Evil: The Origins of Genocide and Other Group Violence* analyzes the sociopsychological causes of mass murder and violence against minorities. Among the motivations Staub identifies for aggression is resentment, inflamed by a sense of injustice or aroused by the scapegoating of minorities, who are accused of enjoying unjustified advantages or privileges and blamed for society's ills.

"A sense of *injustice* that arises from unfavourable comparison of one's relative well-being and of the balance between one's efforts and rewards or between one's own and one's group's rights and privileges and those of other people or groups can give rise to resentment, anger, and violence. The experience of injustice motivates aggression of many kinds: revolutions and other social movements, criminal and other violence. . . . It is not the actual injustice that is the source of resentment, but the perception of injustice. Those identified as responsible will often be perceived as evil and deserving punishment."[343] An important role in this context is played by ideology, which offers a vision of a better world and serves to justify atrocities.[344]

There is a long but seldom-discussed history of mass murders of the rich and "privileged" groups in society. As George Gilder writes in his classic work *Wealth and Poverty,*

> On every continent and in every epoch the peoples who have excelled in creating wealth have been the victims of some of society's greatest brutalities. Recent history has seen, in Germany, the holocaust of Jews; in Russia, the pogroms of Kulaks and Jews; in northern Nigeria, the eviction and slaughter of tribesmen; in Indonesia, the killing of near a million overseas Chinese; in China itself, the Red Guard rampages against the productive; in Uganda, the massacre of whites and Indians; in Tanzania, their expropriation and expulsion; in Bangladesh, the murder and confinement of the Biharis. And as the seventies drew to a close, much of the human wealth and capital of both Cuba and Southeast Asia was relegated to the open seas. Everywhere the horrors and the bodies pile up, in the world's perennial struggle to rid itself of the menace of riches—of the shopkeepers, the bankers, the merchants, the traders, the entrepreneurs.[345]

In general, minorities targeted for genocide have been victims of prejudice long before the genocide and have been scapegoated for complex social developments that were otherwise incomprehensible to the majority of people. In crisis situations, this long-standing hatred would then erupt in violent aggression against the scapegoated. Even though a majority of the population was usually not directly involved in the persecutions and mass murders of the scapegoated minorities, the murderers were confident that most would look the other way and prefer to remain ignorant of these barbaric acts.

Before such minorities were singled out for murder, they would be subjected to a long process of dehumanization—treated as mere "character masks" of the system, or simply as "pigs," as the RAF (Red Army Faction) terrorists in Germany called the rich in the 1970s, for example, before murdering the spokesmen of the boards of Deutsche Bank and Dresdner Bank and the president of the employers' association. As scions of capitalism, they were first scapegoats for "inhuman capitalism" and the injustices of this world and then finally "liquidated."

CHAPTER 7

PRESERVING SELF-ESTEEM: COMPENSATION THEORY

As early as childhood and adolescence, members of society form images of the rich and poor, as demonstrated by an empirical study conducted by Carol K. Sigelman with 6-, 10-, and 14-year-olds in the United States. During interviews, children and young people were shown pictures and reports about one poor person and one rich person and asked why the rich man was rich and the poor man was poor.

Even at the age of six, children already perceive the rich man as "more competent" than the poor man, but they can hardly comprehend the differences between the two. Although they understand that both have different professional positions, they do not yet associate this fact with personality traits. As they grow older, they begin to associate certain personality traits with the rich and others with the poor. Increasingly, they associate wealth and poverty with categories such as ability and level of effort.[346] Sigelman's study partially confirms previous research: "On balance, it seems that the tendency to view rich people more positively than poor people may emerge quite early but strengthen once children adopt an individualistic or equity perspective on income inequality and begin to believe that rich people work harder and/or have more ability than poor people."[347]

Not only children, but also adults perceive wealthier people as more intelligent and successful. Helga Dittmar reports on an experiment that tested people's first impressions of the wealthy and the less wealthy. According to her hypothesis, material possessions signal socioeconomic status, but they also lead people to draw broader conclusions about the possessions' owners.[348] Two comparison groups of students, one with higher social status, the other with lower status, were shown five-minute videos. In one, actors were shown in a more affluent setting with more expensive material possessions; in the other, they were shown in a less affluent setting with less expensive possessions—although the differences were deliberately not very extreme. The students were asked to assign 30 personal qualities to the actors in the videos, such as intelligent, successful, friendly, warm, and so forth. The result? "The wealthy person was seen as more intelligent, successful and educated, as well as more in control of their life and environment than the less privileged character. A similar, but less pronounced, trend emerged also for forcefulness. In contrast, the poorer person emerged as warmer, friendlier and more self-expressive."[349]

It is only natural that social groups, when they perceive out-groups as economically more successful and intelligent, should develop compensation strategies to maintain their own self-esteem. It is also only natural that members of higher social strata can more easily accept the criteria for societal rankings—for example, economic success or education—because they themselves are at the top of the hierarchy.

We know that people constantly and automatically—often unconsciously—compare themselves with others. If the results of this comparison are unfavorable, the inferior comparer develops strategies to compensate. "Even if forced to compare with others, we may act on our disappointment by lowering our standards, no longer comparing so much, or even changing domains: academics suddenly matter less, for instance, and athletics suddenly matter more."[350]

Other studies show that members of upper social classes have a greater tendency to differentiate themselves from other groups on socioeconomic and cultural grounds, whereas members of lower social classes have a greater tendency to rely on moral criteria. This emphasis on moral criteria serves as an alternative yardstick for workers and the lower middle classes, allowing them to place themselves above those who are superior to them in the socioeconomic and cultural dimensions.[351]

For his dissertation, Patrick Sachweh conducted qualitative interviews with members of the working class in Germany. Those interviews confirmed his thesis. He reports that his interviewees "in particular" criticized "the egoism, greed, ruthlessness, and arrogance of the privileged classes."[352] This criticism was evident from, for example, descriptions of rich people who gave stingier tips than less wealthy people despite having more money. The egoism and miserliness said to be shown by those who have "real money" contrasted sharply with interviewees' own sense of responsibility for, or solidarity with, those of lower incomes.[353] He writes:

> By denying "others" a certain quality (e.g., being considerate) or assigning a negative attribute to them (e.g., self-centered), one can also highlight one's own qualities and define oneself in a more favorable light (here, for example, as "showing solidarity"). In addition, the "rich" are not only seen by lower class interviewees as selfish, ruthless and stingy, but also greedy and extravagant. . . . This image of the "immoral rich" contrasts above all with the self-definition of interviewees from the lower classes and the attribution of greater solidarity among the disadvantaged social classes. This suggests that members of the lower classes (ordinary employees, workers, the unemployed) employ moral principles to distinguish themselves from the rich "above them," who are perceived as immoral.[354]

The interviewees in Sachweh's study explained that material status symbols (such as a large house or car) were not so important to them and said that extremely wealthy people were no happier or more satisfied than the rest of the population. "The latter point in particular is cited by some respondents and serves to relativize the importance of material well-being."[355] This strategy of relativization was evident from the following statements: "They may be better off financially, but I doubt that they are better off in human terms. So, I think, only as far as material security is concerned, they are certainly better. Um, whether they are happier people, I doubt it."[356] Here it becomes clear, according to Sachweh, that the reference to people who are materially wealthier, but therefore not necessarily happier, serves to accentuate individuals' satisfaction with their own achievements in life.[357]

Sachweh observes that when individuals believe that not everyone in a privileged socioeconomic position is necessarily more content, it allows them to more readily accept the condition of their own existence, even if this condition is associated with noticeable material restrictions: "nonsocioeconomic distinctions can also be emphasized when one deems material status symbols to be generally irrelevant and minimizes their importance."[358]

A qualitative study conducted by Thomas J. Gorman in the United States confirms that this is a general strategy, widespread in other societies, that aims to maintain self-esteem by first relativizing the importance of economic success and then compensating by highlighting one's own superiority in other domains (better morals, better family life, etc.). Gorman's interviews revealed that working-class respondents had strong misgivings about the middle class and the rich. Workers saw themselves as superior to other groups in the sense that they themselves were more family oriented, and they criticized those at a higher level for being oriented too much toward educational and career objectives.[359]

Some of the working-class respondents "felt that those with socioeconomic advantages lack important qualities. A clerical worker said: 'Money can buy everything but not love and happiness, really. I would rather be low in money and have that happiness than be rich and miserable. I'd like to be comfortable; *they* don't know what to do with their money' (35, female, unemployed clerk, high school [education])."[360]

In summarizing his findings, Gorman notes that working-class individuals experience "self-doubt" and a "lack of self-confidence."[361] Their denigration of privileged classes is by no means directed only against the truly rich, but more generally against the "suits." "The middle-class, college graduate's manner of dress—especially the business suit—is another aspect of middle-class behavior that made some of the respondents angry. . . . One working-class man said, 'I hold resentment for some people who wear suits. I call them "suits." I think they look down on me because I work with my hands and not sit behind a desk' (age 34, male, unemployed bridge painter, high school [education])." Similarly, a working-class woman said, "'A man comes in a three-piece suit and orders something and acts like he's better than you are. My job is not sitting behind a desk; I'm on my feet, I'm as good as he is.' (age 43, female, waitress, less than high school [education])." According to Gorman, the problem is not the suit as a piece of clothing but what the suit symbolizes to the worker. "The business suit represents the ability of members of the middle class to command respect for their kind of work. The business suit in our society proclaims loudly that the wearer is involved in dignified work."[362]

The lashing out by white working-class Americans against members of the middle and upper classes or elites described by Gorman can help explain the phenomenon that has recently been referred to as the rise of angry white men. In 2017, Gorman wrote *Growing Up Working Class: Hidden Injuries and the Development of Angry White Men and Women* and found "working-class men and women with damaged selves and little confidence in their ability to help them navigate professional social worlds . . . . The 'hidden injuries of class,' as a concept, is now part of accepted wisdom in the social sciences."[363]

Disparaging members of the middle-class and rich people allows members of the working class to compensate for their own feelings of inferiority. This compensation strategy was also confirmed in a qualitative study by Michèle Lamont, which explored the question of how working-class Americans perceive privileged classes and the rich. Her central finding was as follows: "While American workingmen identify with and positively evaluate the upper half, its positional attributes (particularly money), and cultural dispositions (particularly ambition), most also have at their disposal a set of standards for evaluating worth that is independent of social status."[364] This alternative set of standards for evaluating worth includes values such as sincerity and rich interpersonal relations, which are given greater weight than money or material possessions.[365] The working class thus evaluate status not according to socioeconomic criteria but according to moral criteria.[366]

According to Lamont, 75 percent of the workers interviewed showed critical dispositions toward the more privileged and the rich. "Workers repeatedly argue that worth should not be judged on the basis of social status, but on the basis of criteria such as the quality of interpersonal relationships. The standards they use to evaluate worth allow them to locate themselves at the top of a hierarchy and to promote criteria of evaluation available to all."[367]

Yet it is clearly not enough for members of the working class to point out that they also have something to offer and to emphasize those qualities on which they score themselves highly. They also need to accuse other social groups—in this case, the more privileged—of corresponding flaws in the fields they have declared relevant. In the interviews Lamont conducted, workers regularly attributed flaws to higher-status individuals, precisely in those dimensions that allow them to locate themselves at the top of a hierarchy: interpersonal relationships, family life, and moral values in general.

Above all, members of the upper classes were accused of a lack of "warmth"[368]—which corresponds to the findings of the stereotype content model presented in Chapter 3. A radio technician described members of the upper classes as "very cold, shallow people . . . concentrating a lot on finance and not that much on personal needs."[369] Particular criticism was leveled at "people above" for their competitiveness, which generated dishonesty. One laborer explained: "When you get that almighty dollar, you hate to lose it. So you step on somebody's feet, or somebody's hand, or somebody's head to make sure you stay on top, which is not the greatest thing in the world. . . . The lower-middle-class people, they got nothing to lose by being honest."[370]

A third of the white workers Lamont spoke to also criticized the high level of ambition that is a cultural disposition of members of the upper classes: "You miss all of life. . . . A person that is totally ambitious and driven never sees anything except the spot they are aiming at."[371] More than two-thirds of the (white) workers Lamont spoke to said they were better than the "upper half" of society because they had a better quality of life.[372]

Among African American workers, this tendency was not quite as strong, although some made statements similar to those of their white counterparts, pointing to the moral flaws and poor quality of life of the rich. A plumber said: "Some rich people . . . they can't live an average life. To me, it means driving around in a BMW, going to a big house in Sands Points and it being empty, [with] my cat Fluffy. Or having a boat with no one to be on it with. Or telling people where I've been and not being able to see or share it with some people."[373]

Sachweh, Lamont, and other researchers agree that workers draw moral boundaries against the upper classes, subordinating socioeconomic status to morality, defining their own worth and that of other groups on the basis of universally available "goods," such as moral qualities or the quality of interpersonal relationships. "This allows them, despite their low socioeconomic status, to position themselves side by side with or even above those who are superior to them in socioeconomic and material terms, thereby maintaining a sense of self-esteem and dignity, even if they cannot keep up with normative standards of success. The members of the middle and upper classes are often criticized by these workers for their superficial personal relationships, a lack of sincerity, excessive ambition, and competitive orientation."[374]

All in all, Sachweh claims that these findings refute the theoretical consideration of L. Richard Della Fave,[375] who argues that people with low socioeconomic status would also have low evaluations of their own social worth.[376] Lamont believes it is time to reassess models like the one proposed by Max Weber, which equates the status of a class with its socioeconomic position in society. As Lamont argues, this conventional view neglects to consider the ways in which individuals evaluate their status and decouple status and worth from social position.[377] Lamont refutes Richard Sennett and Jonathan Cobb's thesis that in the United States, "the working man is deprived of dignity because it can be acquired only through upward mobility and the achievement of the American dream."[378]

In their classic study *The Hidden Injuries of Class*, Sennett and Cobb develop the argument that the self-esteem of workers in an (apparently) egalitarian society suffers because when they don't climb the social ladder, they blame their own personal deficits. Working-class success stories square with the prevailing ideology in America, demonstrating that it is possible to rise through the ranks, thus implicitly conveying this message: "If you don't like poverty, you too can leave it *if* you are good enough [and], if *I* don't escape being part of the woodwork, it's because I didn't develop my powers enough. Thus, talk about how arbitrary a class society's reward system is will be greeted with general agreement—with the proviso, that in my own case I should have made more of myself."[379]

According to Sennett and Cobb, the working classes interpret inequality as a result of their own failings. "If I believe that the man I call 'Sir' and who calls me by my first name started with an equal fund of powers, do not our differences, do not all the signs of courtesy and attention given to him but denied me, do not his very feelings of being different in 'taste' and understanding from me, show that somehow he has developed his insides more than I mine? How else can I explain inequalities?"[380]

Lamont criticizes the thesis of "hidden injuries," contrasting it with her interpretation that workers do not, in fact, feel inferior but have developed an alternative value system based not on economic success but on moral criteria, which in some dimensions even allows them to feel superior to members of the upper classes. In my opinion, Lamont's criticism is unjustified: in fact, there is no contradiction at all between her findings and the theses put forward by Sennett and Cobb. It is naive to oppose traditional status definitions, in which economic and professional success or education play a central role, by offering other "alternative definitions of success,"[381] in which values such as "interpersonal relationships," "warmth," "morality," or "better family life" can't easily coexist with economic success. It is obvious that this is merely a compensation strategy used by members of the lower classes, who, having little in the way of material resources or education, stress the importance of other values, which allow them to claim superiority over the upper classes.

The assertion that one is morally superior is, of course, impossible to objectively prove. And at the same time, the psychological compensation function of such claims is clear: claiming that the rich have worse family lives, are morally inferior, or generally do not have healthy interpersonal relationships allows one to compensate for an inferiority complex and place oneself above those with higher social status.

The common feature of the domains in which Gorman's, Lamont's, and Sachweh's interviewees claimed to be superior to the rich is that they are largely based on subjective interpretation. Using objective measures, it is easy to demonstrate who has more money or is better educated, which leaves little room for debate or subjectivity. The same cannot be said when it comes to determining who has the most fulfilling interpersonal relationships or the most satisfying family life. It is questionable whether, for example, the lower classes generally have better family lives or morals than the upper classes. Nevertheless, in the interviews, this statement is either postulated abstractly or interviewees cite individual examples from their lives that seem to confirm this.

It is interesting in this context to consider the findings of Joan C. Williams. She examined the "class culture gap" between the working class and the professional-managerial elite. Her use of the term "working class" is somewhat confusing: when she refers to the working class, she means people who are neither rich nor poor and who would typically describe themselves as middle class. The people who call themselves the upper middle class she calls the professional-managerial elite.[382]

As Williams reports, workers likewise tell a story of their own moral advantages. They "see themselves as doing the real work," thereby differentiating themselves from "pencil pushers," who don't do any real work, because what they do "isn't hard, it isn't unpleasant, it isn't boring or frustrating," as the daughter of a carpenter who herself became a professor explained.[383] According to Williams, the working class strongly emphasizes the importance of morality and of family. Many of the working-class Americans she cites are very religious, and family is described as much more important to them than ambition and career advancement.[384]

So far, what Williams found lines up with Lamont's and Sachweh's findings. Where she differs is in claiming that workers are more hostile toward the educated than toward the rich. "Workers typically admire the rich but resent the educated because their goal is not to lose their way of life but to continue it, with more money." Workers, she found, would often be very derogatory toward academics, doctors, lawyers, or teachers. "Resentments stem in part from unsatisfying or even humiliating encounters with professionals with whom workers lack the social capital to communicate effectively or who downright disrespect them. . . . In contrast, most workers never encounter the truly wealthy and so carry no sense of class affront."[385]

The fact that Donald Trump attracted so many working-class votes would perhaps make her thesis plausible. It is interesting, by the way, that the author, who was writing long before Trump was elected president, said that the Democrats had failed to understand which values were central to working-class dignity in America (family and religion). This is one reason why the working class's attitude is increasingly shifting to the right.[386]

In summary, research in the United States and Germany suggests that the nonrich employ compensation strategies to maintain their self-esteem. These strategies aim, on the one hand, to question the correlation between economic success and life satisfaction and, on the other hand, to give greater weight to certain values, such as interpersonal relationships, morality, and family life. But that's not all. In order for the nonrich to be able to position themselves above the rich, it has to be widely accepted that members of the lower classes can be just as good (or perhaps even better) when it comes to these values. The working-class stereotypes of the rich, namely, that they are cold and self-centered and have unfulfilling family lives, unsatisfactory interpersonal relationships, and poor morals, serve to assert the superiority of the working class and to compensate for feelings of inferiority.

Evaluations of the rich are not relativized by what psychologists call the "halo effect." Usually, a positive perception of a certain dimension of a person's personality is transferred to other dimensions of their personality. This process does not apply to comparisons of social groups, as we know from the stereotype content model theory (see Chapter 3).[387] The rich are viewed ambivalently, often in extremes that do not correspond to reality. As Susan Fiske writes, "They seem more than human, as though they are above regular humans in some ways (such as sheer intelligence), but inferior in the ways that make a person a regular human. The rich are seen as failures at being warm, as though they are incapable of experiencing complex emotions, being self-aware, having ups and downs, and being typically human. Envy up, toward the unsympathetic winners (rich people), is thus clearly established."[388] According to Fiske, rich people only become likable when they donate their wealth.[389] Whether this is really the case is debatable, for even those rich people who make generous donations are often accused of doing so for selfish reasons—as shown in later chapters.

Compensation strategies are used against people who are either generally more successful or superior in certain domains. For example, beautiful women are sometimes accused of being stupid; professional footballers are often accused of lacking intelligence; and the scientist, whose intelligence is not in doubt, is said to be unworldly and unable to cope with everyday life. Apparently, some people are not willing to accept the simple fact that other people are superior in certain areas. When comparing themselves with higher achievers, in order to maintain their self-esteem, people tend to attribute flaws and failings to the high achievers in other domains, and these domains are also claimed to be more relevant.

The attribution of competence traits to out-groups while denying them positive moral traits has far-reaching consequences. We know from perception research that our impressions of other people and out-groups generally rely more on moral traits than on competence traits. Bogdan Wojciszke, Róża Bazinska, and Marcin Jaworski demonstrate that "morality-related information" plays a more important role in perception than "competence-related information." The researchers confirm that morality and competence are the two key factors in determining our perceptions of out-groups—and some three-quarters of all our perceptions are determined by these two components.[390]

Wojciszke, Bazinska, and Jaworski conducted experiments to measure whether perceptions of out-groups are based more on categorizations related to "morality" (fair, generous, good-natured, helpful, honest, righteous, sincere, tolerant, truthful, and understanding) or "competence" (clever, competent, creative, efficient, energetic, foresighted, gifted, ingenious, intelligent, knowledgeable, and resourceful). They found that of the top seven traits, six are morality traits (helpful, sincere, fair, understanding, truthful, and honest), and only one is a competence trait (resourceful). "Judgements of M traits emerged as a relatively better predictor of global impression than judgements of specific C traits."[391]

The researchers explain this finding in terms of evolutionary biology. All organisms have at least one mechanism for differentiating agreeable environments from adverse environments. "If the main function of global evaluative impressions is to distinguish between persons who should be approached and persons who should be avoided, it is clear why M categories occupy a privileged position in impression formation. These categories are instrumental in locating others on the approach–avoidance dimension to a higher extent than any other concept (C traits included)—a decision about whether a person is moral amounts to a direct settlement of whether the person is beneficial rather than dangerous."[392] Only after this basic decision has been made do competence traits come into play, because they help to decide *how* beneficial or dangerous another person or group is.

As seen from the research presented at the beginning of this chapter, workers tend to judge rich people as competent but morally questionable. And because workers attach greater significance to their own moral judgment, they do not arrive at a balanced judgment but at a generally negative judgment of superior persons or social groups.

The sociopsychological concept of the "hidden injuries of class," as first developed by Sennett and Cobb in the early 1970s, has been repeatedly confirmed (most recently by Gorman's works quoted earlier) but could possibly be taken further. Sennett and Cobb's attention was focused on deficits in the self-esteem of economically less successful blue-collar workers in a society that measures value in terms of individual achievement and financial success. But what about members of the educated middle class, against whom—as has been shown—the prejudices of workers are partially directed? What effect does it have on *their* self-esteem if, despite their higher education, they are all too often the economic losers in a capitalist system in which a less educated entrepreneur can become far richer than someone with a higher level of education? Put yourself in the shoes of someone who has been told time and again that higher education is the key to success—and has then been frustrated as other people climb higher and higher up the economic ladder despite lacking education. Wouldn't this frustration likely lead to feelings of inferiority and resentment against economically more successful people, just like the "hidden injuries" of the working class as they compare themselves with the middle and upper classes? It is to this question that we will now turn.

CHAPTER 8

EXPLAINING SUCCESS: INDIVIDUAL ABILITY OR EXTERNAL CIRCUMSTANCES?

How do people explain the wealth of the rich? In principle, three factors play a role, but they are weighted differently:

1. *External circumstances.* This factor includes favorable elements, such as inheritance or family relationships. Surveys also mention structural or societal elements, such as the economic or tax systems.
2. *Individual traits and talents.* This factor includes positively eval- uated traits, such as ambition, intelligence, and social skills, but also negative traits, such as ruthlessness and dishonesty.
3. *Luck.* This factor includes advantageous but coincidental occurrences.

It is obvious that financially successful and less successful people tend to have different explanations as to why some people get rich. Logically, one would suspect that the less financially successful are more likely to explain wealth in terms of external circumstances, negative individual traits, or luck, whereas the more financially successful would cite posi- tive individual traits.

Studies in the United States

Michael W. Kraus, Paul K. Piff, and Dacher Keltner investigated the correlation between social class, on the one hand, and explanations of social outcomes, on the other. They claim that subjective socioeconomic status (SES), that is, the subjective social class rank of a person within a society or hierarchy, is a more accurate measure for this purpose than objective SES indicators such as income. To measure subjective SES, the researchers used a 10-point scale that allowed test participants to indicate their own class rank. According to the authors, subjective SES is only moderately correlated with objective indexes of class affiliation.[393] The researchers carried out several studies, including one with students and a nationwide survey.

In one of the studies, participants were asked to explain a series of positive and negative social outcomes and to express their opinion on a seven-point scale as to whether these events were caused by contextual factors or whether the people influenced by these events were responsible for their own outcomes.[394] Among others, the prompts included "Having low income," "Failing a class at school," and "Being laid off at work." From the participants' responses, a composite measure was developed to show how strongly they endorsed contextual explanations. The study showed that lower subjective SES was significantly associated with contextual explanations rather than dispositional explanations for positive and negative social outcomes.

Participants' sense of control over their life circumstances was also assessed, using their responses to 12 items, including "I can do just about anything that I really set my mind to," "Whatever happens in the future mostly depends on me," "There is little I can do to change many of the important things in my life," and "I sometimes feel like I am being pushed around in my life."[395] Researchers found that participants with lower subjective SES tended to explain social outcomes in terms of contextual factors because of a reduced sense of control over their own lives.

In other words, those who self-identified as poor tended to blame external circumstances for their situation, whereas the self-identified rich tended to attribute social outcomes to how people think and act.

This result stands to reason, because people prefer to claim the credit for their successes and to blame others or circumstances for their failures.

Kraus and colleagues offer an explanation that could be summed up using the words of Karl Marx: "Being determines consciousness." According to the researchers, members of the lower classes often experience uncertainty, constraints, and threats, whereas members of the upper classes experience the opposite, that is, control, freedom, and choice. This difference in experience results in two diametrically opposing interpretations of the world, which the authors call "solipsism" and "contextualism." "Solipsism" is defined as an individualistic cognitive and relational orientation to the world, with "internal states, goals, and emotions" playing the central role, whereas "contextualism" is understood as "external orientation to the environment motivated by managing external constraints, outside threats, and other individuals."[396]

Unfortunately, the authors do not ask whether the relationship between cause and effect could possibly (also) be reversed. Perhaps people are more successful in life when they see themselves as masters of their own destinies and less successful when they see themselves as victims of external circumstances and societal ranking. Social theorists from David Hume to F. A. Hayek have speculated along these lines, though research to establish a causal direction between SES and attitudes is difficult to conduct. Presumably both apply: being determines consciousness—in the sense described by the authors—but consciousness also determines being.

In 1980, sociologist James R. Kluegel and psychologist Eliot R. Smith published a frequently cited study based on a representative survey in the United States. One of the questions the researchers asked was why there are rich people in the United States.

The authors distinguished between individualistic and structural explanations for wealth and emphasized the dominance of individualistic explanations in the United States. Figure 8.1 depicts (in percentages) the personal characteristics mentioned by respondents as being very important/somewhat important/not important. Similarly, Figure 8.2 depicts the external, structural factors respondents mentioned as being very important/somewhat important/not important.

Figure 8.1

Individualistic explanations for wealth

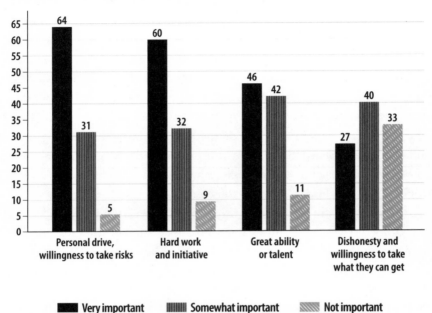

Source: James R. Kluegel and Eliot R. Smith, *Beliefs about Inequality: Americans' Views of What Is and What Ought to Be* (New York: Aldine de Gruyter, 1986), p. 77.
Note: All data are in percentages of respondents.

Among the individualistic explanations for wealth, it is noticeable that positive personality traits and attributes, such as hard work and initiative, willingness to take risks, and great ability or talent, were rated as far more important than the leading negative personality trait (dishonesty), even though only one-third of the respondents said that dishonesty did *not* play a role in financial success.

With regard to which population groups prefer which explanatory approaches, this study also highlighted significant differences:

- In general, individualistic explanations (i.e., those that focus on individual ability and personality traits) were favored by those with higher status, including people with higher incomes, whites, and older people.[397] "Individual causes of

Figure 8.2

Structural explanations for wealth

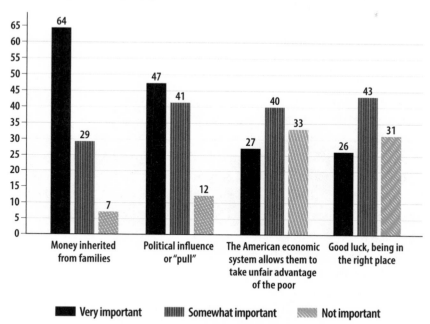

Source: James R. Kluegel and Eliot R. Smith, *Beliefs about Inequality: Americans' Views of What Is and What Ought to Be* (New York: Aldine de Gruyter, 1986), p. 77.
Note: All data are in percentages of respondents.

wealth portray the wealthy in a more positive light. Males, the old, whites, those with high incomes, and Westerners are more inclined to see individual causes of wealth. . . . The advantaged see wealth as achievable by individual talents and efforts and thus as potentially attainable by themselves."[398]

- Structural causes for wealth were more often cited by women, the young, nonwhites, and those with lower incomes, although income played a lesser role than race. Nonwhites were much more inclined to structural explanations than whites.[399] "Structural causes are thus perceived by people who are themselves likely to be distant from the wealthy and perhaps from chances to personally obtain wealth. Those for whom wealth is unlikely personally seem to see the wealthy

in negative terms and see wealth itself as the result of structural factors—one might call them biases in this context—
rather than individual efforts and abilities."[400]

"Structuralists" also tended to favor similar explanations for poverty.
They were more likely to explain poverty by "low wages in some businesses and industries," "failure of private industry to provide enough jobs," or
"prejudice and discrimination against blacks." Overall, however, in both a
1969 survey and a 1980 survey in the United States, "individualistic" explanations for poverty prevailed, including "lack of thrift and proper money-
management skills" (1969: 90 percent, 1980: 94 percent); "lack of effort
by the poor themselves" (1969: 91 percent, 1980: 92 percent); and "lack of
ability and talent" (1969: 88 percent, 1980: 88 percent).[401] Individualistic
explanations for poverty were even more widespread in the 1980 survey
than individualistic explanations for wealth, which means that people were
willing to attribute financial success more than poverty to structural factors.
       In 1998, Gallup conducted a survey of 5,000 people in the United
States that asked similar but not identical questions;[402] it, too, asked why
some people are rich and others poor (Figure 8.3).
       According to Gallup, views as to why some people are poor have changed
over time: in the mid-1960s, the majority still thought people were poor
due to a lack of effort, whereas in 1989 and 1990, the majority of respondents blamed circumstances beyond a person's control.[403] Women are more
likely to blame poverty on external circumstances than men (46 percent and
35 percent, respectively). And those who describe themselves as "have-nots"
are more likely than the "haves" to attribute both wealth and poverty to
external circumstances and less likely to cite strong effort or lack of effort.
       Clearly, respondents do not want to come across as hardhearted,
which is why they are less likely to blame the poor for their own
situation—and one-third are unwilling to acknowledge that wealth is a
result of personal effort.
       When more general questions are asked about why some people are
more successful, that is, when the questions are not explicitly about why
some people are poor and others rich, the picture shifts considerably.
The Gallup survey also included the following statement: "I am going
to read several reasons why some people get ahead and succeed in life

Figure 8.3

Why are some people poor and some rich?

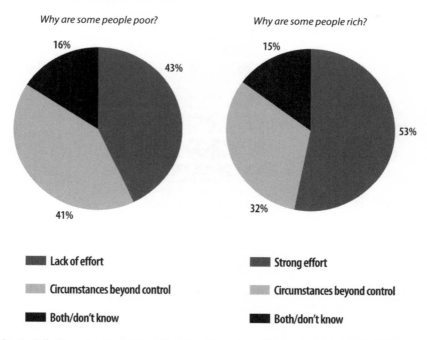

Why are some people poor?

16%

43%

41%

Why are some people rich?

15%

53%

32%

▪ Lack of effort	▪ Strong effort
▫ Circumstances beyond control	▫ Circumstances beyond control
▪ Both/don't know	▪ Both/don't know

Source: Gallup News Service, "Have and Have-Nots: Perceptions of Fairness and Opportunity," July 6, 1998.
Note: All data are in percentages of respondents.

and others do not."[404] Respondents were asked to evaluate the importance of a variety of factors in determining a person's success in life. Figure 8.4 depicts the factors that were rated as most important, that is, scoring 4 or 5 on a five-point scale.

It is striking that, overall, the most frequently cited explanation for success was hard work and initiative, compared with only 43 percent of respondents who said that "lack of effort" was a main cause of poverty. A similar number of respondents attributed poverty to factors beyond the individual's control. The Gallup researchers thought "sympathy for the downtrodden" might explain why respondents prefer to blame poverty on external circumstances. It is my sense that blaming the poor for their poverty is largely considered politically incorrect and hardhearted, while—at least in the United States in 1998—a narrow majority was nonetheless prepared to attribute economic success to "strong effort."

Figure 8.4

Perceived reasons why some people get ahead and succeed in life

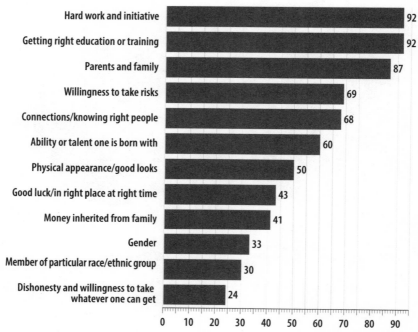

Source: Gallup News Service, "Have and Have-Nots: Perceptions of Fairness and Opportunity," July 6, 1998.
Note: All data are in percentages of respondents.

Opinions continued to differ as to whether wealth is primarily the result of hard work, ambition, and education or whether it has more to do with family background and knowing the right people, as a 2011 Pew survey shows (Figure 8.5).

From 1987 to 2012, the Pew Research Center regularly asked respondents whether they agreed or disagreed with the following statement: "Success in life is pretty much determined by forces outside our control."[405] Whenever this question was asked, a majority of Americans disagreed. In 1987, 38 percent of respondents agreed with the statement, compared with 35 percent in 2012. The strongest agreement was registered in 1988 and 1993 (41 percent). The proportion of those who disagreed with the statement was 57 percent in 1987 compared with 63 percent in 2012. The strongest disagreement was in 1999 and 2003 (67 percent).

Figure 8.5

Pew social trends, December 2011

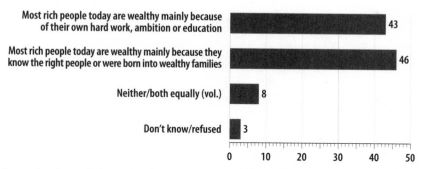

Source: Pew Research Center, Social & Demographic Trends, *Rising Share of Americans See Conflict Between Rich and Poor,* January 11, 2012.
Note: All data are in percentages of respondents.

However, the statement elicited a very different response depending on the individual respondent's level of income. As expected, agreement with the opinion that success in life is determined primarily by external factors—that is, factors beyond a person's individual control—was lowest among higher-income groups and much higher for members of lower-income groups.[406]

STUDIES IN GERMANY

Only one major empirical study has been conducted in Germany to explore general perceptions of the rich. This single study is based on several sets of primary data gathered by a research group from the Institute for Social and Political Analysis in the Department of Social Sciences at Goethe University in Frankfurt as part of the "Attitudes toward the Welfare State" project. The study was based on a representative survey of 5,000 people, which was mainly conducted in 2007.

One question was designed to find out why respondents believe some people are rich (Table 8.1).

Just like the American researchers cited earlier in this chapter, Wolfgang Glatzer and colleagues differentiate between individual and structural explanations for wealth. Individual explanations include factors such as "natural ability or talent," while structural explanations include factors such as "injustices in our economic system." An analysis

Table 8.1

Reasons why some people get rich (Germany)

"I will now mention a few reasons why there are rich people in Germany today. By rich I mean people who can afford almost anything. For each of these reasons, please tell me how often you think this is a reason why someone in Germany is rich: very often, often, sometimes, rarely or never."

	Very Often	Often	Sometimes	Rarely/Never
They know or have relationships with the right people	35	47	13	5
They have better opportunities	28	52	14	6
Natural ability or talent	18	50	22	11
Injustices in our economic system	18	36	26	21
Dishonesty	16	36	27	21
Hard work	15	38	24	24
Luck	7	22	33	39

Source: Wolfgang Glatzer et al., *Reichtum im Urteil der Bevölkerung: Legitimationsprobleme und Spannungspotentiale in Deutschland* (Opladen: Verlag Barbara Budrich, 2009), p. 65.
Note: All data are in percentages of respondents.

of the explanations preferred by various societal groups confirms both logical expectations and the findings of numerous American studies:

1. The more positive respondents' assessment of their own economic situation and the higher the status they award themselves in the social hierarchy, the more they tend to prefer individual explanations for wealth. Subjective assessments were even more important than actual income, although a clear correlation also exists here: higher earners were far more likely to favor individual explanations for wealth.[407]

2. This correlation is even stronger for structural explanations for wealth. Respondents who subjectively assessed their own social status as lower, who were less satisfied with their economic situation, who earned less, or who were unemployed tended to favor structural explanations of wealth.[408] As one would expect, the survey's east German respondents, even 18 years after the fall of the German Democratic Republic, also tended to favor structural explanations for wealth.

Furthermore, respondents who favored individual explanations for wealth tended to reject structural explanations—and vice versa.[409]

STUDIES IN THE UNITED KINGDOM, AUSTRALIA, AND FRANCE

In 1979/80, Adrian Furnham interviewed 200 British people to find out how they explain wealth.[410] Furnham rightly criticized earlier studies for asking respondents to state their opinions about rich people without first clarifying what precisely the researchers meant by rich. "Thus any differences that may occur might be more as a result of the subject's definitions of wealth than their different belief about the cause of wealth."[411] Because people's concepts of "rich," "wealthy," and "affluent" vary greatly, my own study clearly defined "rich" as referring to millionaires (for more on this matter, see Chapter 10).

Furnham's second major methodological criticism of earlier studies was that, in seeking to explain the causes of wealth, a vast majority of studies differentiated exclusively between individual and structural/societal explanations. Furnham rightly criticized these studies for failing to make any distinction between positive and negative individual explanations. "Thus, as regards wealth, positive individualistic explanations such as thrift and hard work are endorsed by a very different set of people [than those] who endorse negative individualistic explanations such as ruthlessness and ambition."[412]

The explanations for wealth mentioned in Furnham's study included the following:

- Individualistic
  1. Careful money management throughout life
  2. Hard work and great effort
  3. High intelligence
  4. Ruthlessness and determination
- Societal
  1. Very high wages in some businesses and trades
  2. Being sent to certain schools and universities
  3. Better opportunities for people from certain families
  4. A taxation system that favors the rich
  5. Strong trade unions that get higher wages

6. Inequality automatically created by the economic system
7. Rewards from society for those who work hard and take
    risks
- Fatalistic
    1. Inheriting wealth from parents or relatives
    2. Good luck in winning money at gambling
    3. Having a lucky break
    4. Being born with good business sense[413]

Furnham's questions and categorizations are only partially convincing, however. For example, many respondents might find it difficult to clearly differentiate between the structural/societal explanation that society rewards hard work and risk taking and the individualistic explanation that people who work hard and take risks become rich.

In Furnham's study, as in the American studies, political attitudes were confirmed as a major factor in different patterns of explaining wealth. Conservative and Liberal Party voters—in contrast to Labour Party voters—favored explanations such as "hard work and great effort among the rich," whereas Labour Party voters favored explanations such as "the rich are ruthless and determined." Labour Party voters were also far more likely to agree that the tax system favors the rich. In general, Conservative Party voters found positive individualistic explanations for wealth to be more important, while Labour Party voters favored societal explanations.[414] On this point, Furnham's findings correspond to the findings of studies conducted in other countries.

In 2013, the University of Birmingham commissioned polling firm Ipsos MORI to ask members of the general British public about the reasons some people are wealthier than others. The answers were again dominated by external factors. According to the survey's respondents, the main reason why some people had greater wealth than others was that they had inherited it (24 percent). A further 19 percent thought that injustice explained why some people were wealthier than others; the same number of respondents said there was no particular reason why some people were wealthier. Some 14 percent thought wealth inequality was just inevitable, and 6 percent thought the rich simply had more luck.

Only one answer was related to personal achievement or ability: 14 percent of respondents thought that the reason for large wealth differentials was that wealthy people had worked hard.[415]

In France, the research institute Ifop conducted an extensive survey for the news and commentary site Atlantico into attitudes toward wealth in France in 2017.[416] Ifop had previously asked the same set of questions in July 1994 and January 2013, which makes it possible to meaningfully compare the three surveys' findings. At the end of October 2017, a representative sample of 1,002 French people ages 18 and older were interviewed. They were asked to select the personality traits and characteristics they regarded as especially important in becoming rich. Participants were able to make multiple selections from a predefined list and ranked their choices in order of importance. The following percentages include the items that were ranked either first or second by the 2017 survey's participants. About half (48 percent) thought that people get rich mainly through "hard work"; one in three (32 percent) regarded "relationships" as important; in third place (29 percent) was "rich parents," followed by being "bold and daring," which was rated important by just over one in five; "intelligence" received a similar score. Fourteen percent selected the negative trait "lack of scruples," which was almost matched by the positive attribute "honesty." "A good education" was selected by 1 in 10 respondents, while 8 percent thought that the rich were "self-centered."

Comparing these results with the findings of the two earlier studies reveals that the proportion of French people who believe that "hard work" is the most important factor in becoming rich has risen (from 40 percent to 48 percent) since 1994. In contrast, in the first survey, only one in five French respondents believed that "relationships" were the decisive factor; this factor has now risen to one in three. The proportion of respondents who think that "rich parents" are the most important factor has fallen from 40 percent to 29 percent.

Responses vary greatly depending on the interviewees' political preferences. Although 70 percent of conservative voters (les Républicains) saw "hard work" as the most important factor in becoming rich, only 37 percent of left-wing voters held the same opinion.

Then again, left-wing voters were twice as likely to highlight the role of having the right "relationships" (38 percent) as conservative voters (19 percent). And although only 6 percent of conservative voters mentioned "lack of scruples," the same item was selected by almost three times as many left-wing voters (16 percent).

Supporters of François Fillon, a very market-oriented presidential candidate who was forced to abandon his campaign because of a scandal, exhibited overwhelmingly positive attitudes toward the rich, as did supporters of Emmanuel Macron. This fact was confirmed by the 47 percent of Macron supporters and 69 percent of Fillon supporters who thought that "hard work" was particularly important in becoming rich.[417]

Anti-capitalist attitudes are particularly strong in France, as another Ifop survey from 2011 demonstrated.[418] The survey revealed that 33 percent of French people believed it was time to abandon capitalism, the highest proportion among 10 countries surveyed.[419]

Nevertheless, in the 2017 Ifop survey, three out of four French people (76 percent) confirmed that the existence of the rich was beneficial for society as a whole (Figure 8.6). The figure for French people under the age of 35 (69 percent) was slightly lower than for those older than 65 (82 percent). It is no surprise that 95 percent of Fillon supporters and 85 percent of Macron supporters believed that the rich benefit society.

Figure 8.6

Statements about rich people (France)

Do you completely agree, mostly agree, somewhat agree, somewhat disagree, or totally disagree with each of the following?

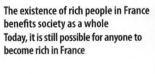
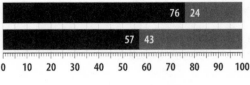

Source: Ifop, "Les Français et la richesse en France en 2017," October 2017, https://www.ifop.com /wp-content/uploads/2018/03/3904-1-study_file.pdf.
Note: All data are in percentages of respondents.

It is remarkable, however, that as many as 66 percent of those who supported the left-wing populist Jean-Luc Mélenchon shared this positive opinion.[420]

Of French respondents, 57 percent believed that it was still possible to become rich in modern France. Among men, the approval rate was as high as 64 percent; among women, it was lower, at 52 percent. No major differences existed between age groups.

However, when we come to analyze our own survey results from 2018 in Part Two of this book, we will see that the generally positive attitudes toward the rich in France are far more critical in relation to taxation and managers' salaries.

In combination, the findings of these international studies demonstrate that explanations for wealth and success vary greatly both between countries and between social groups. Americans are more likely to explain wealth in terms of individualistic causes and personality traits. But even here, as in other countries, clear differences exist according to both social status and political affiliation. Higher earners, those who position themselves at the top of the social hierarchy, and conservative voters tend to emphasize the importance of personal ability and character traits as explanations of wealth and success. In contrast, less financially successful individuals, those who rank themselves lower in the social hierarchy, and left-wing voters tend to emphasize external, societal conditions.

CHAPTER 9

THE RICH: AN ADMIRED BUT MISTRUSTED MINORITY

Before moving on to examine the findings of the international survey I commissioned into attitudes toward rich people (from Chapter 10 onward), it makes sense to review some of the findings of previous surveys. The first question to consider is: To the general public, who actually qualifies as rich?

Who's Actually Rich, Anyway?

In 2007, a survey was conducted in Germany to find out what net monthly income and what level of assets would be required to classify someone as "rich." The median monthly income above which the survey's respondents considered someone to be rich was €5,000. The mean value was much higher, at €26,694, although it was distorted by some respondents' mentioning absurdly high net monthly incomes (up to €10 million per month). Excluding the top 10 percent and the bottom 10 percent of responses, respondents' answers were strongly concentrated within the €2,000 to €20,000 monthly net income range.[421]

The study reported even greater divergences in respondents' assessments of the level of assets required to describe someone as rich. The median value was €500,000, while the mean was €34 million. One interviewee said that individuals could only be described as rich if they were worth at least €100 billion, which suggests that many people simply have no realistic concept of extremely large numbers; no one in the world was worth €100 billion in 2007, and only one person has achieved such wealth today. Again, excluding the top and bottom 10 percent of responses, the interviewees' assessments of who qualified as rich ranged from €50,000 to €2 million.[422]

A classic sociological thesis states that the richer an interviewee, the higher the threshold the interviewee will set in defining wealth,[423] which certainly seems plausible. A correlation analysis reveals that interviewees' incomes do influence the point at which they perceive someone to be rich. However, the variables of region, age, and gender also revealed correlations. A regression analysis used to control the other variables revealed the two clearest correlations:[424] "The most decisive factors in assessing at which income level someone can be assumed to be rich would thus appear to be socioeconomic status in the form of disposable income and a predisposition to social equality."[425]

In 2011, Gallup asked the American public how much savings, including real estate and investments, they would need to have to consider themselves rich. Although 29 percent would feel wealthy with less than $500,000, 38 percent said they would need between $500,000 and $1 million, and another 24 percent said over $1 million.[426]

In 1948, 1996, and 2011, Gallup asked how much income would make someone rich. In 2011, 25 percent of Americans thought that an income of less than $100,000 would suffice, compared with 22 percent who said it would take more than $750,000 per year to qualify as rich. In every year Gallup asked this question, including in the 1948 and 1996 surveys, Americans provided a broad range of answers to define the point at which someone can be described as rich.[427]

In 2012, the Pew Research Center published a survey titled "Yes, the Rich Are Different." When asked how much income it would take for a family to be considered wealthy in their area, most Americans said that a family of four would need at least $100,000. Roughly a third of the survey's respondents set the bar considerably higher, at $250,000 or more.[428]

These surveys in Germany and the United States confirm that people have widely differing perceptions of the level of income and assets it takes to consider someone rich. To avoid the problems associated with such massive variations in personal definitions of wealth, our survey in 2018 defined in more detail that when we refer to the rich or the wealthy, we are referring to individuals with assets worth at least one million dollars (or euros or pounds), excluding a person's primary residence.

HOW MANY AMERICANS DREAM OF GETTING RICH—AND HOW MANY EXPECT TO MAKE IT?

Between 2001 and 2003, American sociologist Juliet B. Schor interviewed 300 children between the ages of 10 and 13 about their consumer habits and desires. Figure 9.1 shows one of the 157 statements presented to the children with their answers in percentages.

Figure 9.1

What children think about money (10–13-year-olds)

"I want to make a lot of money when I grow up."

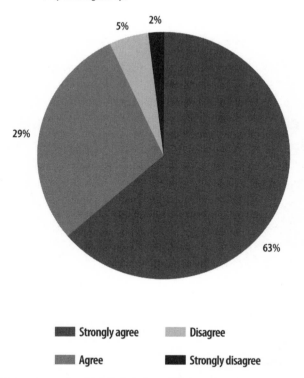

Source: Juliet B. Schor, *Born to Buy* (New York: Scribner, 2004), p. 149.
Note: All data are in percentage of respondents. Percentages do not add up to 100 because of rounding.

Figure 9.2

What children think about money (10–13-year-olds): Comparison between neighborhoods

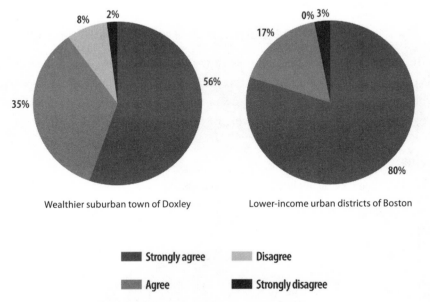

"I want to make a lot of money when I grow up."

Wealthier suburban town of Doxley   Lower-income urban districts of Boston

■ Strongly agree   ■ Disagree

■ Agree   ■ Strongly disagree

Source: Juliet B. Schor, *Born to Buy* (New York: Scribner, 2004), pp. 150–51.
Note: All data are in percentage of respondents. Percentages do not add up to 100 because of rounding.

The first set of interviews was conducted in the suburban town of Doxley, located about 30 minutes outside Boston, with a very high median household income and high housing prices. The second set of interviews took place about a year later, in two urban schools in Boston. These locales provided a sharp contrast to Doxley, with far more low-income residents and less homeownership. The desire to become rich later was strong among children in both socially contrasting areas, but it was markedly stronger in the neighborhoods with more low-income residents (Figure 9.2).[429]

The children were more likely to want to earn a lot of money when they grew up than they were to wish that their parents earned more money—in spite of the fact that the latter would be far more important in terms of their consumer desires (Figure 9.3).

Figure 9.3

Consumer Involvement Scale (Children, 10–13-year-olds): Parents' earnings

"I wish my parents earned more money."

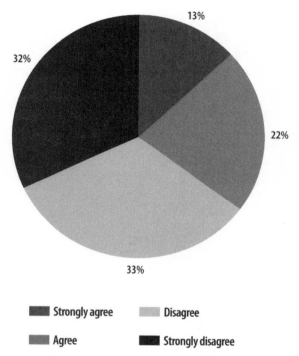

Strongly agree   Disagree

Agree   Strongly disagree

Source: Juliet B. Schor, *Born to Buy* (New York: Scribner, 2004), p. 149.
Note: All data are in percentage of respondents.

So, although almost 92 percent of the children want to earn a lot when they are older, only 35 percent want their parents to earn more. In more affluent Doxley, only 32 percent of the children wished their parents earned more; in the less affluent urban districts of Boston, the figure was understandably higher, at 43 percent—but even here, a clear majority of 57 percent of children disagreed or disagreed strongly when asked if they wished their parents earned more money.[430]

The fact that dreaming of becoming rich later in life is not a reflexive desire born out of the children's current consumer aspirations is confirmed by another of Schor's findings, which is that 79 percent of the

Figure 9.4

Consumer Involvement Scale (Children, 10–13-year-olds): Possessions

"I have pretty much everything I need in terms of possessions."

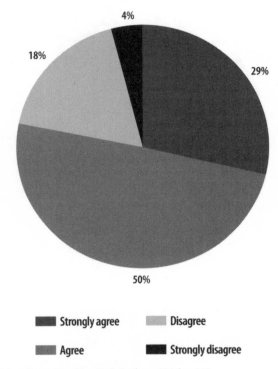

Source: Juliet B. Schor, *Born to Buy* (New York: Scribner, 2004), p. 149.
Note: All data are in percentage of respondents. Percentages do not add up to 100 because of rounding.

children interviewed were satisfied with the amount of possessions they have (Figure 9.4).[431]

And how about older Americans? In 2006, Gallup asked a representative sample of Americans whether they dreamed of getting rich (Figure 9.5).[432] Overall, only 37 percent said they do. Interestingly, the figure was significantly higher among men between the ages of 18 and 49 with 59 percent of younger men reporting dreaming about getting rich. In contrast, it is perhaps not all that surprising that only 27 percent of men ages 50 and older still reported harboring dreams of getting rich.

Figure 9.5

Gallup survey: Americans' attitudes about wealth

For each of the following statements about money, please say whether you strongly agree, agree, disagree or strongly disagree.

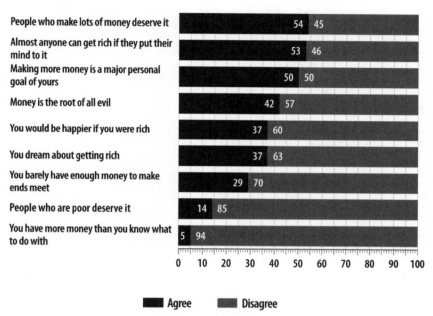

Source: Jeffrey M. Jones, "Most Americans Do Not Have a Strong Desire to Be Rich," Gallup News Service, December 11, 2006.
Note: All data are in percentages of respondents.

After all, those who haven't gotten rich by then have probably largely given up the hope that they could still make it.

The differences between the genders are clear: although 45 percent of men dream of getting rich, only 30 percent of women do so. According to this survey, American women also have a far more skeptical attitude toward the rich than men. Although 61 percent of American men believe that people who make lots of money deserve it, only 47 percent of American women agree (Table 9.1).

However, one can assume that the percentage of Americans who want to get rich is significantly higher than 37 percent. It is highly likely that many have simply given up hope of achieving riches as they have gotten older. This phenomenon has been confirmed by other researchers

Table 9.1

Attitudes toward money, by gender

	Men (%)	Women (%)
People who make lots of money deserve it	61	47
Almost anyone can get rich if they put their mind to it	59	48
Making more money is a major personal goal of yours	57	44
You would be happier if you were rich	45	30
You dream about getting rich	45	30
People who are poor deserve it	19	9

Source: Jeffrey M. Jones, "Most Americans Do Not Have a Strong Desire to Be Rich," Gallup, December 2006.
Note: Figures indicate the percentage who agree with the statement.

who have asked the same or similar questions regarding expectations of getting rich.[433] In another Gallup poll conducted in 2003, 51 percent of Americans ages 18 to 29 said that they would become rich one day, compared with 36 percent of those ages 30 to 49 years, 22 percent of 50- to 64-year-olds, and a mere 8 percent of those over 65 (Table 9.2).

This discrepancy is certainly plausible. Logically speaking, a 20-year-old has a far higher theoretical possibility of getting rich than a 65-year-old who has not yet become wealthy. It is highly likely that a greater proportion of older Americans share the dream of getting rich, but they probably no longer expect it to happen, because they have become somewhat disillusioned during the course of their lives. Of male

Table 9.2

Percentage of Americans who expect to be rich, by age group (2003)

	Very/somewhat likely to be rich (%)	Already rich (%; vol.)
Overall Age	31	2
18–29	51	0
30–49	36	1
50–64	22	4
65+	8	2

Source: David W. Moore, "Half of Young People Expect to Strike It Rich, but Expectations Fall Rapidly with Age," Gallup News Service, March 11, 2003.

Americans under the age of 30, as many as 58 percent expect to be rich one day, plus the 1 percent that are already rich.

Gallup asked the same question about people's expectations of ever being rich in 2018. Once again, the results were similar. It was clear that people become dramatically less optimistic about ever being rich as they get older. Although 52 percent of 18- to 29-year-olds expected to be rich one day, this belief was shared by only 39 percent of 30- to 49-year-olds, 23 percent of 50- to 64-year-olds, and just 10 percent of those over the age of 65. It is interesting to note that only 27 percent of white Americans believe they will ever be rich, compared with 40 percent of nonwhite Americans. And, at 36 percent, the proportion of Republican voters in the 2018 survey who expected to be rich was slightly higher than that of Democrats. Overall, 32 percent of adult Americans believe it is likely that they will be rich at some point in the future.[434]

The percentage of respondents who expect to become rich has changed little over time. Gallup had already asked the same question in 1990 and 1996, and asked it again in 2012 and 2018. In all of these surveys, about a third of respondents agreed that it is likely they will be rich later in life (Table 9.3).[435]

Gallup's findings tally with survey results from CBS News and the *New York Times*. Between 1983 and 2015, a majority of Americans agreed that it was possible to start out poor, work hard, and get rich,

Table 9.3

Percentage of Americans who expect to be rich, by age group (1990–2018)

Looking ahead, how likely is it that you will ever be rich?

	Very/somewhat likely (%)	Not very likely (%)	Not at all likely (%)
2018, May 28–June 3	32	34	32
2012, May 3–6	28	40	32
2003, January 20–22	31	37	31
1996, April 25–28	34	37	27
1990, May 17–20	32	32	35

Source: Frank Newport, "Partisan Divide on Benefit of Having Rich People Expands," Gallup News Service, June 8, 2018.
Note: Percentages based on those who do not already consider themselves rich.

although the proportion who believed this has changed over time. The lowest level of agreement with this statement (57 percent) was registered in 1983, and the highest level (84 percent) was recorded in 2000. In 2015, 64 percent believed that hard work was a route out of poverty and into wealth. The proportion of Americans who disagreed with this sentiment fluctuated between 13 percent (2000) and 38 percent (1983). In the 2015 survey, 33 percent of Americans did not believe in this statement, which is commonly seen as the essence of the American dream.[436]

Accordingly, most Americans rejected the following statement: "Hard work offers little guarantee of success."[437] Pew has regularly asked Americans whether they agreed that hard work offers *little* guarantee of success in life. In surveys conducted between 1987 and 2012, some two-thirds of Americans rejected this skeptical view. In 1987, 68 percent rejected it, compared with 63 percent in 2012.

As expected, large variations in opinion on this statement exist between low-income and upper-income groups. In 1987, 78 percent of very high earners rejected the view that hard work offers little guarantee of success in life, in contrast to only 54 percent of low earners. And in 2012, 76 percent of respondents in the upper-income group rejected this statement, compared with a significantly lower 46 percent of the low-income cohort. The fact that high earners are more likely to reject the view that hard work contributes little to success is as predictable as the fact that low earners are less likely to do so. It is striking, however, that almost half of low earners reject the notion that hard work offers little guarantee of success.

Two lines of explanation are possible for the variations in levels of rejection:

1. Firsthand experience has taught higher earners that hard work does lead to success, and they are happy to ascribe their success to their own efforts; lower earners have either experienced life differently or are unwilling to attribute their own economic failings to a lack of hard work and personal effort.

2. In my opinion, there is an equally valid, although less fre-
    quently cited, explanation: individuals who believe that
    success or failure is determined by external circumstances
    or forces beyond their control are less likely to make a real
    effort than individuals who believe that success or failure are
    primarily the result of personal effort.

Intelligent and Industrious—but Also Dishonest and Greedy

Between 1992 and 2012, Pew repeatedly asked Americans whether they
admired people who get rich by working hard. Across eight individual
surveys (in 1992, 1994, 1997, 1999, 2002, 2003, 2009, and 2012), the
percentage of respondents who said they admire the hardworking rich
fluctuated between 87 percent and 90 percent.[438]

There were high levels of admiration for the hardworking rich across
all social groups in the Pew surveys. Even in the survey's lowest-income
group, between 82 percent and 88 percent of all respondents agreed
that they admire people who got rich through hard work, with 1999
being the only outlier; in that year, only 75 percent agreed.[439] In the
upper-income bracket, the figure fluctuated between 88 percent and
93 percent. Among men and women, people with high and low educational attainment, Republicans and Democrats, and people of different
ages, only minor variations appeared in the percentage of respondents
who admired people who got rich through hard work.

However, admiration is only one side of the coin, as other surveys
show. In 2012, Pew asked, "How are the rich different from average
Americans?" (Figure 9.6).[440]

These findings confirm the hypothesis that people have an ambivalent attitude toward the rich: many admit that the rich are more intelligent and work harder, but at the same time, they perceive the rich as
greedy and dishonest.

The survey found that Republicans and Democrats have very different views of the rich. A much higher share of Republicans (55 percent)
than Democrats (33 percent) said that rich people are more likely to
be hardworking compared with the average person. Similar differences

Figure 9.6

How are the rich different from average Americans?

Percentage saying rich people are more likely/less likely than the average person to be ...

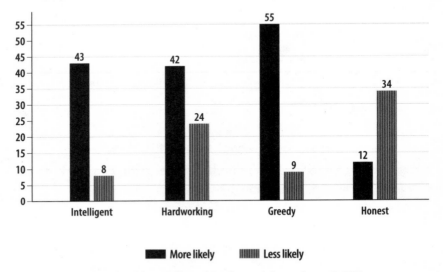

■ More likely   ⫼ Less likely

Source: Kim Parker, "Yes, the Rich Are Different," Pew Research Center, August 2, 2012.

along party lines emerged when respondents were asked whether rich people are more likely than the average person to be greedy (65 percent of Democrats and 42 percent of Republicans agreed) or intelligent (49 percent of Republicans and 38 percent of Democrats agreed). And the number of Republicans who thought the rich were honest was low, at 18 percent, but still twice as high as among Democrats (8 percent).[441]

When asked whether the rich are more likely to be intelligent, there was little variation in the answers from members of different social classes. Their responses to other questions, however, did differ: 51 percent of upper-class Americans considered the rich to be hardworking people, compared with only 44 percent of the middle class and 35 percent of the lower class. And lower-class Americans are much more likely than those in the upper or middle classes to view the rich as dishonest or greedy.[442]

In Germany, none of the Allensbach Institute's various surveys directly addressed popular perceptions of the rich, but they did investigate perceptions of entrepreneurs and top-tier managers, asking what

Figure 9.7

Positive statements about entrepreneurs (Germany, 1999–2009)

Positive attribute and the percentage agreeing

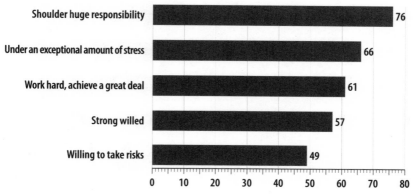

Source: Allensbach Institute surveys 4218, 7013, 7059, 7082, 10018, and 10033.

people think about the business class in general. In the surveys conducted in 1999, 2001, 2004, 2005, 2008, and 2009, positive statements about entrepreneurs were met with broad approval (Figure 9.7).[443] In contrast, Figure 9.8 shows responses to negative statements about entrepreneurs.

In 2008, the Allensbach Institute asked whether an anti-business sentiment existed in Germany.[444] While 14 percent of the survey's respondents said that there was a "very anti-business sentiment," 55 percent felt that the sentiment was "somewhat anti-business." Only 18 percent said there was little or no anti-business sentiment.

Entrepreneurs were perceived in a more positive light than top-tier managers, as revealed by an Allensbach survey from 2008 (Figure 9.9).[445] In another survey, only 27 percent saw managers as "capable, competent," and only 9 percent saw them as "trustworthy, serious." These results correspond to 37 percent of respondents who said that a "very hostile mood toward managers" exists in Germany and 48 percent who said the mood toward managers is "somewhat hostile." Only 7 percent said that no anti-manager sentiment existed in Germany.[446]

In the 2009, 2013, and 2017 surveys, clear majorities agreed that the state should dictate maximum salaries for managers. This statement was

Figure 9.8

Negative statements about entrepreneurs (Germany, 1999–2009)

Negative attribute and the percentage agreeing

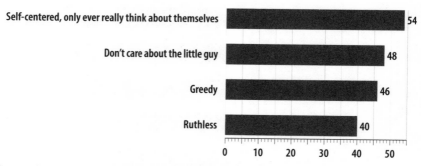

Source: Allensbach Institute surveys 4218, 7013, 7059, 7082, 10018, and 10033.

Figure 9.9

Statements about managers (Germany, 2008)

Statement and percentage approving

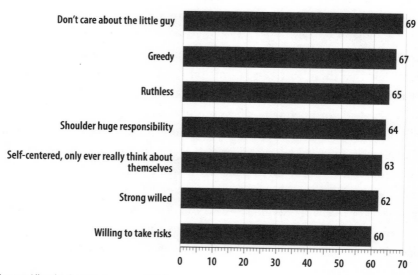

Source: Allensbach Institute survey 10018.

supported by 58 percent, 56 percent, and 54 percent of respondents in the respective surveys, compared with only about one-third of respondents who said that setting salary caps was not the job of the state.[447]

The dissatisfaction expressed by respondents in all of these surveys about "excessive manager salaries" is related to a specific understanding (or lack of understanding) of the concept of performance. Patrick Sachweh cites studies from different years according to which three-quarters of the German population regarded managers' salaries as being too high.[448] He argues—and cites other studies that support his position—that although a relatively broad consensus exists among the general population that salaries should bear some relation to performance, people have very different ideas when it comes to the concept of just rewards. "In particular, individuals with low socioeconomic status usually understand 'performance' in relation to the conscientious completion of a defined quantity of tasks within a specific period of time and are hardly in a position to deviate from this mindset in order to formulate a more far-reaching, abstract concept of performance."[449]

This view is evident from a number of the statements made by Sachweh's interviewees, such as "What's fair is when someone gets what they deserve, what they are entitled to as a result of their own hard work, you understand? And . . . if someone puts a lot of effort into something, and they get the right pay off at the end, then that is fair, isn't it?"[450] According to Sachweh, such opinions are underpinned by the view that exceptional performance, in this case in the form of a large workload, justifies an exceptional reward.[451] This view is held across all social classes. In contrast, feelings of injustice arise when "someone receives a greater reward with less effort."[452]

Furthermore, Sachweh found that people generally accepted that lengthy periods of professional training or studying should be reflected in higher incomes.[453] It would seem that workers and salaried employees primarily equate earnings to the time they spend working (i.e., in the form of hourly wages). They also accept that higher education should lead to higher wages, as a form of compensation for the many years in which a student earns nothing. However, top-tier managers' incomes are

not determined by the time they spend on a task, by their academic qualifications, or by any vocational training they have completed. Rather,
managers' salaries are the market prices for scarce commodities such as
leadership skills, strategic thinking, contacts, creativity, and experience.
Relatively few people possess such qualities, and the principle of supply and demand thus determines top-tier salaries. The time a person
spends in a job, or what that person has studied, is irrelevant. Thus, it
is not these factors that are used to determine how much top executives earn in compensation. Executives are paid not for their time input
but for achieving a specific financial result, which can be measured, for
example, in the total value of transactions they conclude (for investment
bankers) or in the development of the company's share price (for senior
executives).

In addition to general considerations of fairness and merit, ideas of
distributive fairness also include considerations of need. According to
Sachweh, who cites related American research, "low-status" respondents
give need considerations more weight, whereas "high-status" respondents place greater weight on merit considerations.[454] We can assume
that, in broader sections of the population, different ideas and perceptions of distributive fairness coexist. After all, in the debate surrounding
excessive executive pay, some have argued that no individual needs such
huge amounts of money because he or she could never hope to spend it
sensibly. From Sachweh's interviews, however, it was clear that people
are willing to grant others a certain degree of luxury and accept salaries that go far beyond satisfying the necessities of life. But Sachweh
does qualify this concession: "On the other hand, a measure of wealth
that goes beyond this is considered problematic, especially if it seems
to be motivated by an obvious striving for social distinction and clearly
goes beyond justifiable needs. Conspicuous patterns of consumption and
behavior are therefore also interpreted as signs of a lack of moral standards on the part of the 'rich.'"[455]

Hardly anyone, Sachweh observes, is in favor of absolute equality,
although a prevailing sense of fairness dictates that the inequalities should
not be too great. "Perceptions and criticisms of what is perceived as
excessive wealth are based on moral judgments, which deem wastefulness

and the profligate spending of money on goods that are not required to directly satisfy needs as illegitimate. Such negative perceptions of this kind of behavior are also aggravated by perceptions of material under-privilege and poverty."[456]

PUBLIC OPINION, IMPLICIT ASSOCIATION

Previous research on intergroup prejudice has revealed that people have two types of attitudes toward social groups: an explicit (conscious) attitude and an implicit (unconscious) attitude. However, this approach has not yet been applied to investigate attitudes toward the rich specifically.[457] Conscious attitudes are measured using conventional surveys, unconscious attitudes with response latency tasks, such as the Implicit Association Test. Implicit attitudes often originate in childhood and often persist long after the emergence of divergent explicit attitudes. Suzanne R. Horwitz and John F. Dovidio also report that there is frequently only weak correlation between explicit and implicit attitudes and that these attitudes may even contradict each other—for example, in the case of racial attitudes.[458]

As measured by existing surveys, the researchers argue, attitudes toward the rich are often not very positive. "Even though people do not openly favor the rich on surveys, in the current research we examine whether people may hold unknown and unacknowledged positive implicit attitudes toward the upper class."[459] The authors refer to research supporting the possibility that children have pro–upper-class tendencies and prefer those who have expensive-looking possessions. The study hypothesized that these positive attitudes toward wealth develop early in childhood and adolescence and would persist in the form of implicit attitudes into adulthood, even if, under the influence of egalitarian values, explicit attitudes toward the rich change in a less positive direction.[460]

The researchers used an Implicit Association Test to measure associations with lexical items, such as "upper class," "millionaire," "rich," "middle class," "average Joe," and "blue collar." Their findings confirmed that implicit attitudes toward the rich are more positive than implicit attitudes toward the middle class. This implicit preference for the rich relative to the middle class was stronger for participants from higher-socioeconomic-status households, but it also occurred in participants who self-identified as middle class, even though adults explicitly espouse more positive attitudes toward the middle class than toward the rich.[461]

In further studies, the researchers measured participants' implicit (unconscious) attitudes toward different socioeconomic status groups. The authors conclude that "wealth attitudes may reflect cultural values that are shared by people with different amounts of personal wealth."[462] The effect of these implicit and explicit attitudes in everyday situations was confirmed by a third study, which asked participants to assign responsibility for causing a road traffic accident involving a Jaguar and a mid-range car (Toyota Corolla).[463] All of these studies confirmed that "compared to other types of intergroup attitudes, attitudes toward the rich have an uncommon structure in which implicit attitudes are relatively positive, despite the fact that our participants generally do not self-identify as members of this social group or express explicit positivity about this group."[464]

In most studies, the rich are presented as a homogeneous group. But in 2005, Andrew N. Christopher and colleagues investigated whether the way in which someone became rich affected the way they were perceived. The researchers presented 312 American students with four different stories about "Lisa," who started out as a regular employee at a large technology company.[465]

1. Over time, Lisa earned several promotions with salary increases and is now a high-level executive.
2. Lisa founded the technology company at which she now works; her company has grown from 2 to 15 employees and is now quite profitable. Lisa earns a very high salary.
3. In Las Vegas, Lisa gambled in some of the casinos and won many games and a lot of money. Thus, Lisa attained the life she currently enjoys.
4. Lisa inherited a large sum of money, which has made her wealthy.

Participants were given a list of the Big Five personality traits and asked to assign them to each of the four different Lisas, that is, the high-income executive, the entrepreneur, the gambler, and the heiress. The findings:

- *Conscientiousness.* Characters who acquired their affluence by external means (i.e., luck or inheritance) were perceived to be less conscientious than those who acquired their affluence by internal means (i.e., promotions or entrepreneurial success).[466]
- *Agreeableness.* The authors had expected participants to perceive characters who acquired their affluence via external means to be less agreeable than characters who had acquired their affluence via internal means.[467] This hypothesis received "only limited support"—with a significance of only $p = 0.091$, it would be more correct to say that this hypothesis received no support.
- *Openness to experience.* Participants perceived the character who acquired her affluence via entrepreneurial means to be more open to experience than the character who owed her affluence to inheritance. However, the gambler was perceived to be just as open to experience as the entrepreneur.[468]

The researchers reported no significant correlation between the four scenarios and the assignment of the two remaining Big Five traits, extroversion and neuroticism.

It is important not to overstate the importance of these findings, especially because the studies were carried out with student groups of slightly more than 50 participants each. But the general approach is correct: unlike in other studies, these researchers do not ask questions about rich people in general; their questions focus on how someone became rich. Our own internationally comparative study contains a question that likewise allows us to differentiate according to the origins of wealth.

THE CARDS ARE STACKED IN FAVOR OF THE RICH

When Americans are asked whether they believe that society as a whole benefits from having a class of rich people, a majority (58 percent) agrees, at least according to a Gallup poll from 2018. In contrast, 39 percent disagree. The proportion of respondents who are skeptical of whether society as a whole benefits from the existence of the rich has risen somewhat since Gallup first asked this question in 1990. At that time, 62 percent agreed that society benefited from the rich and 32 percent disagreed. The most recent results have changed little from 2012.[469]

The general attitude of Americans toward the rich, however, is decidedly ambivalent. On the one hand, Americans acknowledge that the rich are important. On the other hand, many Americans perceive the rich as profiteers with unjustified advantages. When Americans are asked whether the tax system benefits the rich and is unfair to ordinary working people, majorities have agreed since the 1980s. And despite revisions to the tax code, whether under George W. Bush or Bill Clinton, a majority has always believed that tax cuts most benefit the rich and that the rich would avoid paying tax increases.[470]

In every Gallup poll between 1992 and 2017, majorities of Americans have said the rich pay too little tax.[471] When the question was first asked in March 1992, 77 percent of Americans agreed that upper-income people were paying too little tax. Only 4 percent said that upper-income people were paying too much, and 16 percent thought they were paying a fair share. In contrast, 57 percent said that middle-income people paid too much tax, and only 5 percent said middle-income people were paying too little tax.

Gallup asked the same question 20 times between 1992 and 2017. Opinions changed very little over the years. In most years, somewhere between 60 percent and 69 percent of Americans said that upper-income people paid too little tax (the figure was slightly lower in 2010 and 2011, at 55 percent and 59 percent, respectively). In 2017, the figure was 63 percent.

In contrast, the 1992 survey reported that 57 percent of Americans thought that middle-income people were paying too much tax. In 2017, the figure stood at 51 percent. The proportion of respondents who believed that middle-income people were paying too little tax hovered between 3 percent and 7 percent in all 20 surveys.

Gallup also asked whether the government should redistribute wealth by imposing heavy taxes on the rich.[472] In the nine surveys between 1998 and 2016, American opinion was always divided (Table 9.4). It was only quite long ago, in 1939, that a significant majority of Americans were against heavy taxes on the rich, although 35 percent then supported heavy taxes as a mechanism for redistributing wealth.

In 15 surveys between 1984 and 2016, Gallup asked whether money and wealth should be distributed more evenly among a larger percentage of Americans. This softer question elicited 60 percent agreement in 1984 and 59 percent in 2016. On the other 13 occasions it was asked, approval was usually around the 60 percent mark, with roughly one-third of Americans consistently rejecting wealth redistribution. As often happens, responses depend on the way a question is asked.

Table 9.4
Should the government redistribute wealth? (United States, 1939–2016)

People feel differently about how far a government should go. Here is a phrase which some people believe in and some don't. Do you think our government should or should not redistribute wealth by heavy taxes on the rich?

	Yes, should (%)	No, should not (%)	No opinion (%)
2016, April 6–10	52	46	2
2015, April 9–12	52	45	2
2013, April 4–7	52	45	3
2011, April 7–11	47	49	4
2009, March 27–29	50	46	4
2008, October 23–26	46	50	4
2008, April 6–9	51	43	5
2007, April 2–5	49	47	4
1998, April 23–May 31	45	51	4
1939, March[a]	35	54	11

[a]Roper/*Fortune* magazine poll.
Source: Gallup News Services, Taxes (Historical Trends).

The skepticism toward wealth redistribution expressed by Americans in numerous surveys is an exception in international comparison, as is revealed by an analysis conducted by Giacomo Corneo and Hans Peter Grüner in 2002 using data from 1992. In 11 countries (Australia, Bulgaria, Canada, Czechoslovakia, Germany [east and west], Hungary, New Zealand, Norway, Poland, Russia, and the United States), respondents were asked whether they agreed or disagreed with the following statement: "It is the responsibility of the government to reduce the differences in income between people with high incomes and those with low incomes."[473]

In almost every one of the 11 countries, very clear majorities agreed that the state was responsible for redistributing wealth.[474] In former socialist countries in particular, this statement met with very strong support (e.g., 65 percent in Russia, 81 percent in Bulgaria). Only two countries registered no majority for redistribution: in the United States, only 39 percent of respondents agreed, and in Canada, only 48 percent agreed. However, even in these two countries, only 42 percent (United States) and 30 percent (Canada) were against redistribution (the rest were undecided). Nevertheless, the sharp contrast with east Germany, for example, where 89 percent were in favor of redistribution and only 6 percent were against, is very clear.[475]

Table 9.5 presents the answers in west Germany, east Germany, and the United States to the question of whether one is in favor of redistribution.[476]

Table 9.5

Should the government reduce income inequalities? (2002)

Country/region	Strongly agree	Agree	Neither agree nor disagree	Disagree	Strongly disagree
Germany (west)	20	46	15	15	5
Germany (east)	42	47	5	6	0
United States	10	29	20	29	13

Source: Giacomo Corneo and Hans Peter Grüner, "Individual Preferences for Political Redistribution," *Journal of Public Economics* 83, no. 1 (2002): 89.
Note: All data are in percentage of respondents.

At the same time, respondents were asked whether they thought their incomes would go up or down if incomes became more equal in their countries. In most countries, respondents thought their own incomes would go up as a result of redistribution. It is striking, however, that in three countries, the number of people who support redistribution was lower than the number who believed they would personally benefit.

This difference was particularly noticeable in the United States: 60 percent of Americans believed that they would benefit from incomes becoming more equal, but only 39 percent supported redistribution. In Australia and Canada, too, the number of people who support redistribution was lower than the number who believed they would personally benefit, although the difference was much smaller than in the United States.[477]

According to Corneo and Grüner, these results prove that we need more than an exclusively economic explanation related to one's immediate interests to help us understand why people either favor or oppose redistribution (although they acknowledge that this factor is the decisive explanation). They therefore tested two alternative explanations: "public values effect," and an explanation that seemed somewhat constructed, which they defined as the "social rivalry effect." According to their hypothesis, people worry that even if they were to personally benefit from government redistribution, so would others. Their response is to oppose political redistribution. These individuals, the researchers proposed, would therefore reject redistribution because it could have a negative effect on their relative social status and standard of living. However, the empirical evidence for these explanations is not convincing, especially as the researchers used only indirect indicators.[478]

What remains is the highly interesting finding that in the United States, the proportion of respondents who supported redistribution is 21 percentage points lower than the number who thought their incomes would go up as a result of government redistribution. Although the researchers do not directly address this question, one may assume that this apparent discrepancy relates to a general skepticism against "big government" in the United States, in combination with a value system in which private assets are highly valued and many people regard taxes and government redistribution programs as a form of theft, which is not the case in other countries.

Although many surveys have asked respondents whether they think current levels of taxation are fair or not, relatively few surveys have asked respondents to identify other benefits enjoyed by the rich that could be described as fair or unfair. The following survey, conducted in Germany in 2007, is one exception. It was based on a welfare state research project for the federal government's Poverty and Wealth Report at the Johann Wolfgang Goethe University in Frankfurt and asked the following: "We're interested in finding out what you think can be considered fair in Germany. Would you please indicate whether you strongly agree, agree, neither agree nor disagree, disagree or strongly disagree with each of the following statements?"[479] Table 9.6 presents the responses.[480]

Table 9.6

The rich enjoy certain advantages. Which are perceived as fair? (Germany, 2007)

	Strongly agree	Agree	Neither agree nor disagree	Disagree	Strongly disagree
• It is fair that people who earn higher salaries can afford to live in better homes than everyone else	40	37	7	9	7
• It is fair that people who earn higher salaries will retire on higher pensions than everyone else	35	35	8	12	10
• It is fair that parents who can afford it should give their children a better education	20	19	8	25	28
• It is fair that people who earn higher salaries should be able to exert greater influence on political decisions than everyone else	6	6	5	29	54
• It is fair that people who earn higher salaries should receive better health-care than everyone else	6	7	4	24	59

Source: Wolfgang Glatzer et al., *Reichtum im Urteil der Bevölkerung: Legitimationsprobleme und Spannungspotentiale in Deutschland* (Opladen: Verlag Barbara Budrich, 2009), p. 73.
Note: Percentages of respondents.

In 2013, Ipsos MORI conducted a survey in the United Kingdom. Among the questions, the researchers were interested in public perceptions of the wealth gap.[481] Figure 9.10 shows what respondents thought about large differences in wealth.

In keeping with this critical view, 72 percent of respondents agreed that the government should restrict maximum salaries and bonuses; 70 percent supported increasing the rate of income tax for high earners; 62 percent supported introducing a tax on properties worth more than £2 million (mansion tax); and 50 percent were in favor of increasing the inheritance tax on estates worth £500,000 or more.[482]

Figure 9.10

Ipsos MORI survey of public perceptions of the wealth gap (United Kingdom, 2013)

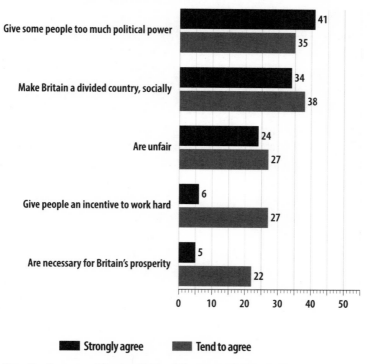

Source: Karen Rowlingson and Stephen McKay, "What Do the Public Think about the Wealth Gap?," University of Birmingham, 2013.
Note: Percentages of respondents.

All of these surveys, especially those in the United States and Germany, reveal an ambivalent attitude toward the rich. Many Americans admire the rich and, as children or young people, set themselves the goal of becoming rich. Later in life, however, most of these aspirational Americans become disillusioned. In every single survey, a majority of respondents believe that the rich pay too little tax, but if you ask Americans whether tax revenues should be redistributed, opinions are divided, whereas in most other countries, clear majorities favor redistribution. And on the one hand, rich people are credited with positive traits, such as intelligence and diligence, but on the other hand, they are also perceived as exhibiting negative traits, such as greed. Surveys have revealed strong anti-business sentiments in Germany and even more pronounced anti-manager sentiments. Managers are regarded as greedy, and a clear majority in Germany is in favor of a state-imposed limit on their salaries.

Unfortunately, the questions asked over the years in all of these countries were not uniform. In Germany, in particular, hardly any surveys have been conducted to explore attitudes toward the rich—previous surveys have focused on the subgroups of top-tier managers and entrepreneurs. Some questions have been asked over and over again; others, which would be of great interest in exploring popular perceptions of the rich, have never been asked at all. For these reasons, I commissioned the first-ever comparative international study, using the same set of items in four countries, to explore popular perceptions of and attitudes toward the rich.

PART TWO

What the Germans, Americans, French, and British Think of the Rich

CHAPTER 10

HOW GERMANS VIEW THE RICH

From April 26 to May 8, 2018, the Allensbach Institute conducted a representative survey of Germans ages 16 and older. In May and June 2018, Ipsos MORI asked the same questions in the United States, France, and Great Britain.

What the General Population Thinks

Prejudice research has repeatedly shown that it is not easy to measure prejudices about minorities with surveys because many people do not dare express critical opinions about some groups even when they know the survey is anonymous. We wanted to know whether that effect also applied to prejudices about the rich. To find out, Allensbach asked, *"It is sometimes said that there are certain groups of people that you have to be careful not to criticize in public. Which of these groups, if any, do you think this applies to?"*

The list included Muslims; immigrants; Jews; blacks; homosexual people; disabled people; people receiving welfare benefits; unemployed people; women; rich people; and Christians. Figure 10.1 presents the results. As shown, about two-thirds of Germans believe that you have to be careful not to criticize Muslims, immigrants, and Jews in public.

---

*Figure and table data in Chapter 10 are from the 2018 Allensbach Institute survey 11085 of Germany.

Figure 10.1

Germany: Whom do you have to be careful not to criticize in public?

Question: "It is sometimes said that there are certain groups of people that you have to be careful not to criticize in public. Which of these groups, if any, do you think this applies to?"

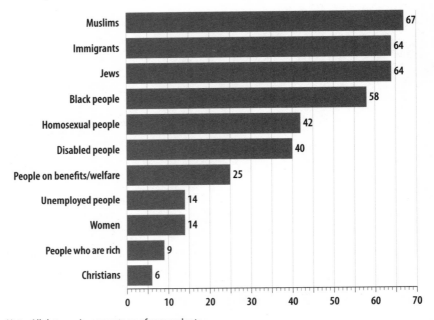

Note: All data are in percentage of respondents.

According to 58 percent of German respondents, the same applies to blacks, whereas 42 percent think that you need to be careful not to openly criticize gay or lesbian people and disabled people. Only 25 percent believe that you have to avoid criticizing people on welfare. In contrast, hardly anyone (only 9 percent of respondents) professed to be worried about appearing tactless by criticizing the rich. Only among interviewees in the lowest-income group (less than €1,500) was the proportion somewhat higher, at 16 percent. Nevertheless, even that figure is significantly lower than the proportion of low earners who think that you have to be careful when making statements about immigrants (70 percent).

These findings support the hypothesis that prejudices based on classism are far more acceptable than prejudices based on ethnicity, religion, or gender.[483] Despite the fact that opinion polls are less than ideal for measuring people's true attitudes toward minority out-groups, they are a reliable instrument for measuring attitudes toward the rich, because there is little reason to fear that interviewees will distort their answers.

To find out what Germans think about the rich, our survey next asked them whether they agreed or disagreed with a number of positive, negative, and neutral statements. To overcome the limitations of previous surveys, the Allensbach Institute clearly informed respondents that the questions about wealthy people referred to people with assets worth at least €1 million, not including the home they live in.

One of the survey's aims was to ask the respondents why they think some people become rich. Based on their responses, participants can be assigned to one of two groups:

1. Some people emphasize the importance of external circumstances beyond a person's control. Thus, many people believe that people become rich primarily as the beneficiaries of inheritance, luck, or an unfair tax system.
2. Other people explain wealth in terms of the personality traits or abilities of people who get rich. These can include both positive traits (e.g., intelligence or industriousness) and negative ones (e.g., ruthlessness).

The first explanation includes the opinion that becoming rich primarily depends on the connections and contacts you have through your parents and family. In response to this statement, 55 percent of Germans agreed. No other explanation for wealth was mentioned as often. Furthermore, 41 percent believed that most rich people become rich only through inheritances, which have nothing to do with their own abilities. And a third of respondents agreed with both of the following two statements: "People who are rich mainly have good luck," and "The rich people in Germany only became rich because there was injustice in our society."

The second explanation for the origin of wealth includes the opinion that many rich people become rich because they take more risks than others tend to (47 percent). We have already mentioned family relationships, which are crucial from the point of view of 55 percent of respondents. Slightly less—49 percent—also see relationships as important but believe that whether or not one gets rich depends crucially on one's ability to establish important connections and contacts on one's own.

On the whole, Germans tended to think that wealth is the product of negative traits and patterns of behavior: 43 percent of German respondents believed that many rich people are rich only because they ruthlessly pursued their own interests—a negative characterization—but just as many believed that becoming rich depends primarily on the abilities and ideas one has. At the same time, 35 percent thought that many rich people obtained their wealth at the expense of others, whereas only 22 percent believed that rich people are generally very industrious throughout their lives.

Even 30 years after reunification, east Germans continued to harbor far more negative attitudes toward the rich than west Germans. In west Germany, one in three believed that the rich have obtained their wealth at the expense of others, whereas almost one in two east Germans (44 percent) believed this to be the case. And although one in four west Germans thought that the rich were generally very industrious, only 14 percent of east Germans agreed. Every second west German believed that many rich people become rich because they took more risks than others tend to, but only one in three east Germans were of the same opinion. When asked whether becoming rich depended primarily on one's abilities and ideas, 45 percent of west Germans, but only 32 percent of east Germans, agreed. The difference was particularly great in the proportions of east and west Germans who agreed that rich people in Germany became rich only because there was injustice in society. Fewer than a third of west Germans, but almost half of east Germans, agreed with that statement.

The overwhelmingly negative picture of the rich can be ascertained from the list of traits that respondents most frequently said apply to rich people. The top five traits mentioned by German respondents were all negative: 62 percent said the rich are self-centered; 56 percent said they are materialistic; 50 percent, ruthless; 49 percent, greedy; and 43 percent, arrogant. Only then did German respondents mention positive traits, such as industrious (42 percent), bold or daring (41 percent), intelligent (40 percent), and visionary or farsighted (39 percent). Traits such as cold-hearted (28 percent) and superficial (18 percent) were also attributed to the rich, whereas only 3 percent considered being honest to apply to them. Here, too, east Germans saw the rich in a far more negative light than west Germans. For example, fewer than half of west Germans perceived rich people as being ruthless and greedy, compared with two-thirds of east Germans.

In terms of Bogdan Wojciszke, Róża Bazinska, and Marcin Jaworski's fundamental distinction between "moral traits" and "competence traits,"[484] the negative traits attributed to the rich are predominantly "moral traits." As we have already seen, our positive or negative perceptions of other people and of out-groups are based on both moral and competence traits, and morality-related information plays a more important role in perception than competence-related information. Even when large numbers of people say that the rich are industrious, visionary, and intelligent, those positive competence traits carry less weight than the negative perception that the rich are dishonest, ruthless, greedy, self-centered, and arrogant.

The overall negative picture of the rich is also confirmed by responses to many other items. When respondents were asked which of 17 statements about the rich they agreed with, the statement that elicited the second-greatest level of agreement was that most rich people are "tax cheats" (51 percent), and in third place was "Those who are very rich and want more and more power are to blame for many of the major problems in the world, [such as] financial or humanitarian issues." In contrast, only one in three believe that society as a whole benefits from the existence of rich people because many of them create jobs, or that many of the rich are entrepreneurs who create new products. Even fewer said that society as a whole benefits from the existence of rich people because they pay high taxes (18 percent) or that the state can afford to pay for the social system because the rich pay higher taxes (10 percent).

This finding doesn't mean that the rich are viewed entirely negatively. Fewer than a third of German respondents agreed with the extreme statement that rich people are good at earning money but are not usually decent people. This may be because some respondents were reluctant to describe members of a whole group of people as lacking decency. Nevertheless, the fact that fewer than half of respondents outright rejected this sweepingly disparaging statement does correspond with the overall negative picture of the rich.

Attitudes toward the rich also varied widely depending on how the rich people in question acquired their wealth. Interviewees were asked which groups of people deserve to be rich, and their responses differed considerably. The groups identified as deserving to be rich included self-employed people (64 percent), entrepreneurs (57 percent), and lottery winners (54 percent). Half of respondents believed that creative people and artists, such as actors or musicians, deserve to be rich. In the case of top athletes and heirs, fewer than a third and one in five, respectively, believed that these groups deserve to be rich (see Figure 10.2).

Figure 10.2
Germany: Who deserves to be rich?

Question: "Which, if any, of the following groups of people do you personally believe deserve to be rich?"

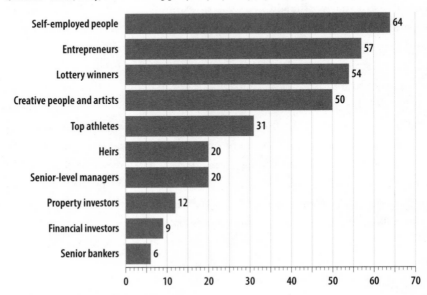

Note: All data are in percentage of respondents.

The headlines about greedy managers, bankers, and financial and property investors have clearly had an effect, because very few respondents believed that such people deserve to be rich. Only one in five thought that senior-level managers deserve their wealth; only 12 percent thought that property investors deserve their wealth; and senior bankers came in last: only 6 percent thought they deserve their wealth. Here again, east and west Germans differed significantly. East Germans were most likely to think that lottery winners deserve their wealth (66 percent)— considerably *more* likely than for entrepreneurs (50 percent). This may be because the respondents also hope to get rich by guessing the right numbers in a lottery one day. In sharp contrast, only 22 percent of east Germans believed that top athletes deserve their wealth, and only 3 percent thought the same for senior bankers.

In Chapter 5, we saw how important zero-sum beliefs are in shaping attitudes toward the rich. In Germany, a plurality (48 percent versus 44 percent) agreed with the statement "The more the rich have, the less there is for the poor." In east Germany, however, a clear majority (almost 60 percent) agreed with this statement, and only 29 percent disagreed. Of those who subscribed to zero-sum beliefs, 63 percent blamed the rich for the world's major problems, an example of scapegoat thinking, compared with only 36 percent of non-zero-sum believers. And zero-sum believers are three times as likely as non-zero-sum believers to think that many rich people obtained their wealth at the expense of others.

The overwhelmingly critical attitude of Germans toward the rich is confirmed by responses to the questions on taxation. More than half of all Germans and almost two-thirds of east Germans thought not only that the rich should pay high taxes but that they should pay very high taxes. In this way, the state can ensure that the gap between the rich and the poor does not become too great. On the other hand, fewer than one-third believed that taxes for the rich should be high but not excessively high, because the rich have generally worked hard to earn their wealth and the state should not take too much away from them. Among zero-sum believers, a sizeable majority—70 percent—were in favor of very high taxes, whereas among non-zero-sum believers, fewer than one-third were in favor of very high taxes.

From many previous surveys, we already knew that most Germans were in favor of government-imposed caps on managers' salaries. But why is that? And to what extent do arguments against such caps find a voice?

In the Allensbach survey, 63 percent of respondents thought it was inappropriate for managers to earn so much more than their employees, because they do not work so much longer and harder than their employees (Figure 10.3). Of all the statements on why managers should not earn so much, this one elicited by far the greatest agreement. It reflects what we might call the prevailing "employee mindset," which dictates that salaries should be determined primarily on the basis of how long and how hard someone works.

Figure 10.3

Germany: Why managers' earnings are perceived as too high

Question: "Here are a few statements about the differences in earnings found between managers who earn 100 times more than their employees. Which of these statements would you agree with?"

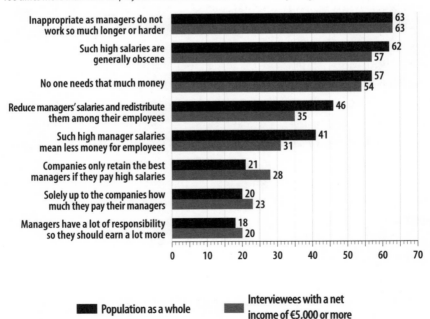

Note: All data are in percentage of respondents.

Employees thus project their own performance and remuneration benchmarks onto senior-level managers and believe that there must be a close relationship between how hard and how long someone works, on the one hand, and the person's salary, on the other. With regard to senior-level managers' salaries, respondents clearly do not see such a link. Thus, they conclude that managers' salaries are excessive, because no manager works 100 times as long or as hard as an average employee. On the other hand, respondents barely understood that senior-level managers' salaries are determined by supply and demand in the market for top-tier executives. Only one in five German respondents agreed that companies can only hire and retain the best managers if they pay very high salaries (the survey specified salaries that are 100 times more than those of an average employee) because otherwise those managers would go to another company that pays more or would work for themselves.

Other arguments, such as that managers have a lot more responsibility, also met with little approval (18 percent). At the same time, 62 percent of all Germans agreed, when prompted, that they found it "obscene" [unanständig] that someone should earn so much money, and 57 percent felt that it was inappropriate for a manager to earn so much more than a normal employee, because no one needs so much money. And in another example of the zero-sum mindset, 41 percent feared that because managers earn so much more than employees, less money is left for employees' salaries.

But can rich people at least improve their image by donating from their wealth? Rich people who believe they can should note that a majority of the population will accuse them of self-interest, rather than altruism, when they donate. For example, they may be accused of seeking to reduce their tax burdens or improve their reputations. Half of all German respondents said that the rich donate to charitable causes primarily because they want to benefit themselves, and only 14 percent believed that the rich support charities primarily because they want to benefit others (Figure 10.4).

When something bad happens to someone else, most people feel sorry for that person. If, however, a millionaire who made a risky

Figure 10.4

Germany: Donations to benefit themselves?

Question: "Some rich people donate a great deal of money to charitable causes. In your opinion, what is the main reason why people do that? Do they primarily donate because they want to benefit others, or primarily because they want to benefit themselves (e.g., for tax relief, to improve their reputation)?"

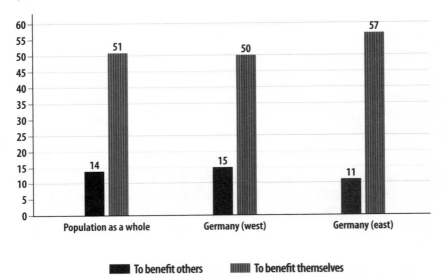

Note: All data are in percentage of respondents. Figures do not add up to 100 percent because "to benefit themselves and others equally" responses have been omitted.

business decision loses a lot of money as a result, then a narrow plurality (40 percent versus 37 percent) reacts with schadenfreude and says, "It serves him right." Schadenfreude is even more pronounced among east Germans (45 percent versus 30 percent). In Chapter 4, which discussed the research on envy, we saw that schadenfreude is directly related to feelings of envy.

After the German interviewees had been asked about their attitudes toward millionaires, we wanted to find out how many of them actually knew a millionaire personally—be it as a family member, a friend, or an acquaintance. This question revealed that 80 percent of our survey's participants have formed their opinions of millionaires without consciously knowing a single one personally (in east Germany, the figure was even higher, at 94 percent). Only 8 percent of respondents knew more than one millionaire personally, and 9 percent knew only one. Those who personally knew at least one millionaire had a much more positive opinion of the rich than those who didn't.

Recall that among the population as a whole, the traits associated with millionaires were mainly negative: 62 percent described the rich as self-centered, 56 percent said they are materialistic, 50 percent thought the rich are ruthless, 49 percent described them as greedy, and 43 percent said they are arrogant. It was only at this point that our respondents start to mention positive traits such as being industrious (42 percent), bold or daring (41 percent), intelligent (40 percent), or visionary or farsighted (39 percent).

The picture is quite different when we consider only the responses from those who personally know one or more millionaires. At least with regard to the millionaire they know best, respondents provided very positive assessments (Figure 10.5): 71 percent considered the millionaire industrious, 71 percent intelligent, 58 percent imaginative, 47 percent optimistic, and 45 percent visionary or farsighted.

And although only 3 percent of the population as a whole considered the rich to be honest, this figure jumped to 42 percent among Germans who personally know a millionaire when asked about that millionaire. Although more than 60 percent of Germans thought the rich are self-centered, only 20 percent thought the same about the millionaires they know personally.

Do Germans personally want to be rich? Considering that 7.7 million Germans regularly play the lottery and another 21 million occasionally buy a ticket (presumably not with the dream of winning just €10, but in the hope of winning the jackpot), it is astonishing that only 2 percent say it is "very important" for them to be rich and 20 percent say it is "fairly important." Two-thirds of Germans claim that it is either not very important or not at all important for them to be rich. However, we will see later that responses to this question from younger and older Germans differ considerably.

Figure 10.5

Germany: General and personal perceptions of millionaires—Five most frequently mentioned traits

Question 1 (General perception: Rich people in general): "Which, if any, of the following are most likely to apply to rich people?"

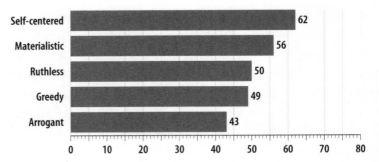

Question 2 (Personal perception: To respondents who know a millionaire personally): "Which, if any, of the following are most likely to apply to the millionaire you know best?"

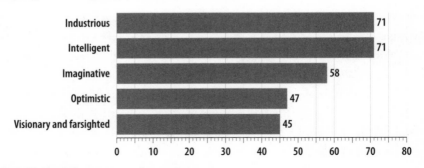

Note: All data are in percentage of respondents.

How Do Enviers and Non-Enviers Think?

The questionnaire on attitudes toward the rich contained three items that can be assumed to capture different aspects of envy and schadenfreude. The first two items were as follows:

1. *"To what extent do you agree or disagree with this statement: 'I think it would be fair to increase taxes substantially for millionaires, even if I would not benefit from it personally.'? Do you strongly agree, tend to agree, neither agree nor disagree, tend to disagree, or strongly disagree?"*

2. *"To what extent, if at all, do you agree or disagree with this statement: 'When I hear about a millionaire who made a risky business decision and lost a lot of money because of it, I think it serves him right.'? Do you strongly agree, tend to agree, neither agree nor disagree, tend to disagree, or strongly disagree?"*

The third item was one of the options in a list:

3. *"I would favor drastically reducing those managers' salaries and redistributing the money more evenly amongst their employees, even if that would mean that [the employees] would only get a few more euros per month."*

These items were included because, as shown in Chapter 4, envy is characterized by the fact that the envier does not primarily want to better him- or herself, but rather begrudges what the other has and desires that it be taken away from the other, even if it would not benefit the envier directly. Accordingly, as envy research has also shown, envy and schadenfreude are closely intertwined.

However, it is possible that agreement with only one item might not be based on envy. Other motives may well play a role in positive responses to it. In fact, none of these three statements is in itself a certain indicator of envy. But if someone agrees with two or all three statements, this person's image of the rich is much more likely shaped by envy than that of someone who agrees with none or only one of the statements. To categorize respondents, it may therefore be more useful to determine *how many* of these statements they agree with rather than which of these statements they specifically agree with.

To facilitate such an analysis, the three questions and statements mentioned were combined to form a quasi-scale. Each participant was assigned a score on the basis of his or her responses to these three questions.

Those who strongly agreed with the first question received one point, while all other respondents were awarded zero; those who strongly agreed or tended to agree with the second question also received one point, while all other respondents were given zero; and those who agreed with the third statement received one point, while those who did not received zero.

In this way, a value between 0 and 3 was assigned to each respondent. The participants were subsequently sorted into groups depending on whether their response behavior was deemed to be strongly (2 or 3 points), weakly (1 point), or barely/perhaps not at all (0 points) shaped by envy.

The reason only "strongly agree" responses to the first question received a score of 1, whereas the same score was also awarded for "tend to agree" responses to question 2, is of a purely pragmatic nature. For the scale to be able to differentiate clearly, the boundaries between qualifying and nonqualifying categories need to be drawn in such a way that all groups are of a comparable size. However, this approach was not possible with the first question, because 41 percent of respondents indicated that they "tend to agree" with the statement. Because the number of respondents who "strongly agree" with the statement was slightly higher (25 percent) than the number who "tend to disagree" or "strongly disagree" (23 percent), those who "tend to agree" were added to the latter group. Methodologically speaking, to decide otherwise would also have been possible and legitimate, and that decision would not have fundamentally affected the explanatory power of the scale.

For the following analysis, I distinguish among three groups, each of which represents an equal proportion of the German population:

1. *Social enviers.* These respondents agreed with at least two of the three questions above. Exactly one-third (33 percent) of respondents belong to this group. Within this group, a distinct subgroup of hardcore enviers agreed with all three questions (11 percent, subsequently referred to as "hardcore enviers").
2. *Ambivalents.* These respondents agreed with one of the envy questions. This group also accounts for approximately one-third of respondents (32 percent).
3. *Non-enviers.* These respondents did not agree with any of the envy questions. This group also represents approximately one-third of respondents (34 percent).

The responses given by these three groups differ considerably for almost all items. To illustrate the differences, I will contrast hardcore enviers with non-enviers. Figure 10.6 highlights the question that elicited the greatest

Figure 10.6

Germany: Statements about the rich by rank on the Social Envy Scale—Largest deviations in percentage points

Question: "Here is a list of things that people have said about rich people. Which, if any, of the statements on the list would you agree with?"

Mentioned more frequently by respondents ranking high on the Social Envy Scale (3 points) than by respondents ranking low on the Social Envy Scale (0 points).

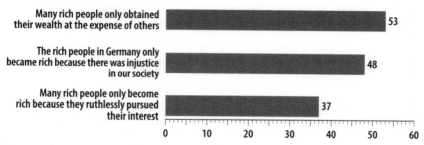

Mentioned more frequently by respondents ranking low on the Social Envy Scale (0 points) than by respondents ranking high on the Social Envy Scale (3 points).

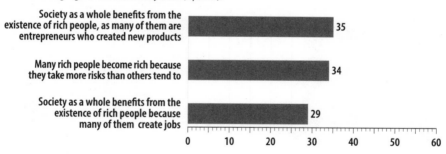

variation in responses between the two groups: 72 percent of hardcore enviers are convinced that many rich people obtained their wealth at the expense of others. Only 19 percent of non-enviers were of the same opinion. The gap in response behavior between the two groups was therefore 53 percentage points. The other greatest differences between hardcore enviers and non-enviers can be seen in their responses to the statements in Figure 10.6 (the figures indicate the differences in percentage points).

We have seen from the stereotype content model, presented in Chapter 3, that the rich are mainly stereotyped as "cold" and that this characterization is associated with envy. This finding corresponds to the fact that two-thirds of hardcore enviers describe the rich as "cold-hearted," in stark contrast to only 14 percent of non-enviers. A remarkable 82 percent of hardcore enviers perceive the rich as "ruthless," compared with only one in three non-enviers.

In Chapter 7, compensation theory was advanced to explain why enviers tend to morally denigrate out-groups in order to protect their own self-esteem in the face of the out-group's economic superiority. This attitude is most pronounced among hardcore enviers, 71 percent of whom believed that "rich people are good at earning money, but are not usually decent people" (Figure 10.7). Among non-enviers, however, only 13 percent agreed with this statement.

Figure 10.7

Germany: Envy and the tendency to deny that rich people are usually decent

Question: "To what extent do you agree or disagree with the following statement: 'Rich people are good at earning money, but are not usually decent people.'?"

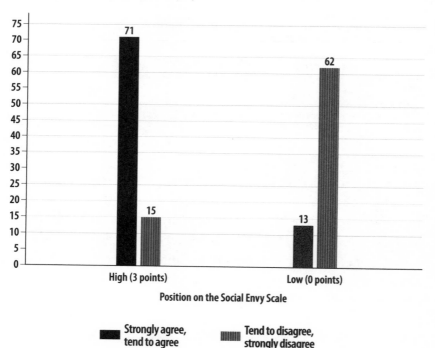

Note: All data are in percentage of respondents.

Figure 10.8
Germany: Who deserves to be rich?

Question: "Which, if any, of the following groups of people do you personally believe deserve to be rich?"

Groups most frequently mentioned by respondents ranking high on the Social Envy Scale (3 points)

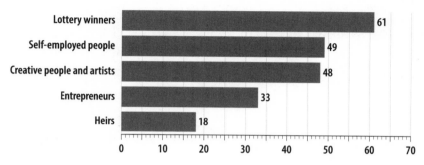

Groups most frequently mentioned by respondents ranking low on the Social Envy Scale (0 points)

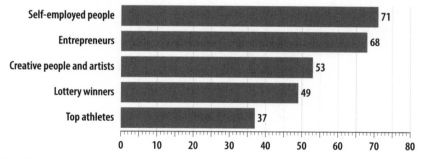

Note: All data are in percentage of respondents.

If we look at which groups hardcore enviers are most likely to think deserve to be rich, then, unlike the population as a whole, they do not rank self-employed people or entrepreneurs at the top (Figure 10.8). Significantly, first place goes to lottery winners: 61 percent of hardcore enviers think that lottery winners deserve to be rich. The enviers ranked lottery winners significantly higher than self-employed people (49 percent), creative people and artists (48 percent), and entrepreneurs (33 percent). Opinions are quite different among non-enviers, who think that self-employed people (71 percent), entrepreneurs (68 percent), and creative people and artists (53 percent) deserve to be rich. Lottery winners rank fourth among non-enviers, at 49 percent.

The fact that enviers think that lottery winners deserve to be rich may seem surprising at first glance, and it definitely needs some explanation. Other rich groups attract particularly vehement criticism because their wealth is allegedly not proportionate to how long and hard they work. This opinion is particularly strong concerning senior-level managers: According to 85 percent of hardcore enviers, "It is inappropriate for managers to earn so much more, as they do not work so much longer or harder than their employees" (Figure 10.9). Not even half as many non-enviers agree with this statement. Only 6 percent of

Figure 10.9

Germany: Social envy and the assumption that income must relate to how long and hard someone works

"I think it is inappropriate for managers to earn so much more, as they do not work so much longer or harder than their employees."

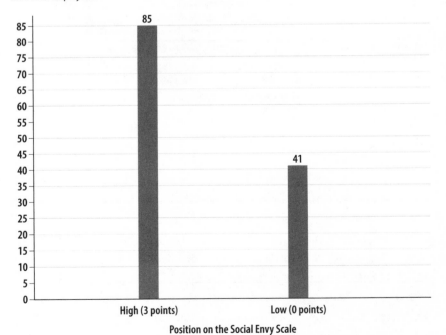

Position on the Social Envy Scale

Note: All data are in percentage of respondents who agreed with the statement.

hardcore enviers think that senior-level managers deserve to be rich, whereas the proportion of non-enviers who think so is more than four times as high.

Why were enviers unwilling to accept that senior-level managers deserve to be rich when they had no problem accepting the fortunes of lottery winners, who became rich purely because they had the luck to pick the right numbers on a lottery ticket? As Helmut Schoeck has already pointed out, envious people are most likely to think that advantages are deserved when the advantages are the result of luck and chance rather than of achievement and merit. After all, if someone else has gained an advantage through luck or chance—unlike when the advantage is based on achievement—it does not lead to the nagging question of why one does not have the advantage oneself. Schoeck even cited lottery winners as an example. The random selection process of a lottery ensures that the winner is not envied: "A wife will not nag her husband for not having bought the right lottery ticket. . . . No one could seriously suffer from an inferiority complex as a result of repeated failure."[485] In terms of self-esteem, it is therefore easier to accept the good fortune of a lottery winner without envy than it is to come to terms with the success of an entrepreneur or a senior-level manager. Moreover, in the case of lottery winners, there is even a remote chance that one could join the ranks of lucky winners oneself at some point.

Less than a quarter of hardcore enviers believed that becoming rich depends on abilities and ideas, in contrast to over half of non-enviers. Of hardcore enviers, only 17 percent believed that rich people are generally industrious throughout their lives, compared with 53 percent of non-enviers (Figure 10.10). And only 14 percent of hardcore enviers believed that rich people are visionary and farsighted, in comparison with 51 percent of non-enviers. The proportion of hardcore enviers who believed the rich to be intelligent is 22 percent, well below the proportion of non-enviers (46 percent). It is therefore clear that enviers consistently deny that the rich could ever have earned their wealth through their own efforts.

Figure 10.10

Germany: Attribution of personality traits by rank on the Social Envy Scale

Question: "Which, if any, of the following are most likely to apply to rich people?"

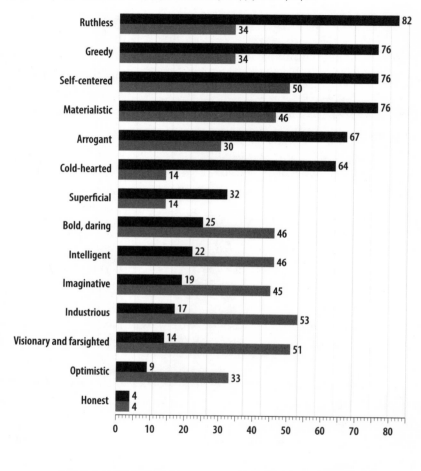

Interviewees who rank high on the Social Envy Scale (3 points)

Interviewees who rank low on the Social Envy Scale (0 points)

Note: All data are in percentage of respondents.

Figure 10.11

Germany: Attribution of personality traits by rank on the Social Envy Scale — Largest deviations in percentage points

Question: "Which, if any, of the following are most likely to apply to rich people?"

Panel A: More frequently cited by respondents ranking high on the Social Envy Scale (3 points) than by respondents ranking low on the Social Envy Scale (0 points)

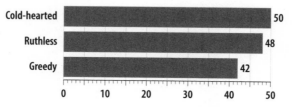

Panel B: More frequently cited by respondents ranking low on the Social Envy Scale (0 points) than by respondents ranking high on the Social Envy Scale (3 points)

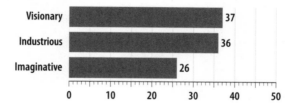

A substantial majority of hardcore enviers disagreed with the statement that many rich people become rich because they take more risks than others tend to. Only one in five hardcore enviers believed this to be true, compared with one in two non-enviers (54 percent). Conversely, 59 percent of hardcore enviers believed that most rich people become rich only through inheritances, whereas the proportion of non-enviers who believed this statement is only half as great.

The clear differences in people's attitudes on most issues depending on how many of the three envy/schadenfreude items they agreed with demonstrate the clear differentiations that can be achieved by our Social Envy Scale.

In general, enviers' responses indicate how deeply mistrustful they are of the rich. When asked whether rich people donate to charitable

Figure 10.12

Germany: Envy and the tendency to accuse rich donors of self-interest

Question: "Some rich people donate a great deal of money to charitable causes. In your opinion, what is the main reason why people do that? Do they primarily donate because they want to benefit others, or primarily because they want to benefit themselves (e.g., for tax relief, to improve their reputation)?"

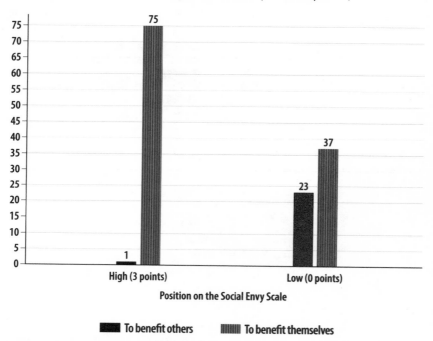

Position on the Social Envy Scale

■ To benefit others   ▥ To benefit themselves

Note: All data are in percentage of respondents.

causes because they want to benefit primarily themselves or others, 23 percent of non-enviers thought that rich people want to benefit others, versus only 1 percent of hardcore enviers (Figure 10.12). In stark contrast, three-quarters of hardcore enviers thought that the rich primarily want to benefit themselves, while not even half as many non-enviers shared their skepticism.

However, another important difference exists: one in four non-enviers knew at least one millionaire personally, whereas only one in ten enviers could say the same. And although 13 percent of non-enviers knew more than one millionaire, only 3 percent of enviers did.

Although our survey provides no direct evidence, we can assume that enviers are not only critical of rich people. Since Gordon Allport, prejudice research has confirmed that people who harbor prejudices against one minority often have negative attitudes toward other groups as well. It is therefore not surprising that, when asked whether there are certain groups you have to be careful not to criticize in public, enviers agreed far more strongly than non-enviers.

What are the sociodemographic compositions of the groups of enviers and non-enviers? Comparing hardcore enviers with non-enviers revealed the following:

- The proportion of men who were hardcore enviers (45 percent) was lower than the proportion of men who were non-enviers (56 percent). Women had a slightly stronger tendency toward social envy than men.

- Younger people were less likely to be socially envious than older people.

- The most influential variable on whether someone was envious, much more influential than income, was education: The less educated were far more highly represented among hardcore enviers (42 percent, compared with 34 percent of the total population and 26 percent of non-enviers). And in the group of non-enviers, 47 percent were highly educated, compared with 35 percent of the total population and 25 percent of hardcore enviers.

- In terms of income groups, the lowest earners were most envious and—as expected—social envy was least pronounced among higher earners. Although 11 percent of Germans have a net monthly household income of €5,000 and more, only 4 percent of hardcore enviers and 14 percent of non-enviers do.

- There are also significant differences in voting preferences among hardcore enviers and non-enviers. Although the share of center-right Christian Democratic Union/Christian Social Union (CDU/CSU) voters in the total population was

36 percent at the time of the survey, it was only 20 percent among hardcore social enviers, compared with 43 percent among non-enviers. In other words, these voters were less envious than the general population. The envious disproportionately favored Germany's left-wing party Die Linke [The Left]: 10 percent of the total population said they would vote for Die Linke, but among hardcore social enviers, this figure was 24 percent. Among non-enviers, in contrast, Die Linke voters represented only 4 percent. Enviers also disproportionately favored the right-wing Alternative für Deutschland (AfD), but comparatively less so. Among the total population, 10 percent said they would vote for AfD, whereas 17 percent of hardcore enviers said they would.

- The relevance of these findings is illustrated by a thought experiment. If only the hardcore enviers in Germany—that is, those who agreed with all three envy statements—were to vote, the center-left Social Democratic Party (SPD), the environmentalist Greens, and the left-wing Die Linke would together receive 56 percent of the vote. Die Linke and the AfD would together win 41 percent of the vote. Conversely, if only the non-enviers—that is, those who did not agree with any of the three envy statements—voted, the CDU/CSU and the market-liberal Free Democratic Party (FDP) would receive a combined 53 percent of the vote. The AfD and Die Linke, on the other hand, would receive only a combined 13 percent.

Zero-Sum Beliefs and Social Envy

We have seen that different population groups rank differently on the Social Envy Scale. However, it remains unclear, for example, if there is a direct correlation between income and a respondent's position on the Social Envy Scale or if there is a confounding variable—that is, if the mathematical correlation should be interpreted as simple cause and effect or if it is actually explained by the influence of a third, background variable on the correlated variables. This possibility is worth consideration, because the variables are themselves interrelated.

For example, older people generally have a lower level of education than younger people. This phenomenon raises the question of which of the two variables, age or education, is the most significant. Do older people rank higher on the Social Envy Scale only because they are, on average, less educated than younger people? Are highly educated people less envious simply because they are disproportionately young? Or are both variables independently linked to a respondent's position on the Social Envy Scale?

The only way to answer these questions is by performing a regression analysis. This statistical modeling process is used to calculate the extent to which, for example, the age of the respondents determines their position on the Social Envy Scale independent of their education, gender, zero-sum beliefs, and other variables.

Table 10.1 shows the results of one such regression analysis. In this case, the dependent variable—that is, the variable for which the factors influencing it were analyzed—is the respondent's position on the Social

Table 10.1

Regression analysis of social envy in Germany

Dependent variable: Social Envy Scale
Influence of independent variables on the dependent variable

	Beta	**Significance**
Zero-sum belief	−.37	***
Education	−.11	***
Personally knows a millionaire	−.08	**
Gender (F)	.05	ns
West/east	.04	ns
Age	.01	ns
Household income	−.01	ns
Immigrant status	−.01	ns
Unsure in everyday situations	−.01	ns

Note: *** $p < .01$; ** $p < .05$; ns = not significant.

Envy Scale. The first column lists the independent variables included in the regression analysis—that is, the variables related to the respondents and their statements whose influence on the Social Envy Scale we want to measure. The table also includes a column of beta coefficients. These coefficients are the most important result of the calculation; they indicate the degree to which the independent variable in question affects respondents' values for the dependent variable. Some beta coefficients are marked with asterisks, which indicate the degree to which the variable in question is statistically significant. Three asterisks indicate a 99 percent probability that the independent variable in question has an influence on the dependent variable; two asterisks indicate a probability of at least 95 percent. For all other results, the probability that the independent variable significantly influences the dependent variable is less than 90 percent. Under such conditions, the result is not considered statistically significant.

Table 10.1 also shows that a number of variables that one would naturally assume to be significant are, in fact, statistically insignificant predictors of respondents' positions on the Social Envy Scale. These independent variables include gender, age, and even household income. Only three variables prove to be significant: education level, the tendency to hold zero-sum beliefs, and whether the respondent personally knows a millionaire. The correlation between voting preferences and social envy was not investigated in the regression analysis.

In Chapter 5, we saw that zero-sum beliefs are a crucial basis for envy. Thus, it is not surprising that 84 percent of hardcore enviers and only 28 percent of non-enviers agree with the following statement: "The more the rich have, the less there is for the poor" (Figure 10.13). And 66 percent of hardcore enviers, but only 22 percent of non-enviers, believe that "if managers earn so much more than employees, there is less money left over for employees' salaries" (Figure 10.14).

Social envy and zero-sum beliefs are closely related, not only theoretically but also empirically. As mentioned above, our regression analysis confirms the strong correlation between zero-sum beliefs and social envy.

Figure 10.13

Germany: Zero-sum beliefs and social envy

Question: "To what extent do you agree with the following statement: 'The more the rich have, the less there is for the poor.'?"

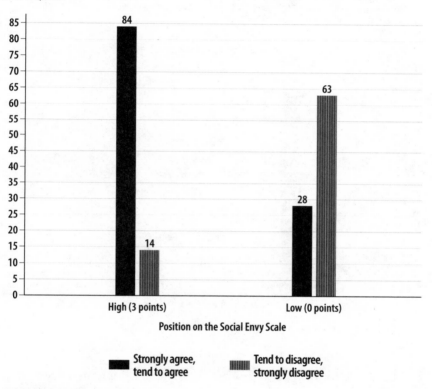

Position on the Social Envy Scale

■ Strongly agree,
   tend to agree

▦ Tend to disagree,
   strongly disagree

Note: All data are in percentage of respondents.

SCAPEGOATERS

Chapter 6 demonstrated that people who harbor negative prejudices against minorities are often also scapegoaters: they designate minorities as scapegoats, and they blame the minorities for crises and other negative developments that people find difficult to explain. In the Allensbach survey, 50 percent of all Germans agreed with the following statement: *"Those who are very rich and want more and more power are to blame for many of the major problems in the world, such as financial or humanitarian issues."*

Figure 10.14

Germany: Social envy and the assumption that high manager salaries are paid at the expense of employees

Question: "Do you agree with the following statement: 'If managers earn so much more than employees, there is less money left over for employees' salaries.'?"

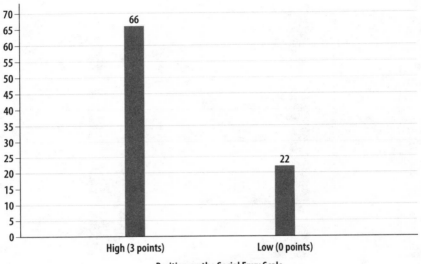

Position on the Social Envy Scale

Note: All data are in percentage of respondents.

Respondents who agreed with this statement, whom I refer to as "scapegoaters," also responded very differently than non-scapegoaters to many other items. For example, 59 percent of scapegoaters believed that many rich people become rich only because they ruthlessly pursued their own interest. Among non-scapegoaters, only 28 percent shared this belief.

One in two scapegoaters (48 percent) thought that rich people in Germany became rich only because there was injustice in society. In response to the same statement, only one in five non-scapegoaters (20 percent) agreed.

Scapegoaters also assigned different personality traits to rich people than did non-scapegoaters (Table 10.2).

Table 10.2

Germany: Scapegoaters have a far more negative view than others of rich people's personality traits

Percentage of scapegoaters and non-scapegoaters who think rich people are . . .:

Personality Trait	Scapegoaters	Non-scapegoaters
Ruthless	63	37
Greedy	65	34
Cold-hearted	39	17

Forty-two percent of scapegoaters believed that the rich are good at earning money but are not usually decent people. Of non-scapegoaters, only 18 percent agreed. And 61 percent of scapegoaters were zero-sum believers, in comparison with only 35 percent of non-scapegoaters.

How Do High and Low Earners View the Rich?

The Allensbach survey distinguished among five income brackets: net monthly household incomes of (a) less than €1,500, (b) between €1,500 and €2,499, (c) between €2,500 and €3,499, (d) between €3,500 and €4,999, and (e) €5,000 and more. There were not always strong differences between the responses given by these income brackets. More similarities than differences were found, for example, in the view that becoming rich depends primarily on the connections and contacts one has through one's parents and family. The same was true of the general level of agreement (about one-third of each income bracket) with the statement that society as a whole benefits from the existence of rich people because many of them create jobs. Even the proportion of respondents who said it is important for them personally to be rich did not vary much between low and high earners. And on the question as to whether bankers and property and financial investors deserve to be rich, disagreement was fairly consistent across all income brackets.

Despite these similarities, responses to many other questions revealed massive differences of opinion between low and high earners, proving that different income brackets often have diametrically opposed world-views. For example, 57 percent of Germans with net household incomes of less than €1,500 ("low earners") believed that most rich people are tax cheats, whereas only 39 percent of those who earn more than €5,000 ("high earners") held this opinion.

The opinion that many rich people have become rich only because they ruthlessly pursued their own interest was approved by 47 percent of the lowest earners but only 29 percent of the highest earners. Only about a third of low earners believed that becoming rich primarily depends on one's abilities and ideas, in contrast to more than half of high earners. And the proportion who believed that many rich people obtained their wealth at the expense of others was more than twice as high among the lowest earners as it was among the highest earners. Almost twice as many low earners as high earners believed that the rich became rich only because of injustice in society.

The differences between income brackets were at their starkest when respondents were asked about the traits most likely to apply to rich people. Only 17 percent of high earners, compared to 42 percent of low earners, perceived the rich as cold-hearted. In contrast, 61 percent of high earners said that rich people are industrious, compared with only 38 percent of low earners.

On the basis of the responses from low earners, it is also probable that members of this group were wondering whether they themselves might one day become rich. This prospect might explain why significantly more low earners than high earners thought that lottery winners and heirs deserve to be rich. On the other hand, significantly more high earners than low earners thought that senior-level managers or entrepreneurs deserve their wealth. It is highly likely that this discrepancy is because high earners have more in common with these groups than do low earners.

Nor is it surprising that, although 62 percent of the lowest earners believed that the rich should pay not just high taxes but very high taxes so that the state can mitigate the gap between the rich and the poor, only one-third of high earners believed the same. Nor is it surprising that only a little more than a third of high earners, but well over half of low earners, were in favor of drastically reducing managers' salaries even if employees would get only a few more euros per month. Even in the case of top athletes, high earners were far more "generous": 41 percent thought they deserved to be rich, compared to only 26 percent of low earners. And although half of high earners reported no schadenfreude when a millionaire lost a lot of money because of a risky business decision, only 30 percent of low earners said they would never think "It serves him right." The fact that, in Germany, little interaction takes place between those at the top and those at the bottom is evident from the fact that 40 percent of high earners knew one or more millionaires personally but only 7 percent of low earners counted a millionaire among their acquaintances.

How Do Younger and Older Germans View the Rich?

Younger Germans are far more likely to want to become rich than older Germans. Almost one in three respondents between the ages of 16 and 29 (referred to here as "younger people") said that it is important for them to be rich (Figure 10.15). In contrast, only 14 percent of those older than 60 ("older people") said the same. Of course, this finding is not entirely surprising. Younger people still have their entire lives and every possibility ahead of them, but those who aren't rich by the age of 60 have usually accepted the fact that even if they wanted to achieve great wealth, they probably never will.

Accordingly, 52 percent of younger people said that rich people who have succeeded through their own efforts were role models who motivated them. In the 30- to 44-year-old age group, almost one in two said the same, but among those over the age of 60, the proportion who see self-made rich people as role models was only 39 percent.

In their responses to positive and negative statements about the rich, younger people were far more likely to agree with positive statements and far less likely to agree with negative statements. The opposite was true of older people. For example, 45 percent of older people believed that many rich people become rich only because they ruthlessly pursue their own interest, compared to 37 percent of younger people.

Figure 10.15

Germany: How important is it to be rich?—Analysis by age group

Question: "For some people, it is important to be rich. How important, if at all, is it for you personally to be rich?"

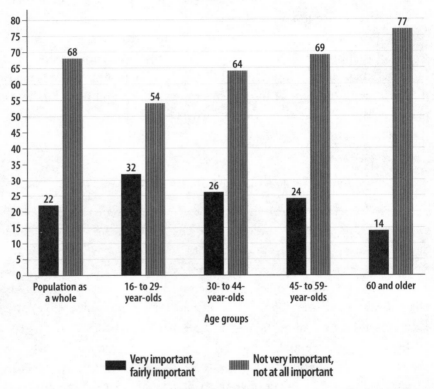

Note: All data are in percentage of respondents. Figures do not add up to 100 percent because "Neither important nor unimportant" responses have been omitted.

Conversely, almost one in two younger Germans thought that becoming rich primarily depends on the abilities and ideas one has, but only slightly more than a third of older people thought so. The difference in approval amounts to more than 10 percentage points. In contrast, the negative statement that many rich people obtained their wealth at the expense of others elicited agreement from 38 percent of older people and 30 percent of younger people.

A look at the list of characteristics that people assigned to the rich is consistent with what we've seen so far: 47 percent of younger people thought the rich are particularly industrious, compared to only 36 percent of older people, and 45 percent of younger people thought the rich are particularly intelligent, compared to only 36 percent of those over the age of 60. The younger generation's view of the rich was more negative than the older generation's on only one point: 27 percent of younger people thought the rich are superficial, compared with only 12 percent of older people.

Significant differences arose when respondents were asked which groups of rich people deserve their wealth. Three-quarters of younger people, but only half of older people, believed that self-employed people deserve to be rich. The situation is similar for entrepreneurs: two-thirds of younger people did not begrudge entrepreneurs their wealth, but only half of older people felt the same. When it comes to top athletes, 41 percent of younger people, but only 25 percent of older people, said they deserve to be rich. When asked whether property investors deserve to be rich, 15 percent of younger people agreed; among older people, the figure was only 9 percent.

The willingness to impose very high taxes on the rich was somewhat more widespread among older people than among younger people. And one in two younger people thought it inappropriate for some managers to earn 100 times more than their employees; among older people, this share was far higher, at three out of four. Less than half of younger people thought that very high manager salaries are inappropriate because no one needs so much money, compared with almost two-thirds of older respondents. In contrast, the proportion of younger people who agreed that companies can only hire and retain the best managers if they pay such high salaries was 28 percent, a full 12 percentage points higher than it was among older people (16 percent).

How Do Men and Women View the Rich?

Although different income and age groups differ significantly in their perceptions of the rich, the opinions of men and women are much more closely aligned. On many items, men and women showed only minor differences, and the pattern to the differences was inconsistent, unlike what we have seen with the differences among different income and age groups. On one question, however, responses did differ: more men (26 percent) than women (18 percent) agreed that it is important for them to be rich. This finding matches up with the fact that 47 percent of men said that rich people who have succeeded through their own efforts are role models who motivate them. The corresponding figure for women was 42 percent.

In all other respects, the picture was inconsistent. A few more men than women thought the rich are intelligent and optimistic, and a few more men than women thought the rich are ruthless. Slightly more women than men were in favor of very high taxes on the rich. However, the differences were small on most issues.

In their assessment of senior-level managers, women were more critical than men, perhaps because there are so few women in German boardrooms. Half of female respondents were in favor of drastically reducing managers' salaries and redistributing the money more evenly among their employees, even if that would mean the employees would get only a few more euros per month. Among men, only 40 percent were in favor of such a measure. And although 64 percent of women felt that very high salaries are generally obscene, only 59 percent of men felt this way. In addition, 61 percent of women and 53 percent of men felt that very high salaries for managers are inappropriate because no one needs that much money. And although 22 percent of men thought that managers have a lot more responsibility than ordinary employees and should therefore earn a lot more, only 15 percent of women thought that more responsibility should result in more money.

However, even though differences exist—usually small ones—on individual questions, men's and women's perceptions of the rich are more similar than different.

How Do Well-Educated and Less-Educated Germans View the Rich?

A comparison of responses according to people's education levels reveals greater differences in how people view the rich. This difference is particularly evident on questions that can serve as indicators of envy: 54 percent of less-educated respondents said they were in favor of drastically reducing managers' salaries and redistributing the money to their employees, even if the employees would get only a few more euros per month. Only 35 percent of better-educated people shared this opinion—a remarkable difference of 19 percentage points.

Similarly, responses to the schadenfreude question differed greatly: 50 percent of less-educated respondents, but only 30 percent of better-educated respondents, agreed that "When I hear about a millionaire who made a risky business decision and lost a lot of money because of it, I think it serves him right." The proportion who advocated a sharp increase in taxes for millionaires (even if they would not personally benefit) was almost 11 percentage points higher for less-educated respondents than it was for better-educated respondents.

The question as to which groups of people deserve to be rich demonstrates that far fewer less-educated Germans thought that most groups (entrepreneurs, self-employed people, etc.) deserve to be rich than did better-educated respondents. Only in the cases of lottery winners and heirs was there hardly any difference on the basis of education level, which could be related to the fact that less-educated people can more easily imagine themselves winning the lottery or inheriting a fortune, whereas the idea of them becoming rich as an entrepreneur is far harder to picture.

In Chapter 7, we saw that although less-educated people and low earners tend to believe that rich people are good at earning money, they are far less positive about the moral traits of the wealthy. This view is confirmed by the Allensbach survey: 39 percent of less-educated respondents thought that rich people are good at earning money but are not usually decent people, whereas only 21 percent of those with a higher education agreed with this statement.

In general, less-educated respondents were more critical of the rich than were those with a higher education. The less educated were far more likely to describe the rich as cold-hearted, superficial, self-centered, materialistic, or ruthless, and they were far less likely to describe the rich as intelligent, farsighted, or imaginative. They were also far more in favor of very high taxes on the rich than were better-educated people, and they believed more strongly that rich people donate to charitable causes primarily to benefit themselves.

When it comes to more abstract matters, less-educated respondents were far more likely than better-educated respondents to arrive at negative judgments of the rich. Although 28 percent of better-educated respondents understood how the salaries of senior-level managers are determined—namely, by supply and demand in the market for top managers—only 17 percent of less-educated people were aware of this connection. And the statement that "society as a whole benefits from the existence of rich people, because many of them are entrepreneurs who created new products" was met with agreement by 39 percent of better-educated respondents but only 26 percent of the less-educated.

In light of their critical attitudes, it is important to note that less-educated people rarely claimed to know any millionaires personally. A meager 4 percent stated that they personally knew more than one millionaire; the proportion was four times higher among the better-educated.

How Do Germans with Different Political Affiliations View the Rich?

The relationship between political affiliation and perception of the rich was more complex than one might think. Some of our findings were as expected—for example, supporters of the left-wing party Die Linke were extremely critical of the rich, and supporters of the free-market FDP were less critical than those of other parties. Three-quarters of left-wing voters would like to see very high taxes on the rich, compared with only one-third of FDP voters (Figure 10.17). And 83 percent of Die Linke voters believed it would be fair to increase taxes substantially for millionaires even if they would not personally benefit from it. In another example, almost half of FDP voters agreed that companies can only hire and retain the best managers if they pay high salaries; however, only one in ten left-wing voters (compared with 21 percent of the population as a whole) agreed with this statement.

But beyond these expected findings, the picture is less clear. For example, one in three supporters of the far-right party AfD thought it "important" for them personally to be rich. Among no other party's

Figure 10.16

Germany: Political orientation and the tendency to attribute negative traits to the rich

Question: "To what extent do you agree or disagree with the following statement: 'Rich people are good at earning money, but are not usually decent people.'?"

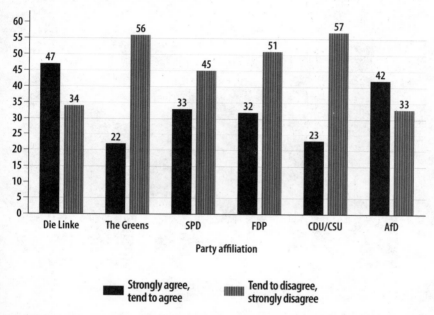

Party affiliation

■ Strongly agree,
tend to agree

▥ Tend to disagree,
strongly disagree

Note: All data are in percentage of respondents. Figures do not add up to 100 percent because "Neither agree nor disagree" responses have been omitted.

supporters was the proportion so high, and only one in ten supporters of Die Linke agreed. On other issues, we saw similarities in the attitudes of right-wing AfD voters and left-wing Die Linke voters. Two-thirds of the supporters of both parties described the rich as self-centered, materialistic, ruthless, and greedy. In comparison, Green Party supporters were not quite as critical—between 40 and 50 percent of Green Party supporters attributed these negative traits to rich people.

We also found similarities between AfD and Die Linke voters in their criticism of high manager salaries: 76 percent of left-wing voters and 74 percent of AfD voters thought it inappropriate, for example, for managers to earn 100 times more than their employees, because they do

Figure 10.17

Germany: Very high taxes for the rich—Analysis by party affiliation

Question: "On balance, which, if any, of the following statements do you agree with MOST?"

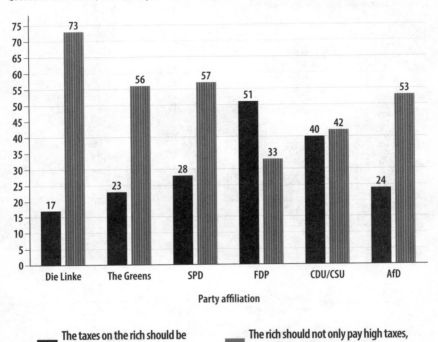

The taxes on the rich should be high but not excessively high

The rich should not only pay high taxes, but they should pay very high taxes

Note: All data are in percentage of respondents. Figures do not add up to 100 percent because "Don't know" responses have been omitted.

not work so much longer and harder than their employees. By way of comparison, one in two SPD or FDP voters agreed with this statement. And on the question of schadenfreude ("When I hear about a millionaire who made a risky business decision and lost a lot of money because of it, I think it serves him right"), about half of Die Linke, AfD, and SPD voters agreed, compared with roughly a third of CDU/CSU, FDP, and The Green supporters (Figure 10.18).

A mixed picture emerges when respondents are asked which groups deserve to be rich. For example, supporters of the FDP and The Greens

Figure 10.18

Germany: Schadenfreude—Analysis by party affiliation

Question: "To what extent, if at all, do you agree or disagree with this statement: 'When I hear about a millionaire who made a risky business decision and lost a lot of money because of it, I think: It serves him right.'?"

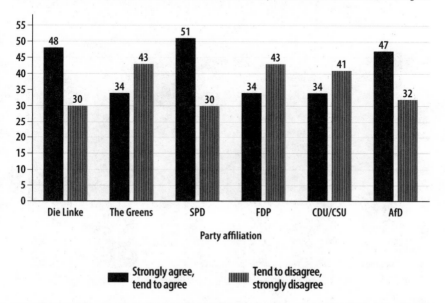

Party affiliation

■ Strongly agree,
tend to agree

▥ Tend to disagree,
strongly disagree

Note: All data are in percentage of respondents. Figures do not add up to 100 percent because "Neither agree nor disagree" responses have been omitted.

appreciated entrepreneurs much more than did the population as a whole. When it comes to property investors, the proportion of FDP voters who thought they deserve to be rich was twice as high as the proportion among the population as a whole, while supporters of The Greens, Die Linke, and AfD were particularly critical of property investors.

With regard to zero-sum beliefs, that is, whether respondents agreed that "the more the rich have, the less there is for the poor," we saw overwhelming agreement among left-wing voters (72 percent), while only slightly more than a third of FDP and CDU/CSU voters shared this view (Figure 10.19).

The correlations were therefore not as clear with regard to political affiliations as they were, for example, with regard to income brackets and age groups. On some issues, Green voters were just as critical of the

Figure 10.19

Germany: Zero-sum beliefs and political affiliation

Question: "To what extent do you agree or disagree with the following statement: 'The more the rich have, the less there is for the poor.'?"

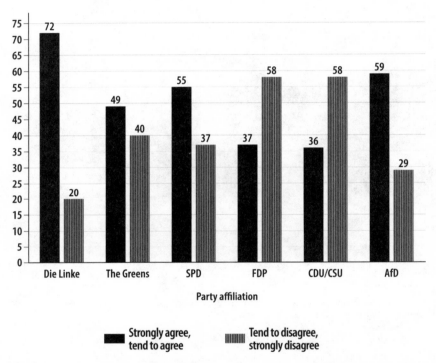

Note: All data are in percentage of respondents. Figures do not add up to 100 percent because "Neither agree nor disagree" responses have been omitted.

rich as left-wing voters, but on other issues, their attitudes were more similar to those of FDP voters. This outcome is probably explained by the fact that Green voters are more similar to FDP voters in education and socioeconomic status, whereas in ideology, they are closer to the left.

HOW DO IMMIGRANTS TO GERMANY VIEW THE RICH?

The data and responses we collected from respondents who have migrated to Germany differ markedly in some respects from those

Figure 10.20

Germany: Donations to benefit themselves—Analysis by party affiliation

Question: "Some rich people donate a great deal of money to charitable causes. In your opinion, what is the main reason why people do that? Do they primarily donate because they want to benefit others, or primarily because they want to benefit themselves (e.g., for tax relief, to improve their reputation)?"

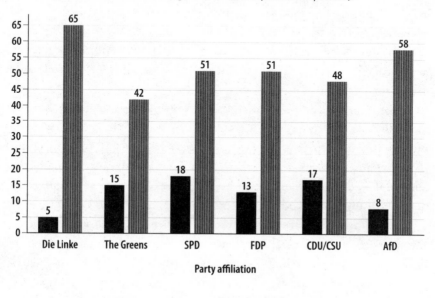

■ To benefit others ▤ To benefit themselves

Note: All data are in percentage of respondents. Figures do not add up to 100 percent because "Don't know" responses have been omitted.

of other respondents.[486] At 30 percent, twice as many immigrants as nonimmigrants say that they personally know a millionaire. And the proportion of immigrants who said that they personally know more than one millionaire, at 19 percent, is almost three times as high as that of nonimmigrants. This difference may be because immigrants generally have larger circles of acquaintances than nonimmigrants. Immigrants to Germany clearly believe that becoming rich depends primarily on the connections and contacts one has through one's parents and family: although 54 percent of nonimmigrants identify this factor as key to getting rich, it was selected by 62 percent of immigrants. Furthermore, 48 percent of nonimmigrants and 64 percent of immigrants believe that the decisive factor in becoming rich is how good one is at establishing important connections and contacts. These responses reflect the particular importance of social, professional, and family relationships in the cultures of many immigrants.

When it comes to assigning personality traits to rich people, very little difference exists between immigrants and nonimmigrants, with the exception of two traits: 18 percent of nonimmigrants versus 25 percent of immigrants consider the rich to be superficial, and 55 percent of nonimmigrants versus 61 percent of immigrants consider the rich to be materialistic.

Immigrants are more likely than nonimmigrants to think that successful people deserve to be rich, especially if they have achieved success through their own efforts. Thus, 73 percent of immigrants (10 percentage points more than among nonimmigrants) believe that self-employed people deserve to be rich. In contrast, fewer immigrants than nonimmigrants said that lottery winners deserve to be rich.

Nonimmigrants' aversion to senior-level managers, senior bankers, and property and financial investors is not shared to the same extent by immigrants—perhaps they are less exposed to German media, where negative sentiments are frequently expressed against those groups. The proportion of immigrants who feel that property investors, senior bankers, and financial investors deserve to be rich is more than twice as high as that of nonimmigrants. And only 19 percent of nonimmigrants believe that senior-level managers deserve to be rich, versus 29 percent of immigrants. Furthermore, 19 percent of nonimmigrants believe that it is solely up to companies to decide how much their managers earn and that the state should have no say in such salaries. In contrast, 28 percent of immigrants believe it should be up to companies alone—free of government interference—to determine top managers' salaries.

CHAPTER II

HOW AMERICANS VIEW THE RICH

Many readers would assume that Americans are less envious than Germans. For this study, Ipsos MORI interviewed 1,084 Americans between June 1 and June 4, 2018, and asked them about their attitudes toward the rich. On the basis of these interviews, we can determine the extent of Americans' envious feelings toward the rich. For this purpose, we developed the Social Envy Scale (see pages 160 et seq.), which measures social envy by assessing interviewees' responses to three statements. The statements presented to the American interviewees were identical to those used with the German participants (see Chapter 10).

How Much Do Americans Envy the Rich?

Of the three statements serving as indicators of social envy, the one that attracted the most agreement from Americans was statement 1: "I think it would be fair to increase taxes substantially for millionaires, even if I would not benefit from it personally." This statement elicited agreement from 47 percent of American interviewees, compared with 28 percent who disagreed. Of course, agreement with this statement alone is not

---

*Figure and table data in Chapter 11 are from the 2018 Ipsos MORI J18-031911-01-02 survey of the United States.

proof of social envy, because other motives (e.g., altruism) could play a role in supporting increased taxes for millionaires.

Statement 2 required the interviewees to declare their opinions on drastically reducing the salaries of top managers and distributing the money to employees, even if it meant the employees would end up with only a few dollars more in their pockets each month. Fewer than a third (31 percent) of American interviewees agreed. And statement 3, which is used to assess levels of schadenfreude, asked the interviewees whether they experience a "serves them right" feeling when a millionaire loses a lot of money as the result of a risky business decision. It elicited agreement from 28 percent of the 1,084 interviewees.

Interviewees who agreed with two or all three statements were likely to harbor far more pronounced feelings of social envy than were those who either agreed with just one of the statements or rejected all three. The hardcore social enviers who agreed with all three statements were few in the United States, totaling just 55, or about 5 percent, of the respondents. Therefore, it is impossible to form subgroups with statistically significant numbers from this group using this scale. This is an important finding in and of itself: it confirms that social envy is not particularly pervasive in the United States. If the subgroup is expanded to include those Americans who agreed with at least two of the statements of envy—that is, the same approach used for Germany—then 215 interviewees can be classified as social enviers, that is, about 20 percent of the total sample.

At the other end of the Social Envy Scale is the group consisting of those who rejected all three statements, which represents almost half (48 percent) of the interviewees. This group is again referred to as the non-enviers, and it is by far the largest group in the United States, followed by the ambivalents, at 32 percent, who agreed with one of the three envy statements and rejected the other two.

The group of social enviers was very different from the general population, and especially from the non-enviers (Figure 11.2). Although 22 percent of social enviers believed that rich people have become rich only because of injustice in society, only 3 percent of non-enviers held the same belief. In general, enviers were far more likely than non-enviers to chalk up the economic success of the rich either to external conditions or to unsavory personality traits. For example, 39 percent of enviers in the United States said that becoming rich depends primarily on the connections and contacts people have through their parents and families, compared with only 16 percent of non-enviers. Of the enviers, 22 percent believed that people who are rich mainly have good luck, a belief shared by only 5 percent of non-enviers. Furthermore, 40 percent of enviers assumed that most rich people become rich only through inheritances, compared with only 11 percent of non-enviers. And although every second envier (52 percent) thought that rich people obtained their wealth at the expense of others, only 14 percent of non-enviers shared that view.

In Chapter 6, we saw that social enviers are far more likely than others to scapegoat the rich for many of the world's major problems.

Figure 11.1

United States: Wealth and social envy I—Positive and neutral statements

Question: "Here is a list of things that people have said about rich people. Which, if any, of the statements on the list would you agree with?"

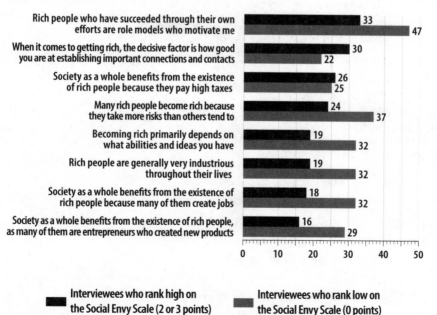

Note: All data are in percentage of respondents.

Figure 11.2

United States: Wealth and social envy II—(Somewhat) negative statements

Question: "Here is a list of things that people have said about rich people. Which, if any, of the statements on the list would you agree with?"

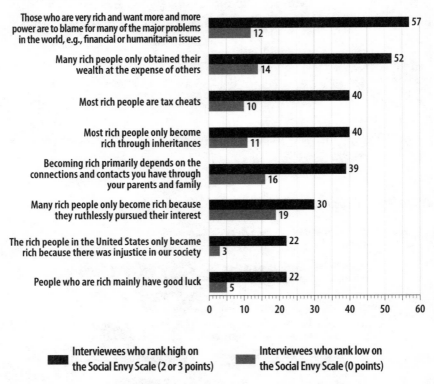

Those who are very rich and want more and more power are to blame for many of the major problems in the world, e.g., financial or humanitarian issues — 57 / 12

Many rich people only obtained their wealth at the expense of others — 52 / 14

Most rich people are tax cheats — 40 / 10

Most rich people only become rich through inheritances — 40 / 11

Becoming rich primarily depends on the connections and contacts you have through your parents and family — 39 / 16

Many rich people only become rich because they ruthlessly pursued their interest — 30 / 19

The rich people in the United States only became rich because there was injustice in our society — 22 / 3

People who are rich mainly have good luck — 22 / 5

■ Interviewees who rank high on the Social Envy Scale (2 or 3 points) ■ Interviewees who rank low on the Social Envy Scale (0 points)

Note: All data are in percentage of respondents.

This view was confirmed by our survey: although only 12 percent of non-enviers believed that the rich are largely responsible for the world's major financial and humanitarian problems, 57 percent of enviers blamed the rich.

When asked which personality traits are most likely to apply to rich people, enviers and non-enviers in the United States also responded very differently. Enviers were far more likely to attribute negative personality traits to rich people (Figure 11.3). They were also far more likely to deny them positive personality traits.

Figure 11.3

United States: Attribution of personality traits by rank on the Social Envy Scale

Question: "Which, if any, of the following are most likely to apply to rich people?"

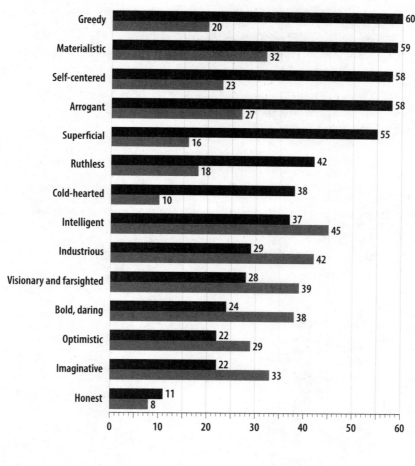

Interviewees who rank high on the Social Envy Scale (2 or 3 points)

Interviewees who rank low on the Social Envy Scale (0 points)

Note: All data are in percentage of respondents.

These findings demonstrate that enviers and non–enviers have diametrically opposed views of the rich.

In Chapter 7, I developed the theory of compensation bias. According to this theory, social enviers concede economic success to rich people while at the same time denying them human qualities. Here, too, we can see the explanatory power of the Social Envy Scale. Of enviers in the United States, 57 percent supported the statement that the rich are good at making money but are rarely decent people (Figure 11.4). Only 27 percent of Americans in general believed this. Of the non–envier group, which makes up half of the survey's interviewees, only 14 percent agreed with this statement.

Figure 11.4

United States: Envy and the tendency to deny that rich people are usually decent

Question: "To what extent do you agree or disagree with the following statement: 'Rich people are good at earning money, but are not usually decent people.'?"

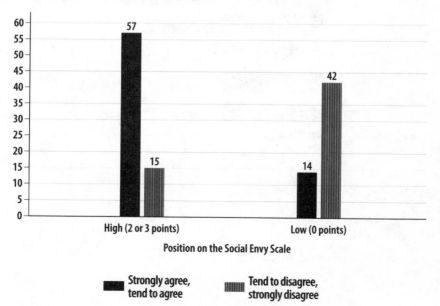

Note: All data are in percentage of respondents. Figures do not add up to 100 percent because "neither agree nor disagree" responses have been omitted.

And although 34 percent of enviers thought that lottery winners deserve to be rich, the figure for non-enviers is much lower, at just 21 percent. As already shown on pages 165–167, enviers are more likely than non-enviers to believe that rich people deserve their wealth if it is the result of pure luck.

In Chapters 4 and 5, we saw just how closely social envy correlates with zero-sum beliefs. The same correlation is evident in the United States. Although two-thirds (67 percent) of enviers agreed with the statement that "the more the rich have, the less there is for the poor," only 18 percent of non-enviers accepted such zero-sum beliefs (Figure 11.5).

Figure 11.5

United States: Zero-sum beliefs and social envy

Question: "To what extent do you agree or disagree with the following statement: 'The more the rich have, the less there is for the poor.'?"

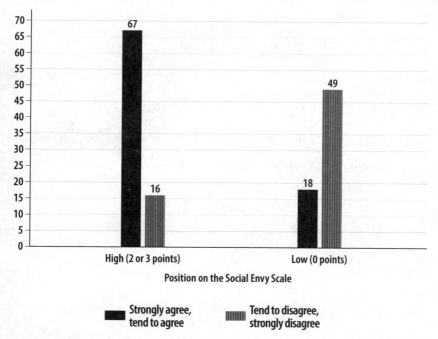

Position on the Social Envy Scale

■ Strongly agree,
tend to agree

▥ Tend to disagree,
strongly disagree

Note: All data are in percentage of respondents. Figures do not add up to 100 percent because "neither agree nor disagree" responses have been omitted.

The relationship between zero-sum beliefs and social envy was also investigated using a regression analysis. The findings of this analysis highlight major similarities between the United States, Germany, France, and Great Britain. According to this regression analysis, the degree to which someone harbors strong levels of social envy depends primarily on how strongly they view life as a zero-sum game. It is also striking that, according to this analysis, an individual's level of household income in the United States has no direct, significant influence on his or her propensity for social envy. Although high earners—as we will demonstrate later—view rich people more positively than low earners in some respects, this connection is rather indirect; that is, it is mediated by other factors. This finding suggests that social envy may be primarily an expression of an inner disposition.

Enviers' tendency to view life as a zero-sum game is also evident in how they much more frequently (55 percent) agreed that when managers earn much more than their employees, less money is left over for the employees' salaries. Among non-enviers, only 21 percent agreed.

The extent of an individual's social envy can be regarded as a key determining factor in their opinions of managers. Social enviers were far more convinced that there needs to be a correlation between

Table 11.1

Regression analysis of social envy in the United States

Dependent variable: Social Envy Scale
Influence of independent variables on the dependent variable

	Beta	Significance
Zero-sum belief	−.27	***
Education	.10	***
Household income	−.03	ns
Gender (M)	−.02	ns
Unsure in everyday situations	−.02	ns
Age	−.01	ns
Personally knows a millionaire	.00	ns

Note: *** $p < .01$; ns = not significant.

how long and how hard someone works and their salary—the same employee mindset that we encountered in the German survey. Among enviers, 61 percent believed that managers should not earn 100 times more than ordinary employees because they do not work so much longer or harder than their employees (Figure 11.6). Of non-enviers, only 24 percent shared this belief. And although 65 percent of enviers thought it "obscene" for managers to earn 100 times more than their employees, only 22 percent of non-enviers thought so.

Rich people who believe that donating a great deal of money to charitable causes will appease widespread feelings of envy are likely to be disappointed by this survey's findings. After all, 50 percent of enviers in the United States thought that rich people donate primarily because they want to benefit themselves (e.g., to improve their reputation or save on taxes). This opinion is shared by just 12 percent of non-enviers.

Figure 11.6
United States: Envy and the "employee mindset"

The percentage of interviewees who agree with the following statement: "I think it is inappropriate for managers to earn so much more, as they do not work so much longer or harder than their employees."

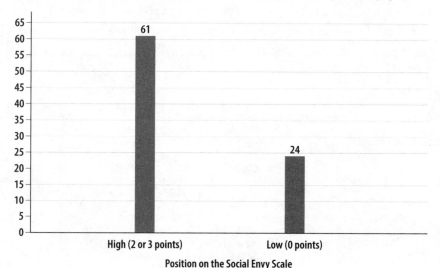

Position on the Social Envy Scale

Note: All data are in percentage of respondents.

But let's not forget, the group of enviers in the United States was relatively small, comprising only 20 percent of the interviewees. And only
5 percent of respondents were hardcore enviers who agreed with all
three envy-related statements.

How Zero-Sum Believers View the Rich

One-third (34 percent) of Americans agreed that "the more the rich
have, the less there is for the poor," whereas 40 percent did not subscribe to this zero-sum belief. Compared with the group who do not
see life as a zero-sum game, the third of Americans whom I refer to as
zero-sum believers also held very different attitudes on a wide range of
other subjects. In general, people with a zero-sum mindset are more
critical of the rich. When asked which personality traits are most likely
to apply to rich people, the two groups provided diametrically opposed
answers. According to zero-sum believers, the five most common traits
of rich people are all negative. In contrast, the top five traits mentioned
by interviewees who do not have a zero-sum mindset are all positive
(Table 11.2).

With regard to their opinions and attitudes toward the rich, significant variation existed between zero-sum believers and non-zero-sum
believers. Four times as many zero-sum believers as non-zero-sum
believers accused rich people of donating to charitable causes primarily

Table 11.2

United States: Which traits are most likely to apply to rich people?—Analysis by
zero-sum beliefs

Zero-sum believers	Other interviewees
1. Self-centered, 54 percent	1. Intelligent, 58 percent
1. Materialistic, 54 percent	1. Industrious, 58 percent
1. Arrogant, 54 percent	2. Bold, daring, 48 percent
2. Greedy, 53 percent	3. Imaginative, 46 percent
3. Superficial, 45 percent	4. Optimistic, 37 percent

to benefit themselves. Two-thirds of non-zero-sum believers said that rich people who have succeeded through their own efforts are role models who motivate them. Among zero-sum believers, not even one in three admired rich people who have succeeded through their own efforts. Half of all zero-sum believers also thought that the very rich are to blame for many of the major problems in the world, compared with only one in ten interviewees who rejected zero-sum thinking.

People who rejected zero-sum thinking were far more likely than others to believe that people who become rich do so because of their personality traits and skill sets: 40 percent of them said that becoming rich depends primarily on one's abilities and ideas. Among zero-sum believers, agreement with this view was only half as widespread (21 percent). Half of all non-zero-sum believers (48 percent) thought that the rich are very industrious throughout their lives, compared with only 19 percent of zero-sum believers (Figure 11.7). At the same time, half of non-zero-sum believers said that many rich people become rich because they take more risks than others tend to. This opinion contrasts sharply with that of the zero-sum believers, who were only half as likely to share this view.

Zero-sum believers attributed wealth either to external circumstances beyond an individual's control or to unsavory personality traits (Figure 11.8). For example, almost one in two zero-sum believers (47 percent) agreed that many rich people obtained their wealth at the expense of others, whereas only 10 percent of non-zero-sum believers held the same opinion. And one in three zero-sum believers thought that most rich people become rich only through inheritances, compared with only 12 percent of non-zero-sum believers.

As shown in Chapters 4 and 5, a strong correlation exists between social envy and zero-sum beliefs. Only 18 percent of American non-enviers were zero-sum believers, in contrast with 67 percent of enviers. Accordingly, 59 percent of zero-sum believers agreed that taxes on the rich should be very high to close the gap between rich and poor. Among interviewees who did not have a zero-sum mindset, only 22 percent advocated very high taxes on the rich. And 79 percent of zero-sum believers went as far as to support increasing taxes on millionaires

Figure 11.7

United States: Wealth and zero-sum beliefs I—Positive and neutral statements

Question: "Here is a list of things that people have said about rich people. Which, if any, of the statements on the list would you agree with?"

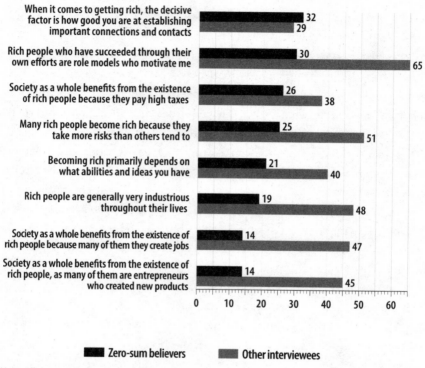

Note: All data are in percentage of respondents.

substantially even if they would not benefit from it personally (and only 8 percent of zero–sum believers outright rejected this statement). A majority of the non–zero–sum believers (55 percent), however, were against raising taxes on millionaires if they would not benefit personally.

Half of zero–sum believers in the United States would be in favor of drastically reducing managers' salaries and redistributing the money more evenly, even if it meant that employees would get only a few more dollars per month. Only 22 percent of non–zero–sum believers supported the same proposal. In the United States, those who saw the world in

Figure 11.8

United States: Wealth and zero-sum beliefs II—(Somewhat) negative statements

Question: "Here is a list of things that people have said about rich people. Which, if any, of the statements on the list would you agree with?"

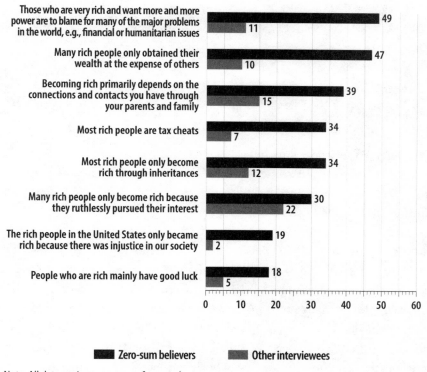

Note: All data are in percentage of respondents.

zero-sum terms were twice as likely to experience schadenfreude at a millionaire's large financial loss than were those who did not think that one person's gain is another's loss.

YOUNGER AMERICANS ARE MORE CRITICAL OF THE RICH

In contrast to Germany, younger Americans harbored far more critical opinions of the rich than their older compatriots. The following analysis is based on interviewees from two age groups: 18- to 29-year-olds

Table 11.3

United States: Which traits are most likely to apply to rich people?—Analysis by age group

American, aged 18–29 years	American, aged over 60
1. Materialistic, 51 percent	1. Industrious, 51 percent
2. Intelligent, 47 percent	2. Intelligent, 45 percent
2. Arrogant, 47 percent	3. Imaginative, 40 percent
3. Greedy, 45 percent	4. Materialistic, 38 percent
4. Self-centered, 41 percent	4. Bold, daring, 38 percent

(younger Americans) and those over 60 (older Americans). Although younger Americans identified four negative personality traits among the top five traits they associated with the rich, older Americans identified four positive traits (Table 11.3).

Although younger Americans were more critical of the rich, more younger Americans than older Americans personally aspire to be rich (Figure 11.9). Among 18- to 29-year-olds, 39 percent said it is important for them personally to be rich, compared with 37 percent of 30- to 44-year-olds, 24 percent of 45- to 59-year-olds, and only 18 percent of those over 60. This finding again comes as no surprise: younger people still have their lives ahead of them, lives full of unlimited hopes and possibilities. In contrast, anyone who is not rich by the time they turn 60 has probably already given up hope of ever being rich. This interpretation is supported by the following findings: 42 percent of younger Americans said that rich people who have succeeded through their own efforts are role models, but 55 percent of older Americans agreed with this statement, despite the fact that most of them have given up on ever being rich themselves.

Even the blunt accusation that rich people are good at making money but are not usually decent people elicited agreement from 40 percent of younger Americans (only 23 percent disagreed). Older Americans, however, saw things very differently: only 15 percent of them shared that opinion, and 50 percent outright rejected it (Figure 11.10).

Figure 11.9

United States: How important is it for you personally to be rich?—Analysis by age group

Question: "For some people, it is important to be rich. How important, if at all, is it for you to be rich? Is it very important, fairly important, neither important nor unimportant, not very important, or not at all important?"

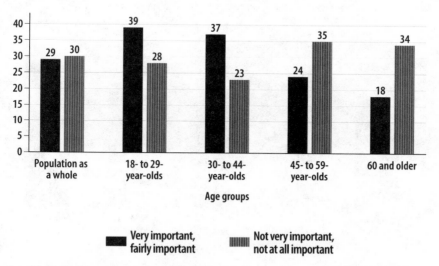

Note: All data are in percentage of respondents. Figures do not add up to 100 percent because "neither important nor unimportant" responses have been omitted.

The zero–sum belief that the more the rich have, the less there is for the poor was shared by 45 percent of Americans ages 18–29, 40 percent of those ages 30–44, 27 percent of those ages 45–59, and just 24 percent of those over 60 (Figure 11.11).

Younger and older Americans also differed strongly in their opinions of high manager salaries: 42 percent of older Americans believed that it is solely up to companies to decide how much managers earn, in contrast to 30 percent of younger Americans. And although 38 percent of younger Americans said that managers' salaries should be reduced and redistributed to employees even if employees would get only an extra few dollars per month, only 28 percent of older Americans supported this redistributive approach. The only exception to this trend was that 40 percent of older Americans thought that salaries of managers who

Figure 11.10

United States: The tendency to believe that rich people are not decent—Analysis by age group

Question: "To what extent do you agree or disagree with the following statement: 'Rich people are good at earning money, but they are not usually decent people.'? Do you strongly agree, tend to agree, neither agree nor disagree, tend to disagree or strongly disagree?"

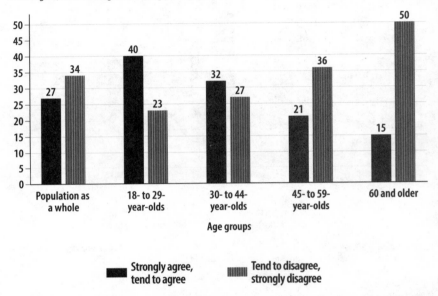

Strongly agree, tend to agree

Tend to disagree, strongly disagree

Note: All data are in percentage of respondents. Figures do not add up to 100 percent because "neither agree nor disagree" responses have been omitted.

earn 100 times more than their employees are "obscene," compared with only 32 percent of younger Americans.

On almost every other question, however, a common tendency is evident: younger Americans were more critical of rich people than older Americans (Figures 11.12 and 11.13). For example, 38 percent of older Americans but 22 percent of younger Americans believed that society as a whole benefits from the existence of rich people because many of them create jobs; 39 percent of older Americans, but only 23 percent of younger Americans, thought that society benefits from the existence of rich people because they pay high taxes; only 14 percent of older Americans, but 39 percent of younger Americans, believed that

Figure 11.11

United States: Zero-sum beliefs—Analysis by age group

Question: "To what extent do you agree with the following statement: 'The more the rich have, the less there is for the poor.'? Do you strongly agree, tend to agree, neither agree nor disagree, tend to disagree, or strongly disagree?"

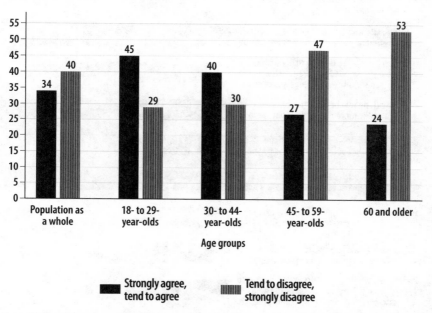

Age groups

Strongly agree, tend to agree

Tend to disagree, strongly disagree

Note: All data are in percentage of respondents. Figures do not add up to 100 percent because "neither agree nor disagree" responses have been omitted.

becoming rich primarily depends on the connections and contacts one has through one's parents and family; and 16 percent of older Americans but 29 percent of younger Americans claimed that most rich people become rich only through inheritances.

From the opposite perspective, 49 percent of older Americans, but only 31 percent of younger Americans, believed that many rich people become rich because they take more risks than do others. And 43 percent of older Americans, but only 27 percent of younger Americans, assumed that rich people are generally very industrious throughout their lives. Finally, 41 percent of older Americans, but only 19 percent of younger Americans, believed that society as a whole benefits from the

Figure 11.12

United States: Attitudes toward the rich—Analysis by age group I: Positive and neutral statements

Question: "Here is a list of things people have said about rich people. Which, if any, of the statements on the list would you agree with?"

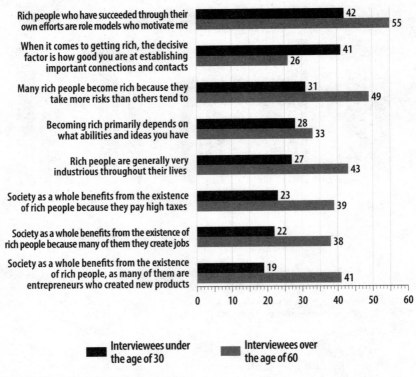

Note: All data are in percentage of respondents.

existence of the rich because many of them are entrepreneurs who cre-ated new products.

From these figures, it is clear why younger Americans so strongly supported Bernie Sanders, the far-left candidate in the Democratic presidential primary of 2016, and his anti-capitalist slogans. Whether younger Americans' attitudes toward the rich will change as they grow older, or whether they will remain critical of the rich, we cannot tell

Figure 11.13

United States: Attitudes toward the rich—Analysis by age group II: (Somewhat) negative statements

Question: "Here is a list of things people have said about rich people. Which, if any, of the statements on the list would you agree with?"

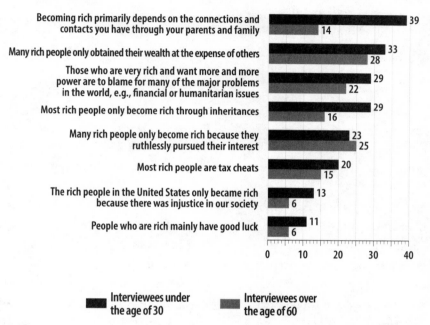

Note: All data are in percentage of respondents.

from our survey; determining this would require a series of regular surveys carried out over an extended period.

Is the American dream of freedom, capitalism, and upward social mobility, which was once shared by an entire nation, now fading? In his book *Becoming Europe*, Samuel Gregg warned that Americans were in danger of "Europeanization" as they progressively abandoned their traditional beliefs in capitalism and their skepticism toward state intervention. Gregg cites opinion polls that suggest that, especially among younger Americans, concerns about state intervention in the economy have diminished.[487]

How Do High and Low Earners View the Rich?

In our survey in the United States, interviewees were divided into the following income brackets (by annual household income in dollars):

- Less than $39,999 (low earners)
- $40,000–$64,999
- $65,000–$89,999
- $90,000–$124,999
- $125,000 and more (high earners)

As one would expect, high earners had more positive attitudes toward the rich than low earners. Four of the five personality traits mentioned most frequently by low earners were negative, compared with only two of the traits mentioned most frequently by high earners (Table 11.4).

Zero-sum beliefs are more common among low earners (39 percent) than among high earners (28 percent). Half of high earners, but fewer than a third of low earners, explicitly rejected zero-sum beliefs. High earners were also more likely than low earners to reject high or very high taxes for the rich. However, the fact that different income groups held similar opinions on a range of topics is far more interesting than the rather unsurprising variations mentioned above. For example, responses to the statement

Table 11.4

United States: Which traits are most likely to apply to rich people?—Analysis by income group

Low earners	High earners
1. Arrogant, 48 percent	1. Intelligent, 50 percent
2. Materialistic, 47 percent	2. Industrious, 49 percent
3. Greedy, 44 percent	3. Materialistic, 36 percent
4. Self-centered, 41 percent	4. Optimistic, 34 percent
5. Intelligent, 37 percent	4. Ruthless, 34 percent

that the salaries of managers who earn 100 times more than their employees are "obscene" did *not* vary significantly between income brackets.

The share of each income bracket that regarded very high manager salaries as "obscene" is as follows:

- Less than $39,999, 36 percent
- $40,000–$64,999, 40 percent
- $65,000–$89,999, 41 percent
- $90,000–$124,999, 44 percent
- $125,000 and more, 33 percent

There were also only minor differences between low earners and high earners when it comes to schadenfreude (Figure 11.14). When asked whether they agreed that a millionaire deserves to lose a lot of money

Figure 11.14
United States: Schadenfreude—Analysis by income group

Question: "To what extent, if at all, do you agree with the following statement: 'When I hear about a millionaire who made a risky business decision and lost a lot of money because of it, I think it serves him right.'?"

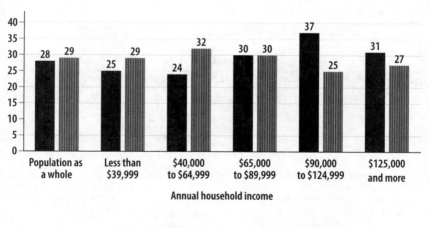

Note: All data are in percentage of respondents. Figures do not add up to 100 percent because "neither agree nor disagree" responses have been omitted.

because of a risky business decision, 25 percent of low earners agreed and 29 percent disagreed. The answers from high earners were similar: 31 percent agreed with the schadenfreude statement, and 27 percent rejected it.

When schadenfreude is analyzed in terms of educational attainment, it appears that well-educated Americans were even more likely than the less educated to react with malicious joy when they hear that a millionaire has lost a lot of money because of a risky business decision. Incidentally, the results of the regression analysis also revealed that well-educated Americans tended to be more prone to social envy. Perhaps this finding is a result of the predominantly left-wing climate at many American universities.

When considering their responses to other questions, however, the different income groups' answers were as expected. For example, low earners did not appreciate that very high salaries may be necessary in order to retain the best managerial talent and prevent managers from moving to other companies or working for themselves. In the income brackets up to $89,000, only 23 percent agreed with this statement. Among interviewees with higher incomes, however, the figure rose to 40 percent.

There is another significant difference between the groups: 65 percent of low earners did not personally know a millionaire, compared with only 28 percent of high earners. Birds of a feather clearly do flock together.

How Does the U.S. Population as a Whole View the Rich?

All in all, a relatively large group of Americans are almost entirely immune to social envy. Almost half of Americans had a distinctly positive attitude toward rich people. This view is reflected in their answers to very different questions:

- Forty-five percent of Americans said that rich people who have succeeded through their own efforts are role models and sources of motivation.
- Forty-eight percent of Americans were non-enviers (see above).
- Forty-four percent of Americans associated rich people, above all, with "intelligence"—which scored highest among the 15 personality traits of rich people that interviewees were asked about.

As detailed in the section on social envy, three groups can be identified: (a) the non-enviers, who viewed the rich positively; (b) the large group of ambivalents, whose views of the rich were neither consistently positive nor consistently negative; and (c) the small group of enviers who exhibited marked social envy or agreed with clearly negative statements about rich people:

- Ten percent of Americans believed that people who are rich mainly have good luck.
- Eight percent of Americans believed that rich people became rich only because of injustice in society.
- Eighteen percent of Americans said that most rich people are tax cheats.
- Twenty-seven percent of Americans said that rich people are good at earning money but are not usually decent people.

Support for higher taxes for millionaires extended beyond the circle of enviers, who are generally critical of the rich. For example, 47 percent of Americans believed that taxes for millionaires should be increased substantially, even if they would not personally benefit, compared with only 28 percent who disagreed.

But rich people, at least those who have become rich through their own efforts, were also the subject of admiration and appreciation from many low earners in the United States. Many members of the lower classes still believe in the American dream of becoming rich through one's own efforts: 37 percent of low earners (who earn less than $40,000 a year) and 43 percent of Americans in the $40,000–$64,999 income bracket said that rich people who have succeeded through their own efforts are role models who motivate them. However, this result was significantly less than the 59 percent in the highest-income group (who earn $125,000 and more per year) who agreed with this statement.

CHAPTER 12

HOW THE FRENCH VIEW THE RICH

From May 28 to June 9, 2018, Ipsos MORI surveyed a representative sample of 1,011 French citizens. The questions asked were identical to those asked in the surveys in Germany, the United States, and Great Britain. The attitude of the French respondents is characterized by their ambivalence toward the rich—pronounced admiration, on one hand, and pronounced envy, on the other.

THE SELF-MADE RICH ARE ROLE MODELS

One of the items that elicited the strongest agreement among French respondents was the statement that "rich people who have succeeded through their own efforts are role models who motivate me." This statement met with agreement from 53 percent of respondents. Among younger respondents (i.e., those between the ages of 16 and 29), the figure was even higher, at 67 percent. Majorities of 30- to 44-year-olds and 45- to 59-year-olds also expressed their agreement. It was only among older French interviewees (i.e., those over the age of 60) that fewer than half of respondents (40 percent) agreed that they view the self-made rich as role models.

★ Figure and table data in Chapter 12 are from the 2018 Ipsos MORI J18–031911–01–02 survey of France.

As expected, levels of agreement with this statement rose with income. But even among low-income respondents (i.e., respondents from households with net incomes of less than €1,200 per month), 48 percent admitted that they admire rich people who have succeeded through their own efforts. Among higher earners (i.e., respondents from households with net incomes of more than €4,500 per month), as many as 66 percent agreed.

Of course, this result does not mean that these respondents have necessarily set themselves the goal of becoming rich. But at least one in four (26 percent) French respondents agreed that being rich is important to them personally. Of younger French respondents (those under the age of 30), some 35 percent said that it is important for them personally to be rich. And it is not surprising that among respondents who want to be rich, admiration for the self-made rich was even higher than it was across the population as a whole: 60 percent of those respondents under the age of 30 said that the self-made rich people are role models for them, compared with only 47 percent of respondents who did not personally believe that being rich is important.

However, a third of French interviewees believed that becoming rich primarily depends on the connections and contacts one has through one's parents and family. When a second variant of this item was presented and respondents were asked in general about the importance of establishing connections and contacts, almost half of French respondents (45 percent) believed this factor to be key to becoming rich.

ACCORDING TO THE FRENCH, WHAT PERSONALITY TRAITS DO THE RICH HAVE?

When our French interviewees were asked about the traits and characteristics they associate with rich people, the top two traits were positive, namely industriousness and intelligence, followed by two negative traits, materialism and arrogance.

However, when the responses are analyzed according to respondents' incomes, significant differences emerge (Table 12.1). Low earners attributed more negative traits to the rich, whereas high earners attributed more positive traits.

Table 12.1

France: Which traits are most likely to apply to rich people?—Analysis by income group

French population as a whole	French respondents with net household incomes under €1,200	French respondents with net household incomes over €4,500
1. Industrious, 45 percent	1. Arrogant, 43 percent	1. Industrious, 65 percent
2. Intelligent, 41 percent	2. Ruthless, 40 percent	2. Bold, daring, 53 percent
3. Materialistic, 40 percent	3. Materialistic, 38 percent	3. Imaginative, 50 percent
4. Arrogant, 37 percent	3. Industrious, 38 percent	4. Intelligent, 47 percent
4. Bold, daring, 37 percent	4. Intelligent, 37 percent	5. Materialistic, 38 percent
	4. Self-centered, 37 percent	

ONLY ONE IN FOUR FRENCH PEOPLE IS NOT ENVIOUS

French interviewees were asked three questions as indicators of social envy:

1. *"I think it would be fair to increase taxes substantially for millionaires, even if I would not benefit from it personally."*

When presented with this statement, 61 percent of respondents agreed. On other issues, too, majorities of the interviewees advocated higher taxes for the rich (more on this below). Only 20 percent disagreed with this statement.

2. *"I would favor drastically reducing managers' salaries and redistributing the money more evenly among their employees, even if that would mean that [the employees] would only get a few more euros per month."*

This form of drastic redistribution elicited support from 54 percent of French respondents, despite the fact that it would be of little benefit to employees but would significantly lower salaries for managers. Even high earners (those with net household incomes of more than €4,500 per month) shared this opinion.

3. *"When I hear about a millionaire who made a risky business decision and lost a lot of money because of it, I think it serves him right."*

The proportion of French interviewees who agreed with this statement was lower than for the two previous statements: one-third (33 percent) agreed, whereas 41 percent disagreed.

Responses to these three questions indicate the strength of social envy across the French population. As with the other countries, we can distinguish among three groups:

1. *Non-enviers* (respondents with low levels of social envy, who disagreed with all three of the above statements): 27 percent
2. *Ambivalents* (who agreed with one statement): 39 percent
3. *Social enviers* (who agreed with two or three statements): 33 percent (including the 11 percent of hardcore enviers who agreed with all three statements)

Thus, the largest group in France was the ambivalents, and this attitude is characteristic of the French. But how did attitudes differ between the two groups at the extremes of the Social Envy Scale? Because France had far more hardcore enviers than the United States or Great Britain, we are able to directly compare the two extreme groups, that is, the non-enviers, who responded negatively to all three statements, and the hardcore enviers, who responded in the affirmative to all three. Once again, one should remember that a number of enviers will be in the "non-envier" group, just as the "envier" group is sure to contain a number of non-enviers. Nevertheless, an interviewee who disagrees with all three of the statements is far more likely to be a non-envier than is one who agrees with two or three of the statements.

Above all, the group of enviers blamed social injustice for the existence of rich people in France. Of hardcore enviers, 53 percent believed that the rich people in France became rich only as the result of social injustice, compared with just 10 percent of non-enviers. And 46 percent of hardcore enviers thought that many rich people obtained their wealth at the expense of others, in contrast to just 14 percent of non-enviers.

Overall, enviers again tended to interpret wealth as the result of external circumstances and not of individual merit or positive traits and specific talents. Of hardcore enviers, 43 percent believed that becoming rich depends primarily on the connections and contacts one has through one's parents and family. Only 24 percent of non-enviers shared this belief. Hardcore enviers were also far more likely (39 percent) than non-enviers (23 percent) to believe that most rich people become rich only through inheritances. On the other hand, only 24 percent of hardcore enviers believed that rich people are particularly industrious, compared with 40 percent of non-enviers. And although 72 percent of hardcore enviers thought that most rich people are tax cheats, only 29 percent of non-enviers thought the same.

In summary, enviers attributed wealth primarily to injustice in society or to negative personality traits, whereas non-enviers placed far greater emphasis on the personal abilities and talents of the rich, as is evident from a comparison of the traits most frequently assigned to rich people by all enviers (not just hardcore enviers) and by non-enviers (Figure 12.1).

In Chapter 7, compensation theory was introduced to explain why enviers deny rich people certain positive traits. Enviers seek to portray themselves in a more positive light than the targets of their envy. Thus, they describe rich people as, for example, being good at earning money but not usually decent people. In France, only one in ten non-enviers agreed with this negative assessment of the rich, compared with one in three enviers (Figure 12.2). Of hardcore enviers, about half agreed with this statement.

When asked which groups of rich people deserve to be rich, the following variations among our French respondents emerged: Although slightly more hardcore enviers than non-enviers believed that lottery winners deserve to be rich, their proportion was lower for entrepreneurs, top athletes, and senior-level managers. However, the differences are particularly striking with regard to financial investors, senior bankers, and property investors: the proportion of non-enviers who believed these groups deserve to be rich (24 percent, 16 percent, and 24 percent, respectively) was far greater than the proportion of hardcore enviers

Figure 12.1

France: Attribution of personality traits by rank on the Social Envy Scale

Question: "Which, if any, of the following are most likely to apply to rich people?"

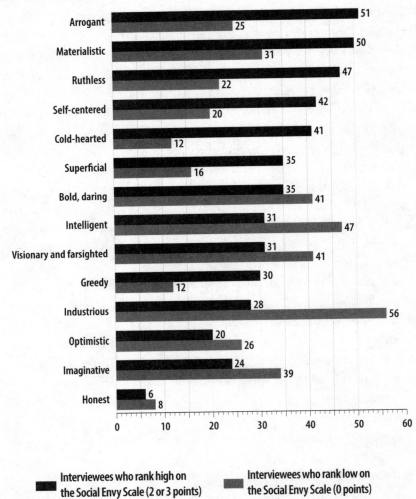

Note: All data are in percentage of respondents.

Figure 12.2

France: Envy and the tendency to deny that rich people are usually decent

Question: "To what extent do you agree or disagree with the following statement: 'Rich people are good at earning money, but are not usually decent people.'?"

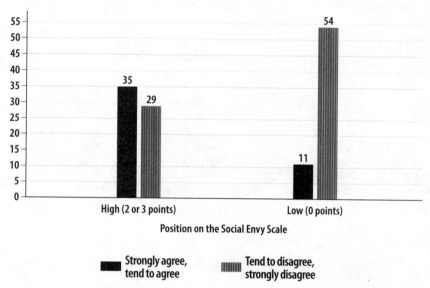

Note: All data are in percentage of respondents. Figures do not add up to 100 percent because "neither agree nor disagree" responses have been omitted.

(11 percent, 5 percent, and 12 percent, respectively) who believed the same.

In general, social enviers thought the rich are incapable of making any kind of positive contribution to society. Even when the rich donate to charitable causes, 44 percent of enviers suspected they do so primarily for selfish reasons (e.g., for tax relief or to improve their reputation), whereas only 8 percent of non-enviers assumed the same (Figure 12.3).

On all of the questions, we can see how accurately the Social Envy Scale differentiates between respondents. Non-enviers and enviers, who were initially distinguished only by their responses to the three social envy statements, have very different perceptions of rich people on all of the other questions, too (Figures 12.4 and 12.5).

Figure 12.3

France: The rich donate to benefit themselves—By rank on the Social Envy Scale

Question: "Some rich people donate a great deal of money to charitable causes. In your opinion, what is the main reason why people do that? Do they primarily donate because they want to benefit others, or primarily because they want to benefit themselves (e.g., for tax relief, to improve their reputation)?"

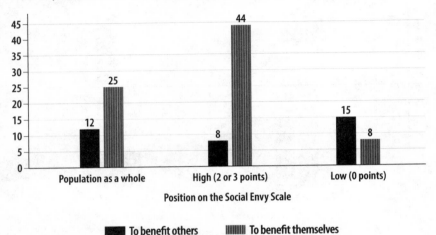

Note: All data are in percentage of respondents. Figures do not add up to 100 percent because "neither agree nor disagree" responses have been omitted.

ZERO-SUM BELIEVERS GENERALLY HAVE NEGATIVE PERCEPTIONS OF THE RICH

In Chapters 4 and 5, we saw the strong correlation between zero-sum beliefs and social envy. This relationship is confirmed by our survey in France: 32 percent of non-enviers perceived the world in zero-sum terms, compared with 41 percent of them who rejected the idea that one person's gain is always another person's loss (Figure 12.6). The reverse is true among enviers: 65 percent of enviers (and 82 percent of hardcore enviers) were zero-sum believers, whereas only 22 percent of enviers (and 12 percent of hardcore enviers) rejected zero-sum beliefs.

What has already been demonstrated for Germany and the United States applies equally to France: whether or not someone subscribes to zero-sum beliefs has a significant effect on that person's responses to the

Figure 12.4

France: Wealth and social envy I—Positive and neutral statements

Question: "Here is a list of things that people have said about rich people. Which, if any, of the statements on the list would you agree with?"

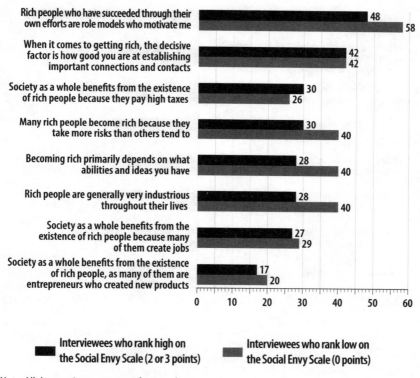

Interviewees who rank high on
the Social Envy Scale (2 or 3 points)

Interviewees who rank low on
the Social Envy Scale (0 points)

Note: All data are in percentage of respondents.

survey's other items. Zero-sum believers generally viewed the rich in a negative light (Figures 12.7 and 12.8).

For French respondents, too, a regression analysis confirms that of all variables, zero-sum beliefs exhibit the strongest correlation with how high a respondent will rank on the Social Envy Scale (Table 12.2). Incidentally, whether or not a French interviewee personally knew a millionaire also plays a key role in determining how socially envious the interviewee was.

Figure 12.5

France: Wealth and social envy II—(Somewhat) negative statements

Question: "Here is a list of things that people have said about rich people. Which, if any, of the statements on the list would you agree with?"

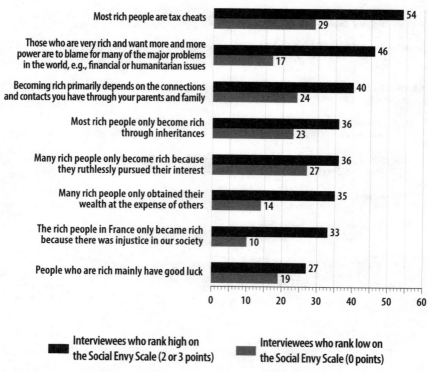

Interviewees who rank high on the Social Envy Scale (2 or 3 points)

Interviewees who rank low on the Social Envy Scale (0 points)

Note: All data are in percentage of respondents.

The French Want Punitive Taxes on the Rich

In 2012, the socialist candidate François Hollande won the French presidential election. During the election campaign, he proposed a marginal tax rate of 75 percent on salaries over €1 million. France's Constitutional Court, however, ruled that Hollande's tax on millionaires was unconstitutional. The tax was later abolished. Despite having to roll back his tax, Hollande was not entirely wrong to assume that the widespread appetite for extremely high taxation of top earners would earn him strong approval among French voters.

Figure 12.6

France: Zero-sum beliefs and social envy

Question: "To what extent do you agree or disagree with the following statement: 'The more the rich have, the less there is for the poor.'?"

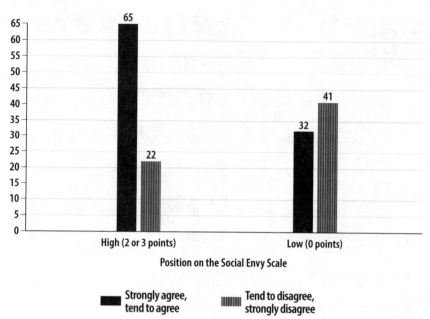

Position on the Social Envy Scale

- ■ Strongly agree, tend to agree
- ▦ Tend to disagree, strongly disagree

Note: All data are in percentage of respondents. Figures do not add up to 100 percent because "neither agree nor disagree" responses have been omitted.

Our survey presented French respondents with two statements:

- *"The taxes on the rich should be high but not excessively high because they have generally worked hard to earn their wealth, and the state should not take too much away from them."*
- *"The rich should not only pay high taxes, but they should pay very high taxes. In this way, the state can ensure that the gap between the rich and the poor does not become too great here in our country."*

Only 19 percent of French interviewees expressed agreement with the first, more moderate statement. Far more, namely 53 percent, agreed with the second.

Figure 12.7

France: Wealth and zero-sum beliefs I—Positive and neutral statements

Question: "Here is a list of things that people have said about rich people. Which, if any, of the statements on the list would you agree with?"

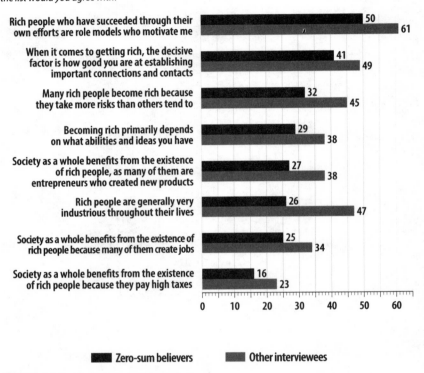

| | Zero-sum believers | Other interviewees |

Note: All data are in percentage of respondents.

It is interesting to note that even among non–enviers, one in three was in favor of very high taxes on the rich; among hardcore enviers, of course, the figure was significantly higher, at 84 percent. And even among high earners (those with household incomes of more than €4,500), support for very high taxes on the rich stood at 45 percent, and only 21 percent wanted moderate taxes on the rich.

The appetite among French respondents for very high wealth taxes is clear when they are asked whether it would be fair to substantially increase taxes on millionaires even if the respondents would not benefit from it personally. On this question, 61 percent of French respondents

Figure 12.8

France: Wealth and zero-sum beliefs II—(Somewhat) negative statements

Question: "Here is a list of things that people have said about rich people. Which, if any, of the statements on the list would you agree with?"

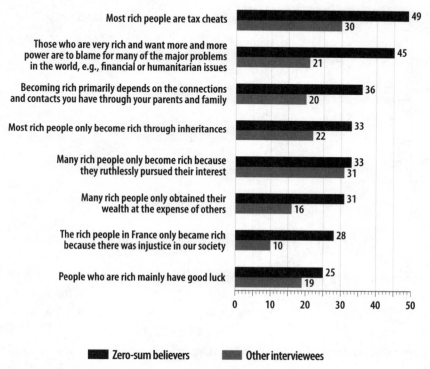

Zero-sum believers   Other interviewees

Note: All data are in percentage of respondents.

supported substantially higher taxes, and only 20 percent were against them (Figure 12.9). Even in the highest-income group, this proposal was supported by 45 percent; among low earners, the figure was 68 percent.

Less than a fifth of French respondents believed that society as a whole benefits from the existence of rich people because the rich pay high taxes. In contrast, twice as many believed that most rich people are tax cheats. It is perhaps no coincidence that the left-wing economist Thomas Piketty (author of *Capital in the Twenty-First Century*), who has called for a marginal wealth tax of 85 percent, is French.

Table 12.2

Regression analysis of social envy in France

Dependent variable: Social Envy Scale
Influence of independent variables on the dependent variable

	Beta	Significance
Zero-sum beliefs	−.20	***
Personally knows a millionaire	−.18	***
Age	.04	**
Household income	−.06	ns
Gender (F)	.05	ns
Education	−.03	ns
Unsure in everyday situations	.02	ns

Note: *** $p < .01$; ** $p < .05$; ns = not significant.

MANY HIGH EARNERS ARE ALSO CRITICAL OF HIGH MANAGER SALARIES

The egalitarian attitude of many French people, including those who earn more, is evident not only from their support for high taxes on the rich but also from their sharp criticism of high salaries for senior managers. When asked whether they think it is inappropriate for some managers to earn 100 times more than their employees, 61 percent of French respondents indicated that, generally speaking, such high salaries are "obscene." What is most remarkable is that there was no difference on this question between less educated and highly educated respondents, nor was there any variation among income groups. Whether low-income, middle-income, or high-income, at least 58 percent of French interviewees share this opinion.

Another unusual finding is that support for drastically reducing managers' salaries and redistributing the money more evenly among their employees, even if the employees would get only a few more euros per month, was virtually as strong (at 56 percent) among respondents with net household incomes over €4,500 per month as it was among the population as a whole (54 percent).

Figure 12.9

France: Substantial tax increases for the rich—Analysis by income group

Question: "To what extent do you agree or disagree with this statement: 'I think it would be fair to increase taxes substantially for millionaires, even if I would not benefit from it personally.'?"

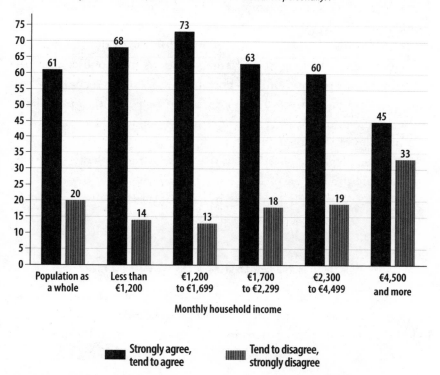

Note: All data are in percentage of respondents. Figures do not add up to 100 percent because "neither agree nor disagree" responses have been omitted.

Even when asked whether they agree that because managers earn so much more than employees there is less money left over for employees' salaries, responses did not vary among income groups, unlike in other countries: 41 percent of low-income French respondents agreed with this statement, as did 39 percent of the highest-income group. When asked whether such high salaries for managers are inappropriate because no one needs that much money, the proportion of respondents with a net household income of over €4,500 per month who agreed (42 percent) was actually slightly higher than the proportion of respondents with net household salaries of less than €1,200 who did so (38 percent).

Differences did emerge, however, when respondents were asked whether it is solely up to companies to decide how much managers should earn. Only 20 percent of low earners agreed, compared with 40 percent of the highest-income group. Only one other question on manager salaries elicited equally large variations in responses from the different income groups: Only 25 percent of low earners recognized that companies can only hire and retain the best managers if they pay salaries of this kind, compared with 44 percent of respondents with net household incomes of €4,500 and more.

Overall, however, one can say that French respondents, including a remarkable proportion of high earners, were both heavily critical of high manager salaries and strongly in favor of substantially higher taxes on the rich.

How Do High and Low Earners in France View the Rich?

The findings discussed in the previous section do not mean that there are no clear differences in attitude between income groups on other issues. Our survey distinguished five distinct groups by monthly household income:

- Less than €1,200
- €1,200 to €1,699
- €1,700 to €2,299
- €2,300 to €4,499
- €4,500 and more

As we have already seen, low earners perceived the rich primarily as arrogant and ruthless, whereas high earners believed the rich are industrious, bold, and daring. Such differences were expected and clearly exist in France just as much as in the other three countries surveyed. What sets France apart is that the differences according to income were not very pronounced on many issues. However, this finding is relativized by the fact that French respondents qualified for the highest-income group with a moderate net household income of €4,500 per month, which is substantially lower than that of the top income groups in our surveys in Great Britain and, in particular, the United States.

Clear variations exist among the income groups in responses to numerous statements, including the item on schadenfreude: *"When I hear about a millionaire who made a risky business decision and lost a lot of money because of it, I think it serves him right."*

Among low earners, a relative majority (42 percent versus 36 percent) agreed with this statement. Among high earners, 50 percent disagreed, and only 24 percent agreed.

According to compensation theory (see Chapter 7 for more details), individuals with low incomes seek to protect their self-esteem by denying moral traits to higher-income individuals. This theory explains why 31 percent of low-income respondents thought that the rich are good at earning money but are not usually decent people, in contrast to 12 percent of French respondents with net household incomes of €4,500 and more. Among low earners, the difference between those who agreed with this statement and those who rejected it is only 2 percentage points; among high earners, the difference is 36 percentage points.

Low earners were also more inclined than high earners to attribute the economic success of the rich to pure luck. Thus, 28 percent of low earners but only 12 percent of high earners thought that people who are rich mainly have good luck. Moreover, 33 percent of low earners but only 15 percent of those in the highest-income group believed that most rich people become rich only through inheritances. And 28 percent of low earners but only 9 percent of high earners believed rich people in France became rich only because of social injustice.

Low earners tend to think that luck, inheritance, injustice, and negative personality traits are the reasons that some people are wealthy. High earners, on the other hand, tend to believe that rich people become rich because they have specific personality traits and abilities.

In the group of French respondents with net household incomes of €4,500 and more per month, 55 percent believed that many rich people become rich because they take more risks than others tend to. Only half as many low earners (28 percent) shared this opinion. And almost half of higher earners (49 percent) agreed that rich people are generally very industrious throughout their lives, whereas less than a third of the lowest-income group (30 percent) concurred with this statement.

Further differences emerged when respondents were asked about the groups they personally believed deserve to be rich. For example, only 31 percent of low earners thought that senior-level managers deserve to be rich, compared with the 43 percent of low earners who did not begrudge lottery winners their wealth. Among the highest-income group, the opposite was true: 47 percent believed that senior-level managers deserve their wealth, but only 32 percent said the same of lottery winners.

It is particularly striking that the percentage of French respondents who personally knew a millionaire (either as a friend, a family member, or an acquaintance) did not vary much by income group: 85 percent of low earners do not count a millionaire among their circle of friends or relatives, a fact that also applies to 72 percent of respondents with net household incomes of €4,500 and more.

Thus, as in the other three countries, responses in France differed depending on respondents' income, although on a number of issues, particularly wealth taxes and manager salaries, the differences between low and high earners in France were surprisingly small.

Young French People Have More Positive Perceptions of the Rich

In the preceding two chapters, we saw that younger Germans viewed the rich more positively than did older Germans but that the opposite was true in the United States. In this matter, the French were similar to the Germans: younger French respondents had more positive perceptions of the rich than did older respondents. In 13 of 16 statements about the rich, French people under the age of 30 expressed more favorable opinions of the rich than did respondents over the age of 60. In some cases, the difference was moderate; in others, it was striking. For example, 45 percent of younger French people agreed that becoming rich depends primarily on one's abilities and ideas (Figure 12.10). The same statement elicited agreement from only 26 percent of older French respondents.

Figure 12.10

France: Attitudes toward the rich—Analysis by age group I: Positive and neutral statements

Question: "Here is a list of things that people have said about rich people. Which, if any, of the statements on the list would you agree with?"

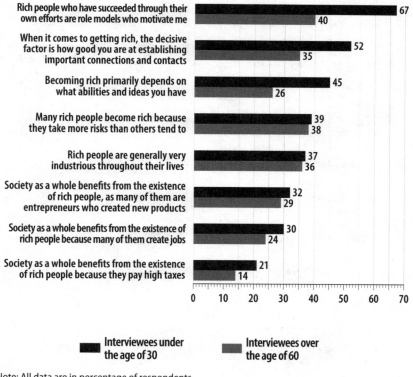

Note: All data are in percentage of respondents.

In contrast, 27 percent of older respondents believed that people who are rich mainly have good luck, compared with only 17 percent of younger French interviewees (Figure 12.11). Furthermore, 33 percent of older respondents thought that most rich people become rich only through inheritances, an opinion that was shared by only 23 percent of younger interviewees.

Figure 12.11

France: Attitudes toward the rich—Analysis by age group II: (Somewhat) negative statements

Question: "Here is a list of things that people have said about rich people. Which, if any, of the statements on the list would you agree with?"

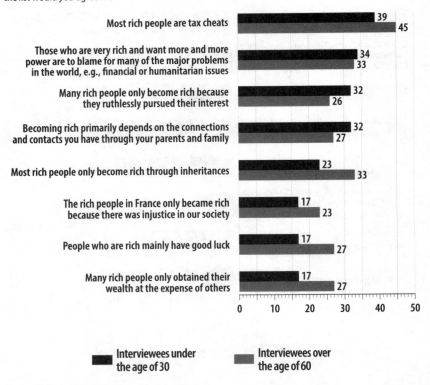

Note: All data are in percentage of respondents.

On most of these statements, younger French people responded more positively than did older interviewees:

- Younger French respondents were far less likely to have a zero-sum mindset and therefore were more likely to reject the theory that the more the rich have, the less there is for the poor (Figure 12.12).
- Older interviewees were far more likely than younger interviewees to support substantial tax increases on the rich.

Figure 12.12
France: Zero-sum beliefs—Analysis by age group

Question: "To what extent do you agree or disagree with the following statement: 'The more the rich have, the less there is for the poor.'?"

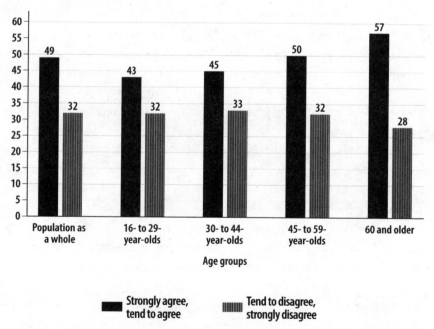

Note: All data are in percentage of respondents. Figures do not add up to 100 percent because "neither agree nor disagree" responses have been omitted.

- Older interviewees were far more likely than younger interviewees to experience schadenfreude when a millionaire
  lost a lot of money.
- Older respondents agreed more frequently than younger
  interviewees that very high salaries for managers were inappropriate because no one needs that much money.

We also asked our French respondents which groups of people they
personally believed deserve to be rich. Without exception, no matter
which group was mentioned—entrepreneurs, self-employed people, top
athletes, creative people and artists, and others—French respondents
under the age of 30 more frequently agreed that the group deserved
its wealth than did respondents over the age of 60 (Figure 12.13). The
greatest differences were registered in relation to top athletes, property
investors, creative people and artists, and senior bankers: a far greater
proportion of younger French people thought that each of these groups
deserve to be rich than was the case among older respondents. Only
27 percent of respondents over the age of 60 believed that senior-level
managers deserve to be rich, compared with 42 percent of those under
the age of 30. The proportion of younger respondents who believed
that senior-level bankers and property investors deserve to be rich was
three times as high as the proportion of those over the age of 60 who
believed the same. Concerning financial investors and top athletes, the
proportion was twice as high among younger French interviewees as
it was among older respondents. No single group was deemed to be
deserving of their wealth by a greater share of older respondents than of
younger respondents.

As previously mentioned, it is not surprising that 67 percent of
younger French respondents agreed that rich people who have succeeded
through their own efforts are role models, compared with only 40 percent
of older French respondents.

Incidentally, opinion polls in France were found to be a more suit-
able instrument for measuring attitudes toward the rich than they were
for measuring attitudes toward other minorities. Our survey revealed
that the French have almost no qualms when it comes to criticizing

Figure 12.13

France: Who deserves to be rich?—Analysis by age group

Question: "Which, if any, of the following groups of people do you personally believe deserve to be rich?"

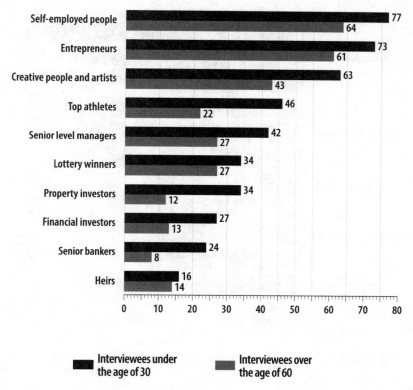

Self-employed people	77 / 64
Entrepreneurs	73 / 61
Creative people and artists	63 / 43
Top athletes	46 / 22
Senior level managers	42 / 27
Lottery winners	34 / 27
Property investors	34 / 12
Financial investors	27 / 13
Senior bankers	24 / 8
Heirs	16 / 14

Interviewees under the age of 30 ■   Interviewees over the age of 60 ■

Note: All data are in percentage of respondents.

the rich in public. When asked which groups of people you have to be careful not to criticize in public, only 28 percent of French respondents mentioned the rich.

Ten other groups were mentioned (Figure 12.14), and, in every case, the psychological barriers surrounding public criticism were higher for those groups than for the rich. The highest-ranking minority in this regard was Muslims (67 percent), followed by homosexual people (57 percent), disabled people (57 percent), and Jews (56 percent).

Figure 12.14

France: Whom do you have to be careful not to criticize in public?

Question: "It is sometimes said that there are certain groups of people that you have to be careful not to criticize in public. Which of these groups, if any, do you think this applies to?"

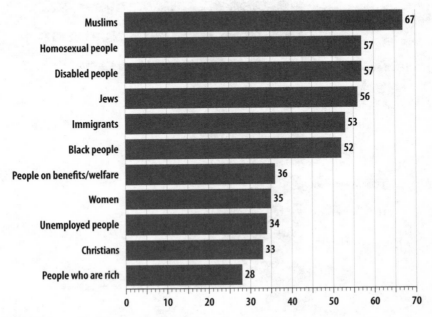

Note: All data are in percentage of respondents.

CHAPTER 13

HOW THE BRITISH VIEW THE RICH

From May 25 to June 10, 2018, Ipsos MORI surveyed a representative sample of 1,002 British adults. The questions asked were identical to those asked in Germany, the United States, and France.

THE BRITISH HAVE MORE IN COMMON WITH THE AMERICANS THAN WITH THE GERMANS OR THE FRENCH

The populations of the United States and Great Britain have more in common than just a language. With regard to enviers, the two countries are also very similar. Using the Social Envy Scale as a basis, the populations of Great Britain and the United States are composed of the groups shown in Figure 13.1: non-enviers, enviers, ambivalents, and hardcore enviers.

As this chapter will demonstrate, the responses of the British population differed considerably from those of Germany and France. Respondents were again assigned to groups according to their responses to the following three statements:

1. *"I think it would be fair to increase taxes substantially for millionaires, even if I would not benefit from it personally."*

---

*Figure and table data in Chapter 13 are from the 2018 Ipsos MORI J18-031911-01-02 survey of Great Britain.

Exactly half of British respondents thought so.

2.   *"I would favor drastically reducing managers' salaries and redistributing the money more evenly among their employees, even if that would mean that [the employees] would only get a few more pounds per month."*

This second statement, which 54 percent of French interviewees agreed with, elicited support from just 29 percent of British respondents.

3.   *"When I hear about a millionaire who made a risky business decision and lost a lot of money because of it, I think it serves him right."*

Agreement with this third statement was also lower among British respondents: 22 percent agreed, 38 percent disagreed, and the rest were undecided.

Figure 13.1

Enviers and non-enviers in Great Britain and the United States

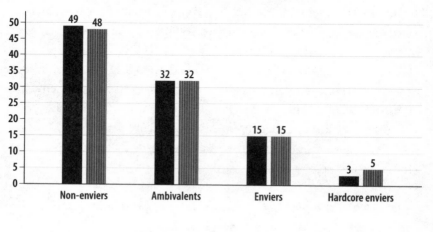

Note: All data are in percentage of respondents.

Because the number of hardcore enviers in Great Britain who agreed with all three statements was extremely small (only 3 percent), the following analyses are based on responses from people who agreed with two or three of these envy statements. In Great Britain, too, the Social Envy Scale achieves a high degree of differentiation. Figure 13.2 shows the responses of enviers and non-enviers when asked which traits most frequently apply to rich people.

Only 10 percent of non-enviers in Great Britain thought that the rich are good at earning money but are not usually decent people, compared with 29 percent of enviers. Only 24 percent of non-enviers thought the rich should pay very high taxes, in stark contrast to 69 percent of enviers. Above all, enviers were far more likely to subscribe to zero-sum beliefs than non-enviers: only 23 percent of non-enviers were zero-sum believers, versus 60 percent of enviers (Figure 13.3).

As was the case for the other three countries, we carried out a regression analysis for Great Britain; it confirmed that zero-sum beliefs have the greatest explanatory power for respondents' positions on the Social Envy Scale (Table 13.1).

On items related to senior-level managers' salaries, it is clear that a far greater number of enviers than non-enviers had an "employee mindset," which associates the amount someone earns only with how long and hard they work. For example, 64 percent of enviers thought it is inappropriate for managers to earn 100 times more than their employees because managers do not work so much longer and harder than their employees (Figure 13.4). This opinion was shared by only 19 percent of non-enviers—those not sharing this opinion probably understand that top-tier salaries are determined not by how long or hard someone works, but by supply and demand in the market for top-tier executives with rare skills and connections.

Among enviers, 67 percent thought that very high manager salaries are "obscene," compared with only 20 percent of non-enviers. And although 59 percent of enviers believed that less money is left over for employees when managers earn so much, only 11 percent of non-enviers shared this view.

Figure 13.2

Great Britain: Attribution of personality traits by rank on the Social Envy Scale

Question: "Which, if any, of the following are most likely to apply to rich people?"

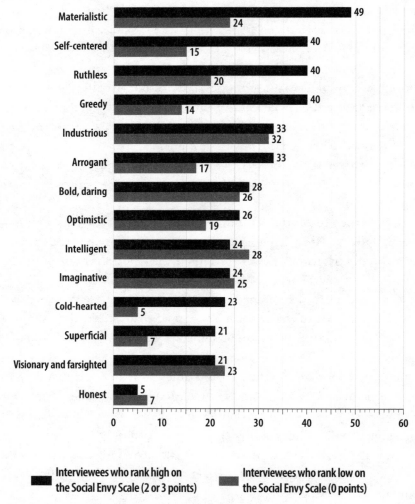

Materialistic — 49 / 24
Self-centered — 40 / 15
Ruthless — 40 / 20
Greedy — 40 / 14
Industrious — 33 / 32
Arrogant — 33 / 17
Bold, daring — 28 / 26
Optimistic — 26 / 19
Intelligent — 24 / 28
Imaginative — 24 / 25
Cold-hearted — 23 / 5
Superficial — 21 / 7
Visionary and farsighted — 21 / 23
Honest — 5 / 7

■ Interviewees who rank high on   ■ Interviewees who rank low on
the Social Envy Scale (2 or 3 points)   the Social Envy Scale (0 points)

Note: All data are in percentage of respondents.

Figure 13.3

Great Britain: Zero-sum beliefs and social envy

Question: "To what extent do you agree or disagree with the following statement: 'The more the rich have, the less there is for the poor.'?"

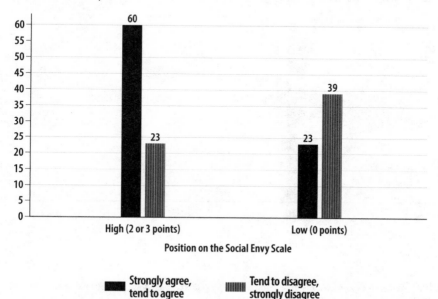

Position on the Social Envy Scale

- ■ Strongly agree, tend to agree
- ▥ Tend to disagree, strongly disagree

Note: All data are in percentage of respondents. Figures do not add up to 100 percent because "neither agree nor disagree" responses have been omitted.

Table 13.1

Regression analysis of social envy in Great Britain

Dependent variable: Social Envy Scale
Influence of independent variables on the dependent variable

	Beta	***p*-value**
Zero-sum beliefs	−.21	***
Gender (F)	−.19	***
Education	.08	***
Age	.08	ns
Household income	−.04	ns
Personally knows a millionaire	.03	ns
Unsure in everyday situations	.01	ns

Note: *** $p < .01$; ns = not significant.

Figure 13.4

Great Britain: Social envy and the employee mindset

Agreement with the statement: "I think it is inappropriate for managers to earn so much more, as they do not work so much longer and harder than their employees."

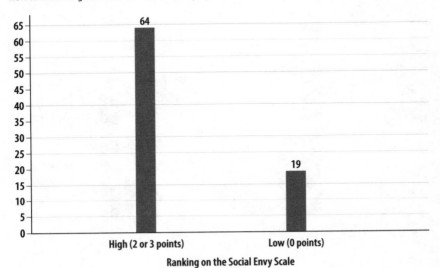

Ranking on the Social Envy Scale

Note: All data are in percentage of respondents. Figures do not add up to 100 percent because "neither agree nor disagree" responses have been omitted.

WHAT DO LABOUR AND CONSERVATIVE VOTERS THINK OF THE RICH?

The differences in perceptions of the rich among left-wing (Labour Party) and center-right (Conservative Party) voters in Great Britain were very clear. Half (48 percent) of Labour voters were zero-sum believers (i.e., they believed that the more the rich have, the less there is for the poor), whereas only 17 percent of Conservative voters adhered to this theory (Figure 13.5).

The proposal that the rich should pay very high taxes was supported by 53 percent of Labour voters but only 21 percent of Conservative voters. And twice as many Labour voters (68 percent) as Conservative voters (34 percent) would favor significant tax increases for millionaires even if they themselves would not benefit.

Figure 13.5

Great Britain: Zero-sum beliefs and political affiliation

Question: "To what extent do you agree or disagree with the following statement: 'The more the rich have, the less there is for the poor.'?"

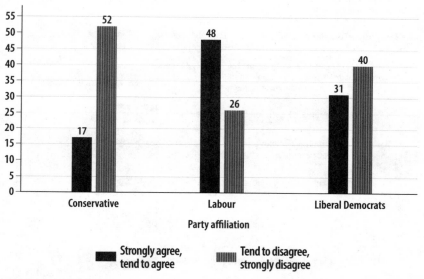

Party affiliation

■ **Strongly agree,**
   tend to agree

▦ **Tend to disagree,**
   strongly disagree

Note: All data are in percentage of respondents. Figures do not add up to 100 percent because "neither agree nor disagree" responses have been omitted.

Labour voters were more likely (33 percent) than Conservative voters (13 percent) to blame the very rich for many of the major problems in the world, and one in four Labour voters (but only one in ten Conservative voters) believed that many rich people obtained their wealth at the expense of others (Figure 13.6). Conservative voters more frequently agreed (45 percent) that society as a whole benefits from the existence of rich people because many of them are entrepreneurs who created new products. The same statement registered agreement from only 20 percent of Labour voters (Figure 13.7).

Conversely, 40 percent of Conservative voters, but only half as many Labour voters (21 percent), believed that becoming rich depends primarily on one's abilities and ideas. And 45 percent of Conservative voters,

Figure 13.6

Great Britain: Attitudes toward the rich—Conservative and Labour Party perspectives: (Somewhat) negative statements

Question: "Here is a list of things that people have said about rich people. Which, if any, of the statements on the list would you agree with?"

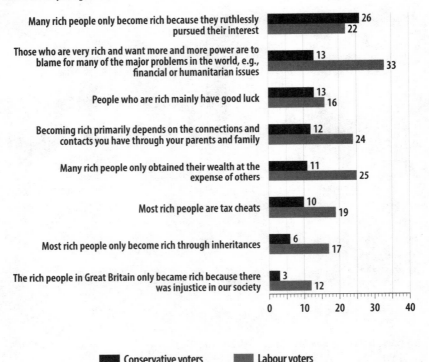

Note: All data are in percentage of respondents.

but only 27 percent of Labour voters, agreed that many rich people become rich because they take more risks than others tend to.

When the British respondents were asked about the traits they most frequently associated with rich people, clear differences emerged. Among Conservative voters, five out of the top six traits attributed to rich people were positive, whereas among Labour voters, four out of the top six traits were negative (Table 13.2).

Figure 13.7

Great Britain: Attitudes toward the rich—Conservative and Labour Party perspectives: Positive and neutral statements

Question: "Here is a list of things that people have said about rich people. Which, if any, of the statements on the list would you agree with?"

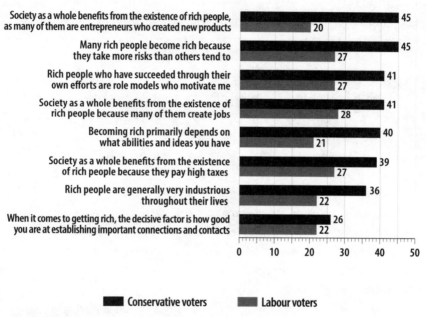

Note: All data are in percentage of respondents.

Table 13.2

Great Britain: Which traits most likely apply to rich people?—Analysis by party

Conservative voters	Labour voters
1. Industrious, 56 percent	1. Materialistic, 35 percent
2. Imaginative, 46 percent	2. Industrious, 30 percent
3. Visionary, 44 percent	3. Ruthless, 26 percent
4. Bold, daring, 40 percent	3. Bold, daring, 26 percent
5. Intelligent, 36 percent	4. Self-centered, 25 percent
6. Ruthless, 32 percent	4. Greedy, 25 percent

One in two (49 percent) Conservative voters personally knew a millionaire (and 29 percent knew more than one), whereas only one in three (34 percent) Labour voters personally knew one or more millionaires. Both Labour and Conservative voters rejected the view that rich people are good at earning money but are not usually decent people, although the degree of rejection varied widely. Among Labour voters, rejection of this negative view of rich people exceeded agreement by only 18 percentage points. Among Conservative voters, rejection was far stronger: the number who rejected the statement exceeded the number who agreed by 44 percentage points.

When asked which groups of rich people deserve their wealth, Labour voters mentioned lottery winners more frequently (32 percent) than Conservative voters (24 percent), whereas Conservative voters mentioned entrepreneurs far more frequently (62 percent) than Labour voters (46 percent).

It almost goes without saying that Labour voters are more critical of high salaries for senior-level managers than are supporters of the Conservative Party. But it is interesting to see which of the statements on senior managers' salaries were the most controversial in the minds of Conservative and Labour voters:

- There was a 22-percentage-point difference (38 percent of Labour voters compared with 16 percent of Conservative voters) in agreement with the following statement: "If managers earn so much more than employees, there is less money left over for employees' salaries."
- There was a 15-percentage-point difference (42 percent of Labour voters, 27 percent of Conservative voters) in agreement with the following statement: "I think it is inappropriate for managers to earn so much more, as they do not work so much longer and harder than their employees." Again, this response reflects the employee mindset, because such attitudes assume that a person's salary should be determined chiefly by how long and how hard they work.

- A difference of 13 percentage points (36 percent of Labour voters, 23 percent of Conservative voters) existed in agreement with the following statement: "I would favor drastically reducing those managers' salaries and redistributing the money more evenly among their employees, even if that would mean that [the employees] would get only a few more pounds per month." This item can be taken as an indicator of envy, because a significant reduction in managers' salaries is offset by only an insignificant increase in salaries for regular employees.

WHAT DO YOUNGER AND OLDER BRITISH PEOPLE THINK OF THE RICH?

As in other countries, younger people in Great Britain are more likely than older people to personally believe that it is important for them to be rich. The difference between young and old becomes even clearer when considering the proportions of each group of respondents who say it is important for them to be rich and those who say it is not at all important. Among 16- to 29-year-olds, the difference between those proportions was only 6 percentage points, whereas for those aged 60 and older, the difference stood at 50 percentage points in favor of respondents who said it is not at all important for them personally to be rich (Figure 13.8).

Unlike in the other three countries, no major differences are discernible in the responses to 17 statements about rich people between younger British interviewees (16- to 29-year-olds) and older British interviewees (60 years and older): specific responses may vary from statement to statement (on some items, the younger respondents were more pro-rich, and on others, they were more critical than their older compatriots), but the percentages of younger and older people who agreed with the individual statements usually differed little.

Nevertheless, younger British respondents were somewhat more critical when asked which traits they most frequently associated with rich people. Four of the top six traits selected by younger British respondents are negative, whereas older British respondents mentioned only two negative traits (Table 13.3).

Figure 13.8

Great Britain: How important is it to be rich?—Analysis by age group

Question: "For some people, it is important to be rich. How important, if at all, is it for you personally to be rich?"

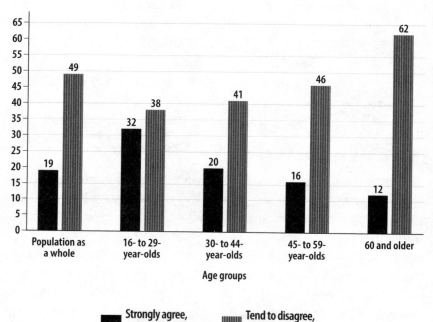

Strongly agree, tend to agree

Tend to disagree, strongly disagree

Note: All data are in percentage of respondents. Figures do not add up to 100 percent because "neither important nor unimportant" responses have been omitted.

Table 13.3

Great Britain: Which traits are most likely to apply to rich people?—Analysis by age group

British, aged 16–29 years	British, over the age of 60
1. Materialistic, 38 percent	1. Industrious, 45 percent
2. Intelligent, 35 percent	2. Imaginative, 34 percent
3. Greedy, 30 percent	3. Materialistic, 33 percent
3. Bold, daring, 30 percent	4. Intelligent, 30 percent
4. Ruthless, 27 percent	5. Bold, daring, 29 percent
5. Arrogant, 26 percent	5. Ruthless, 29 percent

Furthermore, the reactions of the older British respondents to the statement that the rich are good at earning money but are not usually decent people were more positive toward the rich than those of younger interviewees. The difference between disagreement and agreement with this item was twice as great among older people (32 percentage points more disagreement than agreement) as among younger people (16 percentage points more disagreement than agreement).

However, when asked which of 10 groups deserve to be rich, it is striking that *all 10 groups* were selected by a far greater proportion of younger British respondents than older respondents. Whether lottery winners, entrepreneurs, self-employed people, top athletes, financial or property investors, creative people and artists, senior-level managers, heirs, or senior bankers, the proportion of younger people who believed that these groups deserve to be rich was always higher than the proportion of older people who said the same (Figure 13.9).

Overall, younger people have fewer issues with differences in incomes. Only 17 percent of younger British respondents, compared to 29 percent of older people, said that it is inappropriate for senior-level managers to earn 100 times more than their employees because nobody needs so much money. And almost twice as many older respondents than younger respondents agreed that such high salaries are "generally obscene" (45 percent versus 24 percent).

Responses from older and younger interviewees in Great Britain differed from those in the other three countries surveyed. In Germany, the United States, and France, we saw clear, age-based trends across all items as to whether people have more positive or negative perceptions of the rich. In Great Britain, in contrast, the picture is not at all uniform, and no clear trend is discernible.

WHAT DO HIGH AND LOW EARNERS THINK OF THE RICH?

Of course, attitudes also differed between low and high earners in Great Britain. What is particularly noticeable, however, is that the differences on many issues were marginal. There were differences of only

Figure 13.9

Great Britain: Who deserves to be rich?—Analysis by age group

Question: "Which, if any, of the following groups of people do you personally believe deserve to be rich?"

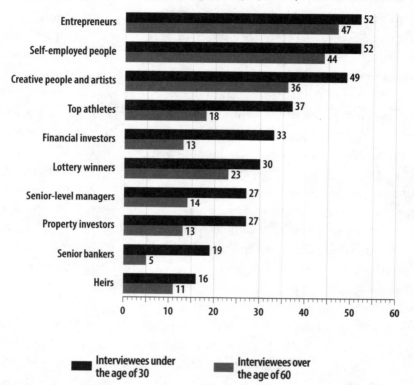

Note: All data are in percentage of respondents.

5 percentage points or fewer between the responses to the following statements from individuals earning less than £11,500 per year and from those earning more than £75,000 per year:

- "Becoming rich primarily depends on what abilities and ideas you have."
- "People who are rich mainly have good luck."

- "Many rich people only become rich because they ruthlessly pursued their interest."
- "Most rich people only become rich through inheritances."
- "Rich people are generally very industrious throughout their lives."
- "Society as a whole benefits from the existence of rich people, as many of them are entrepreneurs who created new products."
- "When it comes to getting rich, the decisive factor is how good you are at establishing important connections and contacts."
- "Those who are very rich and want more and more power are to blame for many of the major problems in the world, e.g., financial or humanitarian issues."
- "The more the rich have, the less there is for the poor." (zero-sum belief)
- "If managers earn so much more than employees, there is less money left over for employees' salaries."
- "I feel such high salaries for managers are inappropriate, as no one needs that much money."
- "I feel that such high managers' salaries are generally obscene."
- "I would favor drastically reducing those managers' salaries and redistributing the money more evenly among their employees, even if that would mean that they would only get a few more pounds per month."

It is striking how small the differences in agreement with the above statements were between low and high earners. Even when respondents were asked whether they think it would be fair to increase taxes substantially for millionaires even if they would not benefit from it personally, the differences between the income groups were smaller than one might expect. The same is also true of the schadenfreude item, which registered only minor variations in responses from the different income groups (Table 13.4).

Table 13.4

Great Britain: Higher taxes for the rich and schadenfreude—Analysis by income group

"I think it would be fair to increase taxes substantially for millionaires, even if I would not benefit from it personally."

Income Group	% in agreement
Less than £11,499	58
£11,500 to £24,999	51
£25,000 to £39,999	45
£40,000 to £74,999	57
£75,000 and more	43

"When I hear about a millionaire who made a risky business decision and lost a lot of money because of it, I think it serves him right."

Income Group	% in agreement
Less than £11,499	29
£11,500 to £24,999	22
£25,000 to £39,999	21
£40,000 to £74,999	26
£75,000 and more	26

When asked which groups most deserve to be rich, it is also striking that the differences in responses between low and high earners were slight for many of the groups.

- Thirty-one percent of low earners and 32 percent of the highest earners thought that lottery winners deserve to be rich.
- Thirty-seven percent of low earners and 38 percent of the highest earners thought that creative people—such as artists, actors, and musicians—deserve to be rich.
- Sixteen percent of low earners and 20 percent of the highest earners thought that senior-level managers deserve to be rich.

- Fifteen percent of low earners and 14 percent of the highest earners thought that heirs deserve to be rich.
- Forty-six percent of low earners and 40 percent of the highest earners thought that self-employed people deserve to be rich.

There are, however, groups who bucked this trend, such as entrepreneurs and top athletes—higher earners were far more likely to think that these two groups deserve to be rich than were low earners.

However, a number of items elicited significantly different responses from low and high earners. For example, twice as many high earners as low earners were convinced that society as a whole benefits from the rich because the rich pay high taxes, and far more high earners than low earners thought the rich are intelligent, industrious, honest, and visionary. And high earners agreed far more strongly that managers should earn a lot more because they have a lot more responsibility and that companies can hire and retain the best managers only if they pay high salaries, because otherwise managers will go to another company that pays more or will work for themselves.

Overall, however, it is interesting to note that the differences between low and high earners in Great Britain were smaller than those in the other three countries.

ZERO-SUM BELIEVERS VIEW THE WORLD DIFFERENTLY

In Great Britain, neither age, income, gender, nor education levels showed numerical differences as great as those found in zero-sum believers versus non-zero-sum believers. Overall, these two groups approach numerical parity in British society. Thirty-six percent of British people adhered to the zero-sum belief ("the more the rich have, the less there is for the poor"), whereas 35 percent rejected it. Only 17 percent of Conservative voters were zero-sum believers versus 48 percent of Labour voters.

The zero-sum believers and their opponents see the world very differently (Figures 13.10 and 13.11).

Figure 13.10

Great Britain: Attitudes toward the rich and zero-sum beliefs I—Positive and neutral statements

Question: "Here is a list of things that people have said about rich people. Which, if any, of the statements on the list would you agree with?"

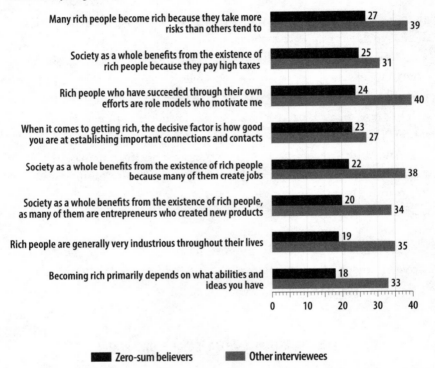

Many rich people become rich because they take more risks than others tend to — 27 / 39

Society as a whole benefits from the existence of rich people because they pay high taxes — 25 / 31

Rich people who have succeeded through their own efforts are role models who motivate me — 24 / 40

When it comes to getting rich, the decisive factor is how good you are at establishing important connections and contacts — 23 / 27

Society as a whole benefits from the existence of rich people because many of them create jobs — 22 / 38

Society as a whole benefits from the existence of rich people, as many of them are entrepreneurs who created new products — 20 / 34

Rich people are generally very industrious throughout their lives — 19 / 35

Becoming rich primarily depends on what abilities and ideas you have — 18 / 33

0   10   20   30   40

■ Zero-sum believers   ■ Other interviewees

Note: All data are in percentage of respondents.

As in our other three surveys, our findings in Great Britain demonstrate precisely how strongly people's attitudes toward the rich are determined by whether or not they are zero-sum believers. If you are looking for a simple test to find out what someone thinks of rich people across a wide spectrum of topics, you don't need to ask them about their income,

Figure 13.11

Great Britain: Attitudes toward the rich and zero-sum beliefs II—(Somewhat) negative statements

Question: "Here is a list of things that people have said about rich people. Which, if any, of the statements on the list would you agree with?"

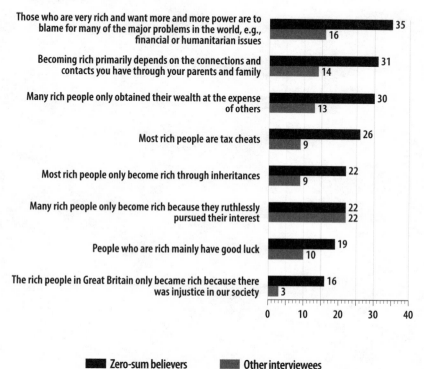

Zero-sum believers   Other interviewees

Note: All data are in percentage of respondents.

education, gender, or age. All you need to do is ask them whether they agree or disagree with the following statement: "The more the rich have, the less there is for the poor." Their answer to this question will allow you to predict with a high degree of accuracy their attitudes on a range of other wealth-related topics.

CHAPTER 14

FOUR NATIONS IN COMPARISON

In this chapter, we will see how levels of social envy differ in the four surveyed countries. The social envy coefficient, which was developed especially for this study, indicates the ratio of enviers to non-enviers in each country. A coefficient of 1.0 means that a country contains equal numbers of enviers and non-enviers. Where the coefficient is less than 1.0, the country has more non-enviers than enviers; where the coefficient is greater than 1.0, it has more enviers than non-enviers. As measured by the social envy coefficient, levels of social envy are highest in France, followed by Germany. Social envy is significantly lower in the United States and Great Britain (Figure 14.1).

The basis for determining the social envy coefficient is respondents' answers to the three statements presented in Tables 14.1, 14.2, and 14.3, which compare the responses from interviewees in each of the four countries.

Table 14.1 shows that although in all four countries at least a plurality of respondents supported the statement on increased taxes on the rich, the gap between those who agreed and disagreed in the United States is much smaller than that in Germany and France, which is probably related to the more skeptical attitudes toward taxation in the United States.

Table 14.2 clearly shows that French and German respondents were more critical of high manager salaries and more in favor of redistribution than were interviewees in the United States and Great Britain.

It is perhaps no coincidence that the word "schadenfreude," which has been so successfully adopted into English, has its origins in the

Figure 14.1

Social envy coefficient: Four-survey analysis

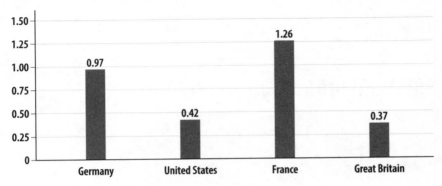

Sources: Allensbach Institute survey 11085, Ipsos MORI J18-031911-01-02.
Note: A coefficient greater than 1.0 indicates that enviers (levels 2 or 3 on the Social Envy Scale) outnumber non-enviers (level 0 on the Social Envy Scale). A coefficient of less than 1.0 indicates that non-enviers outnumber enviers.

German language: Germany is the only country in which the number of interviewees who agreed with the schadenfreude statement was (slightly) higher than those who disagreed, as shown in Table 14.3.

For the purpose of this study, the interviewees who did not agree with any of these three statements are classified as "non-enviers," and those who agreed with one of the three statements are classified as "ambivalents." The term "envier" refers to interviewees who agreed with two or three of the statements, a subgroup that also encompasses "hardcore enviers,"

Table 14.1

Increased taxes on the rich—Four-country analysis

"I think it would be fair to increase taxes substantially for millionaires, even if I would not benefit from it personally."

	Agree (%)	Disagree (%)	Difference (% points)
Germany	65	23	42
United States	47	28	19
France	61	20	41
Great Britain	50	22	28

Sources: Allensbach Institute survey 11085, Ipsos MORI J18-031911-01-02.

Table 14.2

Attitudes in all four countries toward managers' salaries

"I would favor drastically reducing managers' salaries and redistributing the money more evenly among their employees, even if that would mean that [the employees] would get only a few more dollars per month."

	Agree (%)
Germany	46
United States	31
France	54
Great Britain	29

Sources: Allensbach Institute survey 11085, Ipsos MORI J18-031911-01-02.

who agreed with all three statements.[488] The social envy coefficient is the ratio between the group of enviers and the group of non-enviers.

Because the same questions were asked in all four countries, we have a good basis for comparison. You can see that the results in the two Anglophone countries were almost identical and that the results in France and Germany were similar (Figure 14.2).

In each of the four countries, a correlation exists between whether an interviewee personally knows a millionaire and the interviewee's opinions of the rich. In the two countries with low social envy coefficients, a far greater proportion of respondents reported personally knowing one or more millionaires—as either family members, friends, friends of friends, or social contacts—than in the countries with higher social

Table 14.3

Schadenfreude—Four-country analysis

"When I hear about a millionaire who made a risky business decision and lost a lot of money because of it, I think it serves him right."

	Agree (%)	Disagree (%)	Difference (% points)
Germany	40	37	+3 approval
United States	28	29	+1 rejection
France	33	41	+8 rejection
Great Britain	22	38	+16 rejection

Sources: Allensbach Institute survey 11085, Ipsos MORI J18-031911-01-02.

Figure 14.2

Breakdown of interviewees by position on the Social Envy Scale—Four-survey analysis

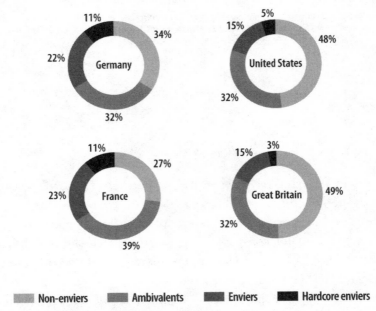

Sources: Allensbach Institute survey 11085, Ipsos MORI J18-031911-01-02.
Note: All data in percentage of respondents. Percentages do not add up to 100 in all cases because of rounding.

envy coefficients. In the United States and Great Britain, where enviers were significantly less common, far more interviewees reported being personally acquainted with one or more millionaires than was the case in Germany and France, where enviers were more common (Figure 14.3).

Note also that the relative proportion of millionaires in the total population is highest in the two countries with the lowest Social Envy Scale scores, namely, the United States and Great Britain, at 13.5 and 12.2 millionaires per thousand people, respectively (Table 14.4).[489] Unsurprisingly, these two countries have the largest percentages of interviewees who claim to personally know a millionaire.

In Germany, however, although the proportion of millionaires in the population is just under 3 per 1,000 fewer than in Great Britain (9.4 versus 12.2, respectively), the proportion of Germans who said they personally know at least one millionaire was only about half as large as that of Great Britain. Compared with British millionaires, German millionaires

Figure 14.3

Personal contact with millionaires—Four-survey analysis

"I personally know one or more millionaires."

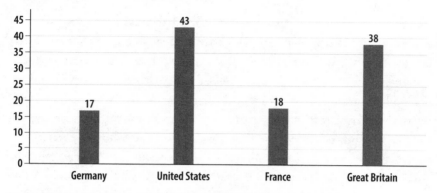

Sources: Allensbach Institute survey 11085; Ipsos MORI J18-031911-01-02.
Note: All data are in percentage of respondents.

are perhaps less likely to identify themselves as such or are more likely to adopt lower-profile lifestyles in order to not flaunt their wealth. This would explain why, despite the fact that the proportion of millionaires is only slightly lower than in Great Britain, Germans were much less likely to say that they personally know a millionaire. Another explanation

Table 14.4

Millionaires and the general population—Four-country analysis

	Number of millionaires (in U.S. dollars, 2016)	Population (2016/2017)	Millionaires per 1,000 inhabitants
Germany	774,600	82,700,000	9.4
United States	4,389,000	325,700,000	13.5
France	290,700	67,200,000	4.3
Great Britain	802,800	66,000,000	12.2

Sources: Number of millionaires: Knight Frank Research, "The Wealth Report 2017," p. 67, https://content.knightfrank.com/research/83/documents/en/the-wealth-report-2017-4482.pdf. Population figures: Germany: Federal Statistical Office (*Statistisches Bundesamt*), https://www.destatis.de/DE/ZahlenFakten/GesellschaftStaat/Bevoelkerung/Bevoelkerungsstand/Bevoelkerungsstand.html; France: Institut National de la statistique et les études économiques, https://www.insee.fr/en/accueil; Great Britain: Office for National Statistics, https://www.ons.gov.uk/peoplepopulationandcommunity/populationandmigration/populationestimates/timeseries/ukpop/pop; United States: U.S. Census Bureau, https://factfinder.census.gov/faces/tableservices/jsf/pages/productview.xhtml?src=bkmk#.

could be that German millionaires are more isolated from the rest of society than are British millionaires.

Germans and Enviers Are More Susceptible to Scapegoating

As shown in Chapter 6, prejudice research has presented a great deal of evidence confirming that minorities are scapegoated for crises and other humanitarian issues around the world. Particularly with regard to economic and financial crises, the causes of which are very complex and are not understood by most people, the general tendency is to blame scapegoats ("greedy bankers," "the superrich," and others). Interviewees in each of the four countries were presented with the following statement: *"Those who are very rich and want more and more power are to blame for many of the major problems in the world, e.g., financial or humanitarian issues."* The following percentages of interviewees agreed:

- United States: 25 percent
- Great Britain: 21 percent
- Germany: 50 percent
- France: 33 percent

In Germany, almost twice as many interviewees agreed with this statement than in Great Britain or the United States. This finding suggests that it would be easier in Germany to exploit preexisting hostility toward rich people in times of severe economic upheaval and that German politicians would be more likely to target rich people than would politicians in Anglophone countries.

Enviers in particular are extremely susceptible to scapegoating, which, incidentally, once again confirms the accuracy of the Social Envy Scale in distinguishing between enviers and non-enviers.

The comparison in Figure 14.4 shows that enviers are far more inclined to scapegoating than non-enviers, with the greatest differences between the two groups registered in the United States and in Great Britain.

Our data also show that respondents in all four countries who agreed with the scapegoating question were far more likely to be zero-sum believers. The statement "The more the rich have, the less is left for the poor" met with approval from 60 percent of scapegoaters in Germany, 65 percent in the United States, 69 percent in France, and 57 percent

Figure 14.4

Tendency to scapegoat—Four-country analysis

"Those who are very rich and want more and more power are to blame for many of the major problems in the world, e.g., financial or humanitarian issues."

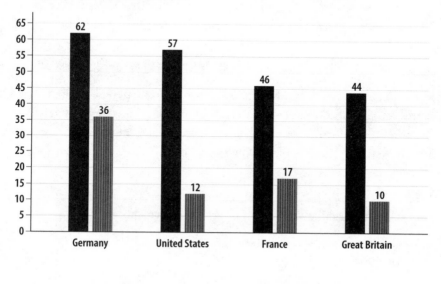

Enviers agreeing   Non-enviers agreeing

Sources: Allensbach Institute survey 11085; Ipsos MORI J18-031911-01-02.
Note: All data are in percentage of respondents. Percentages do not add up to 100 in all cases because of rounding.

in Great Britain. In contrast, non–scapegoaters were less likely to agree: only 35 percent in Germany, 24 percent in the United States, 41 percent in France, and 30 percent in Great Britain.

Scapegoaters and non-scapegoaters also have very different views of the personality traits of the rich. For example, scapegoaters were more likely to think the rich are greedy than non-scapegoaters: Germany (65 percent versus 34 percent), the United States (60 percent versus 22 percent), France (36 percent versus 12 percent), and Great Britain (39 percent versus 17 percent).

The statement "Many rich people only obtained their wealth at the expense of others" met with approval from 52 percent of scapegoaters in Germany, 61 percent in the United States, 37 percent in France, and 46 percent in Great Britain, compared with only 19 percent, 14 percent, 18 percent, and 11 percent of non-scapegoaters, respectively.

Scapegoaters in all four countries were also more likely to agree that you have to be careful not to criticize Jews in public, a view shared by 70 percent of scapegoaters in Germany, 49 percent in the United States, 60 percent in France, and 63 percent in Great Britain. The percentages of non-scapegoaters in the four countries who shared this view were 57 percent, 40 percent, 53 percent, and 45 percent, respectively.

DIFFERENCES BETWEEN YOUNGER AND OLDER INTERVIEWEES IN THE FOUR COUNTRIES

In the previous chapters, I have shown that younger people in the United States are far more critical of the rich than are older people, whereas in the three European countries, the opposite is true. Figure 14.5 contains a more detailed analysis of this phenomenon.

Figure 14.5
Envy in the four countries—Four-survey analysis by age group

Index of enviers (2 or 3 points on the Social Envy Scale)
Index value: Population as a whole = 100

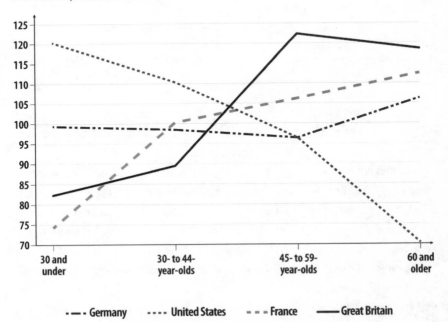

Sources: Allensbach Institute survey 11085; Ipsos MORI J18-031911-01-02.

Figure 14.6

The rich as role models—Analysis by nationality and age group

"Rich people who have succeeded through their own efforts are role models who motivate me."

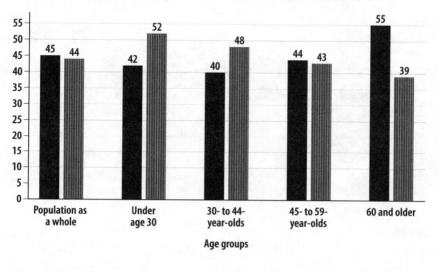

Sources: Allensbach Institute survey 11085; Ipsos MORI J18-031911-01-02.
Note: All data are in percentages of respondents in agreement.

Differences between the generations are evident from the interviewees' responses to many of the survey's questions, including whether rich people are motivating role models (Figure 14.6). Younger German (and French) interviewees agreed with this statement far more frequently than did their older compatriots, whereas in the United States, the reverse was true.

The most confrontational statement presented to the interviewees was "Rich people are good at earning money, but are not usually decent people." In all four countries, pluralities of both younger and older interviewees disagreed with this statement—with one exception. In the United States, a clear majority of young Americans thought that the rich are not usually decent people. At the same time, no other subgroup rejected this statement as strongly as older Americans (Table 14.5). The difference in disagreement or agreement with this statement between younger and older Americans is 52 percentage points. In Great Britain, the difference

Table 14.5

The compensation theory: Differences in age by country

"Rich people are good at earning money, but are not usually decent people": Percentage agreement/ disagreement of younger and older interviewees

	Agree (%)	Disagree (%)	Difference (% points)
Germany			
Younger (16–29)	31	46	+15 rejection
Older (60+)	32	48	+16 rejection
United States			
Younger (18–29)	40	23	+17 approval
Older (60+)	15	50	+35 rejection
France			
Younger (16–29)	17	39	+22 rejection
Older (60+)	25	42	+17 rejection
Great Britain			
Younger (16–29)	20	36	+16 rejection
Older (60+)	15	47	+32 rejection

Sources: Allensbach Institute survey 11085; Ipsos MORI J18-031911-01-02.

in disagreement between younger and older interviewees is 16 percentage points in favor of older interviewees, and little difference existed between younger and older interviewees in Germany and in France.

In Great Britain and Germany, older interviewees more so than younger interviewees favored drastically cutting very high manager salaries and redistributing the surpluses to employees even if the employees would end up with only a few more pounds or euros per month (Table 14.6). The United States is the only country in which this idea gained significantly greater approval among younger respondents than among older respondents.

Zero-sum beliefs were also rejected by a clear majority of older Americans, in sharp contrast to the large majority of younger Americans who believed that one person's gain is always another person's loss (Table 14.7). In Great Britain, younger interviewees were also more inclined to hold zero-sum beliefs than were older interviewees, although the difference was much smaller than in the United States. In Germany,

Table 14.6

Attitudes toward managers' salaries by country and age

"I would favor drastically reducing those managers' salaries and redistributing the money more evenly among their employees, even if that would mean that [the employees] would only get a few more dollars [euros, pounds] per month."

	Agree (%)	Difference (% points)
Germany		
Younger (16–29)	41	
Older (60+)	48	+7 older
United States		
Younger (18–29)	38	
Older (60+)	28	+10 younger
France		
Younger (16–29)	54	
Older (60+)	52	+2 younger
Great Britain		
Younger (16–29)	28	
Older (60+)	31	+3 older

Sources: Allensbach Institute survey 11085, Ipsos MORI J18-031911-01-02.

however, there was no difference in opinion between younger and older interviewees. And in France, older interviewees held much stronger zero-sum beliefs than did younger interviewees.

An analysis of the Social Envy Scale by country and age group shows that in Great Britain, Germany, and France, the proportion of enviers under age 30 was slightly lower than the proportion in the population as a whole. In the United States, the proportion of enviers under age 30 was higher than in the population as a whole. Consequently, the proportion of non-enviers in that group was lower. Among older Americans (60+), the proportion of enviers was lower than in the population as a whole.

Notwithstanding these findings, the proportion of younger people in all four countries who said that it is important for them personally to be rich or to become rich was significantly higher than the corresponding proportion of older people (Table 14.8).

Table 14.7

Zero-sum beliefs among younger and older interviewees

"The more the rich have, the less there is for the poor."

	Agree (%)	Disagree (%)	Difference (% points)
Germany			
Younger (16–29)	50	44	+6 approval
Older (60+)	49	43	+6 approval
United States			
Younger (18–29)	45	29	+16 approval
Older (60+)	24	53	+29 rejection
France			
Younger (16–29)	43	32	+11 approval
Older (60+)	57	28	+29 approval
Great Britain			
Younger (16–29)	45	27	+18 approval
Older (60+)	29	40	+11 rejection

Sources: Allensbach Institute survey 11085; Ipsos MORI J18-031911-01-02.

Table 14.8

Subjective importance of being rich by age and country

"For some people, it is important to be rich. How important, if at all, is it for you personally to be rich?"

Countries	Important to be rich (%)
Younger (Under age 30)	
Germany	32
United States	39
France	35
Great Britain	32
Older (60+)	
Germany	14
United States	18
France	28
Great Britain	12

Sources: Allensbach Institute survey 11085; Ipsos MORI J18-031911-01-02.

DIFFERENCES BETWEEN MEN AND WOMEN

The desire to be rich is more prevalent among men than among women in all four countries (Table 14.9).

A more nuanced picture emerges when the Social Envy Scale is used to analyze the variations between male and female interviewees in all four countries:

Germany: Women Are More Envious Than Men

Social envy is slightly more pronounced among German women than it is among German men. Although women accounted for 51 percent of all German respondents, they represented 57 percent of enviers (i.e., those who gave two or three affirmative responses to the three envy statements). The proportion of women among the non-envier group was 45 percent. In contrast, 49 percent of interviewees were male, but men represented 55 percent of non-enviers.

Table 14.9

Subjective importance of being rich by gender and country

"For some people, it is important to be rich. How important, if at all, is it for you personally to be rich?"

Countries	Important to be rich (%)
Men	
Germany	26
United States	35
France	30
Great Britain	22
Women	
Germany	18
United States	24
France	24
Great Britain	15

Sources: Allensbach Institute survey 11085; Ipsos MORI J18-031911-01-02.

United States: Men Are More Envious Than Women

In the United States, social envy is less prevalent among women than among men. Of the survey's American respondents, 51 percent were women, and women composed 44 percent of the envier subgroup. In contrast, the proportion of male respondents was 49 percent, but men represented 56 percent of enviers.

France: Women Are More Envious Than Men

In France, social envy is somewhat stronger among women than among men. Although 52 percent of the French survey's respondents were female, women made up 57 percent of the envier subgroup. Men represented 48 percent of all respondents but 43 percent of enviers.

Great Britain: Men Are More Envious Than Women

In Great Britain, social envy is moderately lower among women than among men. Of the British survey's respondents, 51 percent were female, but women represented 47 percent of enviers. Men accounted for 49 percent of respondents but 53 percent of enviers. Regression analysis revealed that the correlation between gender and envy is stronger in Great Britain than in any of the other three countries. Of all variables, gender—followed by zero-sum belief—has the greatest explanatory power for determining where an individual British interviewee ranks on the Social Envy Scale.

DIFFERENCES BY EDUCATION

As a rule, less-educated interviewees were more critical of the rich than were the better educated. Combining the figures for all four countries, less-educated interviewees more frequently agreed that "rich people are good at earning money, but are not usually decent people" than did better-educated respondents (Table 14.10). In France and in the United States, the number of less-educated respondents who agreed that the rich are not usually decent people exceeded the number of such respondents who disagreed. Among the better educated in both countries, the opposite was true. In Great Britain, a larger proportion of better-educated

Table 14.10

Compensation theory by education and country

"Rich people are good at earning money, but are not usually decent people."

	Agree (%)	Disagree (%)	Difference (% points)
Germany			
Less educated	39	40	+1 rejection
Better educated	21	60	+39 rejection
United States			
Less educated	30	29	+1 approval
Better educated	28	36	+8 rejection
France			
Less educated	36	30	+6 approval
Better educated	14	48	+34 rejection
Great Britain			
Less educated	17	32	+15 rejection
Better educated	14	46	+32 rejection

Sources: Allensbach Institute survey 11085; Ipsos MORI J18-031911-01-02.

interviewees than of the less educated rejected the statement (i.e., they rejected the claim that the rich are not usually decent people). Calculating the percentage point difference between approval and rejection of this statement in the four countries reveals that, on average, rejection is 2 percentage points higher than approval among the less educated and 28 percentage points higher among the better educated.

The same differences are also evident in relation to zero-sum beliefs. The statement that "the more the rich have, the less there is for the poor" elicited more agreement than disagreement from the less educated in all four countries surveyed, with an overwhelming majority agreeing in France and only a very narrow majority agreeing in the United States (Table 14.11). In contrast, better-educated interviewees in Germany and (albeit very narrowly) in the United States rejected this statement; in France, a narrow majority of the better educated agreed; and in Great Britain, equal proportions of better educated interviewees expressed agreement and disagreement.

Table 14.11

Zero-sum thinking by education and country

"The more the rich have, the less there is for the poor."

	Agree (%)	Disagree (%)	Difference (% points)
Germany			
Less educated	51	40	+11 approval
Better educated	43	49	+6 rejection
United States			
Less educated	34	32	+2 approval
Better educated	38	39	+1 rejection
France			
Less educated	67	21	+46 approval
Better educated	41	36	+5 approval
Great Britain			
Less educated	37	26	+11 approval
Better educated	36	36	

Sources: Allensbach Institute survey 11085; Ipsos MORI J18-031911-01-02.

Taking into account the percentage point difference between agreement and disagreement in all four countries, the less educated were, on average, 17.5 percentage points more likely to subscribe to zero-sum beliefs than to reject them, compared with a difference of just -0.5 percentage point among better-educated interviewees. What is striking, however, is how pronounced zero-sum beliefs are in France. A very large majority of less-educated French interviewees believed that one person's gain is automatically another person's loss, and a narrow majority of the better educated also viewed life as a zero-sum game.

In Germany, the clearest difference between the less educated and the better educated relates to schadenfreude. A clear majority of less-educated Germans replied that it serves a millionaire right when he loses a lot of money because of a risky business decision (Table 14.12). In contrast, better-educated Germans clearly rejected this statement. In France, a narrow majority of the less educated said yes to this schadenfreude question, where-as a clear majority of the better educated did not. And in Great Britain,

Table 14.12

Schadenfreude by education and country

"When I hear about a millionaire who made a risky business decision and lost a lot of money because of it, I think it serves him right."

	Agree (%)	Disagree (%)	Difference (% points)
Germany			
Less educated	50	28	+22 approval
Better educated	30	48	+18 rejection
United States			
Less educated	19	30	+11 rejection
Better educated	35	28	+7 approval
France			
Less educated	39	37	+2 approval
Better educated	29	45	+16 rejection
Great Britain			
Less educated	24	31	+7 rejection
Better educated	22	40	+18 rejection

Sources: Allensbach Institute survey 11085; Ipsos MORI J18-031911-01-02.

the better educated were far more likely to reject the notion of anti-wealth schadenfreude than were the less educated. The only exception was the United States, where the better educated were more likely to gloat over rich people's failures than were the less educated, in stark contrast to the three European countries. This may be because a disproportionately large number of better-educated Americans are young—and, as we have seen, younger Americans (unlike their European peers) are more critical of the rich.

WHO DESERVES TO BE RICH—AND WHO DOESN'T

In all four countries, the survey's respondents were asked the following question: *"Which, if any, of the following groups of people do you personally believe deserve to be rich?"* Table 14.13 presents a comparison of the results.

In all four countries, entrepreneurs and self-employed people were at the forefront, although interviewees also thought that creative people (such as actors, musicians, and artists), top athletes, and lottery winners

Table 14.13

Who deserves their wealth?

	Germany	United States	France	Great Britain
1	Self-employed people	Entrepreneurs	Self-employed people	Entrepreneurs
2	Entrepreneurs	Self-employed people	Entrepreneurs	Self-employed people
3	Lottery winners	Creative people and artists, such as actors or musicians	Creative people and artists, such as actors and musicians	Creative people and artists, such as actors or musicians
4	Creative people and artists, such as actors or musicians	Property investors Lottery winners (tie)	Lottery winners	Lottery winners
5	Top athletes	Financial investors	Senior-level managers	Top athletes
6	Heirs		Top athletes	Financial investors

Sources: Allensbach Institute survey 11085; Ipsos MORI J18-031911-01-02.
Note: Order of the most frequently mentioned groups in the four countries, who, according to the inteviewees, deserve their wealth.

deserve to be rich. Financial investors, who appear in the top six in the United States and in Great Britain, come in second to last in Germany and are also far behind in France.

SURVEY RESPONSES: THE RICH ARE RUTHLESS AND ARROGANT, BUT ALSO INDUSTRIOUS, INTELLIGENT, AND DARING

What personality traits do people in the four countries associate with the rich? When asked which traits are most likely to apply to rich people, the most frequent answers were as shown in Table 14.14.[490]

Of the six most frequently mentioned personality traits, five were negative in Germany and four were positive in Great Britain and in the United States. In France, positive and negative traits were evenly balanced.

In all four countries, "honesty" was the personality trait least frequently attributed to rich people. The percentage of interviewees in each country who described rich people as "honest" was as follows:

- Germany: 3 percent
- United States: 8 percent
- France: 7 percent
- Great Britain: 7 percent

Table 14.14

Personality traits attributed to the rich by country

	Germany	United States	France	Great Britain
1	Self-centered	Intelligent	Industrious	Materialistic Industrious (tie)
2	Materialistic	Materialistic	Intelligent	Intelligent
3	Ruthless	Industrious	Materialistic	Bold, daring
4	Greedy	Bold, daring	Arrogant Bold, daring (tie)	Ruthless
5	Arrogant	Arrogant	Ruthless	Imaginative
6	Industrious	Visionary		

Sources: Allensbach Institute survey 11085; Ipsos MORI J18-031911-01-02.
Note: Order of the most frequently cited personality traits of rich people in the four countries.

Figure 14.7

Number of most frequently mentioned positive and negative personality traits of the rich—Four-survey analysis

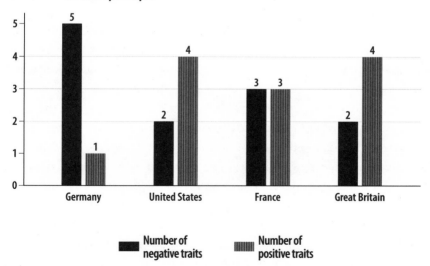

Sources: Allensbach Institute survey 11085; Ipsos MORI J18-031911-01-02.

The research findings presented in Chapter 7 show that judgments of "moral traits" (M traits) generally play a greater role in forming impressions of out-groups than do judgments of "competence traits" (C traits). As we have already seen, the attribution of competence traits but not moral traits to out-groups has far-reaching consequences. We know from perception research that our impressions of other people and of out-groups generally rely more on moral traits than on competence traits. It has been shown that, as a rule, morality-related information plays a more important role in perception than does competence-related information. Researchers have demonstrated that morality and competence are the two key factors in determining our perceptions of out-groups. Some three-quarters of our perceptions are determined by these two components.[491]

An experiment conducted by Bogdan Wojciszke, Róża Bazinska, and Marcin Jaworski measured whether impressions of out-groups are based more on categorizations related to "morality" (e.g., honesty) or on those related to "competence" (e.g., intelligence). Their findings confirmed that six of the top seven traits that people use to form global impressions of other people are morality traits and that only one is a competence trait. "Judgments of M traits emerged as a relatively better predictor of global impression than judgments of specific C traits."[492]

The positive traits most frequently attributed to rich people in our surveys were all competence traits, particularly intelligence and industriousness. The most frequently attributed negative traits, namely arrogance and self-centeredness, were all moral traits, as was the most infrequently attributed trait of all, honesty. Someone who is intelligent, industrious, bold, and daring but is also ruthless, arrogant, self-centered, and dishonest represents a threat; in contrast, someone with the opposite traits—unintelligent, lazy, and cowardly but honest, good-natured, and altruistic—would be harmless. And because positive or negative impressions of others are based more on moral traits than on competence traits, it helps the rich little if they are perceived as intelligent and industrious but also as ruthless and dishonest. Such a combination may even contribute to mechanistic dehumanization responses, as discussed in Chapter 3.

How Envious and Non-Envious People View the Rich: Analysis by Country

Enviers and non-enviers differ vastly in their opinions of rich people, and the accuracy of the Social Envy Scale in distinguishing between the two groups is evident from their attributions of personality traits to the rich.

Table 14.15 presents the personality traits most frequently attributed to the rich by enviers (those who agreed with two or three of the three envy statements).

Only 2 of the 25 traits mentioned by enviers were positive—industrious and bold or daring—compared with 23 that were negative. Among enviers in all four countries, honesty was the least frequently mentioned personality trait: only 3 percent of enviers in Germany, 8 percent in the United States, 6 percent in France, and 5 percent in Great Britain believed that rich people are honest. The traits attributed most frequently to the rich by non-enviers (those who agreed with none of the envy statements) are shown in Table 14.16. Only 5 of the 24 traits mentioned by non-enviers were negative, whereas 19 were positive.

As with enviers, honesty was the trait mentioned least frequently by non-enviers in all four countries: 4 percent of non-enviers in Germany,

Table 14.15

Personality traits most frequently attributed to the rich by enviers

	Germany	United States	France	Great Britain
1	Self-centered	Greedy	Arrogant	Materialistic
2	Ruthless	Materialistic	Materialistic	Self-centered Ruthless Greedy (tie)
3	Materialistic	Self-centered Arrogant (tie)	Ruthless	Arrogant Industrious (tie)
4	Greedy	Superficial	Self-centered	
5	Arrogant	Ruthless	Cold-hearted	
6	Cold-hearted		Superficial Bold, daring (tie)	

Sources: Allensbach Institute survey 11085; Ipsos MORI J18-031911-01-02.
Note: Order of personality traits most frequently attributed to the rich by enviers in the four countries.

Table 14.16

Personality traits most frequently attributed to the rich by non-enviers

	Germany	United States	France	Great Britain
1	Industrious	Intelligent	Industrious	Industrious
2	Visionary	Industrious	Intelligent	Intelligent
3	Self-centered	Visionary	Bold, daring Visionary (tie)	Bold, daring
4	Materialistic Intelligent (tie)	Bold, daring	Imaginative	Imaginative
5	Bold, daring	Imaginative	Materialistic	Materialistic
6		Materialistic		Visionary

Sources: Allensbach Institute survey 11085; Ipsos MORI J18-031911-01-02.
Note: Order of personality traits most frequently attributed to the rich by non-enviers in the four countries.

8 percent in the United States, 8 percent in France, and 7 percent in Great Britain saw honesty as a trait they would apply to rich people.

HARD WORK AND DEDICATION OR SUPPLY AND DEMAND: WHAT DETERMINES MANAGERS' SALARIES?

If I were asked about the traits and characteristics that contribute most to the high incomes and wealth of the rich, I would personally rate factors such as "creativity" (for entrepreneurs) or "scarce/rare skills" (for top managers, top athletes, artists, etc.) far ahead of "industriousness."

The rich do work longer hours than the average population, so in this respect the respondents who viewed the rich as particularly "industrious" were right. In 2012, Melanie Böwing-Schmalenbrock surveyed 472 wealthy Germans (average net wealth €2.3 million, median €1.4 million)[493] and found that the rich work an average of 46 hours per week, compared with an average of 39 hours for the middle class. And those who have become rich through self-employment work an average of about 50 hours per week.[494] Therefore, rich people in Germany work, on average, 18 percent to 43 percent more per week than do members of the middle class. However, those extra hours alone cannot explain why the wealth of the interviewees in Böwing-Schmalenbrock's study was more than 40 times higher than the average wealth of the population as a whole.

From wealth research, we know that a majority of rich people became rich as entrepreneurs.[495] In many cases, they had outstanding business ideas and were particularly creative. Creativity, however, was not among the traits of the rich most frequently mentioned by our respondents—industriousness was mentioned far more frequently.

Given the fact that, as shown above, a clear majority of respondents in all four countries surveyed did not know a single millionaire personally, most respondents must have formed their image of the rich either from media depictions of the rich or by projecting their own experiences onto them. Consequently, to the average employee, earning more is a question of being more industrious, such as by working overtime. Personal experience teaches employees that the amount someone earns depends on how long and how hard they work. People with positive attitudes toward the rich may therefore assume that rich people are particularly industrious, whereas significantly fewer of those who are more critical of the rich—as our survey's findings demonstrate—consider the rich to be particularly industrious.

Respondents' attitudes toward rich people are strongly influenced by their assumptions regarding the key factors that determine an individual's income. This effect can be seen in the opinions expressed by the interviewees about managers' salaries. The level of a manager's salary is not determined, as one may suppose, by the number of hours he or she works, but by supply and demand in the market for top-tier managerial talent. However, most people don't recognize this connection, especially not low earners, as our survey data indicate. In all four countries, respondents were presented with the following two statements:

- Statement A: *"I think it is inappropriate for managers to earn so much more [based on the example of managers who earn 100 times more than their employees], as they do not work so much longer and harder than their employees."*
- Statement B: *"Companies can only hire and retain the best managers if they pay salaries of this kind [based on the example of managers who earn 100 times more than their employees], otherwise these managers will go to another company that pays more or they will work for themselves."*

Statement A implies that salaries are ultimately determined, or should be determined, by how hard and long someone works, and that very high salaries—that is, those not in direct proportion to extra effort—are "unfair." Statement B, on the other hand, assumes that supply and demand in the market for top-tier managers is the main determinant of a manager's salary.

As you can see in Figure 14.8, agreement with statement A prevails in all four countries, which implies that most respondents feel that working harder and longer should play a decisive role in determining an individual's salary. Table 14.17 shows how low earners and high earners differed in their responses to the two statements.

Figure 14.8

Attitudes toward high manager salaries in the four surveyed countries

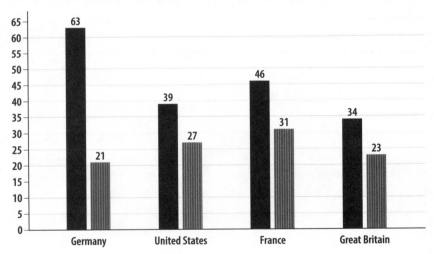

A. I think it is inappropriate for managers to earn so much more, as they do not work so much longer and harder than their employees.

B. Companies can only hire and retain the best managers if they pay salaries of this kind, otherwise these managers will go to another company that pays more or they will work for themselves.

Sources: Allensbach Institute survey 11085; Ipsos MORI J18-031911-01-02.
Note: All data are in percentages of respondents.

Table 14.17

Difference in agreement with statements A and B between lowest- and highest-income groups

	Agreement with A (%)	Agreement with B (%)	Difference (% points)
Germany			
Lowest income	69	16	+53 approval
Highest income	63	28	+35 approval
United States			
Lowest income	42	22	+20 approval
Highest income	35	40	+5 rejection
France			
Lowest income	53	25	+28 approval
Highest income	45	44	+1 approval
Great Britain			
Lowest income	37	17	+20 approval
Highest income	46	35	+11 approval

Sources: Allensbach Institute survey 11085; Ipsos MORI J18-031911-01-02.

The differences in perspective according to income become clear when we calculate the average variation in agreement with statements A and B in each of the four countries. The "industrious" statement elicits far more agreement from low earners than does the statement alluding to supply and demand:

- 29 percentage point difference in favor of industriousness among low earners
- 20 percentage point difference in favor of industriousness among the population as a whole
- 10 percentage point difference in favor of supply and demand among higher earners

Far more respondents in the lower-income groups appear to believe, perhaps from personal experience, that working harder and longer has a direct effect on all incomes (more overtime = higher wages), and thus they agree with statement A. In contrast, respondents in higher–income groups appear to have learned, either directly or from their friends and family, that it is not only working longer and harder but also possessing the scarce skills that meet supply and demand in the market, which determine salaries and remuneration. As a result, higher earners are much more likely than lower earners to endorse statement B.

Having both an "employee mindset" and an understanding of the laws of supply and demand in the market for top-tier managers are not mutually exclusive, as demonstrated by the fact that some of our respondents agreed with both statement A and statement B. Nevertheless, it is clear that respondents who agreed with statement A generally have a very different way of thinking than do respondents who endorsed statement B: respondents who

Figure 14.9

United States: Correlation between entrepreneurial and employee mindsets I

(In percent)

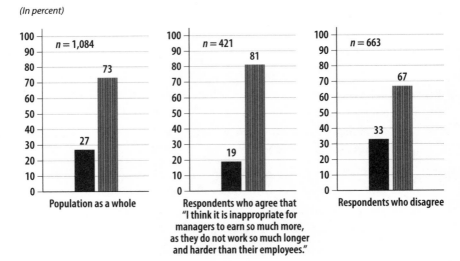

Respondents who agree that "Companies can only hire and retain the best managers if they pay salaries of this kind, otherwise these managers will go to another company that pays more or they will work for themselves."

Respondents who disagree

Source: Ipsos MORI J18-031911-01-02.

Figure 14.10

United States: Correlation between entrepreneurial and employee mindsets II

(In percent)

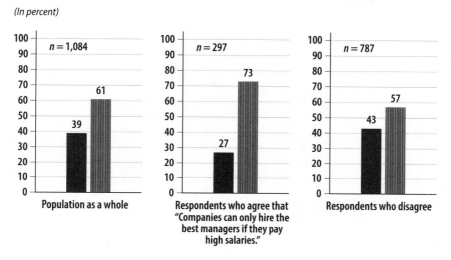

Respondents who agree that "I think it is inappropriate for managers to earn so much more as they do not work so much longer and harder than their employees."

Respondents who disagree

Source: Ipsos MORI J18-031911-01-02.

are inclined to an "employee mindset" and agreed with statement A are less likely than other respondents (19 percent versus 33 percent) to agree that companies can only hire and retain the best managers if they pay very high salaries. Also, having an "employee mindset," on the one hand, and understanding the laws of supply and demand in the market for senior-level managers, on the other, are not entirely mutually exclusive; respondents who agreed with statement A less frequently agree with statement B, and vice versa. Respondents who understand that companies can only hire and retain the most talented managers if they pay very high salaries are significantly less likely to have an "employee mindset" than are those who do not (27 percent versus 43 percent).

The correlations between the responses to the two statements in Germany are similar to those found in the United States. The differences in response behavior in France and Great Britain point in the same direction as those in the United States and Germany, but they are much weaker.

PART THREE

Media Representations of the Rich

CHAPTER 15

THE RICH IN THE MEDIA: EXECUTIVE PAY, BANKERS' BONUSES, AND THE GAP BETWEEN RICH AND POOR

In Chapter 10, we saw that 80 percent of Germans said they could not name a single millionaire among their relatives or acquaintances. And only 8 percent actually knew more than one millionaire. Nevertheless, almost everyone has strongly held opinions about millionaires—and most of them, as we found in the surveys, are negative. We have seen that people who have personal contact with millionaires had far more positive perceptions of rich people than did those who do not report personally knowing any millionaires.

On the one hand, people's opinions are shaped by personal experience. On the other, opinions are also formed on the basis of media reports. This and the following chapters therefore deal with representations of the rich in the media. I will combine my own analyses with those of researchers who have specialized in systematically evaluating media using accepted scientific methods.

MEDIA CONTENT ANALYSIS BY MCT MEDIENAGENTUR

The company mct Medienagentur conducted a content analysis of 582 news articles published between April 25, 2001, and March 28, 2018. Its analysis focused on the following subjects:

- Coverage of managers' salaries and severance payments
- Articles on bankers' bonuses

- Coverage of the German government's poverty and wealth reports
- Coverage of the billionaires' Giving Pledge campaign
- Reports on discussions surrounding Thomas Piketty's book *Capital in the Twenty-First Century*
- Articles on the Panama Papers, as discussed in Chapter 16
- Articles on the Paradise Papers, as discussed in Chapter 16

Researchers at mct Medienagentur analyzed two major German national daily newspapers, *Frankfurter Allgemeine Zeitung (FAZ)* and *Süddeutsche Zeitung*; two national weekly news magazines, *Der Spiegel* and *Stern*; and three regional newspapers, western Germany's *Rheinische Post*, southern Germany's *Nürnberger Nachrichten*, and eastern Germany's *Sächsische Zeitung* (Table 15.1).

Six of the seven analyzed topics also featured prominently in the American, British, and French media, as confirmed by random samples of several thousand articles. As the following chapter demonstrates, some 400 journalists from 100 media outlets in 80 different countries reported on the Panama Papers and the Paradise Papers. Leading

Table 15.1

Analyzed media

Title, percentage of articles	Circulation (Q1 2018)	Notes
Frankfurter Allgemeine Zeitung: 20	263,904	Second-largest quality national newspaper
Süddeutsche Zeitung: 33	369,607	Largest quality national newspaper
Der Spiegel: 4	803,133	Largest German news magazine
Stern: 5	664,192	Second-largest German news magazine
Nürnberger Nachrichten: 11	254,365	Largest regional newspaper in Bavaria
Rheinische Post: 18	285,753	Second-largest regional newspaper in Germany
Sächsische Zeitung: 10	215,664	Second-largest regional newspaper in Saxony

Sources: mct Medienagentur, "Stereotypes of the Rich," July 2018. Circulation information is from IVW Digital, http://www.ivw.eu.
Note: Based on 582 articles.

newspapers and magazines in the United States, Great Britain, and France have also been extremely critical in their coverage of managers' salaries, bankers' bonuses, and increasing inequality. For our detailed analysis, however, we limited ourselves to representations of the rich in German media.

Using a specially developed codebook, mct Medienagentur analyzed the media's valence and slant when portraying rich people. "Valence" refers to the intrinsic attractiveness or averseness of an event, object, or situation. For example, reports on financial crime will always have a negative valence, regardless of how the journalist or the people quoted in the article personally evaluate the subject matter.

Valence is distinct from "slant," which refers to the bias a journalist gives to a report, for example, by including an explicitly personal evaluation of a situation or by giving preference to certain sources. Although valence and slant frequently align, this is not always the case, as we shall see.

The valence recorded by mct Medienagentur's analysis relates only to representations of the rich (Table 15.2). Thus, valence deals with whether an event that affects rich people would generally be regarded as positive or negative and with whether the resulting media coverage portrays rich people in a positive or a negative light. If something positive was reported as happening to a rich person, but it happened in a negative context, the valence would be coded as positive even if the coverage made it clear that many other people were negatively affected

Table 15.2

Character of the events in which rich people were represented (valence)

Valence	Percentage
Negative	59
Ambivalent	26
Positive	15
Total	100

Source: mct Medienagentur, "Stereotypes of the Rich," July 2018.
Note: Based on a sample of 290 articles.

Table 15.3

Evaluation of rich people (slant)

Slant	Percentage
Negative	79
Ambivalent	12
Positive	9
Total	100

Source: mct Medienagentur, "Stereotypes of the Rich," July 2018.
Note: Based on a sample of 170 articles.

by the same event or situation. The valence of media coverage of the rich was registered only when rich people were the subject of media coverage and something was reported as having a positive or negative effect on them (290 articles). The coverage was classed as ambivalent when the events affecting the rich were described as having roughly equal positive and negative aspects.

Assessments of slant in media representations of the rich are based on the statements in the analyzed articles that specifically referenced the rich (Table 15.3). Slant and valence can differ, for example, when a rich person is reported as concluding a profitable deal (positive valence) but a competitor (or a journalist, a politician, or another figure) accuses the individual of greed in the same article (negative slant). The slant of media coverage of rich people was only registered when the articles contained statements about the rich (170 articles). So, how often are valence and slant out of alignment, as described above, and how often do they correspond? Table 15.4. discusses the matter.

According to mct Medienagentur, a majority of articles dealing with rich people in a positive context nevertheless have a negative slant, thereby demonstrating that the overwhelmingly negative bias in these articles is not primarily due to the character of the events or situations being reported on. Rather, the negative bias often arises from value judgments made by journalists or the people they interview. To some degree, this finding is unsurprising in view of the widespread negative opinions that our surveys disclosed in Part Two.

Table 15.4

Relationship between valence and slant

	Valence			
	Negative, 84 articles	Ambivalent, 41 articles	Positive, 25 articles	Total, 150 articles
Slant	%	%	%	%
Negative	93	66	56	79
Ambivalent	7	29	4	13
Positive	0	5	40	8
Total	100	100	100	100

Source: mct Medienagentur, "Stereotypes of the Rich," July 2018.
Note: Based on a sample of 150 articles with both identifiable valence and identifiable slant. For example, 56 percent of the articles with a positive valence nevertheless had a negative slant.

A more detailed analysis reveals that this negative slant is equally pronounced in both informative articles, such as factual news reports, and opinion pieces, such as editorials and op-eds; the incidence of negative slant in each category stands at over 80 percent (Table 15.5). This finding would seem to contradict the assumption that negative representations of the rich in the media are most likely to be found in negative opinion pieces on events and situations that would otherwise be given more or less neutral coverage.

Table 15.5

Slant in media representations of the rich

	Genre			
	Informative 133 articles	Opinion 23 articles	Other 14 articles	Total 170 articles
Slant	%	%	%	%
Negative	81	83	57	79
Ambivalent	11	9	36	12
Positive	9	9	7	9
Total	101	101	100	100

Source: mct Medienagentur, "Stereotypes of the Rich," July 2018.
Note: Based on 170 articles with identifiable slant. Percentages do not add up to 100 in all cases because of rounding.

Table 15.6

Slant of subjective statements from politicians, journalists, and others

Slant	Responsible for the article's slant			Total 170 articles
	Author 116 articles	Politician 19 articles	Other 35 articles	
	%	%	%	%
Negative	83	90	60	79
Ambivalent	12	0	20	12
Positive	5	11	20	9
Total	100	101	100	100

Source: mct Medienagentur, "Stereotypes of the Rich," July 2018.
Note: Based on 170 articles with identifiable slant. Percentages do not add up to 100 in all cases because of rounding.

In addition to an article's slant, mct Medienagentur also analyzed who made the positive or negative statements about the rich and what role subjective judgments, both positive and negative, played into those statements (Table 15.6). The sources of such biased statements were assigned to three groups: (a) the author of the article, (b) a politician, and (c) another person (a scientist, business figure, journalist as expert, or other). Subjective statements made by politicians (90 percent) and the authors of the articles (83 percent) were particularly negative. The other sources were not quite as negative (60 percent).

The term "frame" refers to how the media present an event, a group, or a person. Frames influence how audiences perceive news events. The media often shape perceptions by emphasizing or understating certain information or by confirming or questioning its value or relevance. Frames provide readers with a field of meaning and suggest certain causal attributions and evaluations.

THE TAX AVOIDANCE FRAME

Tax avoidance was the subject of 176 analyzed articles. In 93 percent of those articles, readers were given the impression that the rich and the superrich typically avoid taxes, whether legally or illegally. In any case, the rich were singled out as politically and morally worthy of criticism. These articles focused mainly on the Panama Papers and the Paradise Papers, which are discussed in more detail in Chapter 16.

THE AVARICE FRAME

We coined the term "avarice frame" to describe articles that represent rich people as being interested only in money and ruthlessly pursuing ever-greater wealth. The avarice frame was documented in 76 of the articles analyzed by mct Medienagentur, equivalent to 13 percent of the articles. Of the articles that contained an avarice frame, an overwhelming majority presented allegations of avarice against the rich as well-founded: 75 percent of the 76 articles gave the impression that the rich were excessively greedy. Most of the avarice frames were found in articles on executive pay and bankers' bonuses, which are discussed in more detail below.

THE INEQUALITY FRAME

The inequality frame suggests that the extent of inequality within the society discussed by the article is constantly increasing. One-third of the articles analyzed by mct Medienagentur contained an inequality frame, thereby giving the impression that the gap between the rich and the poor is widening. This frame appeared especially in articles on the German government's poverty and wealth reports, the annual Oxfam reports, and discussions surrounding Piketty's book. These articles created the impression that inequality is extremely relevant (83 percent). For example, *Stern* magazine wrote about one of the Oxfam reports that "the gap between the rich and the poor is increasing, and poses a very real threat to global peace."[496]

"EXCESSIVE" EXECUTIVE PAY AND SEVERANCE PACKAGES

The articles analyzed by mct Medienagentur reported extensively on senior managers' salaries and severance packages (Figure 15.1). The dominant tenor of these articles was that both were too high and represented a serious problem.

Figure 15.1

Slant of articles on high manager salaries and severance payments

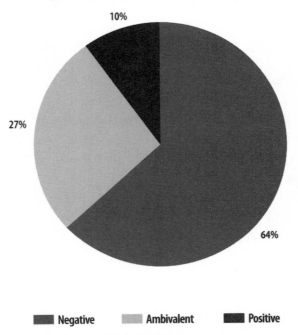

Source: mct Medienagentur, "Stereotypes of the Rich," July 2018.
Note: Based on a sample of 74 articles. Percentages do not add up to 100 because of rounding.

The analyzed articles frequently featured negative and highly emotive terms such as "greed," "gambling," "excess," "filling their pockets," and "obscene." In many cases, articles contained sweeping generalizations, such as referring to a prevailing and "increasing insatiability on the executive floors" or describing managers generally as "criminals."[497] The fact that German companies are extremely well positioned in international markets and that Germany is one of the world's leading exporters is easily lost among the reports of executive failures and greed. This imbalance is worthy of criticism, even when we allow for the fact that the media's job is to report on rare occurrences rather than common ones.

According to mct Medienagentur, about half (49 percent) of the articles that reported on very high senior managers' salaries did so in an extremely generalized manner. In *Stern* magazine, for instance, the editor in chief Hans-Ulrich Jörges wrote that "Germany's business leaders—ruthlessly and in blind ignorance of the consequences—have set social millstones in motion that will grind and crush any moderate political party that campaigns on issues of social equality. . . . Top managers behave as if they live on a different planet, beyond law and order. Business ethics? Swept away by greed, a slavish devotion to the bottom line and the arrogance of globalizers. Only nine percent of Germans still trust managers of large corporations."[498]

To some extent—as in this example—these statements are value judgments made by journalists themselves. In others, the assessments are provided by politicians or by other sources cited in the articles. The issue of senior managers' salaries is equally prominent across both national and regional media. In the period under study, for example, senior managers' salaries and severance payments were discussed in relation to a referendum against "fat cats" in Switzerland, calls from the center-left Social Democratic Party (SPD) and trade unions for caps on executive pay, and reports of very high salaries or severance payments for corporate board members.

A series of arguments have been put forward to justify the recurring accusations that managers' salaries are too high. Managers' salaries are frequently presented as multiples of regular employees' salaries. In February 2017, for example, *Rheinische Post* reported that the Hans Böckler Foundation, which is closely aligned with Germany's trade union movement, calculated that the senior executives of publicly traded corporations in Germany earned an average of 57 times more than their employees in 2014. The "worst performers" were Volkswagen and Deutsche Post, which had board members earning, respectively, 141 and 132 times more than an average employee.[499] The article quotes a highly critical union leader: "The astronomical figures of the past, with salaries in the tens of millions, are both socially unacceptable and impossible to justify if the principle of performance and responsibility is not to be taken ad absurdum as the yardstick for fair remuneration."[500]

When criticizing high manager salaries, the following eight main arguments appear again and again among the analyzed articles:

1. Journalists frequently cite extremely high salaries, despite the fact that only a very small number of German CEOs are actually paid such large amounts. The adjectives used, such as "astronomical," suggest that salaries of this magnitude are almost impossible for an average employee to comprehend. *Rheinische Post* quoted Karl-Josef Laumann, head of the CDA (Christian Democratic Workers' Association): "Every union representative with a seat on the supervisory board must know that it would take 200 years for his colleagues on the production line to earn a salary in the tens of millions."[501] Incidentally, this line of argument proves that curbs on executive pay would not prevent senior managers' salaries from being perceived as excessive: in this specific case, the criticism was directed at an executive compensation limit of €10 million for members of Volkswagen's Executive Management Board, which had been introduced with the argument that even higher remuneration would "be difficult to explain to people."

   A lengthy article in *Sächsische Zeitung* addressed the question "At what point do salaries become obscene?" Sums such as €17 million were referred to as being "so unimaginably high that they violate most people's sense of common justice on a fundamental level." The article's author asked whether such feelings may be an expression of pure envy before proceeding to give a lecture on the thoughts of the American philosopher John Rawls on the concept of "justice." The article concluded that "this outrage has nothing whatsoever to do with envy."[502]

2. Many articles argued that the gap between regular pay and executive pay has "widened significantly" in recent years.[503] Comparisons of managers' salaries and average incomes are a major feature of numerous articles. These comparisons are used to demonstrate the supposed injustice of managers' salaries.

Some articles, however, provided a platform for dissenting voices and space for a different frame of reference to assess whether managers' salaries are too high. An *FAZ* article from March 2018, for instance, pointed out that consolidated profits had risen even faster than executive pay the previous year. According to the article, the CEOs of Germany's top 30 publicly traded corporations saw their pay packages grow by 3.5 percent in 2017 compared with an increase in profits of 36 percent. Thus, the salary increases for top-tier executives would appear to be "moderate."[504] It is characteristic of the overall tenor of the discourse surrounding executive pay that this qualification was made only in relation to another, supposedly even greater grievance. The article conceded that the "spotlight of publicity . . . exerts a moderating influence on CEOs' greed" but went on to quote a remuneration consultant who said that "the greatest remuneration scandals still happen in the shadows." This quote was also used as the headline for the entire *FAZ* article. The "grievance" referred to is that, for example, investment bankers earn significantly more than the members of a bank's management board even if the bank as a whole incurs a loss.[505]

3. Such high salaries are claimed to bear no relation to managers' workloads and responsibilities. "Nobody can tell me that what a boss does is worth 300 times more than the work of their other employees," the head of the DGB (Federation of German Trade Unions), Michael Sommer, was quoted as saying.[506] The language frequently used in this context is especially revealing. After all, rather than using neutral language to refer to a board member *being paid* 300 times an average salary, for example, CEO salaries are discussed in relation to the fact that no CEO's work "is *worth* 300 times more than that of their other employees."

Stern magazine, for example, quoted the organizer of the Swiss "fat cat initiative," Marco Kistler, who called for managers' salaries to be capped at 12 times that of their lowest-paid staff. "It's not just about the sums themselves, but about the value you attach to your employees," Kistler was quoted as saying. "Is it right to say, 'Look, I'm worth 300 times more than you?'"[507] His choice of words insinuates that the value of a person is measured solely in terms of their pay.

Across the media, professors are cited as experts and are invited to comment on the severity of grievances surrounding executive pay. *Sächsische Zeitung* featured comments from Oxford political theory professor David Miller: "Differences in people's economic performance due to personal talents and effort are not so great as to justify very large inequalities of reward on the scale that we now see."[508] *Stern* magazine quoted German historian Hans-Ulrich Wehler: "Top managers have succeeded in increasing their incomes by 400 percent, they now earn 300 times as much as their skilled workers; in 1989, they earned 20 times a skilled worker's salary. . . . In modern history, no other class has lived out its greed with so little restraint." Wehler went on to describe current levels of executive pay as "obscene."[509]

4. It is also argued that such high salaries are impossible to "explain" to the public. Even before the diesel scandal and the uproar surrounding manipulated emission measurements, then-Volkswagen-boss Martin Winterkorn admitted that a €20 million salary was "difficult to explain . . . to people," which is why the company revised its remuneration policies in 2013 and introduced a cap on bonuses.[510] It is striking that the same journalists and politicians who stoke public anger against high manager salaries also argue that it is "difficult to explain" such salaries to the population at large.

5. In addition, it is sometimes argued that such salaries are so excessively high that no one could "sensibly" spend so much money in a single lifetime. For example, a journalist reporting on Daimler CEO Dieter Zetsche's salary and retirement

fund wrote, "But there is no way Zetsche can spend that much money sensibly before the end of his hopefully long retirement."[511]

6. It is also frequently argued that top-tier managers benefit from their companies' positive developments through stock options, bonuses, and the like, but allegedly do not shoulder any of the risk for negative outcomes. "In boardrooms up and down the land, executives are engaged in a race to fill their pockets while simultaneously indemnifying themselves against any personal liability should things go wrong," said North Rhine-Westphalia's then-finance-minister Norbert Walter-Borjans (SPD).[512] Despite having previously opposed state curbs on executive pay, *Rheinische Post* published an editorial claiming that when fraud had been uncovered (as was the case at VW), high manager salaries and severance payments were "scandalous." The editorial declared, "It is clear that the time is now ripe to extend the scope of managers' personal liability."[513] It also quoted the chair of The Green's parliamentary group, Katrin Göring-Eckardt, as saying that there must finally be "genuine personal liability for management blunders."[514]

    When people debate the issue of personal liability, they typically fail to distinguish between malicious intent or gross negligence, on the one hand, and honest business mistakes, on the other. In fact, Germany already has very extensive liability laws concerning corporate management. Managers' liabilities are governed by the general provisions in Section 93 of the German Stock Corporation Act, which sets out the duty of care and the responsibilities of members of companies' management boards. Accordingly, members of these boards who violate their duties of care are liable with their entire personal assets and bear the burden of proof in the event of a dispute as to whether or not they have employed the care of a diligent and conscientious manager. Thus, it is up to board members themselves to disprove any accusations that they have breached their legal duties. And, according to the case law of Germany's Supreme Court, supervisory boards are generally obliged to enforce liability claims against board members and have very little discretion in such matters.

The impression created during the public debate on liability, however, is often that managers are not liable at all for negative outcomes. When people demand that senior-level managers should be liable to the same extent as independent entrepreneurs, who, for example, are liable for any loans they take out with their entire assets, people fail to recognize that entrepreneurship and top-tier management naturally have different risk profiles. This difference is also evident in the fact that independent entrepreneurs in companies with comparable numbers of employees, turnover, and, above all, profits, earn many times more than employed managers. An entrepreneur's significantly higher earnings reflect the higher risk associated with their endeavor. However, none of the analyzed articles put these relationships into context.

7.   Articles repeatedly cited cases of board members making serious mistakes—or even committing fraud—and still seeing their salaries increase. For example, in March 2018, the *FAZ* reported that "Volkswagen triggered the 'Dieselgate' scandal. While aggrieved car owners are left out in the cold, VW is earning billions and its senior managers are raking it in."[515] The article stated that VW set new sales records and doubled its profits in 2017. The compensation package for the management board rose by almost a third, to €50 million, despite the new remuneration policy that capped the CEO's salary at €10 million.[516] In an editorial, the *FAZ* said that members of VW's management board were being paid "what they deserve according to the group's quite demanding remuneration rules." Nevertheless, the editorial ended with the following question: "What might the owner of a VW diesel think when he sees

these figures and hears that the company is not prepared to pay for a hardware upgrade for his dirty old diesel car?"[517] Anton Hofreiter, the parliamentary leader of The Greens in the German Bundestag, was even more drastic in his assessment of the situation. The *FAZ* quoted him as saying that "shareholders and managers are stuffing their pockets with record profits, but there is no money left over to upgrade older diesel cars."[518] Even Germany's chancellor, Angela Merkel, was critical of the situation and said she "had been taken somewhat by surprise" by the substantial salary increases, especially at VW.[519]

8. At times, senior-level managers and the rich are generally blamed for the financial crisis and its aftermath, which makes their very high salaries seem particularly inappropriate. As one editorial observed, "What's more, since the financial crisis, there has been a general sense of anger that taxpayers have been called on to clean up mistakes that were often the result of pure, unadulterated greed. Disproportionately high incomes and severance payments for top-tier executives have severely damaged confidence in the economy."[520]

This criticism of high manager salaries and severance payments appears convincing for several reasons, even if the arguments put forward by the critics are not persuasive in their own right, largely because the criticism comes from more than just the usual suspects, such as trade unions or left-wing politicians.

The media also frequently cite representatives from the DSW (Deutsche Schutzvereinigung für Wertpapierbesitz) shareholders' association or the market-oriented Federation of Family Businesses. An article in *Sächsische Zeitung* in March 2012 pointed out that calls for curbs to executive pay were being voiced by "impartial stakeholders." This claim was supported by comments from the DSW and the Association of Family Entrepreneurs. The article was published under the headline "Would You Like a Little Bit More?" A photo above the article showed a man in a suit, unshaven and with a cigar casually hanging from the corner of his mouth. The caption read, "A cliché, yes. But when managers earn a hundred times more than their employees, they also get to smoke cigars, too."[521]

In March 2012, *Sächsische Zeitung* cited the Federation of Family Businesses' call for executive compensation to be capped at €5 million. According to the association's president, Lutz Goebel, "This is more than enough to get all the best people." He continued, "No top-tier manager is worth 300 or 400 times as much as a regular employee. Such high salaries breach all moral standards and take a wrecking ball to all established salary structures." The same article featured a state-ment from the DSW: "Above €10 million, salaries become socially unacceptable."[522] And the commercial lawyer Michael Adams asked, "Must a CEO earn 50 times as much as the German chancellor? Or 180 times more than a professor, or 15 times as much as a Nobel Prize winner?"[523]

Classism research in the United States has demonstrated that gener-ally no sense of solidarity exists among the poor, because each subgroup of the poor seeks to distance itself from the others.[524] One can assume that the same applies to the rich. Entrepreneurs, in particular, want to set themselves apart from corporate managers and bankers, whose image is clearly worse. However, when voices from within their own social class support criticism of the rich in the media, it lends the criticism an air of justification and objectivity from the reader's point of view.

What's more, criticism of high salaries is echoed across the polit-ical spectrum. An article headlined "Calls for Moderation Intensify" contained the following statement: "Just six months ahead of federal elections, there's no better hot-button issue than managers' salaries for politicians who are looking to make a name for themselves as champions of social justice. Politicians from every single party agree: 'Something needs to be done.'"[525] Clearly, given the highly charged atmosphere created by constant references to "excess" and "obscene manager sala-ries," not a single political party was willing to argue against prevailing opinion and deny the need for regulation in this area. Thus, the media limited their coverage to discussing the various *methods* that could be implemented to remedy the supposed grievance.

Even articles that oppose state-imposed ceilings on senior managers' salaries are often critical of other groups of rich people. One editorial, for example, bemoaned the uproar surrounding high manager salaries but lamented the fact that no one is outraged by top soccer players earning tens of millions each year.[526]

Entrepreneurs and investors also attract criticism—albeit less frequently—when it comes to their incomes. *Stern* magazine, for example, compared the salary of BMW's then-CEO Norbert Reithofer (€7.25 million) with the dividends received by the company's largest stockholders, the Quandt family: "The Quandt family can only chuckle about the annual salary of their employee, Reithofer. Last year they received 112 times as much—€815 million." Such income from capital investment is described as "income decoupled from performance" and as privileged from a tax point of view because it would only be subject to the final withholding tax of 25 percent. All in all, the article states, the rich are "exempting themselves from financing the state."[527]

Stern attempts to prove the injustice of this situation with a survey, which included the following leading question: "Is it fair that a lower tax rate should apply to interest and capital gains than to wages?"[528] Entirely predictably, 72 percent of the survey's participants said it was unfair. It is highly likely that many respondents did not know that the money had already been taxed at the company level before it was paid out as a dividend to BMW's shareholders and that the total tax burden on shareholders, at around 48 percent, was therefore comparable with the top tax rate paid on other income in Germany.

There are frequent reports of substantial severance payments when companies part ways with managers before the end of the managers' regular contracts. One example that attracted intensive media coverage relates to former constitutional judge and Hessian SPD justice minister Christine Hohmann-Dennhardt. She was tasked with clearing up the 2016 Dieselgate scandal as a member of VW's Board of Management, but she left the company after just one year as a result of internal disputes. She received a severance payment of €12 million.

Some articles called for understanding, explaining that VW had only been able to hire Hohmann-Dennhardt from Daimler because the company had offered her €7 million in compensation for the stock options she lost when she left Daimler. Such factual arguments, however, were often undermined by snide remarks, such as, "In truth, such stock options are part of the help-yourself attitude common in boardrooms across Germany." When it was pointed out that Hohmann-Dennhardt was not receiving a cent more than she was contractually entitled to, *Der Spiegel* magazine responded, "That might be true," before going on to claim that boardrooms are only governed by one principle: "Everyone takes as much as they possibly can."[529]

The argument that VW was only able to persuade Hohmann-Dennhardt to switch jobs because the company was prepared to honor her previous employer's obligations, and that the severance payment was therefore fully justified, was dealt with very briefly, if at all. In this case, as with previous cases of contractually agreed-upon severance payments, Hohmann-Dennhardt was called upon to decline the payment. The general secretary of the IG Metall union, Jörg Hofmann, who had personally approved the contract as a member of VW's supervisory board, did later concede that the severance payment was contractually justified. "But that's not how integrity works," he said. "It would have been appropriate for Ms. Hohmann-Dennhardt to decline parts of the severance package or, for example, to donate the money to a charitable foundation."[530]

According to mct Medienagentur's analysis, not even one in ten of the articles (9 percent) provided readers with background information on the legal basis for severance payments. In addition, references to legal obligations were brusquely dismissed in many of the articles. For example, one of the articles on the Hohmann-Dennhardt case in *Süddeutsche Zeitung* adopted a slightly ironic tone and reported that "Contracts must be honored, says the former constitutional judge. She knows her way around the finer points of the law." Nevertheless, the article observed, for almost all of the company's 600,000-strong workforce and for the vast majority of employees in the private sector, €12 million is an "astronomical sum." Still, this article at least found space to explain in detail the legal basis for Hohmann-Dennhardt's considerable severance payment.[531]

Of course, some media offer a different interpretation, even if they are clearly in the minority. For example, *Nürnberger Nachrichten* published an article on the Hohmann-Dennhardt case under the headline "Golden Handshakes? Sometimes They're for the Best." The business ethicist Markus Beckmann asked whether it is better to bite the bullet and dismiss a senior executive like Hohmann-Dennhardt or "let her carry on for years as part of a team that can't deliver the kind of progress you are looking for—and end up paying her the same anyway."

Rarely do articles clarify—as that article does—that very high salaries and severance payments are a result of supply and demand on the competitive market for top-tier executives. "Labor markets, just like any other markets, are governed by the principle of supply and demand," explained Beckmann. "A high wage is therefore a signal that certain qualities—for example a specific skill-set or the ability to deliver what is expected—are highly sought after and extremely rare." According to Beckmann, that is why it is not possible to introduce salary caps in a free, international, and competitive economy. "This also means that if I, on a personal level, think that a certain salary is unfair, I have to live with it."[532]

It is extremely rare for articles to argue that managers' high salaries—just like those of top athletes—are the result of supply and demand in a tight market. Many articles are colored by the same implicit salary expectations that are frequently seen in population surveys (see Chapter 10 for more on this topic). As we have seen, 63 percent of Germans think it is inappropriate for managers to earn so much more because, after all, they do not work so much longer and harder than their employees. This opinion is the most strongly supported when respondents are asked why managers shouldn't earn as much as they do, and it reflects the "employee mindset," which believes that salaries should be determined primarily by how long and how hard someone works.

The fact that, according to our survey, 54 percent of respondents think lottery winners deserve to be rich—compared with only 20 percent who say the same about senior-level managers—is certainly also a result of negative media coverage, which highlights every time a manager receives a high severance payment despite having failed to fulfill expectations. Only senior bankers are singled out as being less deserving of their wealth—a paltry 6 percent of Germans say that senior bankers deserve to be rich.

THE "GREEDY BANKER"

In the wake of the financial crisis, which peaked in 2008 with the collapse of the investment bank Lehman Brothers, bankers have had a particularly hard time in terms of public opinion. The causes of the financial crisis are complex and difficult for most people to understand, so it is easier for the media and politicians to offer simple explanations and clearly identifiable scapegoats for what happened.[533] As a result, "greedy bankers" who "gambled on a massive scale" are commonly singled out for blame. Banks and bankers are demonized in many of the analyzed articles (Figure 15.2). For example, an article published by *Stern* magazine in May 2012 features a compilation of—anonymous—quotes from bankers and former bankers in London.

A recruitment manager comments that "perhaps 5–10% of traders could be described as psychopaths, I suppose, a few more as nutcases or addicts. . . . Apart from these categories, I'd say most people in finance are moulded by the system. They morph." Another anonymous voice confesses: "These days I am cheating, lying, manipulating—all in the name of targets. The crazy thing is, I am good at this. I get bonuses."[534]

Anyone who doesn't succeed in investment banking can fall back on a simple explanation: "I found out that I'm not a big enough asshole to make it there." Another stock trader describes her colleagues as "simply very boring. . . . What do they do when they're off? Sit in fancy restaurants, stare at their Porsches, stare at people staring at their Porsches?" Another eyewitness—this time, a "partner at a major accountancy firm"—also talks about investment bankers: "The problem is greed . . . there really is a lot of greed around. What's driving the greed? I'd say the competitive macho culture, all that testosterone."[535]

In another article in *Stern* in 2013, this time under the headline "*Lüge in Zeiten der Gier*" ("Lies in the Time of Greed"), editor in chief

Figure 15.2

Slant of reports on high bankers' bonuses

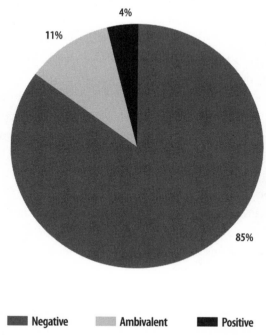

Source: mct Medienagentur, "Stereotypes of the Rich," July 2018.
Note: Based on a sample of 53 articles.

Jörges observed that a planned cap on bankers' bonuses would have no impact because "investment banking is organized greed." He quotes Swiss psychiatrist Thomas Noll, who says that "stock traders are more egocentric and prone to lying than psychopaths." Jörges's conclusion: "As long as we don't kill off speculation, the gravy train will keep on chugging along."[536]

Sächsische Zeitung ran a major article on the plans to curb banker bonuses titled "A Clear-Cut Case of Market Failure." The article reports that "bonuses in the millions are a symbol of the same greed that led to the financial crisis. . . . A ceiling for bonuses is as easy to justify as a statutory minimum wage, which strips companies of the freedom to pay people four euros an hour."[537]

Der Spiegel, however, was skeptical about the planned European Union cap on bankers' bonuses. The news magazine pointed out that the proposed cap would apply to only a fraction of bankers and would be very easy to circumvent. It concluded that the proposed cap "would achieve very little—although it would also do very little harm." The motivation behind the cap—which was also the article's headline—was "Putting a Lid on People's Anger": "And nothing incites people's anger more than the flood of reports about bankers, who even throughout the financial crisis they caused, were paid many multiples of normal salaries." However, the article concedes that capping bankers' bonuses would be counterproductive, because banks would simply raise fixed salaries in response.[538]

In an interview in *Süddeutsche Zeitung Magazin*, a personnel consultant defended plans to increase bonuses: "I think the regulations are, at least to some extent, counterproductive. It was clear that capping bonuses would lead to increases in fixed salaries. This is an unwelcome development, whether from a shareholder's point of view or from a social perspective. After all, this cap decouples payments and performance once and for all." On the other hand, the same interviewee suggested that it would make sense for banks to be able to claw back bankers' bonuses under certain circumstances: "After all, anyone who takes a risk should also be liable for the fallout. Just like real entrepreneurs."[539]

In spite of the small number of more nuanced opinions that are aired, the problem with the vast majority of media coverage is that the simplest explanation for the financial crisis is accepted, namely, that "greedy bankers" chasing bonuses caused it. Misdiagnosing the roots of a problem in this way means that the therapy prescribed to treat it will not work—and this is the real danger here.

THE OXFAM REPORTS

Oxfam publishes its global wealth reports every year in January, to coincide with the annual meeting of the world's economic elite in Davos, Switzerland. Unsurprisingly, Oxfam's reports attract considerable media attention. The quality of the reports, however, is in inverse proportion to the attention they generate. The spectrum of media coverage of the reports ranges from uncritical regurgitation of the reports' central claims to sharp criticism of the methods used in the reports.

A number of more nuanced articles also appear, but even those frequently appear under banner headlines featuring key claims lifted directly from Oxfam's reports. For example, in January 2017, the economic section of the *FAZ*, one of Germany's most respected daily newspapers, opened with the banner headline "Just Eight Men Are Richer than Half the World." The article was accompanied by a large photo of Bill Gates and Warren Buffett and a graphic detailing the estimated assets of the eight richest men in the world.[540] It began by recounting the central theses of the Oxfam report, which claimed that social inequality across the world was far more extensive than had been previously thought: "Last year the eight richest men in the world together owned 426 billion dollars, which is more than the 3.6 billion people who make up the poorest half of humanity, who currently own 409 billion dollars in wealth." The article pointed out that the previous year's Oxfam report had attracted widespread attention with its central claim that the wealth of the 61 richest people in the world corresponded to that of the poorer half of the world's population. Matters would appear to be getting worse, at least at first glance.[541]

Oxfam, the newspaper continued, had incorporated new data into its 2017 report. If the same data and calculations had been used in the previous year's report, Oxfam admits that report would have shown that 9 billionaires owned the same wealth as the poorest half of the planet, rather than 61. The article also pointed out that the calculation itself was questionable because the "poorest half of the planet" includes an astonishing number of people in the developed world—for example, in the United States—who have taken out loans to buy houses or finance their studies. The paper cited criticism from Mark Littlewood of the London-based Institute of Economic Affairs, which regularly criticizes Oxfam's reports: "It is misleading at best to label the average university graduate who has accumulated £50,000 of debt among the world's poorest, without any consideration of their future earning potential."[542] The article itself was quite nuanced, as was the editorial on the same page. But why would such a highly reputable newspaper decide to give pride of place in its economics section to Oxfam's dubious report? And why would the newspaper accompany its article with a headline and graphics that uncritically parrot Oxfam's central thesis—even when the article itself adopts a more balanced and critical tone?

The fact that journalists can take a different approach was demonstrated by *Süddeutsche Zeitung*, Germany's highest-circulation daily newspaper, which also reported extensively on the Oxfam study on the same day but did so with a far more appropriate headline: "No, Eight People Do Not Own as Much as Half the World." The article criticizes the Oxfam study as follows: "Last year, Oxfam claimed that the 61 richest people in the world own as much as the poorest half of the planet. And now it's just eight! Isn't that proof that the world is going to the dogs? No. It just proves that the number 'eight' is surely wrong." As the newspaper pointed out, the study compares apples with oranges. According to Oxfam's calculations, a German pensioner with a small car loan is poorer than a farmer in Burundi. The newspaper wrote that Oxfam had defended its report with the surprisingly feeble argument that "our report does not claim to be scientific, nor does it pretend to be."[543]

Despite the serious shortcomings of Oxfam's reports, their findings receive prominent media coverage year after year, with large numbers of articles uncritically regurgitating Oxfam's central claims. This regurgitation is especially common in regional media. When the 2016 report was published, many regional media outlets in Germany simply reproduced an article on the report from Deutsche Presse-Agentur (DPA), Germany's largest news agency. One major regional newspaper ran the headline "The Gap Is Widening All the Time." The article opened with "The gap between rich and poor is growing all over the world," and it backed up this claim with the fact that Oxfam's previous report had found that 80 people owned as much as the poorest half of the planet, a figure that had since fallen to just 61. The newspaper featured a direct quote from an Oxfam spokesperson: "We live in a world that makes the rules for the super-rich."[544] Another major regional paper headlined its reporting

"Half the World Belongs to the Rich."[545] and one of the leading newspapers in southern Germany went as far as to publish the DPA article on its front page under the headline "Study: 62 Rich People Own as Much as Half the World."[546]

Even after word spread that Oxfam's studies were not based on credible data and methods, the reports were not retracted or corrected, as is common practice among journalists. In January 2018, *Die Zeit*, Germany's leading weekly newspaper, ran an article under the headline "Social Inequality: The Rich Shape Our Politics." The article began by presenting figures from the Oxfam report, with dramatic comparisons used to provide sensational emphasis: "A seamstress in Bangladesh earns as much in her whole life as a CEO of a large fashion group earns in just four days."[547] The article did point to the weaknesses of Oxfam's data and methodology, but it adopted a conciliatory tone: "The organization confesses that its calculations have unavoidable minor shortcomings." And an Oxfam spokesperson was quoted in the article as saying, "Whether it's eight, 42 or 61 people who own the same wealth as half of the world's poor, there's great inequality among individuals."

But a study should have more to offer than just general outrage over a "fundamental imbalance" between rich and poor; it should also provide additional—new and accurate—information and data. The article in *Die Zeit*, which began with the sentence "Inequality is growing worldwide, warns Oxfam," ended with a quote from an Oxfam spokesperson: "The concentration of extreme wealth at the top is not a sign of a thriving economy, but a symptom of a system that is failing."[548]

When Oxfam's methodological failings were exposed, *Stern*—Germany's second-most-popular weekly news magazine—dismissed the concerns, stating that Oxfam's report was "not a scientific study based on the latest statistical methods" and that such criticism was not, in any case, relevant. According to the magazine, the important takeaway is the dramatic nature of developments "because, regardless of whether there are 8 or 61 superrich, the trend Oxfam identifies is real. The gap between the rich and poor is growing and this threatens social stability."[549]

Yet this trend, as we have seen, was the product of nothing more than a change in data and methodology.

A simple thought experiment suggests that such widespread coverage of Oxfam's dubious reports in reputable newspapers probably has a lot to do with the fact that Oxfam's central claims and its general thrust against "the superrich" are closely aligned with the editorial viewpoints of large swathes of the media. Imagine if a right-wing organization published a study on immigration that used apparently questionable methods and based its conclusions on unsound data. The "study" would not even be mentioned, and rightly so—or, if it were, it would be only as evidence of right-wing demagoguery.

If you Google the keywords "Eight rich people own as much as . . . ," you are greeted not only by millions of hits but also by a huge number of hits demonstrating uncritical acceptance of most of Oxfam's figures.

Thomas Piketty and the Gap between Rich and Poor

The overwhelming success of French economist Thomas Piketty's 2013 book *Le capital au XXIème siècle*, which was published in English in 2014 as *Capital in the Twenty-First Century*, proved just how strongly the concepts of "inequality" and the "gap between rich and poor" resonate with the media—and beyond.

Piketty's complaint is that modern economics and social sciences no longer focus on the "distributional question": "It is long past the time when we should have put the question of inequality back at the center of economic analysis."[550] One of Piketty's core theses is that the gap between rich and poor widened further at the beginning of the 21st century, although he does concede that "it is by no means certain that inequalities of wealth are actually increasing at the global level."[551]

Other authors have published comprehensive critiques of Piketty's data set and methodological errors,[552] forcing him to retract some core claims of his book.[553] This criticism from academia, however, did nothing to dent the popular success of his book, which was hailed as the most convincing proof that the gap between rich and poor was widening.

The general tone of media coverage was that Piketty's work was a groundbreaking contribution to modern criticism of capitalism. In the context of mct Medienagentur's analysis, the book's media resonance is of particular interest: the company analyzed articles on Piketty's book in German media and found that two-thirds of them shared his main thesis.

Süddeutsche Zeitung devoted several major articles to the book, including almost a whole page in October 2014:

> Thomas Piketty's brilliant book is now available in German and has triggered a global debate on the distribution of wealth. . . . There is an era before Piketty's book, and there is an era thereafter. . . . He has consummately uncovered the lines of development from the 18th century to the present with a brilliant depth of focus. . . . Even readers who already thought they were well versed on issues of economic inequality will have their eyes opened by Piketty's work. His abundance of data gives us a real idea of the shocking facts hidden at the top of society behind abstract notions of "inequality" of incomes and wealth.

The newspaper approvingly endorsed calls for the French economist to be awarded "the Nobel Prize for his work" and praised his "unprecedented diligence" and "decades of factual research" (according to Piketty, he spent 15 years researching the book). The review ended on a note of resignation, speculating that Piketty's radical proposals for a tax on global wealth "will be dismissed as unrealistic, batted aside with the usual cold snarl."[554]

In May 2014, the *FAZ* also devoted almost a whole page to Piketty and asked, "How Can Europe Ever Become Strong and Beautiful Again?" The article began, "Thomas Piketty is the new rising star among intellectuals. Based on his research on inequality, he proposes original and ingenious solutions to ensure that financial burdens are distributed more fairly across society." The author supported Piketty's call for an exorbitantly high global wealth tax:

> Piketty's equal distribution of financial burdens would secure the future of our hard-won model of civilization, a model that would otherwise erode if left to itself. It is our task to extend this historical

moment, which has so far lasted for forty years, beyond its natural expiration date, so that the democratic, social, and cultural constitutional state does not sink back into the hands of the oligarchs, the drug bosses and commodity kings, the boys with the black SUVs. And Piketty also reminds us in his book that it has always been unjust tax systems that served as the spark to ignite revolutions."[555]

The *FAZ* also published several lengthy articles on Piketty's theses, including one critical report describing Piketty as a rock-star economist who had taken America by storm.[556]

Stern magazine joined the hype that had coalesced around Piketty and published a glowingly positive article about his book. It stated that the French economist had supplied proof for the thesis that "the middle class can work as hard and long as it wants—they won't reap the rewards. At the end of the day, the wealthy will take their money. Just like under the feudal system of the 18th century." The article was full of praise: Piketty is "super cool, very relaxed." And "nobody has made it as far as Piketty." His theses met with total approval. "The best trick pulled by the rich was to tell the poor: 'Just wait, you will all benefit from our wealth in the end.' . . . Piketty has now demonstrated: Prosperity does not trickle down. It coalesces at the top. . . . Piketty's approach is empirical and rational. This makes him a real threat to the rich." The article ended with Piketty's proposal for a global wealth tax of between 5 and 10 percent on assets over €100 million and the following call for action: "It's daring, but we need to do it."[557]

Under a headline claiming that *"Das Kapital frisst die Zukunft"* ("Capital Is Eating the Future"), *Der Spiegel* published a three-page interview with Piketty in which he explained his proposal for a global wealth tax.[558] A month later, *Der Spiegel* ran an interview with the left-wing economist Peter Bofinger, who agreed with Piketty that "wealth and prosperity are increasingly being distributed unequally." However, Bofinger questioned the correctness of Piketty's capital formula and said, "He puts forward a theory—but then disproves it with his own numbers." It is strange, Bofinger observed, "that his magic formula does not apply to the most extensively documented 100 years in which the market economy has really come into its own. In fact, the opposite is true. If I were to discover that my theories and my figures diverged to such a massive extent, I would have sleepless nights." *Der Spiegel*'s interviewer followed up by saying that they had actually expected Bofinger to sympathize with Piketty. "After all, you are considered to be the only left-winger on the German council of economic experts." Bofinger's response: "As an economist, I can't turn a blind eye to a fundamental contradiction just because I agree with the basic thrust of the argument."[559]

In the wake of mounting criticism from within the scientific community, several articles appeared in Piketty's defense, including one in *Süddeutsche Zeitung*, which clearly stated that "Thomas Piketty's book *Capital in the Twenty-First Century* has been wrongly criticized."[560]

One of Piketty's main arguments—namely, that the primary evil of the modern world is rising global inequality and that between 1990 and 2010 the gap between rich and poor widened—attracts very little critical attention from the media. One could argue that it is precisely in these decades that more than one billion people worldwide have been able to lift themselves out of bitter poverty thanks to the spread of capitalism—especially in China, but also in India and other parts of the world. Piketty should have asked what is more important: that more than one billion people have escaped poverty and are no longer starving, or that the wealth of multimillionaires and billionaires increased at an even faster rate during the same period?

In my book *The Power of Capitalism*,[561] I demonstrate that the sharp rise in the number of millionaires and billionaires in China in recent decades and the massive improvements in living standards for more than 800 million people in China are simply two sides of the same coin. They are the outcomes of the same process, namely, the transition from socialism to capitalism, from a planned economy to a market economy.

For anti-capitalists like Piketty, the economy is a zero-sum game in which some (the rich) win and others (the middle class and the poor) lose.[562] In *The Power of Capitalism*, I suggest the following thought experiment: Let's assume you live on an island where three rich people have a fortune of $5,000 each, while 1,000 others have only $100 each. The total wealth of the island's residents is $115,000. Now you decide between two alternatives.

In the first, because of economic growth, the total wealth of the island's residents doubles to $230,000. The wealth of the three rich people triples to $15,000 each; they now own $45,000 between them. Meanwhile, the wealth of the island's remaining 1,000 residents grows by 85 percent, to $185 per capita. The gap in wealth between the richest and the poorest residents has widened considerably.

In the alternative scenario, the total wealth of $115,000 is split evenly among all 1,003 residents—$114.66 per capita. As one of the poor, with a baseline wealth of $100, which of the two societies would you prefer—economic growth or equal distribution? And what would happen if, as a consequence of economic reforms aimed at creating greater equality, the island's total wealth shrank to a paltry $80,000, or less than $79.80 per capita?

Of course, you may well object that the best outcome would be economic growth and a higher general standard of living in tandem with greater equality. And that's exactly what capitalism achieved in the 20th century, as even Piketty admits. But the thought experiment above is still useful as a way to demonstrate a fundamental difference between two competing value systems. Somebody who prioritizes fighting inequality over raising the standard of living for the majority will make different choices from somebody who prioritizes the opposite.

THE GIVING PLEDGE: THE SUPERRICH AND CHARITABLE DONATIONS

There are few circumstances in which the rich are the subject of positive media coverage. One such occasion could have been the Giving Pledge, a campaign launched in June 2010 by two high-profile billionaires, Bill Gates and Warren Buffett. The aim of the Giving Pledge is to encourage wealthy individuals to donate their wealth. The campaign kicked off in August 2010, when 40 American billionaires promised to donate at least half of their fortunes to charitable causes. The initiative attracted support from New York City's mayor at the time, Michael Bloomberg, and George Lucas, the creator of the *Star Wars* and *Indiana Jones* film franchises. They were soon joined by 100 more billionaires, including Facebook founder Mark Zuckerberg.

What kind of coverage did the Giving Pledge attract? In Chapter 10, we saw that a majority of people assume that the rich donate to charitable causes primarily to benefit themselves, such as by reducing their taxes or improving their reputations. Half of our surveys' respondents said that the rich donate primarily to benefit themselves, and only 14 percent believe that the rich want to help others first and foremost with their donations.

For its survey, mct Medienagentur analyzed 16 different articles on the Giving Pledge. In those articles, journalists mentioned 37 motives for making charitable donations. These motives can be divided into altruistic motives, such as the desire to help "reduce educational inequalities," and self-centered ones, such as the desire to use charitable donations to lower one's taxes. Among the 37 motives mentioned in the articles, 13 are altruistic, 16 are self-centered, and 6 are neutral (e.g., that in the United States, it is simply "good manners to donate to charitable causes").[563]

According to the analysis conducted by mct Medienagentur, the overall slant of coverage devoted to the Giving Pledge campaign was either positive or somewhat positive. Three articles were negative and two were ambivalent, versus ten that were positive or somewhat positive. It is noticeable, however, that very few articles, only three in all, were overwhelmingly positive. Many of the more positive articles still found space to air critical remarks alongside the positive content. The following criticisms of the Giving Pledge campaign were identified:

- There is no "measure of success." Many of the signatories were already active philanthropists, "so it is unclear to what extent the Giving Pledge campaign will encourage more donations."[564]
- In some articles, praise for the donations was relativized by criticism of individual donors. *Süddeutsche Zeitung*, for example, wrote about the initiator of the campaign, Warren Buffett: "His obsession with the stock market and his refusal to communicate with his family ultimately cost him his marriage."[565] In another article, this time under the headline "The Great Philanthropists," the *FAZ* criticized

Warren Buffett's company for profiting from the use of derivative financial instruments and that "despite his apparently outstanding analysis of undervalued companies, he is also a major gambler."[566]

• Donations were described as undemocratic because individual billionaires, not the state, decide which causes to support. *Der Spiegel* cited the German shipping magnate Peter Krämer, who advocates an increase in taxes for the rich: "I simply don't want a handful of billionaires to decide whether fishing grounds in Alaska, golf resorts in Florida, or the fight against AIDS are the most deserving of financial support." In his opinion, philanthropic initiatives such as the Giving Pledge campaign are equivalent to giving up on the concept of a centralized state, "which is democratically legitimized and should know where money most urgently needs to be spent."[567] *Süddeutsche Zeitung* ran an article headlined "Charity with a Catch": "There is no control over objectives, resources or methods. . . . Even if there are no moral or practical arguments against the rationality of venture philanthropy, it is still another step into a political parallel world without control mechanisms."[568] On the topic of the Giving Pledge campaign, *Stern* magazine inquired critically: "Does this still qualify as kindness? Or should we feel threatened by a dictatorship of altruists?" According to the article, there was "a deep mistrust of what motivates the rich to give away money at all" in Germany. The article ended with a reminder from Princeton professor Peter Singer: "Much as we may applaud what Gates and Buffett are doing, we can also be troubled by a system that leaves the fate of hundreds of millions of people hanging on the decisions of two or three private citizens."[569]

• It was claimed that the fundraising campaign was also motivated by a desire to "polish the tarnished image of capitalism," as the *FAZ* noted in August 2010.[570] And the appeal for donations was "not just an appeal for selflessness," according to *Süddeutsche Zeitung*: "The campaign also helps the superrich themselves. It improves the image of a social class that has increasingly decoupled itself from the rest of the country [the United States] in recent years and has therefore been caught in the crosshairs of criticism." The article went on to explain that "popular anger at the rich" had lately intensified: "Seen in this light, the Giving Pledge campaign comes at a particularly opportune moment. It demonstrates a sense of social responsibility that the country has so painfully missed. The campaign was deliberately designed to have a high profile."[571]

- According to the critics, the Giving Pledge's donations simply prove that a very small group of individuals own far too much wealth. *Die Zeit* cited public policy professor and former U.S. secretary of labor Robert Reich, who observed that the fundraising campaign reminds us that "so much money is concentrated in so few hands." This factor was cited as further proof that we had returned to the 19th century, when "a handful of corporate chieftains known as 'robber barons' presided over all this—collecting great riches at the expense of workers who toiled long hours often in dangerous conditions for little pay."[572]

There were, however, a number of dissenting voices. In the *FAZ*, two guest authors wrote an article that appeared under the headline "Are Donors Turning Their Backs on Charitable Foundations?" They addressed the risk that "potential donors are being driven away because their motives and justifications are being over-scrutinized. As the article observed, many people now equate charitable foundations with tax-saving schemes. "This is unfair to the foundations—which is bad enough on its own. But it would be a tragedy for society if potential donors were to turn their backs in disillusionment because they and their donations are treated with suspicion instead of gratitude and recognition."[573] In another guest article in the *FAZ*, the authors criticized the Giving Pledge campaign for the fact that, in Germany at least, it had "primarily aroused objections and misgivings about the effectiveness of the work done by foundations and donors."[574]

Although reports on the Giving Pledge campaign were naturally kinder to the rich than were articles on other issues, they were also colored by strong levels of animosity. As we shall see, this animosity is all the more pronounced in articles on subjects that lend themselves to critical bias against the rich, namely media coverage of the Panama and Paradise Papers.

CHAPTER 16

"TO HELL WITH THE RICH": THE PANAMA AND PARADISE PAPERS

In April 2016, an international research team of 400 journalists published excerpts from what they called the "Panama Papers." Because this was the "largest international investigative journalism project of all time"[575] and "the wealthy and superrich of this world" were denounced all over the media, I have decided to devote this entire chapter to the investigations, which focused on offshore shell companies in Panama. *Süddeutsche Zeitung*, one of the major German national daily newspapers, which had been offered stolen data detailing the shell companies, referred to it as the "biggest data leak in history,"[576] a "data leak from which truth suddenly flows."[577] In fact, "data leak" is a decidedly euphemistic term that allowed the media to avoid acknowledging that in reality, the "leak" was a hacker attack against the Panamanian law firm of Mossack Fonseca.

At no point did the newspaper clarify whether these shell companies were fronts for illegal or merely dubious activities. The *Frankfurter Allgemeine Zeitung (FAZ)*, the second major German national daily newspaper, stated, "There are legal and illegal reasons why someone would not want to conduct their business openly. There are also both legal and illegal methods for minimizing taxes." To support this argument, the newspaper quoted a statement from the lawyer of Formula One racing driver Nico Rosberg, who justified registering a company in the British Virgin Islands in terms of liability laws and the option of acting internationally.[578] At this point, the *FAZ* reported, the Panama Papers investigation had "not uncovered any tangible crimes."[579]

An op-ed in the *FAZ* was one of the very few articles to provide more than just a cursory, vague, and very general explanation of the legitimate reasons to form a shell company. In fact, the *FAZ* provided some examples: in some countries, shell companies are used to guard against kidnapping or blackmail, and buyers of real estate, works of art, or innovative companies can use shell companies to prevent the prices of their targets from skyrocketing.[580] It was rare indeed for the media to mention such legal motives and specific examples. The tone of the media campaign, which was supported by numerous outlets, was otherwise unambiguously critical: "Above all, the media live from the assumption that the existence of shell companies is generally reprehensible. As a result, the prominent figures from the worlds of politics, sports, and business who are mentioned in connection with such companies are placed under general suspicion."[581]

But the *FAZ* also published articles expressing a range of very different opinions. In an article that appeared three days later under the headline "Are We Not Allowed to Moralize Anymore?," which was clearly published to differentiate from articles that the journalist's colleagues had published in the same newspaper, the author observed that it was a sign of "blind faith in authority" when the right to criticize was declared "sacrosanct" as long as it was also briefly mentioned that the behavior being reported on was legal.[582] The question of legality is totally irrelevant, said one person interviewed by *Süddeutsche Zeitung*, because "slavery was also legal for a very long time. Let's not forget that men could legally go to market and sell their wives."[583]

The interview was part of a series called "*Die Geheimnisse des schmutzigen Geldes*" ("Secrets of the Dirty Money").[584] One of the articles in this series begins with the statement that "shell companies are the purest expression of globalized capitalism."[585] According to another article in the series, the revelations contained in the Panama Papers represented the "unmasking of the dark side of capitalism."[586] The articles referred to "the rich" and "the superrich" and placed them all under the same general suspicion.

The Panama Papers even featured extensively in regional media. For example, *Nürnberger Nachrichten* published an article titled "United by Greed: What Connects Despots, Criminals and the Rich."[587]

THE PANAMA PAPERS: THE RESEARCH

The story of the "largest international investigative journalism project of all time" is told by Bastian Obermayer and Frederik Obermaier, two journalists from *Süddeutsche Zeitung*, in their 390-page book *The Panama Papers: Breaking the Story of How the Rich and Powerful Hide Their Money*, which was published in English in 2016. An anonymous informant, whose motives they did not know, gave them more than 11 million internal documents,[588] which had apparently been stolen during a hacker attack, from Mossack Fonseca.

In the book, the two journalists extensively describe how they and about 400 other journalists from more than 100 media organizations in over 80 countries[589] set about investigating stories originating from the data. The case of Germany, for example, proceeded as follows: "Basically, we make an inventory of public life in the Federal Republic of Germany. We list all the leading politicians, business executives, sportspeople and public figures. We look for the super-rich, criminals and swindlers, and we try to compile the names of as many individuals implicated in scandals as possible. . . . Our data stretches back into the 1970s."[590] The data leak, they explain in their book, is "bigger than any leak that *any* journalist has ever seen."[591] The data leak included "detailed information concerning about a quarter of a million offshore companies" from all around the world.[592] To search through all the data, the journalists bought ever more powerful and expensive computers (including a server farm for €17,484.36[593]) and special forensic software, Nuix, which is also used by the U.S. Securities and Exchange Commission.[594]

The journalists strategically timed the publication of their findings, adopting an approach similar to those used by major global brands for their international advertising and public relations campaigns. Partner newspapers were sought all over the world, and work on the stories was tightly coordinated. The investigative journalists' findings were published in 20 languages.[595] *Süddeutsche Zeitung* had an illustrator working exclusively on the project, and there was even a "Making of" film.[596]

The journalists spent over a year on their research. In a presentation to colleagues from all over the globe, their plan was to "grab our audience's attention immediately by outlining the magnitude of the leak."[597]

To put the size of the leak into perspective, they calculated how many Bibles would be filled if all of the documents were printed out: probably "more than 700,000."[598] When they shared that information with the assembled journalists, the entire room was won over: "Our haul really does look very impressive and the room quietens down immediately."[599] According to the two journalists, their work was at least partly financed by the International Consortium of Investigative Journalists (ICIJ), an initiative of the Center for Public Integrity. The Center is a project financed by donations; one of their main donors is the left-leaning billionaire George Soros.[600]

The two investigative journalists gave intensive thought to how they could attract attention to their campaign. Clearly, they felt that the facts alone were not enough. They even engaged in what they call "old-school investigating" to gather background information that would make the story more interesting. They conducted extensive research into Erhard Mossack, the father of the founder of the law firm, despite the fact that he was in no way connected with the matters at hand. It turned out that the father had been in the Waffen SS and had possibly worked with the Central Intelligence Agency in the aftermath of World War II. When the two journalists told their colleagues, the colleagues listened with fascination, because "Nazis are always news, the CIA is always news, but the two combined is fantastic."[601]

They continue to describe the scene: "It feels as if we've stepped into a pastiche of a hacker film. All the blinds are down, there are laptops on two tables and on all sides cables snake, external hard drives wink, screens flicker and computers hum. . . . We place our laptops beside theirs and dive into this strange universe."[602] Almost as if they were really in a film, they dreamed up lurid headlines for future articles. When they were looking for the perfect working title for their investigative campaign, they were inspired by another article called "Evil LLC."[603]

Every scandal needs its victims. According to professor of mass communications Hans Mathias Kepplinger, the most successful media campaigns frame events according to a hierarchical offender-victim schema: "The offender is powerful and unscrupulous, the victim is powerless and scrupulous."[604]

Because the victims in the campaign on the Panama Papers are not obvious—unlike, for example, in environmental scandals—the journalists consulted Jean Ziegler, a Swiss professor emeritus of sociology,[605] whom they describe as "not the type to mince his words; he's the voice of the poor and a nightmare for the high and mighty."[606] They also describe him as "a loud, likeable admonisher in a world that has remained strikingly silent about the offshore underworld for far too long."[607] Ziegler offered them an explanation for why governments had not taken stronger action against the machinations of the superrich: "Because the governments have been under pressure from banks, secret services, global corporations and the super-wealthy: the 'world dictatorship of globalized financial capital.'"[608]

In Africa, the journalists found the victims that are so crucial for turning any scandal into a sensation: "An invisible machine is working to plunder the continent. A coalition of corrupt dictators, unscrupulous large corporations and ruthless banks, all working hand in hand, united by their greed."[609]

The authors of the book say little about the legality of the means by which the data were acquired and whether the publication of these data can be justified from a data protection and personal rights perspective. They vaguely speak of "stolen data" and describe their fear of smuggling it across the U.S. border.[610]

So, what is the result of the largest international investigative journalism project of all time? To quote, the Papers contained information on letterbox companies (also known as shell, mailbox and offshore companies) and documents belonging to:

- Arabian heads of state[611]
- African despots, Eastern European oligarchs, Latin American rulers, and members of international Mafia networks[612]
- Venezuelan socialists, supporters of Hugo Chávez[613]
- Associates of the Russian head of state, Vladimir Putin[614]
- African politicians[615]
- Drug lords, financial fraudsters, Mafiosi, arms smugglers, tax evaders, sanction breakers, and pretty much every type of fraudster[616]

The fact that these individuals owned letterbox companies should not be all that surprising. The list of Western politicians and business leaders was far shorter; the revelations had the greatest impact in Iceland, where numerous senior politicians were forced to resign.[617] The 11 million documents contained references to just 3,500 offshore company owners from the United States and included copies of just 200 American passports. The explanation for this disparity, according to one article, is that Americans have enough options within their country to evade taxes. "According to industry experts, just because the 'Panama Papers' primarily contain references to dubious investments made by foreign figures does not mean that wealthy Americans are not involved."[618]

What about the superrich, who were the subject of so much coverage throughout the journalistic campaign? The book says, "If the volume of secrets is large enough, it is, statistically speaking, almost bound to contain some good stories."[619] The authors explain that the number of "very rich and very famous families in the data is in the three figures."[620] However, "good stories" about the superrich, whom the journalists' campaign sweepingly condemn, are extremely rare. In a lone sentence, the authors fleetingly refer to an essential fact: "There are of course many reasons for using an offshore company and of course owning one is not in itself a criminal offence."[621] Thus, the mere fact that a name appears in the data is evidence neither of an illegal act nor of anything morally questionable.

Very few pages of the book are dedicated to the "regular" superrich and the CEOs of large companies. On the subject of Germany, the book reports:

> We see, for example, a number of men from the boardrooms of the biggest German companies buying offshore companies in the British Virgin Islands to hold their villa in Mallorca or the Caribbean, or because the former owner only wanted to sell the villa to them that way. One of them even sends us excerpts from his tax return to prove that foul play wasn't involved. Another is quick to tell us on the phone that he would "happily pull his trousers down" because he's got nothing to hide, and invites us to a meeting with his tax adviser.[622]

The journalists never tell us whether they accepted this invitation or whether they even reviewed the excerpts from the tax return (and, if they did, what they found).

The only prominent Germans directly referenced are Ferdinand Piëch, members of the Porsche family, and Silvia Quandt, all of whom are named as the directors of companies in Panama. At the time, however, they all explained either that the companies were part of structures that were never used and that didn't create any tax advantages anyway or that they couldn't explain why their names were found among the data.[623]

Readers are also left in the dark as to whether the journalists, who had all of the law firm's data at their disposal (including confidential emails and internal documents), looked into the explanations provided by Piëch, the Porsches, and Silvia Quandt, and, if so, what they discovered. One can assume, however, that nothing came of it, because otherwise the authors would certainly have reported it. Names are mentioned simply because they were on a list, even though there is not the slightest indication that the named individuals had acted dubiously, let alone illegally. Readers are nonetheless left with the impression that these individuals are in the same league as Russian oligarchs, African despots, Mafiosi, money launderers, and the rest of "the world's biggest scumbags."[624]

In their coverage of the Panama Papers investigation, numerous media outlets published articles peppered with vague, unsubstantiated assumptions. For example, a headline in *Nürnberger Nachrichten* in April 2016 was "Do Offshore Companies Own Real Estate in Nuremberg?" Clearly, the editorial staff were keen to establish a local link to global events for their readership in Nuremberg. However, in the article itself—an interview with a Green politician—no reference whatsoever is made to the provocative question raised by the headline. Instead, the article merely states, "If you want to find out how much real estate in Nuremberg is held by offshore companies, you won't be able to. Because the local land registry office won't tell you."[625]

Tax Cheating: The Rule for the Rich, the Exception for the Nonrich?

According to Kepplinger, one essential characteristic of the media's coverage of scandals is that the media do not report about "the relative frequency with which such events occur."[626] By citing (supposedly) substantial figures and stringing numerous individual examples together, the media create the impression that a certain pattern of behavior is typical for a specific group—in the case of the Panama Papers, the rich. *Süddeutsche Zeitung* published an article on April 5, 2016, under the banner headline "Lost in Paradise." In large letters, the article opened, "Holders of the Federal Cross of Merit, brothel barons, senior executives: Many thousands of Germans used the services of Mossack Fonseca—including a scatterbrained billionaire, who in the end no longer knew where his offshore company was even registered."[627] In the body of the article, however, it soon became clear that the proven number of cases is comparatively low and can be estimated at best very roughly. The talk was no longer of "many thousands of Germans," but, far more vaguely, "In total—based on estimates from Mossack Fonseca's internal lists—a high four-digit number of Germans may have taken advantage of the services provided by the Panamanian law firm. Several hundred German addresses can be found in the documents alone." The papers included about 200 copies of identity documents issued by the German authorities, although "by all indications," according to the article, only a small minority of the law firm's clients had actually provided copies of their identity documents.

Far more relevant than the number of individual cases, however, is what it actually means for someone to have been a client of the Panamanian law firm. The presumption of innocence, a fundamental tenet of due legal process, was casually brushed aside. Even without the slightest grounds for suspicion, those named in the leaked data, which was illegally acquired through a hacker attack, were lumped together with Mafiosi, drug dealers, and corrupt politicians.

But let's get back to the question of just how widespread the use of such letterbox companies by the rich is. *Süddeutsche Zeitung* reported that "the Panama Papers also show what role offshore companies play in the world of the superrich: Hundreds of millionaires and billionaires hoard their wealth in Mossack Fonseca's tax minimization structures, including 29 of the billionaires on the *Forbes* list of the 500 richest people in the world."[628]

You could, of course, formulate the same facts very differently: the names of more than 94 percent of the superrich on the *Forbes* list do not appear even once in the more than 11 million documents in the leaked data. And of those who do appear, many probably have motives that are not at all disreputable. Then again, there are many companies like Mossack Fonseca, so it is practically impossible to determine precisely what percentage of the superrich take advantage of such off-shore companies, and of this percentage, it is equally impossible to determine precisely how many individuals are associated with illegal activities.

However, in the articles and the book that accompanies them, the journalists state in general terms—without providing even rudimentary proof—that "in the parallel world of the rich and the super-rich, it may be the norm for accounts, shares, houses, yachts and so on to be held by offshore constructs that are, in part, spread across multiple continents and countries." Although owning letterbox companies is not illegal, they add, "We can, however, certainly draw the conclusion that a two-tier system seems to have established itself internationally, whereby some people pay their taxes in the conventional way, while others, because they have the means to do so, decide for themselves when, how much and indeed whether they pay taxes at all." For the wealthy, they continue, there are "no rules at all."[629] This is, of course, absurd. There are rules for the superrich, the same as there are for ordinary citizens; it is simply the case that some of the wealthy, like some ordinary citizens, disregard those rules.

These generalizations are usually entirely uncorroborated. In an article titled "SOS for Tax Compliance," the following argument was put forward: "Rich people move their money to Panama, Joe Public pays his cleaning lady in cash," although the article did immediately add, "Whoever equates the millions of dollars being whisked out of the taxman's grasp by the tax fraud of the privileged with the tax fraud committed by the 'little man' fails to recognize the mechanisms of routine taxation."[630] In a series of counterarguments, the article cited the results of a representative survey in which 80 percent of respondents stated that they had never evaded taxes. The author went to great lengths to explain why such results should be accepted as entirely credible.[631] Thus, the author seemingly established that tax evasion is an exception among members of the general population—while at the same time creating the completely unsubstantiated impression that tax evasion is extremely widespread, common, and normal among the rich.

Some media take the easy route and declare the entire matter to be a "systemic issue." They blame capitalism itself, claiming that its very nature is corrupt. A lengthy essay on the Panama Papers headlined "Financial Porn" published in *Der Spiegel* opened with the following statement: "Politicians, bankers and CEOs have always been greedy. What is it about our legal and economic system that enables them to live out their greed?" The author's answer: "Corruption is not a random deviation within the global capitalist system—it is a fundamental element of how the system works. The reality described by the Panama Papers is that of class separation. The Panama Papers expose the fact that wealthy people live in a world where different rules apply. A world where the legal system and the authorities not only protect the rich, but go as far as to systematically undermine the rule of law to accommodate them."[632]

The same issue of *Der Spiegel* also contained an article on the Panama Papers called "Islands of Anarchy" that was equally critical of capitalism: "Another reason the Panama Papers are so powerful is because they seem to confirm widespread misgivings about the globalized economy, against a capitalism in which the rich become richer and the poor become ever poorer. And in which the top one percent of the population can do whatever it wants."[633]

In a subtle way, the article did mention that letterbox companies are neither illegal nor illicit, a fact that was immediately relativized. Rather than stating that letterbox companies are legal, the author wrote that they are "not illegal—yet." The article did concede that there are legitimate reasons for owning an offshore company, but it failed to mention a single one: "Of course it is not illegal—yet—to hide your money in letterbox companies, provided it has been taxed at home. There may also be entirely legitimate reasons for doing so. Experts, however, have so far only been able to come up with a handful of convincing motives."[634]

It is well worth analyzing such passages word for word: An entirely legal activity is described as "not illegal—yet." The journalist does not write that there are legitimate reasons, or explain what they are; instead, he writes merely that such motives *"may"* exist. The author then proceeds to relativize what is already a qualified concession by citing unnamed "experts" who have "only been able to come up with a handful of convincing motives."

Media Content Analysis by mct Medienagentur

For this research project, mct Medienagentur's team systematically analyzed 195 articles on the Panama Papers published in 2017 by *Süddeutsche Zeitung, FAZ, Der Spiegel, Rheinische Post, Nürnberger Nachrichten,* and *Sächsische Zeitung.* A majority of the articles appeared in *Süddeutsche Zeitung,* which played the lead role in the global Panama Papers investigation.

Many of the analyzed articles do briefly mention that the mere appearance of a name in one of the more than 11 million documents—thus suggesting that an individual was or is a client of the law firm—should not be taken as evidence of illegal activities. Nevertheless, 86 percent of the articles create the impression that there is something disreputable about each of the individuals named in the leak (Figure 16.1). This fact is often suggested in the articles' headlines.

Some articles do point out that there is nothing illegal about owning an offshore company, although such references are usually strongly relativized. Characteristically, in the context of a brief general explanation of the legality of letterbox companies, there is rarely a detailed discussion of the possible legitimate reasons for owning such a company. Further, mct Medienagentur's analysis revealed that the term "letterbox company" itself is given a negative connotation, or is at least used not as a neutral term but in a decidedly negative context, in 92 percent of the analyzed articles (Table 16.1).

Tax-planning structures are not in and of themselves morally or legally objectionable. In fact, according to case law, they are a legitimate right of every taxpayer. In the public debate, however, legal tax arrangements are often conflated with illegal tax evasion. In 90 percent of the articles on the Panama Papers, tax structures are presented as illegitimate, often because journalists use terms such as "tax cheating" instead of the neutral term "tax planning."

Figure 16.1

The "shadiness frame" in articles on the Panama Papers

Does an article create the overall impression that the activities dealt with in the Panama Papers are dubious or even illegal?

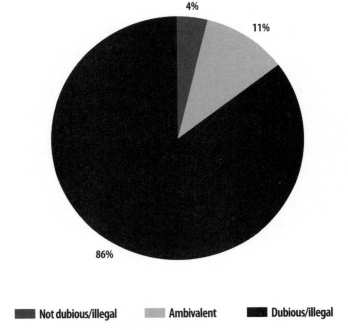

Not dubious/illegal   **Ambivalent**   **Dubious/illegal**

Source: mct Medienagentur, "Stereotypes of the Rich," July 2018.
Note: Based on a sample of 168 articles. Percentages do not add up to 100 in all cases because of rounding.

Table 16.1

Valence of references to "letterbox companies" in articles on the Panama Papers

Overall, does the article present letterbox companies in a negative or a more positive light? The analysis is based on more than just explicit statements: it is enough if the term "letterbox company" is conflated with illegality.

Valence	Percentage
Negative	92
Ambivalent	7
Positive	1
Total	100

Source: mct Medienagentur, "Stereotypes of the Rich," July 2018.
Note: Based on a sample of 158 articles.

As Kepplinger has shown,[635] a key characteristic of media reports on scandals is that they do not provide quantitative terms of reference. No attempt is made to establish the prevalence of a certain pattern of behavior; instead, the articles list large numbers of individual examples, thereby creating a certain, potentially misleading, impression. In the case of the Panama Papers, this meant that readers were usually left none the wiser about the relationship between legal and illegal activities.

Frequent mentions of dubious individuals (Mafiosi, money launderers, dictators, etc.) create the impression that a majority of owners of letterbox companies are money launderers or tax evaders—even if this

Figure 16.2

Relationship between legal and illegal activities in the Panama Papers

Does the article indicate the relationship between the legal and illegal activities revealed by the Panama Papers?

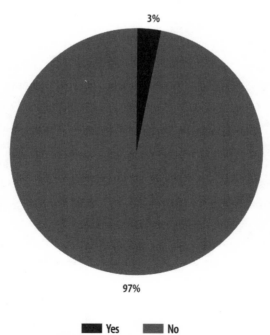

Yes   No

Source: mct Medienagentur, "Stereotypes of the Rich," July 2018.
Note: Based on a sample of 192 articles.

idea is not stated explicitly. Because the Panama Papers' researchers fail to provide information on the number of offshore companies used for legal versus illegal activities, *Stern* decided to cite a "guesstimate" from Social Democratic Party politician Peer Steinbrück: "I would guess that nine out of ten of these companies are used for deliberate tax fraud."[636] So much for quantitative rigor.

THE PARADISE PAPERS

Many media outlets published similar articles when the same international research team continued its revelations in November 2017 with the Paradise Papers. Once again, *Süddeutsche Zeitung* had received confidential documents from anonymous sources with unknown motives. A majority of the documents were from two companies specializing in services related to offshore companies: Appleby, a law firm founded in Bermuda, and Asiaciti, a smaller trust company headquartered in Singapore. In addition, the newspaper had received internal data from the company registers of 19 tax havens, including Bermuda, the Cook Islands, and Malta.

The Paradise Papers contained data from 21 sources. A total of 13.4 million documents were involved. "The documents," the journalists stress, "allow us to glimpse into a world specifically tailored to the needs of large corporations, the rich and the superrich."[637]

Once again, the team of journalists worked with the ICIJ, which had been involved in the Panama Papers project. The leaked documents were analyzed by 382 journalists from 67 countries.[638] Reports focused on the purportedly large number of politicians who were involved: "This is the political elite: the data contains the names of more than 120 politicians from almost fifty countries."[639] That is, on average, about two politicians per country. Is that number really so remarkably high? Many of these people, who at best can be said to have been clients of a certain law firm, had clearly done nothing wrong. As with the coverage of the Panama Papers, many of the full-page articles contained no more than a very brief (but crucial) caveat that just because someone's name appeared in one of the documents did not "necessarily mean that they can be accused of legal or moral misconduct."[640] Nevertheless, the bold headline above the series, "*Die Schattenwelt des großen Geldes*" ("The Shadowy World of Big Money"), made a far bolder claim than any caveat buried in a subordinate clause. After all, "Shadowy World" more than implies that the subject at hand is questionable and disreputable.

Researchers at mct Medienagentur analyzed 76 newspaper articles on the Paradise Papers (Table 16.2 and Figure 16.3). They determined the valence of media coverage of letterbox companies and the frames used to represent specific cases. In 91 percent of the articles, the term "offshore company" had a negative valence, and 78 percent of the articles created the impression that the activities dealt with in the Paradise Papers were shady or even illegal.

Incidentally, mct Medienagentur's analysis reveals that 83 percent of the articles completely failed to explain what offshore companies are and what purposes they serve. However, by emphasizing certain owners of offshore companies, such as drug dealers and corrupt politicians, the media creates a general impression of suspicion, especially because 78 percent of the articles failed to caution readers not to automatically assume that the individuals mentioned in the leak had done anything wrong. According to mct Medienagentur's analysis, only 5 out of 272 articles specifically highlighted the danger of drawing such erroneous conclusions.

Table 16.2

Paradise Papers: Valence of coverage of offshore companies

Overall, does the article present offshore companies in a negative or a more positive light? The analysis is based on more than just explicit statements: it is enough if the term "offshore company" is conflated with illegality.

Valence	Percentage
Negative	91
Ambivalent	9
Positive	0
Total	100

Source: mct Medienagentur, "Stereotypes of the Rich," July 2018.
Note: Based on a sample of 51 articles.

Figure 16.3

Paradise Papers: The "shadiness frame"

Does the article create the overall impression that the activities dealt with in the Paradise Papers are dubious or even illegal?

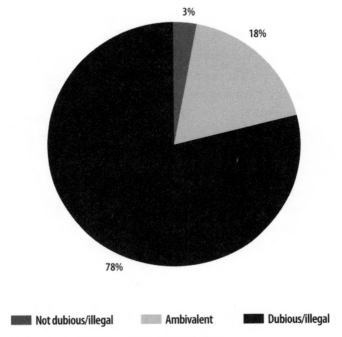

Not dubious/illegal   **Ambivalent**   **Dubious/illegal**

Source: mct Medienagentur, "Stereotypes of the Rich," July 2018.
Note: Based on a sample of 60 articles. Percentages do not add up to 100 in all cases because of rounding.

Generalizations: The Rich and the Superrich

As was the case with media coverage of the Panama Papers, articles on the Paradise Papers also referred sweepingly to "the rich" and "the superrich," thereby creating the impression that this group of individuals regularly engages in illegal activities. To back up this claim, *Süddeutsche Zeitung*, for example, quoted Brooke Harrington, an American professor of economic sociology, who said that the tax haven system makes it possible not only to avoid taxes "but also to circumvent laws that do not suit the rich. For example, they are able to 'live the dream' and enjoy 'the benefits of society without being subject to any of its constraints': 'For the superrich there's a world beyond the law.'"[641]

This line of interpretation was developed further in a large op-ed in *Süddeutsche Zeitung*. Under the headline "Paradise of the Rich," the article opined that tax havens have long since ceased to be "just filthy corners of the world" and have now become "meeting places of the business elite, among whom Irish-Dutch-Caribbean tax structures are just as widely accepted as pornography, for example."[642] The counterargument, namely, that "they should not be subjected to invasive media reports because they have done nothing illegal," is dismissed as mirroring the "spirit of the tax havens, which demands that the beneficiaries of the system should be left alone."[643]

Only very few articles placed the issues of tax avoidance and tax evasion in a broader context. The fact that tax avoidance is widespread across all sectors of society and is not limited to the rich is addressed in only 9 of 272 articles on the Panama and Paradise Papers, according to mct Medienagentur's analysis. "Only idiots and the poor pay taxes," claimed Jakob Augstein, one of Germany's most famous publicists, in *Spiegel Online*. His article ran under the headline "To Hell with the Rich."[644] This example demonstrates the massive disconnect between media coverage of the rich and that of other minorities: readers would rightly be outraged if a prominent journalist wrote an article for a reputable media outlet calling for Muslims, refugees, or gay people, for example, to be damned "to hell."

According to Augstein, the very fact that the practices described in the Paradise Papers are not illegal is precisely the scandal: "And the most beautiful thing—at least from the point of view of the rich: Many of these practices are completely legal. . . . No wonder: Illegality is not the scandal here—the scandal is the law."[645] The most remarkable thing about this article is the way it is constructed. First, the article refers sweepingly to "the rich" and accuses them collectively of lacking morals. Second, the fact that the activities described in the Paradise Papers are not illegal is twisted from a defense into a major accusation, supposedly proving that the laws have been written to benefit the rich. As Augstein wrote,

> The world of the rich is exposed; a world in which people lack morals, solidarity and a sense of duty—but possess huge amounts of money and power. Compared to this rarified world, the lives of everyone else,

who bear the burden of the state and taxes, are in fact hell. But there is something else that paradise lacks: a bad conscience. After all, a rich person who decides they don't want to share doesn't even have to break any laws. The laws are made for them. We can't quite be certain yet but, ultimately, the only thing illegal about the Paradise Papers could be their provenance.[646]

In articles such as this one, the lack of illegality in the revelations is itself held up as a general indictment of the capitalist system and of the rich: "The system is chronically ill. It is immoral and indecent. Anger is growing. The only problem is that the anger is directed at the wrong targets. The hatred of the defrauded is aimed at those fleeing war rather than those fleeing taxes. Our planet is a paradise for assholes."[647]

Just a few days after Augstein's article was published, the same argument was made in a *Zeit Online* article, which ran under the headline "Where Is the Anger?" This article's author also complained that popular anger was directed not against the rich but against refugees: "Recently, it seems that more and more people are angry at politicians, at the elites. Not because the top one percent has been siphoning off huge sums of money for decades, but rather for fear that those at the very bottom—immigrants—might take something away from them in the future. Thus, the proverbial 99 percent have their common enemy."[648]

The article in *Zeit* called for solidarity in the common "struggle against the real injustices in our society and around the world. . . . It is these injustices that deserve our anger." The author was disturbed by the lack of anger directed at the rich, which he explained was probably due to the fact that "our society supposedly rewards the brightest and the best" and thus "the ultrarich are more likely to be treated with reverence or envy, rather than anger." He complained that "100 years after the October Revolution, not much remains of the promise of social utopia and alternative systems."[649]

Even in less one-dimensional articles on the Paradise Papers, linguistic patterns insinuate that the rich routinely employ the practices that are being denounced. An article in *Der Spiegel*, for example, was more balanced, reporting that the indignation at the revelations was "understandable, but in some respects it comes too late." The article went on to point out that many of the tax avoidance practices described "would no longer work today." What the Panama Papers and Paradise Papers reveal, the article explained, was akin to "a glance in the rearview mirror."[650] Nevertheless, the article's title was "The Games Rich People Play." And it continued: "The data describe how the rich and superrich, celebrities and corporations try to put themselves beyond the reach of tax authorities. It's a rich man's game."[651]

An op-ed in the *FAZ* criticized the coverage of the Paradise Papers in large sections of the media. In particular, the article dismissed the argument that although the activities described in them might have been legal, they were not legitimate. "But in tax matters, the idea of decency does not take us very far. You can engage in almost endless debates about what is morally correct or not. But the only thing you can really demand is that everyone adheres to the law. We are all free to organize our affairs to ensure that we do not have to pay any more taxes than we absolutely have to."[652]

However, this position was not typical of the rest of the media's coverage. The dominant tone was one of accusation and of pillorying the rich and the superrich. Claims such as those made by Augstein that only the "poor" pay their taxes while the rich avoid them were very rarely challenged.

The media could easily have referred to the Federal Republic of Germany's official tax statistics. A simple comparison of the taxes paid by the lowest and the highest income deciles, for example, would reveal that the lowest 10 percent of earners pay no income tax at all and supply only 2.0 percent of total tax revenue, whereas the highest 10 percent pay 48.2 percent of the income tax and are responsible for 37.2 percent of total tax revenue.[653] The top 1 percent contributes more than 20 percent of income tax receipts.[654] The blanket claim that only the poor pay their taxes while the rich avoid them is therefore not supported by the figures.

In any case, even if the media had mentioned such facts, it would probably have had little effect, because media consumers—as Kepplinger has proved—classify events according to preexisting schemes or frames of interpretation. Such internalized schemes are often the direct result of previous exposure to media reports. Scientific research has shown that "media consumers are more likely to retain information from attitude-consistent sources than from counterattitudinal ones, interpret neutral information according to existing frames, and believe that they have read, seen or heard attitude-consistent information that was not actually present."[655]

The same analysis applies to the issue of whether rich people are "tax cheats." Of the 16 statements about rich people in our survey, the one that attracted the second-highest level of agreement from our German respondents was that "Most rich people are tax cheats," at 51 percent. Among hardcore social enviers, the figure was 71 percent. For media consumers who already believe that the rich avoid paying their fair share of taxes, media campaigns like the ones for the Panama and Paradise Papers confirm preexisting frames; they also create frames of interpretation that will serve as the basis for future media exposure on the same subject.

A majority of the journalists involved in these campaigns appear to have been far more interested in confirming these preexisting frames than in asking critical questions. The data were obtained illegally, and the very act of storing and publishing them can also be viewed critically, observes Kepplinger: "The exclusive access some media enjoyed to millions of emails, documents, bank statements, etc., data that belong to what we can presume are predominantly non-criminal actors, is also remarkable because so many media outlets have consistently objected to the state collecting and retaining similar data. They have always argued that this would primarily involve collecting data from entirely innocent individuals."[656] It would, perhaps, have been entirely logical for the media to conduct a self-critical examination of whether and in what circumstances it was acceptable not only to store stolen data but also to publish the names contained in the data.

The analysis by mct Medienagentur reveals that only 6 percent of the 272 articles highlighted the privacy issues surrounding the publication of the Panama and Paradise Papers. The media campaigners apparently believed that the end (their good cause, i.e., exposing the machinations of the rich and superrich) justified the means—a principle that does not apply in formal criminal proceedings, where there are clear restrictions on the methods that can be used to convict a suspect. Media campaigns such as those surrounding the Panama and Paradise Papers, however, resemble show trials more than the rule of law: even a vague suspicion (such as the fact that a wealthy individual was a client of a specific law firm) is enough to secure a preliminary conviction. In this context, protesting that a rich person hasn't actually broken the law is not enough to lift the shadow of suspicion. On the contrary, pointing out that a rich person has done nothing illegal is taken as evidence that the capitalist system itself is morally bankrupt and that we live in a world in which the rich write the laws to benefit themselves.

CHAPTER 17

ONLINE COMMENTS ABOUT THE RICH

Any analysis of how the rich are portrayed in the media would be incomplete without at least some impressions from the internet. Perhaps more so for this chapter than for any other, it is important to point out that the following represents little more than a preliminary step in the study of stereotypes of the rich. There are no scientific articles or other scholarly analyses about how the rich are represented in internet forums or online media. This chapter takes the first step toward filling that gap with two illustrative analyses. The first analysis was supported by Dr. Alexander Knuppertz and Malte Paulmann;[657] the second is by mct Medienagentur. A total of 2,250 online comments were analyzed.

GUESTBOOK POSTS FOR A TV TALK SHOW ABOUT THE RICH

The first analysis focuses on an evaluation of internet guestbook entries for an episode of the TV show *Hart aber fair* (*Hard but Fair*). This program airs on Monday evenings at 9:00 p.m. on Germany's principal publicly owned television channel (*Das Erste*) and is one of the most watched political talk shows in Germany. The analyzed broadcast was watched by 3.37 million viewers. Those viewers correspond to an audience share

---

*Figure and table data in Chapter 17 are from the author's own research.

of 12.4 percent. The number of viewers was sufficient for third place in the daily charts of May 7, 2018.[658]

The title of the episode was "Der Club der Reichen—wie viel Ungleichheit verträgt Deutschland?" ("The Rich Club—How Much Inequality Can Germany Tolerate?"). The live debate on *Hart aber fair* was preceded by a documentary called *Ungleichland—Wie aus Reichtum Macht wird* (*Land of Inequality—How Wealth Becomes Power*), which followed the self-made millionaire and entrepreneur Christoph Groener through his day-to-day life. He reports about his career, from his beginnings as a construction worker and his first experiences with real estate all the way to his large-scale real estate projects in Berlin, Cologne, Frankfurt, and other German metropolises.

Guests in the *Hart aber fair* debate included (left-wing) sociologist and elite researcher Professor Michael Hartmann; the chair of the Social Democratic Party youth organization Jusos, Kevin Kühnert; Free Democratic Party member of the Bundestag, Hermann Otto Solms; business journalist Bettina Weiguny; and the aforementioned real estate developer, Groener.

From May 5 to May 8, 2018, viewers were able to leave comments in *Hart aber fair*'s online guestbook. A total of 1,263 comments were posted in the guestbook, and each comment was limited to a maximum of 1,000 characters. Editors removed 142 comments because they did not comply with the broadcaster's official netiquette.[659] Another five comments were deleted because readers duplicated their posts in full or in part. Therefore, out of the 1,263 comments originally posted, 1,116 were analyzed.

The following method was used to analyze them. After an initial review, 38 topic categories were formed, to which the individual comments would be assigned. Because many viewers made comments that were either unclear or unrelated to the show's topic, two special categories were created and were excluded from the final content analysis. All 1,116 comments were assigned to the individual categories.

To make the analysis more straightforward, the 38 topic categories were combined into 7 main categories (Tables 17.1 and 17.2). Of those categories, five are anti-rich in terms of content and two are pro-rich. This imbalance is because 84 percent of the comments were hostile to the rich.

Table 17.1

Seven main categories by content

Anti-rich	Pro-rich
Capitalism is unjust	Envy of the rich gets on my nerves
The rich are exploiters	General pro-rich/pro-capitalism (other)
Pro-redistribution	
Rich people have character weaknesses	
General anti-rich/anti-capitalism (other)	

Of the 1,116 comments, 597 contained statements that could be analyzed in terms of "attitudes toward the rich" (Figure 17.1). Thirty-nine percent had no relation to the topic, instead containing complaints about general grievances in the country or the incompetence of politicians without making any specific reference to the rich. A further 8 percent of comments were so opaque that they could not be assigned to any of the designated categories.

The remaining 597 comments were assigned to seven main categories (Figure 17.2); 84 percent of the comments were anti-rich. Almost 30 percent of the commenters believed that the rich obtained their wealth unjustifiably at the expense of others, such as by paying too-low wages. Seventeen percent generally found it unfair that some people are richer than others, and 6 percent explicitly demanded the redistribution of wealth.

In 67 comments (11 percent), the content referred mainly to entrepreneurs exploiting their employees by paying unreasonably low wages (Figure 17.3). Many of the commenters argued that employees enrich entrepreneurs through their work, or at least support them in becoming rich, and that employees should therefore be paid higher wages. In this context, commenters often demanded a significant increase in the statutory minimum wage.

Another 55 comments (9 percent) focused primarily on the rich using their power to lobby for their own interests. In this context, politicians were often criticized for pursuing policies for their rich "clients" and for being so strongly influenced by lobbyists.

Table 17.2

Subcategories, sorted by anti-rich and pro-rich

Comments: Anti-rich

Capitalism is unjust

Gap exists between rich and poor
Society is becoming more and more divided
A large part of society is neglected
Managers are paid too much
There is no equality of opportunity
Wealth is unevenly distributed

The rich are exploiters

Rich people pay too-low wages
Financial markets damage society
Bankers/banks damage society
The rich use tax loopholes
Rich people influence government policy in their favor
The rich are privileged
The rich flee from "unsafe" countries/flee from Germany

Pro-redistribution

Rich people should pay more taxes
Other comments in favor of redistribution

The rich have character weaknesses

The rich are immoral
The rich are aloof from the rest of society
The rich have no respect for blue-collar workers
The rich are materialistic
The rich are greedy/self-indulgent
The rich are cold-hearted
The rich are self-centered
The rich are dishonest
The rich are manipulative
The rich are "actually poor"
The rich have no sense of social responsibility/are irresponsible
The rich are narcissistic/arrogant

Anti-rich/anti-capitalism (other)

General anti-rich comments
Anti-capitalism
Pro-socialism

(Continued)

Table 17.2

Subcategories, sorted by anti-rich and pro-rich *(continued)*

Comments: Pro-rich

Envy of the rich gets on my nerves

There is equality of opportunity
The rich are wrongly pilloried
Rich people who have worked hard for their wealth deserve it
The rich should not be taxed more heavily
The envy debate gets on my nerves

Pro-rich/pro-capitalism (other)

Pro-rich
Pro-capitalism
Anti-Marxism/socialism

Figure 17.1

Analysis of selected comments by opinion expressed

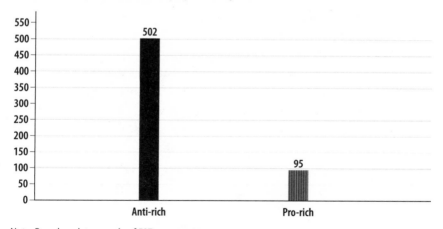

Note: Based on data sample of 597 comments.

Figure 17.2

Allocation of selected comments into the seven main categories

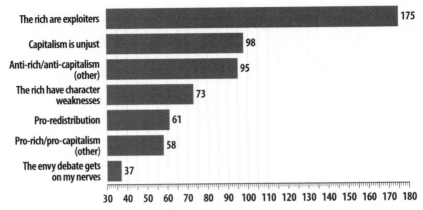

Note: Based on data sample of 597 comments.

Forty-seven comments (8 percent) called for the rich to pay more taxes. After all, according to the commenters, even if the rich were to pay higher taxes, they would still have more than enough to live on.

A majority of the comments were written in a measured tone (Figure 17.4). In contrast, comments related to alleged character weaknesses of the rich tended to be more sharply worded. However, the picture was somewhat distorted by the deletion of any comments that did not comply with the website moderator's netiquette, which is sure to have affected a disproportionately large number of comments with a sharp tone.

In the following section, one typical comment is cited for each of the 20 most frequently occurring subcategories. Where a comment addresses numerous topics, only the dominant passage is included.

Anti-Rich
The rich are exploiters
"Let's not forget, Mr. Groener's wealth was also built on the backs of others, such as unpaid craftsmen, poorly paid employees and off-the-books workers."

General anti-rich comments
"The middle class is being destroyed in Germany! This is how our democracy dies! Housing shortages and unaffordable housing. If the

Figure 17.3

Selected comments by subcategory (top 20)

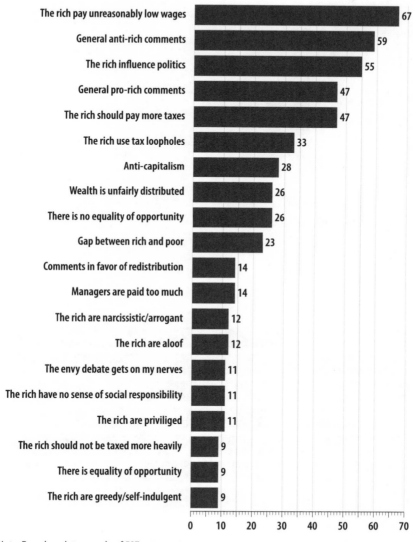

Note: Based on data sample of 597 comments.

Figure 17.4

Analysis of selected comments by tone

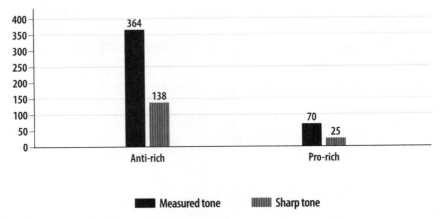

Note: Based on data sample of 597 comments.

Figure 17.5

Tone of comment of seven main categories

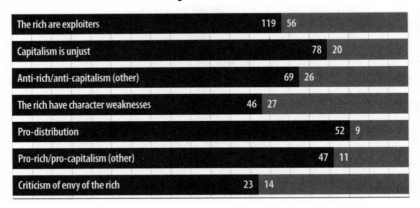

Note: Based on data sample of 597 comments.

problem is not solved quickly . . . our democracy will be transformed into a dictatorship. The rich and superrich only make it happen faster!"

The rich influence politics in their favor

"Money equals power—great wealth means great power—unbelievable wealth equals appalling power over society and the state. The state borrows money from these (undeserved) rich, is dependent on them, ergo the ultra-rich are systemically important and are always rescued. And, by the same measure, people think it is fair for a 'high achiever' to get a pension of €3,000. Not per month, but per day!"

The rich should pay more taxes

"As far as I'm concerned, you should only be able to leave single-digit millions to your heirs—nobody needs more than €5 million to live comfortably. Anything above this amount should be taxed at 90% and people shouldn't be allowed to take their wealth to other countries."

The rich use tax loopholes

"In good times, before things go belly up, the rich secure their 'hard-earned' property (house) by transferring its ownership to a limited company. For a certain group of people, there are almost always back doors/loopholes."

Anti-capitalism comments

"Turbo-capitalism and the greed for profit and power are responsible for almost all of the catastrophes in the world. The power of capital determines our lives. Look at the weapons lobby in the USA, arms sales to war zones, global warming due to environmental pollution, plastic waste in the seas, etc."

Wealth is unequally distributed

"When I was a young man (25 years old), there were 35 people who owned more than the rest of the world. Today I'm 72 and according to 2016 statistics, only 8 people own more than the rest of the world?!?"

There is no equal opportunity

"The wealth of the parents is passed on to the children in the same way that poverty is passed from parent to child. This has nothing to do with envy. It's a question of equal opportunities, which is no longer the case thanks to neo-capitalism."

Gap between rich and poor

"The fact is, the gap is there. It's sad that those who have an unbelievable amount hold on even tighter to their (unearned) fortunes. No one can truly earn billions. Nothing anyone does is worth soooo much. And, if it has not been earned, you have to ask yourself what gives someone the right to be so rich."

Comments in favor of redistribution

"Is this really about taking money from the rich? The crux of the matter is that their wealth is increasing exponentially, which is unfair, and that this needs to be stopped and redistributed through taxation!"

Managers are paid too much

"When managers' salaries go through the roof, no one seems to be bothered. But as soon as anyone calls for the wages of the workers who provide the salaries for the managers to be increased, then it's the same old story: 'Oh no, we can't do that, we'd have to offshore the jobs.' Politicians need to take a stand and get rid of all the lobbyists who start wailing as soon as anyone calls for the minimum wage to be raised to 12.50."

The rich are narcissistic/arrogant

"My problem isn't that there are so many rich people. No, what's bad is that they come across as so arrogant and unsympathetic."

The rich are aloof

"It's unbelievable that people with money (e.g., Mr. Groener) always think they are entitled to dictate to everyone else/stick their oar in. When people object, they take offense. The cheek! Just goes to show how people at the top think and act, this permeates everything . . . and it's really sad that they actually seem to believe what they say, crude, aloof."

The rich have no sense of social responsibility

"Other than that, I have the feeling that the common good doesn't interest business owners and they're shirking their responsibilities."

The rich are privileged

"Why do the rich (and their lackeys?) always think that they are more privileged than their fellow citizens????"

The rich are greedy/self-indulgent

"Dear people, let the greedy have their beautiful millions. Maybe, like me 4 years ago, they'll go to a doctor with a cold and come back with a diagnosis of cancer. Then—and only then—will man's unbearable greed be transformed into THINKING. Until then, any discussion is pointless because there will be no insight."

Pro-Rich

General pro-rich comments

"Entrepreneurs invest effectively and economically to make a profit. This is where most jobs are created. We are an industrial country, God save our entrepreneurs, we have to reduce bureaucracy. This is the only way we can make progress."

The envy debate gets on my nerves

"Our society is full of bleating, envious sheep! In the USA, you are 'a good performer' or just successful. There, people are appreciated for their achievements, in contrast to our leftist, envy-addled republic. Our desire for success is increasingly being replaced by 'redistribution dogmas.' Ultimately, this will harm us all because people who are willing to work hard bring our country forward, not lazy people."

The rich should not be taxed more heavily

"More and more intelligent people are leaving our country. Our state is not able to use taxpayers' money sensibly, just look at Berlin. We should all celebrate the fact that there are still 'rich people' who invest and help our country. And they should now pay even higher taxes? This is the wrong way."

There is equal opportunity

"There have never been more opportunities to get a good education than there are today. And there has never been more funding and support than there is today. Or do you really believe that life was better and fairer 30, 50, 70 years ago? By no means. Today everyone has access to education in Germany. There are so many more ways to get a degree than ever before."

READER COMMENTS ON ARTICLES IN TWO ONLINE MEDIA OUTLETS

Having been interviewed by an online medium (*Telepolis*) that tends to attract left-wing readers and having written guest commentaries in a medium that is popular among conservative readers (*Tichys Einblick*), I noticed that both media attracted large numbers of comments on my contributions that contained evaluations of the rich. I therefore commissioned mct Medienagentur to systematically evaluate these reader comments (Table 17.3).

The analysis included 1,134 online comments on contributions by Rainer Zitelmann in the Heise Forum (*Telepolis*) and on *Tichys Einblick* (rolandtichy.de). Of these comments, 30 percent appeared in *Tichys Einblick* and 70 percent in *Telepolis*. The number of comments on each of the contributions varied greatly.[660]

Table 17.3

Number of reader comments by contribution

Contribution	Date	Platform	n	%
Why intellectuals don't like capitalism	3/10/18	*Telepolis*	356	31
I'm honored to be branded a neoliberal	3/3/17	*Telepolis*	307	27
Sahra Wagenknecht twists the narrative	2/28/18	*Tichy*	143	13
Annual salaries don't really matter to these people	2/26/17	*Telepolis*	126	11
DSW—Capping manager salaries	3/6/18	*Tichy*	64	6
South Korea—Capitalism is good for people	2/12/18	*Tichy*	40	4
International study—Why do so many people support redistribution?	1/30/18	*Tichy*	34	3
Current *Forbes* list—Two-thirds of the top 15 are self-made entrepreneurs	3/11/18	*Tichy*	31	3
Criticism of business damages confidence	1/2/18	*Tichy*	27	2
Ingvar Kamprad—Farewell to the Ikea founder	1/28/18	*Tichy*	6	1
Total			**1,134**	**101**

Note: Percentages do not add up to 100 because of rounding.

On average, readers' comments were 769 characters long, although comments on *Telepolis* contributions averaged 813 characters, which was significantly longer than comments on *Tichy* (on average 670 characters). Of the analyzed comments, 19 percent referred directly to the author's original contribution under which they were posted; 72 percent of the comments were made in response to other comments in the same comment area; 34 percent of the comments addressed the topic of the original post; 39 percent referred to a related topic; and 21 percent addressed the author (and author's comments[661]) directly.

Judgments of the Rich

In 233 of the analyzed comments (21 percent), the commenter expressed an opinion on the rich (Table 17.4). Of those opinions, 73 percent were explicitly or somewhat negative, 11 percent were ambivalent, and 16 percent were explicitly or somewhat positive. On a five-point scale (where 1 equals unambiguously negative and 5 equals unambiguously positive), the mean value for opinions of the rich is 2.3 (i.e., significantly lower than 3, which is the middle of the scale).

It is interesting to note that there was no statistically significant difference in opinions of the rich in reader commentaries on *Tichy*, which tends to be read more by conservatives, compared to those on *Telepolis*, which attracts more left-wing readers.

Table 17.4

Opinions on the rich, wealth, and capitalism in comments on *Telepolis* and *Tichys Einblick*

Opinion	*Telepolis* n = 140 %	*Tichy* n = 93 %	Total n = 233 %
Negative	76	69	73
Ambivalent	10	13	11
Positive	14	18	16
Total	100	100	100

The following passages are representative of the most frequently expressed negative opinions on the rich, wealth, and capitalism:

The rich are often antisocial or are psychopaths (20 comments)

- "Poor psychopaths go to jail; rich psychopaths join the board of traded companies."
- "This kind of unscrupulousness shows precisely why we cannot allow unfettered capitalism—because the unscrupulousness of many business people knows no limits."
- "In many cases, it's only possible to earn your first millions if you have very few scruples, let others work for very little money, don't always obey the law and are willing to cheat your business partners from time to time."
- "These are the worst kind of people, mostly narcissists."
- "The IMPORTANT things a 'successful entrepreneur' needs are brutality and zero shame."

The rich exploit workers and employees (5 comments)

- "And then talk about whether those at the top really made it by 'their own' efforts, or whether they only succeeded by pulling a fast one or exploiting their employees."
- "The 'hard' working worker (endowed with valuable human capital) is fobbed off with crumbs while the person standing next to him doing nothing (AKA the manager) gets it all."
- "The problem is not the neighbor's oversized car, it's the fact that he only gets his oversized car—or the bonus he buys it with—by squeezing his employees out of their rightful pay."

The failure of managers is inconsistent with their high salaries (5 comments)

- "I am immediately reminded of the former head of Deutsche Bank AG, Joe Ackermann. He made a lot of money, but he left a pile of rubble behind."
- "In quite a few cases (former managers of Daimler, Siemens, Holzmann, Telekom—the list goes on and on), it would indeed have been better if they had done nothing more than

simply keeping their companies ticking along instead of trying to live out their visions."

Rich people don't do enough to justify their wealth (4 comments)

- "Consider Deutsche Bank: The share price is tumbling, profits are nowhere to be seen. Shareholders get a pittance—the investment bankers pocket a billion. And all to keep the 'best' people. I don't know whether to laugh or cry."
- "However, I remain of the opinion that top managers are nowhere near as ingenious as is generally claimed when justifying their salaries."
- "In response to the paragraph you quote, I merely want to point out that we are not talking about supermen who fill such posts and earn such huge salaries. Rather, in my experience, they tend to be blowhards and brown-nosers."

Capitalism is based on oligarchy and nepotism (3 comments)

- "Whenever you hear about salaries in the millions, it's always the same names. This is certainly no coincidence, but intent. It is always the same people who are given such posts, in politics and business."
- "The capitalists own almost all the media in a country, they use them to manipulate the citizens for their benefit. The capitalists also use their lobbyists to craft and enforce laws that serve their interests."

Capitalism leads to feudalism (3 comments)

- "Therefore, ultimately, it doesn't matter if someone gets 10 million or more, because the gap between rich and poor will be so wide at some point that we'll be back to the feudal system."
- "We have seen the circumvention of state structures and procedures and the formation of informal social hierarchies and associations of individuals (elite networking). So absolutely correct: capitalism resembles feudalism."

Capitalism has unpleasant side effects (3 comments)
- "Let's not forget: The capitalist system regularly extracts a tremendous price in human blood. Wars, the destruction of countries and the privatization of wealth that previously belonged to the general public are not 'accidents.'"
- "And thirdly, the problem with capitalism is not that it could not be made to work—the problem is that the collateral damage it causes in the permanent cycle of crises extends so far that it becomes inhuman."

The following passages are representative of the most frequently expressed positive opinions on the rich, wealth, and capitalism:

The rich are industrious, accomplish a lot, and are willing to take risks (6 comments)
- "The rich people I know work longer and harder than anyone else."
- "I think those who invest so much work, talent and innovation into their professions deserve high salaries."

Commentators object to the view that being rich is per se morally reprehensible (3 comments)
- "What's more, and this annoys me the most, is the fact that the rich are always deemed to be morally inferior, even if they treat their employees better than poor entrepreneurs do."
- "So, if being poor is morally better than being rich, everyone should be poor? That doesn't make any sense, man!"

How do readers express their opinions about the rich? Opinions can be positive, neutral, or negative and can be directed at more than just rich people. They can also be expressed in a sharp or a measured tone. In light of the fact that it makes little sense to distinguish between a measured tone and a sharp tone in comments stating neutral opinions, the following classification of readers' opinions emerges (Table 17.5).

Table 17.5

Readers' opinions of the rich

Opinion	*n*	Percentage
Positive, measured	88	8
Positive, sharp	7	1
Neutral	121	11
Negative, measured	144	13
Negative, sharp	131	12
Other focus, measured	423	37
Other focus, sharp	152	13
Unclear	68	6
Total	**1,134**	**101**

Note: Percentages do not add up to 100 because of rounding.

Having identified 290 sharply expressed opinions among the 1,134 comments, it is worth examining the overall aggressiveness of the reader comments. Of the analyzed comments, 73 percent were either explicitly or somewhat peaceable, 20 percent were less peaceable or somewhat aggressive, and 7 percent were aggressive. No comment was classified as extremely aggressive. There was no correlation between the platform (*Tichy* versus *Telepolis*) and the aggressiveness of the contributions. However, there was a correlation between a reader's opinion of the rich and the aggressiveness of his or her comments (Table 17.6).

These two analyses can provide only a first impression. However, they show that the predominantly anti–rich tenor that was evident in the survey of Germany (see Chapter 10) and the similarly critical tenor of media reports in Germany (see Chapters 15 and 16) correspond to the negative tenor of statements on the internet.

Naturally, criticism on the internet is often more pronounced than responses to questions in a general survey, and it often sharper than criticism in the media. However, the critical opinions expressed in the analyzed online comments correspond to the stereotypes we have come to

Table 17.6

Correlation between opinion of the rich and aggressiveness

	Rich-valence			
	Negative $n = 170$ %	**Ambivalent** $n = 26$ %	**Positive** $n = 37$ %	**Total** $n = 233$ %
Aggressiveness				
Peaceable	62	85	87	69
Moderate	29	15	14	25
Aggressive	9	—	—	6
Total	100	100	101	100

Note: Percentages do not add up to 100 in all cases because of rounding.

know in the previous chapters: rich people are immoral, greedy, arrogant, and aloof; senior managers' salaries are far too high; rich people avoid paying taxes; the gap between rich and poor is constantly widening; and government redistribution should be used to ensure that wealth is distributed more equitably.

One topic that our survey did not touch on and that is frequently voiced as a complaint on internet message boards is that the rich exert far too great an influence on politics through lobbying. Revealingly, we discovered no major differences in the anti-rich tone of the comments left on conservative versus left-wing online media. Clearly, criticism of the rich is widespread not only among left-wing outlets.

CHAPTER 18

THE RICH IN HOLLYWOOD MOVIES

In addition to daily newspapers, magazines, and the internet, views of rich people are also heavily influenced by television series and movies. To examine the influence of these global media, a team[662] developed criteria for analyzing the portrayal of rich characters in popular movies. First, they ranked the 20 top-grossing feature films worldwide in each of the past 28 years.[663] From 1990 to 2017, this amounts to 560 movies. Because there are no reliable figures to determine which blockbusters were actually seen by the largest audiences, the analysis is based on box-office earnings. In almost all cases, high box-office revenues correspond to high viewer figures. Factors such as inflation or population expansion do not influence this selection, because the ranking is based on the films released within the same year (see Table 18.1).

An Analysis of 43 Movies

The total of 560 films was reduced in several systematic steps. Animation, documentaries, fantasy, horror, science fiction, and superhero movies were excluded, because it is often difficult to determine the precise wealth of the rich characters depicted in films of these genres. Although fantasy films do feature rich characters, the analysis focused on films in which real, measurable wealth is portrayed.

From the remaining films, the next analytical step involved select-
ing those that feature rich characters. Films in which wealth is acquired
exclusively through crime or other illegal activities were excluded at
this stage, because the portrayal of "professional" criminals is inherently
negative and is thus of limited significance to this investigation. Thus,
films such as *Bugsy* (1991), *Heat* (1995), and a number of James Bond
movies, such as *Spectre* (2015), were excluded.[664]

This systematic process resulted in a sample of 33 films. To ensure
that films from earlier decades and from previously excluded genres were
not completely disregarded, this sample was expanded to include one well-
known and randomly selected movie from each of the following genres:
animation, fantasy, horror, science fiction, and superhero, along with one
movie from each of the following decades: the 1950s, 1960s, 1970s, and
1980s, that is, movies made before the period under investigation.

This approach produced a final sample of 43 movies, all of which
were analyzed in detail (Table 18.1). Of these films, 41 were produced,
coproduced, or distributed entirely (or at least to a significant extent) by
Hollywood studios (e.g., Warner Bros., Paramount Pictures, 20th Century Fox) or their subsidiary studios. Only *The Intouchables* (France) and
The King's Speech (Great Britain) were produced outside the United States.

The plot of each film was summarized, and a codebook was used to
analyze the portrayal of rich characters in each movie. For example, the
genders and professions of rich characters were recorded for each movie.
The codebook was the basis for a deeper analysis and was used to record
the qualities and traits with which these characters were depicted: likeable, obnoxious, competent, incompetent, warm-hearted, cold-hearted,
self-centered, greedy, arrogant, imaginative, reckless, superficial, daring,
visionary, moral, immoral, manipulative, and so on.

The codebook was used to record the traits and qualities attributed
to rich characters both at their first appearance and at the end of the
movie. In addition, the analysis determined whether the rich character
had a counterpart, that is, a contrasting character who served as a foil.
Such a counterpart was not necessarily a rich character's direct oppo-
nent or antagonist; in some cases, the counterpart was simply a person with whom the broad movie audience could more easily identify.

Table 18.1

Movies analyzed

Pretty Woman, rank 3, 1990	*Casino Royale* (James Bond), rank 4, 2006
Sleeping with the Enemy, rank 10, 1991	*The Devil Wears Prada*, rank 12, 2006
Father of the Bride, rank 14, 1991	*Ocean's Thirteen*, rank 16, 2007
The Naked Gun 2½: The Smell of Fear, rank 15, 1991	*Quantum of Solace* (James Bond), rank 7, 2008
The Bodyguard, rank 2, 1992	*Sex and the City*, rank 11, 2008
Basic Instinct, rank 4, 1992	*The King's Speech*, rank 12, 2010
Schindler's List, rank 4, 1993	*The Intouchables*, rank 15, 2012
Indecent Proposal, rank 6, 1993	*The Wolf of Wall Street*, rank 17, 2013
Sliver, rank 19, 1993	*The Great Gatsby*, rank 20, 2013
Forrest Gump, rank 2, 1994	*Fifty Shades of Grey*, rank 11, 2015
Braveheart, rank 13, 1995	*Kingsman: The Secret Service*, rank 18, 2015
Ransom, rank 6, 1996	*Hannibal*, rank 10, 2001, Horror
The First Wives Club, rank 14, 1996	*Iron Man*, rank 8, 2008, Science Fiction
Evita, rank 20, 1996	*The Dark Knight*, rank 1, 2008, Superhero
Titanic, rank 1, 1997	*Up*, rank 6, 2009, Animation
Die Another Day (James Bond), rank 4, 2002	*Doctor Strange*, rank 11, 2016, Superhero
You've Got Mail, rank 12, 1998	*Some Like It Hot*, 1959, 1950s
The Mask of Zorro, rank 15, 1998	*Once Upon a Time in the West*, 1968, 1960s
Notting Hill, rank 7, 1999	*The Towering Inferno*, 1974, 1970s
The World Is Not Enough (James Bond), rank 8, 1999	*Wall Street*, 1987, 1980s
Erin Brockovich, rank 13, 2000	*All the Money in the World*, 2017
Something's Gotta Give, rank 11, 2003	

Sources: Nash Information Services, The Numbers (website), https://www.the-numbers.com; Worldwide Boxoffice.com (website), http://www.worldwideboxoffice.com.

Such counterparts must have had an indirect or direct relationship to the rich protagonist. The codebook was also used to record the characteristics of these counterpart characters.

EIGHT MOVIES OVER 50 YEARS

For the purposes of illustration, and before moving on to the findings of the full analysis, the plots of eight of the analyzed movies are presented in more detail below.

Once Upon a Time in the West *(1968)*

A mysterious, harmonica-playing gunman tangles with assassins paid by a rich railroad mogul. As it turns out, Harmonica (Charles Bronson) has a score of his own to settle with Frank (Henry Fonda), the ruthless leader of the band of killers, who once sadistically murdered Harmonica's older brother.

Frank is now in the service of the gravely ill railway tycoon Mr. Morton, who, given his approaching death, means to complete his railroad line to the Pacific before he dies. But Morton is frustrated by the widowed McBain, who owns a key piece of land along the route, which McBain bought in the hope of becoming wealthy himself. His land, Sweetwater, would provide indispensable water for the railroad's steam locomotives.

Frank and his gang shoot McBain and his three children. Morton is upset about the killings, not so much for moral reasons but because, in his view, this primitive approach leads only to unnecessary complications. He shows Frank a bundle of money: "You see Frank, there are many kinds of weapons, and the only one that can stop that, is this."

The film's rich character, Morton, is not portrayed as cruel or even unpleasant. He is depicted as amoral, desperate to realize his vision and build his business and willing to use all means to do so, even the murder of innocent people, including children. He is obsessed, unwilling to stop at anything in pursuit of his entrepreneurial visions.

The Towering Inferno *(1974)*

During the opening ceremony of a colossal skyscraper in San Francisco, a fire breaks out and the building becomes a deathtrap—all because a negligent building contractor, Duncan (William Holden), and his far-worse son-in-law, Simmons (Richard Chamberlain), have ignored the building code in order to save several million dollars in material and labor costs on the tower's safety measures. Star architect Roberts (Paul Newman) and fire chief O'Halloran (Steve McQueen)—horrified by Duncan and Simmons' machinations—try to save as many people as possible, including two children. Duncan regrets his mistakes; Simmons remains unrepentant.

This all-star disaster movie (Faye Dunaway, Fred Astaire, and O. J. Simpson are among those fighting for their lives as the flames draw ever nearer) is about gigantism and the danger that comes when "bigger, taller, greater" becomes a self-serving exercise while the drawbacks are ignored. The only thing that matters to ruthless developer Duncan and his unscrupulous son-in-law Simmons is making more money and making it fast. Duncan wants to rescue his construction company by cutting costs; Simmons simply wants to become even richer. Duncan experiences a catharsis during the fire and comes to regret his greed, but it is too late. He, too, will die in the flames—just like Simmons, the intransigent villain.

The "good guy" is Roberts, a friend of Duncan's. As a star architect, we can also assume that he is rich, although his wealth is not mentioned even once. Roberts is an idealist; he is not interested in material things, he is not greedy, and he even wants to take six months off once he has finished working on the Glass Tower project. He is one of the film's two main heroes, together with the fire chief O'Halloran and he rescues many of the people trapped in the skyscraper from certain death in the blazing inferno. He not only survives but promises to seek O'Halloran's advice before his next construction project, clearly demonstrating that for him, safety comes first—not size, architectural statements, or even profit.

This film deals with greed and its consequences. Because of their avarice, Duncan and Simmons are responsible for many deaths. The rich are again portrayed as stopping at nothing, including fatalities, in pursuit of their own financial gain.

Wall Street *(1987)*

A young and ambitious New York stockbroker, Bud Fox (Charlie Sheen), wants to be among the most successful traders on Wall Street. His father, Carl Fox (Martin Sheen, who is Charlie Sheen's real-life father), works in Queens as a mechanic and union official for the financially troubled airline Bluestar.

After speaking to one of his wealthy clients on the phone, Bud turns to his colleague, Marvin, and says, "You know what my dream is? To be on the other end of that phone." Marvin responds, "Oh, you got it, baby, where the real cheesecake is."

Through perseverance, charm, and guile, Bud gets to know the star of the New York stock market, the unscrupulous speculator and major investor Gordon Gekko (Michael Douglas).

Marvin describes Gordon Gekko as follows: "He had an ethical bypass at birth."

Gekko is impressed by Bud's hunger and talent and takes him under his wing: "Give me guys that are poor, smart, and hungry, and no feelings." He teaches Bud all the tricks in the book, including insider trading. As he says, "I'm going to make you rich, Bud Fox."

In no time at all, Bud is rich and has abandoned his initial scruples. But everything changes when Gekko buys Bluestar Airlines, the company Bud's father works for. Having promised Bud that he would buy and restructure the company, Gekko goes back on his word and decides to break it up and sell it in individual parts, thereby driving hundreds of working families to ruin. In an argument with Bud, Gekko says, "It's all about bucks, kid. The rest is conversation."

With the help of one of Gekko's old rivals, Bud counterattacks. A no-holds-barred showdown on the stock exchange ensues as Bud and his allies manipulate trades in Bluestar shares, driving Gekko to financial ruin. Bud is arrested and accused of fraud and insider trading. But as part of a deal with the authorities, Bud wears a wire and gets Gekko to talk about several of their illegal stock market transactions, thereby securing the evidence needed to arrest Gekko.

Gordon Gekko's most famous lines are these: "The point is, ladies and gentlemen, that greed, for a lack of a better word, is good. Greed is right. Greed works." Gekko embodies the stereotype of a greedy, rich stockbroker. He is an expert in his field, has no scruples about driving other people to ruin, and uses illegal methods to amass ever-greater wealth. Based on the framing of his character, rich people can never have enough.

Pretty Woman (1990)

Edward Lewis (Richard Gere) is a businessman who became rich as a corporate raider but doesn't really care about interpersonal relationships.

He has just broken up with his girlfriend, who complained that he treated her like a "beck-and-call girl." After a party, he borrows his lawyer's luxury sports car to drive back to his hotel in Hollywood, gets lost, and stops to ask for directions from the beautiful and vivacious prostitute Vivian Ward (Julia Roberts), who is standing at the side of the road looking for johns. They start a conversation, and Edward ends up hiring Vivian for a whole week.

Vivian does not condemn Edward's conduct and business practices, which she doesn't really understand anyway. Of course, she is impressed by his luxurious lifestyle. Despite her humble background, Vivian impresses Edward with her authenticity and natural humanity. Edward is unworldly in many respects—for example, he doesn't really know how to drive the Lotus Esprit he borrowed from his lawyer. During their "business relationship," initially limited to one week, Vivian holds a mirror up to Edward by comparing his business to the behavior of the crooks she presumably knows from the red-light scene:

> EDWARD: "Well, I don't sell the whole company. I break it into pieces and sell that. If it's worth more than the whole."
> VIVIAN: "So, it's like stealing cars and selling them for the parts."

She does this in a completely naive, innocent way, without condemning or even judging Edward. She shows him another way of being and working. Edward changes the way he deals with his business partners and with Vivian during the course of the film, thereby redeeming and reinventing himself. "You and I are such similar creatures, Vivian. We both screw people for money," he says to her at one point in the movie.

Edward abandons his plan to take over and carve up a family business. Instead, he decides to restructure it together with its owners. Edward wants to stay with Vivian, but on his terms, not in a steady relationship or marriage. His initial proposal hurts Vivian, so she leaves him, having fulfilled her side of their bargain. Edward goes after her, locates her, and they find happiness together. The romantic fairy tale has its happy ending.

In summary, the corporate raider Edward Lewis is initially unscrupulous in his greed. Profit is his only interest, and he is even willing to bribe politicians to satisfy his greed. Only through his relationship with a woman who is considered to be for sale and yet cannot be bought does he find redemption, by deciding to help restructure the company he originally wanted to buy and dismantle. The moral of the story is that an unscrupulous rich man can be brought back to a virtuous path by someone who only at first glance appears to live outside mainstream concepts of morality.

Indecent Proposal (1993)

Architect David Murphy (Woody Harrelson) and his wife Diana (Demi Moore), a real estate agent, stand to lose everything they own when a recession hits. They go to Las Vegas and try in vain to win the money they need to complete their dream house and turn their finances around. While in Vegas, the couple meets billionaire John Gage (Robert Redford). He approaches Diana as she is trying on a very expensive dress that she cannot afford. He offers to buy it for her, but she rejects his proposal: "The dress is for sale. I am not."

Shortly afterward, they meet again at the casino and Gage asks Diana to gamble for him. Diana wins $1 million. As a thank you, Gage rents a suite and invites the couple to a cocktail party.

David and Gage play pool while Diana watches, a key scene that precedes Gage's indecent proposal:

> DIANA: "Well, some things aren't for sale."
> GAGE: "Such as?"
> DIANA: "We can't buy people."
> GAGE: "That's naive, Diana. I buy people every day."
> DIANA: "Oh, in business, maybe, but not when real emotions are involved."
> GAGE: "You're saying you can't buy love? That's a bit of a cliché."
> DIANA: "It's absolutely true."

Gage then offers the couple $1 million for a single night with Diana. Without hesitation, David and Diana dismiss the offer. Gage asks them to consider his proposal overnight. The next morning, they accept the offer. Gage and Diana fly off in a helicopter to his luxury yacht, where they have the following conversation:

> GAGE: "You think I have to buy women?"
> DIANA: "Why me, then?"
> GAGE: "I bought you because you said you couldn't be bought."
> DIANA: "I can't be bought. We're just gonna fuck, as I understand it."
> GAGE: "You might enjoy it."
> DIANA: "Don't bet on it."

David and Diana get the money but, having narrowly missed their bank appointment, Gage buys their house and land. David and Diana's marriage soon falls apart because of their growing mistrust, frequent quarrels, and, above all, David's jealousy.

Gage, who has fallen in love with Diana, keeps trying to win her over. She finally succumbs to his charms and moves in with him. It looks as if Gage was right and love can be bought. In the end, however, Gage realizes that Diana is still very attached to David and tells his chauffeur, "She never would have looked at me the way she did at him." Wanting to do the right thing by Diana, Gage ends the romance. Diana thanks him with a parting kiss. She goes to the pier where David proposed to her, where she meets David and reconciles with him.

The film's message is that rich people think that money can buy anything, but they are mistaken. True love is not for sale. Even though billionaire Gage initially manages to wrap Diana around his finger, first with his money and later with his charm, he has to admit that even his billions don't allow him to manipulate her feelings. The film gives comfort to everyone who is not rich: "Money alone does not make you happy."

Titanic (1997)

While searching the wreck of the *Titanic* in 1996, a treasure hunter, Brock Lovett (Bill Paxton), who is looking for a legendary diamond, the Heart of the Ocean, recovers a safe containing nude drawings of a young woman. The woman is 101-year-old Rose Dawson Calvert (Kate Winslet), one of the survivors of the *Titanic*'s catastrophic voyage.

Brock contacts her, and she tells the explorer of her experiences on the doomed ship.

At the outset of their passage from Southampton to New York, Rose—usually a clever, art-loving, and vivacious young woman—appears depressed and blasé. She is horrified at the prospect of spending the rest of her life with her rich, superficial, and loveless fiancé, Cal Hockley, who in a rage becomes violent toward her. While in Europe, she bought paintings by then-undiscovered artists, including Monet and Picasso. Cal mocks her for her fascination with artists who will "never amount to a thing."

The life of the rich is portrayed as contrived and a kind of prison— contributing to Rose's final break with her milieu as she watches a little girl being formally trained in table manners by her mother. This sight makes Rose think of her impending marriage, which she doesn't want but has been urged into by her widowed mother for financial reasons ("Do you want to see me working as a seamstress? Is that what you want? Do you want to see our fine things sold at an auction, our memories scattered to the winds?").

Rose also contemplates suicide. Whether she really intends to jump off the *Titanic*, as it seems, or whether she just slips off the railing but actually "wouldn't a jumped," as the young painter and bon vivant Jack Dawson (Leonardo DiCaprio), her savior, insinuates, is not important. She wants to free herself of the constraints of her social position. Finally, she swaps the sun deck of life at Cal's side for life with Jack in third class—because down there, although people are less educated, they are more honest, cheerful, enterprising, and spontaneous. Despite the massive pressure from Cal and her mother, she wants to live like Jack and travel the world with him, without a plan, without rigid conventions or rules. In place of stilted conversation over liqueurs in the ship's upper-class salon, Rose chooses beer and tap dancing on the wooden planks of the lower deck. She starts an affair with Jack, has him draw the nudes that Brock finds decades later in the wreck, and, on the night the "unsinkable" ship collides with the iceberg, she sleeps with Jack.

In the ensuing chaos, Cal frames Jack as the apparent thief of the 51-carat Heart of the Ocean diamond, which Cal had given to Rose. In reality, Cal hid the diamond in the pocket of a coat (which he later mistakenly throws over Rose to appear as a devoted gentleman). Jack is arrested and imprisoned in a cabin that quickly floods with water. For a brief moment, Rose questions Jack's innocence. But finally, she is convinced that he's not guilty and in the general panic frees him as he is about to drown.

Despite the fact that Cal has bought himself a place in a lifeboat, he chooses to stay on the sinking *Titanic* to hunt for Rose, who he is now convinced has betrayed and left him. He wants to persuade her to go with him. Whether he, the otherwise so successful businessman, has real feelings for the young woman or simply wants to claim victory in the battle for Rose is left to the audience to decide. However, Cal demonstrates that his feelings for Rose are not entirely pure when he tries to shoot her and Jack after they turn him away.

Rose and Jack make their escape from Cal, but the *Titanic* is sinking ever faster. Cal pretends to be looking after a crying, abandoned child, which allows him to board a lifeboat reserved for women and children. Jack and Rose remain on board the sinking *Titanic*. Rose manages to save herself by clambering onto a wooden plank, but there is no room on the plank for Jack. Jack freezes to death in the water because he, the gentleman in rags, sacrifices himself to save Rose.

Later, on a rescue ship, Rose sees Cal again as he searches for her through the rows of survivors. She hides from him and tells her rescuers that her name is Rose Dawson. At the very end of the film, Rose finds the giant diamond in the pocket of the coat Cal mistakenly threw over her shoulders. She throws the treasure into the ocean. As Rose narrates her story to the end, viewers find out that Cal shot himself a few years after the demise of the *Titanic* when he lost his fortune in the Great Depression.

Throughout the film, the wealthy Cal is portrayed in a very stereotypical way: ruthless and self-centered. His fiancée leaves him for his antagonist, the hitherto unsuccessful but loving artist, who in the end sacrifices his life to save her. Here, too, the audience is left with the comforting message: "Money alone does not make you happy."

The Wolf of Wall Street *(2013)*

The film biography of the U.S. stockbroker Jordan Belfort (Leonardo DiCaprio) is, in many respects, almost a sequel to *Wall Street*. Belfort

embodies the stereotype of the rich, extremely greedy, and unethical investment banker. This image is evident from the first scene of
the film, which is set in the 1980s. In an advertisement for the firm
Stratton Oakmont, values such as integrity, seriousness, and stability are
feigned. Immediately afterward, the audience is given a glimpse behind
the scenes: together with his employees, Belfort is shown playing the
degrading game of midget tossing, in which small people are thrown as
living arrows onto oversized dartboards.

Breaking the fourth wall, Belfort boasts about his wealth and lists
how many drugs he takes every day. While he's doing coke, he says,
"But of all the drugs under God's blue heaven, there is one that is my
absolute favorite. And I'm not talking about this [he points to a huge
amount of coke in front of him]. I'm talking about this [he waves money
in front of the camera]." He claims that money makes him a better person
and that he always wanted to be rich.

Belfort began his career as a Wall Street stockbroker at L. F.
Rothschild, a tradition-steeped bank. His boss, Mark Hanna, quickly
taught him that his only goal should be not securing the best returns for
his clients, but getting rich quickly on their commission payments.

During a stock market crash, Belfort loses his job. Then, in a job
interview, he becomes aware of the almost unregulated penny stock
market, where the commissions, up to 50 percent, are much higher than
the paltry 1 percent commission on standard stocks. Belfort uses his sales
talent to enter the market and earns a small fortune very quickly.

He meets Donnie Azoff and, with his friends, founds Stratton Oakmont,
an over-the-counter brokerage house that sells risky penny stocks to wealthy
clients. To increase turnover, Belfort becomes increasingly involved in illegal trading. Stratton Oakmont buys majority stakes in low-value stocks and
then spreads untruthful rumors to pump up the stocks' value.

Belfort quickly attracts the attention of the Federal Bureau of Investigation. He tries to bribe FBI agent Patrick Denham. When Denham
refuses to accept the bribe, Belfort shows his arrogant, condescending
side. As Denham and his colleague are leaving, Belfort calls after them,
"Good luck on that subway ride home to your miserable wives. I'm
gonna have Heidi lick some caviar off my balls in the meantime."

Despite his bravado, Belfort is alarmed. Together with the other founders of Stratton Oakmont, he spirits his accumulated assets to safety in Switzerland. Nevertheless, the FBI secures more and more incriminating evidence against him. Belfort comes close to making a deal with the authorities and resigning as president of Stratton Oakmont. However, his ego will not allow him to go through with the deal. Instead, he flees the United States and runs the company from his yacht, which he moors in the Mediterranean. He uses an English aunt's identity to create a bank account to hide his wealth.

When the aunt suddenly dies of a heart attack, Belfort has to go to Geneva on short notice to sort things out, rather than flying to London for the funeral. In order to secure his money, he even risks the lives of everyone on board his yacht when he forces his captain, despite storm warnings, to head for the Italian coast, from where he wants to travel to Switzerland. The yacht sinks, but, fortunately, the entire crew is rescued—including Belfort.

Back in the United States, Belfort is arrested. To avoid a longer prison sentence, he cooperates with the authorities and betrays his friends. Stratton Oakmont is shut down, and everyone who was involved in its fraudulent business practices is also arrested. Following his stint in prison, Belfort works as a sales and motivational trainer.

The message of the film is striking: rich people only ever think about money. Everything they do is directed at satisfying their greed for more money. They are even willing to cheat and defraud others. Belfort embodies the stereotype of the arrogant, greedy investment banker. In order to amass an ever-greater fortune, he will use any means at his disposal. He becomes involved in illegal business activities and is even prepared to risk the lives of the people around him in his pursuit of money.

All the Money in the World (2017)

In this thriller, which follows true events from the year 1973, a mother fights like a lioness for her son—not only against his kidnappers, but also against his grandfather, J. Paul Getty, portrayed by Christopher Plummer.[665] Getty is an oil magnate and the richest man in the world; he claims to love his grandson but is not prepared to pay a ransom to his kidnappers, who initially demand $17 million and later $4 million.

As Getty, Plummer delivers the archetypal distorted picture of a rich man. He brushes off his former daughter-in-law Gail, the mother of 16-year-old John Paul Getty III (called "Paul"), and pours champagne as he claims, "My financial position has changed. . . . I have no money to spare." His argument: at most, he could deduct $1 million from his tax bill by ransoming his grandson. At the same time, however, this billionaire is prepared to pay $1.2 million for a valuable, stolen, sacred painting of the Blessed Mother with the Child Jesus. Not even after the kidnappers brutally cut off one of the teenager's ears and send it to a newspaper's editorial office is the unsympathetic Mr. Getty willing to soften his stance.

However, the film's audience is also led to understand that the old man is insecure and anxious about losing his entire fortune. He likes "things, objects, artifacts, paintings," he tells Fletcher Chase, his security man and chief adviser: "They are exactly what they appear to be. They never change. They never disappoint. There's a purity to beautiful things that I've never been able to find in another human being." Getty is also extremely suspicious. When Gail divorces Getty's heroin-addicted son and tells him that she rejects any alimony payments ("I don't want your money"), Mr. Getty is bewildered by her decision. "What's your game?" he asks her. "Everybody wants my money!"

The stingy billionaire is also exposed as a liar and braggart. The very first time he and Paul meet, he gives Paul, at that time still a little boy, what he claims is a valuable Minotaur figurine, allegedly from the year 460 BCE. He bought it for $11.23: "I picked it up at the black market in Heraklion. Some old cripple wanted 19 dollars for it. It took me one hour to bring him down to his bottom line. Yes, today, at auction, I hazard it could bring 1.2 million." He goes on to tell the boy, "You see? Everything has a price. The great struggle in life is coming to grips with what that price is." But when Gail tries to sell the figurine in her desperation to raise the ransom for Paul, she discovers that it is worth only $15, a mass-produced souvenir from a museum shop.

J. Paul Getty endures pressure from the media, Chase, and probably also what's left of his conscience; he eventually pays $4 million at the last minute to secure Paul's freedom, then dies of heart failure, alone, surrounded by his art treasures. The change of heart comes too late for any catharsis or redemption. In fact, even one of the kidnappers cares more for the boy than does his grandfather, going as far as to save Paul's life during the dramatic liberation scene.

Because of the way Getty's oil empire is structured, as a charitable family foundation, the previously arrogant Getty lawyers have to ask Gail to run the company after the death of the patriarch until Paul reaches the age of majority. The following conversation takes place between Gail and the lawyers:

> LAWYER: "You see, the estate was structured as a charitable family trust."
> GAIL: "Did he ever give any money to charity?"
> LAWYER: "No. No. The trust enabled Mr. Getty to build his fortune without paying taxes."

Gail takes the helm and, from that day on, the Getty Foundation charts a more noble course.

FRAMING THE RICH IN THE 43 ANALYZED MOVIES

Certain frames recur frequently when rich people are depicted in movies. Where a frame appears, it does not have to be central to the plot or theme of the film. At the same time, it is also not an insignificant episode within the film; rather, it is an open or underlying frame of interpretation concerning the characterization of rich people.

Frame: Rich People Will Stop at Nothing in Pursuit of Their Economic Goals

- *Once Upon a Time in the West*: A railway tycoon hires bandits who murder innocent people, even children, when they stand in the way of his economic goals.
- *The Towering Inferno*: Building contractors skimp on fire protection out of greed, which leads to a catastrophic fire in which many people die.
- *The Mask of Zorro*: A rich man plans to sacrifice hundreds of miners in order to reach a treasure.

- *Casino Royale*: A banker hires an assassin to blow up a pro-totype airplane. He wants to make a fortune by speculating on stock in the airplane's manufacturer. He is even willing to accept the death of all those involved.
- *The World Is Not Enough*: A rich industrialist plans to deto-nate a nuclear bomb in Istanbul so that his oil pipeline will be the only one in the region, allowing him to earn a lot of money through this monopoly.
- *Kingsman: The Secret Service*: An internet billionaire wants to use technology to manipulate everyone in the world to kill one another—and thus prevent global overpopulation and become their ruler himself.
- *Quantum of Solace*: An entrepreneur wants to install a mem-ber of the military as the head of state of Bolivia in order to get access to water reserves. He will stop at nothing to achieve his goal.

Frame: The Rich Have Only Profit on Their Minds—It's All about Satisfying Greed

- *Wall Street*: A rich stockbroker wants to take over an air-line, dismantle it, and sell it in parts. This tactic will drive hundreds of workers' families to ruin.
- *The Wolf of Wall Street*: An investment banker and his company buy penny stocks and then spread false news and rumors in order to increase the shares' prices and thus make a fortune.
- *Ocean's Thirteen*: A rich casino owner cheats his less-rich business partner in order to acquire his casino; even his partner's heart attack does not deter him.

Frame: Money Alone Doesn't Make You Happy—You Can't Buy Everything with Money

- *Indecent Proposal*: A billionaire is forced to concede that true love cannot be bought.
- *Notting Hill*: Despite her wealth, a rich actress is not happy until she meets her true love, a bookseller.

- *The Great Gatsby*: The force driving a man to become a millionaire by any means is his love for a beautiful woman, whom he ultimately cannot win over.

- *Titanic*: Despite his wealth, an arrogant rich man has to face the fact that his fiancée chooses a good-hearted have-not.

- *Sleeping with the Enemy*: A beautiful woman renounces her wealth and leaves the golden cage of her marriage (which is not surprising, considering her husband's psychopathic character).

- *Fifty Shades of Grey*: Although a billionaire can hire women to satisfy his fetish for bondage sex, he can't resist falling in love with a young student whom he draws into his world.

Frame: Rich People Can See the Error of Their Ways and Regain Their Humanity—Thereby Shedding the Typical Negative Characteristics Associated with the Rich

- *Pretty Woman*: A corporate raider who wanted to take over and dismantle a family business, using unfair methods, is transformed into a better person by a prostitute and her human nature.

- *The Bodyguard*: An arrogant and upstanding pop star is redeemed by the encounter with her bodyguard, a man with both feet on the ground.

- *Schindler's List*: A rich man is transformed from a cool, calculating businessman and exploiter who profits from the National Socialist system and war into a compassionate man who saves many lives.

- *Iron Man*: An owner of an armaments company becomes a victim of his own technology and barely escapes with his life. After his personal transformation, his company no longer produces weapons.

- *Basic Instinct*: A wealthy heiress who is also a successful author and suspected serial killer cannot bring herself to kill the police detective who (almost) uncovers her crimes because she falls in love with him.

Frame: Rich People Use Their Wealth to Exert and Manipulate Power and Influence

- *Hannibal*: A rich and child-molesting heir of a cattle baron uses his power and contacts to attempt to murder his enemy, the serial killer Hannibal Lecter, in a sadistic, years-long plan.
- *Die Another Day*: A rich man wants to use a satellite weapon in orbit to cut a path through the minefield separating North and South Korea in order to enable North Korea to invade South Korea.

MORAL AND COMPETENCE TRAITS

In Chapter 7, we saw that in most situations, positive or negative perceptions of people are determined mainly by so-called M traits (moral traits), which suggest whether the intentions of an individual or group are good or bad. The second dimension of perception is competence, which concerns the extent to which the individual or group is able to implement those intentions. Competence traits are also called C traits.

For our analysis, we first had to determine the proportions of characters with negative or positive M traits in each of the 43 films. The characters who were depicted as callous, selfish, greedy, or ruthless and who exhibited immoral or unethical behavior had negative M traits. Positive M traits were associated with characters presented as warm-hearted or honest and who demonstrated morally and ethically positive behavior. After determining whether the rich characters in the movies had positive or negative M traits (M+ or M−, respectively), the same classification was made for simple, nonrich characters in the movies, who often served as counterparts to the rich characters. Finally, we analyzed whether the aforementioned characters were presented as competent (C+) or incompetent (C−). This analysis involved establishing whether the characters were ambitious, capable, intelligent, or purposeful or were incompetent, less capable, or less intelligent. If a character could not be clearly classified into one of these two categories, we determined whether he or she had at least one of the three other C+ traits (imaginative, farsighted, and daring). Depending on the results of these steps, the characters were classified as either competent or incompetent.

Figure 18.1

Portrayals of rich characters at the start of each film

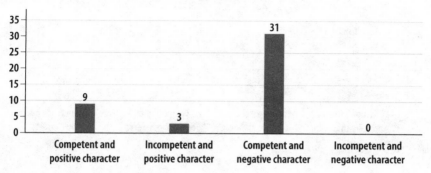

Note: Data based on sample of 43 films.

At the beginning of each movie, the most important rich character is portrayed as presented in Figure 18.1.

Figure 18.2 presents how the most important rich character is portrayed at the end of each film.

The rich characters' most common negative M traits are as follows:

• Arrogant (29 films)
• Obnoxious (23)
• Callous (22)
• Amoral (22)
• Self-centered (21)

Figure 18.2

Portrayals of rich characters at the end of each film

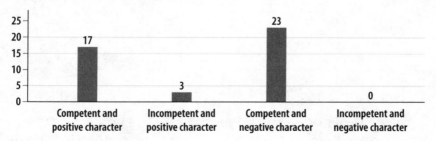

Note: Data based on sample of 43 films.

Figure 18.3

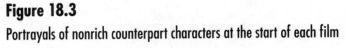

Portrayals of nonrich counterpart characters at the start of each film

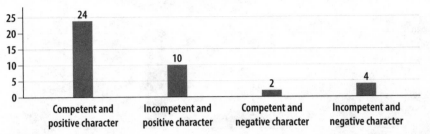

Note: Data based on sample of 40 films.

In 47 cases, the primary rich character is shown to be competent at both the beginning and the end of the film. The characters' positive C traits are distributed as follows:

- Imaginative, creative (29)
- Bold, daring (26)
- Visionary (24)

In this respect, there are clear contrasts between the wealthy characters and the nonwealthy counterpart characters. Figure 18.3 presents the portrayals of the nonwealthy counterpart characters at the beginning of each film.[666]

Figure 18.4 presents the portrayals of the nonwealthy counterpart characters at the end of each film.

The most common positive M traits of the nonrich counterpart characters are as follows:

- Likeable (42)
- Warm-hearted (34)
- Honest (31)
- Moral (31)

Generally speaking, wealthy antagonists and protagonists are predominantly portrayed as competent and intelligent in the first acts of

Figure 18.4

Portrayals of nonrich counterpart characters at the end of each film

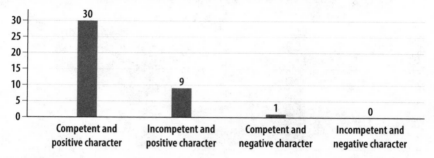

Note: Data based on sample of 40 films.

each movie, although in 31 of the movies, they are also depicted as exhibiting morally questionable tendencies. In 21 of the movies, this immorality is maintained all the way through to the final credits. In 11 of the films, the rich characters experience some form of character evolution. Rich characters are initially portrayed as morally deplorable in 9 of the movies before undergoing a catharsis or redemption. In two of the movies, the opposite happens, and the main rich character actually changes for the worse. The most frequent reason that a rich character "sees the light" is love, as in *Pretty Woman* and *An Indecent Proposal*: the rich character meets someone, falls in love, and changes for the better. In some of the analyzed movies, such as *Iron Man* and *Doctor Strange*, it is a stroke of fate that leads to change: the rich character experiences a serious setback or life-altering event that leads the character to a change of attitude and outlook. Finally, a guilty conscience can also play a role, as in *The Towering Inferno*: the rich character realizes that he has behaved badly and sees the light.

GENDER DISTRIBUTION AND PROFESSIONS

From the lists of the richest people in the world published by *Forbes*, it is clear that the vast majority of the superrich are men. A majority of the small number of women who appear on such lists have inherited their fortunes as the widows or daughters of rich men. In the analyzed movies,

Figure 18.5

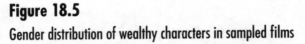

Gender distribution of wealthy characters in sampled films

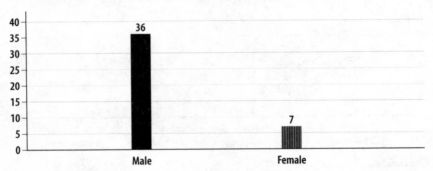

Note: Data based on sample of 43 films. Male characters' professions include entrepreneurs (13), businessmen (4), stock traders (2), and movie producers (2). Female characters' professions include editor-in-chief (1), singer (1), actor (1), and author (1).

too, the rich characters are predominantly male (Figure 18.5). In this respect, they reflect reality. The rich women in the films tend to be singers, actors, or writers, whereas the rich men are entrepreneurs, businessmen, or stock traders.

Overall, the film analysis confirms what we have seen in our examination of representations of the rich in newspapers and magazines. Rich people are by no means portrayed in an exclusively negative light. They are predominantly depicted as intelligent and competent but at the same time as having negative traits: they are self-centered, ruthless, avaricious, and willing to harm other people if it aids their own pursuit of money. Such depictions differ markedly from those of the nonrich counterpart characters, who are predominantly portrayed in a positive light.

CONCLUSION

Since Walter Lippmann's seminal work, *Public Opinion*,[667] was published almost 100 years ago, scholars have conducted extensive research into prejudices and stereotypes. In doing so, researchers have devoted far more attention to some kinds of stereotypes than to others.[668] Particular attention has been devoted to racial and gender prejudices. Much less research has been carried out to investigate prejudices based on social class or class affiliation. To deal with such prejudices, researchers coined the term "classism" as a new field of study alongside sexism and racism.

Several studies have shown that prejudices and stereotypes based on social class are more pronounced than those based on ethnicity or gender. According to classism researchers, not only has there been less research into class-based stereotyping than into stereotyping based on gender, ethnicity, or other characteristics, but what research has been carried out has overwhelmingly focused on attitudes about the lower class.

A majority of classism researchers have a narrow perspective, focusing predominantly on "downward classism," that is, on prejudices related to the working class and the poor, whereas "upward classism," or prejudices concerning the rich, has been almost completely neglected. The works of many classism researchers are also characterized by ideologically driven advocacy for the poor and the working class, combined with considerable resentment directed at the rich and at the capitalist system as a whole. Explicitly or implicitly, these researchers assume that poor people are never responsible for their poverty and that the rich have not earned their wealth. To these researchers, media reports about the personal failures of poor people—or even the deserved successes of rich people—are an expression of classism and are therefore worthy of criticism. From their point of view, people in capitalist societies may never be responsible for their own fate; rather, they are either the innocent victims (the poor and the working class) or the undeserving profiteers (the rich).

Without being aware of it, classism researchers are frequently guilty of doing precisely what they criticize in others: as members of the middle class, they draw their conclusions on the basis of their own value system.

Part One of this study summarized the results of scholarly research into prejudices and stereotypes. One of the most fruitful approaches in the literature, as we have seen, is the stereotype content model, which postulates that emotional impressions of other social groups (i.e., out-groups) form along two dimensions, those of warmth and of competence.

In all interpersonal and intergroup encounters, we are predisposed to first assess a stranger's or an out-group's intentions to either harm us or help us. What goals are these groups or individuals pursuing? Is the stranger or the out-group friendly or unfriendly toward our in-group? This is the dimension of warmth. The second assessment is of competence: to what extent is the stranger or out-group capable of acting on their perceived (good or bad) intentions?

Research conducted using the stereotype content model shows that rich people and businesspeople are dehumanized, likened to cold automata and robots, and envied. Under stable social conditions, the threats faced by envied groups and the damage for society as a whole are limited compared with the risks faced in unstable situations. However, history demonstrates repeatedly that at times of social unrest, such envied groups come under sustained, dangerous, and sometimes deadly attack. A vicious cycle forms: the more suffering is inflicted on envied groups, the more envious people gloat. The specific form of "mechanistic dehumanization"[669]—which construes groups such as the rich as unemotional and heartless and hence associates them with cold, soulless machines—is a prerequisite for persecuting or even killing members of such groups, especially in exceptional situations such as crises or wars. Although mechanized automata may be rational and competent, they lack human values and emotions, which means they are not worthy of pity.

When out-groups—such as the rich—are credited with intelligence, diligence, or other high competence traits but not with moral traits, it has far-reaching consequences. We know from the field of perception research that people base their assessments of other people and social groups primarily on moral traits, whereas competence traits play a distinctly secondary role. If people tend to judge the rich as competent but morally questionable, then the moral judgment has a much higher weight, and the attribution of competence leads not to a more balanced overall assessment but to an overall negative assessment.

Many people tend to deny the rich moral qualities. I explain this phenomenon with a psychological mechanism that I call "compensation theory." In order to maintain self-esteem, it is not enough for some individuals to point out that they also have something to offer, or to highlight those aspects in which they think they are doing particularly well. This strategy can only work when other social groups—in this case, the upper class—are accused of having corresponding failings or deficiencies in the aspects that the individual has declared relevant. The "nonrich" pursue a number of compensation strategies, calling into question whether economic success is a key factor in determining people's levels of contentment and satisfaction and prioritizing other values, such as interpersonal relationships, morality, and family life.

But that is not all. In striving to feel superior to the rich, people generally need to believe that they are just as good (or perhaps even better) in all of the areas they deem relevant. The stereotypes that the rich are cold, have unrewarding family lives and generally unsatisfactory interpersonal relationships, and are selfish and have poor morals serve to promote one's own sense of superiority and to compensate for feelings of inferiority.

The common feature of the domains in which members of "socially disadvantaged" classes claim to be superior to the rich is that they are largely based on subjective interpretation. Using objective measures, it is easy to demonstrate who has more money or is better educated. The same cannot be said for who has the most fulfilling interpersonal relationships or the most satisfying family life. Such determinations rely far more on subjective interpretation of, for example, the quality of someone's marriage, which is almost impossible for an outsider to judge.

Zero-sum beliefs are a major cause of prejudice against the rich. Psychologists have shown through experiments that people often believe they are playing zero-sum games, even when that is objectively not the case. This zero-sum belief is one of the keystones of envy and resentment of the rich. When people believe that any increase in the wealth of the rich automatically worsens the situation of the nonrich, they necessarily regard the fight against poverty as synonymous with the fight against the rich, or with the fight to redistribute wealth.

When the rich are vilified as the cause of poverty, they fulfill a scapegoat function, especially at times of social crisis. "Scapegoating" is the term used to describe a strategy by which members of out-groups are held responsible for the problems faced by an in-group. As demonstrated throughout history, when people are unable to explain negative events, they tend to blame specific out-groups for their problems.

The inventory of previous research in Part One of this book established a theoretical foundation for the empirical studies presented in Parts Two and Three. One study's key aim was to examine variations in social envy among the four countries surveyed. For the first time, an international comparative survey was conducted to find out what the populations of Germany, the United States, France, and Great Britain think of rich people. Because social envy cannot be measured via direct questions ("How envious are you?"), the survey's participants were presented with statements that were designed to serve as indicators of social envy. The same questions were asked in all four countries, producing a solid basis for comparison.

The comparisons were based on the social envy coefficient developed for this study, which indicates the ratio of enviers to non-enviers in any given country. A value of 1 means that the number of social enviers and non-enviers is equal. A value less than 1 indicates that there are more non-enviers than enviers; conversely, a value greater than 1 indicates more enviers than non-enviers. As the social envy coefficient demonstrates, social envy is highest in France (1.26), followed by Germany (0.97). It is significantly lower in the United States (0.42) and in Great Britain (0.37).

Clear differences emerged between social enviers and non-enviers in their positions on dozens of statements. When social enviers were asked about the personality traits they associate with rich people, they highlighted self-centeredness, ruthlessness, materialism, arrogance, greed, cold-heartedness, and superficiality. Only 2 of the 25 personality traits most frequently mentioned by social enviers were positive, whereas 23 were negative. In contrast, non-enviers most frequently described rich people as industrious, intelligent, bold, imaginative, and visionary—but also as materialistic.

One of the survey's questions was designed to find out how susceptible people in the four countries were to scapegoating. The interviewees were presented with the following statement: "Those who are very rich and want more and more power are to blame for many of the major problems in the world, such as financial or humanitarian issues." In Germany, 50 percent of interviewees agreed with this statement, roughly twice as many as in Great Britain and in the United States (25 percent and 21 percent, respectively). This finding suggests that in times of severe economic upheaval, it would be easier to exploit preexisting hostility toward rich people in Germany and that German politicians would be more likely to target rich people than would those of Anglophone countries. In France, 33 percent of interviewees agreed with the same statement.

In particular, social enviers are extremely susceptible to scapegoating, which goes to prove how well the Social Envy Scale distinguishes between enviers and non-enviers. In Germany, 62 percent of enviers tended to scapegoat other groups, compared with just 36 percent of non-enviers. In the United States, France, and Great Britain, responses to the scapegoating statement confirmed an even larger gap between social enviers (57 percent, 46 percent, and 44 percent, respectively) and non-enviers (12 percent, 17 percent, and 10 percent, respectively).

Those who subscribe to scapegoating are also more inclined to zero-sum beliefs. When asked to respond to the statement, "The more the rich have, the less there is for the poor," a majority of scapegoaters in all four countries agreed—60 percent in Germany, 65 percent in the United States, 69 percent in France, and 57 percent in Great Britain—compared with just 35 percent, 24 percent, 41 percent, and 30 percent, respectively, of those not susceptible to scapegoating.

Another key finding of this study is that younger Americans are much more skeptical of the rich than are older Americans, whereas in European countries, the opposite is true. These generational differences were revealed by many of the survey's questions, including one that asked whether rich people are regarded as role models. In Germany, as in France, this question elicited a far more positive response from younger people than from older people, whereas in the United States, it was the other way around.

The fact that younger Americans view the rich far more critically than older Americans is also evident from the personality traits they assign to rich people. Although four of the five personality traits most frequently mentioned by younger Americans in relation to rich people are negative (materialistic, arrogant, greedy, and self-centered), four out of the five traits mentioned by older Americans are positive (industrious, intelligent, imaginative, and bold and daring).

In Germany, France, and Great Britain, many more older people than younger people are strongly in favor of drastically cutting back very high manager salaries and redistributing them to employees, even if it would mean that each employee would get only a few extra euros or pounds per month. The United States is the only country in which younger interviewees are far more likely to embrace this idea than are older interviewees.

A substantial majority of older interviewees in the United States reject such zero-sum thinking, in stark contrast to their younger fellow Americans, who overwhelmingly favor it. In Germany, age is not a factor in zero-sum thinking, whereas in France, older interviewees are far more inclined to think in terms of a zero-sum game than are their younger compatriots.

In all of the surveyed countries, a significantly higher proportion of younger people than of older people say that it is important for them personally to be rich or to become rich. The reason for this is obvious: at a young age, with a long life ahead of you, you are more likely to still entertain the dream of becoming rich someday. The survey's responses clearly show that this hope diminishes with age. After all, anyone who is not rich by the time they turn 60 will have realized that it is unlikely to happen to them now. Also, in all countries, more men than women say that it is important for them to be rich.

Formal education is also a key factor influencing opinions on the rich. As a rule, less-educated interviewees are more critical of rich people than are better-educated interviewees. In general, less-educated people in all four countries more frequently agree with the statement that "rich people are good at earning money, but are not usually decent people" than do better-educated interviewees. In France and the United States, the proportion of less-educated interviewees who agree that the rich are not decent people is greater than the proportion who disagree. The exact opposite is true of better-educated people in both countries. In Great Britain, better-educated interviewees also reject the statement that the rich are not decent people far more strongly than do the less-educated.

In previous surveys on attitudes toward rich people, the rich have usually been treated as a homogeneous group. In fact, however, the population's attitudes on rich people vary depending on how those people acquired their wealth. In the four countries, the interviewees were asked, "Which, if any, of the following groups of people do you personally believe deserve to be rich?" In all four countries, entrepreneurs and self-employed people were the highest-ranked groups, followed by creative people (such as musicians and artists), top athletes, and lottery winners. Financial investors, whom Americans and Britons also ranked highly, came in second to last in Germany and were also far behind in France.

Can the rich at least improve their image by donating to charity? Rich people who believe they can should note that, in all four countries, they will be accused of self-interest rather than altruism—for example, of seeking to reduce their tax burdens or improve their reputations.

One of the positive stereotypes of rich people is that they are particularly industrious. Although this view is to some degree confirmed by empirical studies, the fact that rich people are especially industrious does not explain the gap between their incomes and wealth and those of the rest of society. For this, one must consider the factors of supply and demand in the markets for managerial talent and other specialized, hard-to-replicate fields. And a major reason that entrepreneurs become wealthy is not because they are more industrious than others but because they have outstanding entrepreneurial ideas. Most people, however, do not understand this link.

According to the survey, a majority of interviewees in all four countries claim not to personally know a single millionaire, which means they either base their stereotypes on what they see in the media or they project their own experience onto the rich. Life teaches average employees that they will earn more if they work harder. Therefore, based on their experience, they believe that the amount of money someone earns—or should earn—depends on how long and hard someone works. People who harbor positive views of rich people may thus assume that their wealth is the product of exceptionally hard work, whereas those who are more critical of rich people—as our survey results demonstrate—far less frequently describe the rich as being especially industrious and criticize the imbalance between the actual number of hours they work and their incomes.

In Germany and Great Britain, the survey also examined the correlation between social envy and electoral behavior or political affiliation. In Germany, although the share of center-right CDU/CSU (Christian Democratic Union/Christian Social Union) voters in the total population was 36 percent at the time of the survey, it was only 20 percent among hardcore social enviers, compared with 43 percent among non-enviers. The opposite is true for supporters of Germany's left-wing party, Die Linke. Ten percent of the total population said they would vote for this party. However, among hardcore social enviers, the figure was 24 percent. Among non-enviers, in contrast, the proportion of left-wing voters was only 4 percent. Supporters of the right-wing Alternative für Deutschland (AfD) tended in the same direction, but less so: among the total population, 10 percent said they would vote for AfD, compared with 17 percent of hardcore enviers.

The relevance of these findings is illustrated by a thought experiment. If only the hardcore enviers in Germany were to vote, that is, only those who agreed with all three envy statements, the center-left Social Democratic Party, environmentalist Greens, and left-wing Die Linke would together receive 56 percent of the vote. Die Linke and the AfD would together win 41 percent of the vote. Conversely, if only the non-enviers voted, that is, only those who did not agree with any of the three envy statements, the CDU/CSU and free-market Free Democratic Party would achieve a combined 53 percent of the vote. The AfD and Die Linke, on the other hand, would score only a combined 13 percent.

In Britain, similar differences exist between left-wing and conservative voters. Almost half (48 percent) of Labour voters subscribed to the zero-sum theory that "the more the rich have, the less there is for the poor." In contrast, only 17 percent of Conservative voters adhered to this theory. Similarly, 53 percent of Labour voters supported very high taxes on the rich, compared with only 21 percent of Conservative voters. And twice as many Labour voters as Conservative voters said they would be in favor of a significant increase in taxes for millionaires even if they would not benefit personally. Labour voters were far more likely (33 percent) than Conservative voters (13 percent) to believe that the superrich are to blame for many of the world's major problems. One in four Labour voters, but only one in ten Conservative voters, believed that many rich people obtained their wealth at the expense of others.

In France, the country with the highest social envy coefficient, egalitarianism prevailed on many issues. It is worth noting that in France, this view was also shared by higher earners. Among the French in the highest-income group, 45 percent supported very high taxes on the rich, and only 21 percent supported moderate taxation. The egalitarian attitude of so many French people is reflected not only in their advocacy for higher taxes for the rich but also in their criticism of excessive executive pay. When asked whether they think it is acceptable for some managers to earn 100 times as much as their employees, 61 percent of French interviewees said that they generally regarded such high salaries as "obscene." Whether low-, middle-, or high-income, at least 58 percent of interviewees shared this view.

And approval for drastically reducing top-tier managers' salaries and redistributing money to employees—even if it would give them only a few extra euros in their pockets—was just as high among French households that earned more than €54,000 per year as it was among the average population. Even among the British, the responses by income group did not vary as much as might be expected. In the face of numerous critical statements about rich people, attitudes hardly differed between low and high earners in Great Britain.

A majority of interviewees in all four countries were not personally acquainted with a millionaire. When people who did have a millionaire in their social circle were asked for their opinions of the millionaire they know, their answers were markedly different from the answers given by the general population. Among the German population as a whole, 62 percent thought that rich people are self-centered, 56 percent said they are materialistic ("think only of money"), 50 percent thought the rich are ruthless, and 49 percent thought they are greedy. Only then do positive qualities such as industriousness, boldness, and intelligence get mentioned.

For interviewees who personally know one or more millionaires, the opposite was true. Those who personally know millionaires rated them very positively: 71 percent considered them both industrious and intelligent, 58 percent regarded them as imaginative, 47 percent as optimistic, and 45 percent as visionary. Across the German population as a whole, only 3 percent thought rich people are honest, compared with 42 percent of those who know at least one millionaire personally. And although more than 60 percent of Germans considered the rich to be selfish, only 20 percent said this about the millionaires they know personally.[670]

Because most people do not know any millionaires personally, media images of rich people play a key role in shaping perceptions of them. Part Three of this book examined portrayals of the rich in the media.

Researchers from mct Medienagentur analyzed depictions of rich people in German media. Using a specially developed codebook, mct Medienagentur analyzed the media's valence and slant when portraying rich people. Valence refers to the intrinsic attractiveness or averseness of an event, object, or situation. It is distinct from slant, which refers to the bias a journalist gives to a report, for example, by including an explicitly personal evaluation of a situation or giving preference to certain sources. Although valence and slant frequently align, this is not always the case, as we have seen.

According to mct Medienagentur, a majority of articles dealing with rich people in a positive context nevertheless have a negative slant, thereby demonstrating that the overwhelmingly negative bias in these articles does not arise primarily from the events or situations being reported on. Rather, the negative bias often arises from value judgments made by journalists or by the people they interview.

Negative slants were equally pronounced in both informative articles and opinion pieces, at over 80 percent. Most strikingly, politicians and journalists themselves expressed negative opinions of rich people in 90 percent and 83 percent of the contributions, respectively.

The surveyed media devoted extensive coverage to executive pay and severance payments. The predominant tenor of the coverage was that executive pay and severance payments were far too high and that this represented a serious problem. Although criticism of high levels of executive pay and large severance payments may appear convincing to many readers, on closer examination, the arguments are less so. One reason these articles seem so convincing to many readers is the sources they quote. Criticism comes not only from expected sources, such as trade unionists or left-wing politicians, but also from representatives of Germany's leading association for private investors, DSW (Deutsche Schutzvereinigung für Wertpapierbesitz), and the generally market-oriented federation of family businesses, Die Familienunternehmer.

Classism research in the United States has shown that there is no sense of solidarity among the poor when each subgroup among them is played against the others and when each subgroup strives to set itself apart from others. One can assume that the same applies to the rich. Entrepreneurs, in particular, want to set themselves apart from corporate managers and bankers, whose image is clearly worse. When, however, voices "from within their own ranks" offer criticism of the rich in the media, it lends the criticism an air of justification and objectivity from the reader's point of view.

Bankers' bonuses are another frequent topic of media coverage. In 85 percent of the analyzed articles, bonuses were depicted in a generally negative light. Newspaper articles talked about "greed," while bankers were described as "fat cats"; large bonuses for bankers were described as "excessive" and as manifestations of "excess" and "self-service" by which bankers "fill their pockets." There are a few more differentiated voices; however, the simple (but objectively highly questionable) explanation continues to be by far the most dominant narrative: that "greedy bankers" with their "noses in the trough" caused the global financial crisis.

There are not many real-world contexts in which the rich and the superrich are the subject of positive reporting. Nevertheless, one such context was the Giving Pledge campaign. In media coverage of the campaign, 37 donor motives were mentioned, including 13 positive and altruistic motives, 16 negative and selfish motives, and 6 neutral motives. Overall, the Giving Pledge campaign was depicted in a positive light, as we have seen. Again and again, however, media coverage stressed that the fundraising campaign was motivated by a desire to "polish the tarnished image of capitalism." Although the reports about the Giving Pledge campaign were naturally more sympathetic in their depictions of the wealthy than were articles on other topics, those articles also reinforced strong misgivings about the rich.

The same was true to an even greater extent in other media coverage, which, on the basis of its subject matter alone, suggested an overtly critical framing of rich people, such as coverage of the Panama and Paradise Papers. Shell companies are frequently used by money launderers, drug dealers, and corrupt politicians from all over the world. It is striking, however, that these articles placed the rich and the superrich under the same general suspicion, putting them on public trial. By highlighting so many individual examples of misdeeds within the broader coverage of the events, the articles created the impression that almost all of the rich use tax loopholes and that they do so for nefarious purposes.

Only in very rare cases did the Panama Papers' journalists refrain from sweeping generalizations when they reported about the rich and the superrich. In and of itself, there is nothing wrong with tax structuring. In fact, the highest courts have consistently ruled that it is the legitimate right of every taxpayer to organize their tax affairs as efficiently as possible within the law.

When the Panama and Paradise Papers were published, only 6 percent of the articles that covered them highlighted the data protection issues associated with the leaks. The campaigners apparently believed that the end (their good cause, that is, exposing the machinations of the rich and superrich) justified the means—a principle that does not apply in criminal proceedings, where there are clear restrictions on the methods that can be used to convict a suspect. Furthermore, in the context of these papers, when it was pointed out that a rich person had done nothing illegal, this itself was taken as evidence that the capitalist system is morally bankrupt and that we live in a world in which the rich write the laws to serve their own interests.

Any analysis of portrayals of the rich in the media would be incomplete if it did not include at least some analysis of online content. The research carried out for this book included an analysis of online comments about an episode of a television talk show, "The Rich Club—How Much Inequality can Germany Take?" Of 597 comments examined, 84 percent were critical of the rich.

As we have seen, quantitative analysis shows that the attitudes expressed in these online comments resembled those that were found in survey data. These analyses can only scratch the surface of the matter. What they do confirm, however, is that the predominant tenor of criticizing the rich, which was evident in the population survey in Germany and in the similarly critical tenor in media reports, corresponds with the negative tenor of online statements about the rich. In fact, criticism of the rich online is often sharper than that measured in representative surveys, and it is also far more pointed than the criticism that appears in offline media.

Public opinions about the wealthy are also influenced by television programs and movies. For this study, criteria were developed to analyze how rich people were portrayed in successful feature films. The analysis found that rich people in Hollywood films were overwhelmingly portrayed as morally deficient, in stark contrast to nonrich characters, who were overwhelmingly portrayed in a morally positive light.

The fact that portrayals of rich people tended to be negative rather than positive was confirmed by the analysis of recurring frames, that is, the frames of interpretation used to portray rich people in the analyzed movies. Rich people were depicted as being prepared to climb over corpses in pursuit of their economic goals, as having nothing but profit on their minds. Everything they did was driven by their desire to satisfy their greed—but they also cheated others and used their wealth to exert and manipulate power and influence.

Viewers were reminded, reassuringly, that money alone does not make people happy and that money cannot buy everything. Still, some of the movies also showed that rich people can redeem themselves and regain their humanity, shedding the negative traits that are so often presented as being synonymous with wealth.

Even though this media analysis revealed that rich people are presented more negatively than positively, it would be remiss to search for the cause of prejudices toward the rich in media coverage alone. As demonstrated in the first part of this book, social envy has even deeper psychological roots. The media have the power to amplify envy and channel it at specific targets, but in doing so, the media are, substantially, reflecting feelings and prejudices that already exist.

In societies that promise equality, people develop psychological strategies to cope with the fact that they are nowhere near as economically successful as others. In addition, throughout world history, minorities have frequently served as scapegoats for grievous events that could not be otherwise explained. The media satisfy people's inherent need for simple, linear explanations (e.g., greedy bankers caused the financial crisis), a need that transcends the media. For example, when movies portray rich people in an overwhelmingly negative light, it is not necessarily because the scriptwriters want to manipulate their audiences but rather because the scriptwriters are tapping into widespread stereotypes and satisfying deeper psychological needs.

The research presented in this book has been a first step in analyzing social envy and prejudice against the rich. It should not be the last step. Among the many topics still deserving of research are the following:

- How people in other countries and cultures—for example, in Scandinavia or Asia—feel about the rich.
- How rich people are portrayed in print media, on television, and in literature, novels, and fairy tales.

Although much of classism research, which most often deals with prejudices directed at the lower classes, has been ideologically driven, some aspects of this research can also be useful to wealth researchers, such as the qualitative findings reported by Reutter and others in their 2009 article, "Perceptions of and Responses to Poverty Stigma." The results of Reutter's study pertain to semistructured interviews, conducted by researchers, of low-income residents of two large Canadian cities. One finding of this study was that:

> . . . although participants were highly critical of others' negative opinions of people living in poverty, many held similar views themselves, thus distancing themselves from other low-income people. In effect, they made distinctions between low-income people who were deserving (including themselves) and those who were less deserving—comparing their own identities with those of others. In making these distinctions, participants discounted the stereotype that all poor people are similar (painted with the same brush), as depicted in their social identity, and at the same time perpetuating the stereotype of individualistic attributions for poverty (as applied to others).[671]

For example, low-income participants who were not claiming government income support distanced themselves from those who were. Low-income interviewees also criticized poor people who abused government income support—believing that this abuse made life more difficult for those who truly deserved assistance. Low-income interviewees further criticized other poor people for badly managing their finances or for not doing any work even though there were many opportunities for employment. Even homeless people distanced themselves from other homeless people who spent their money irresponsibly.[672]

Such processes, which classism researchers refer to as "cognitive distancing," should be investigated in the future to determine their prevalence among rich people. My hypothesis is that similar forms of cognitive distancing can be observed among the rich, for example, when "old money" disparages "new money," or when some rich people flash their wealth and are criticized by others who live comparatively modestly, or at least discreetly. Entrepreneurs distance themselves from executive managers, who, in turn, do the same to bankers.

Just as there is a pecking order among lower-income groups, there is also a pecking order among the rich—and this order may prevent the rich from developing a sense of solidarity, because each subgroup (e.g., entrepreneurs) wants to distance itself from another subgroup (e.g., investment bankers or executive managers). By doing so, an entrepreneur may hope that, despite widespread prejudices in society, he or she will be perceived as one of the "good rich." Further research should therefore examine in-group prejudice among the rich, which remains very little studied.

As shown in Chapter 1, research alone cannot eliminate prejudices and stereotypes, as they are inherent features of human perception. The prejudices I have described in this book not only harm the rich but also damage society as a whole. If people do not understand the real causes of crises and negative events, choosing instead to believe simple explanations and blame the rich as scapegoats, this error gets in the way of finding real solutions to very real problems.

When economic policy is driven by social envy, it can lead to significant declines in prosperity and social trust and prevent sorely needed political and economic reforms. In exceptional situations, such as serious economic crises or wars, extreme prejudice can lead to the persecution or even the physical annihilation of the persecuted group, thereby eradicating social systems based on economic freedom and giving rise to repressive systems that actually increase poverty.

But even on a personal level, people who harbor social envy and negative stereotypes of the rich are harmed by these beliefs. Anyone who firmly believes that it is impossible to become rich through honest work and who is convinced that wealth can be achieved only by deceiving and harming other people—provided they have no moral scruples and are prepared to take high risks—is only one step away from trying to become rich through criminal actions.

For others, the same negative beliefs may create unconscious blockades that prevent them from becoming wealthy. People who think of the rich as selfish and cold-hearted and who believe that wealth can only be attained at the expense of the poor are probably far less likely to become rich than are people who inwardly affirm the idea of becoming rich and who regard wealth as something positive and compatible with high moral and ethical standards. It would certainly be interesting if researchers were to investigate how enviers are harmed by their own feelings of social envy and their negative stereotypes toward the rich.

To date, the rich have attached little importance to actively confronting the prejudices directed against them. Despite having the financial resources to do so, they have so far not sponsored scientific research into prejudices against the rich. Therefore, the rich bear a fair share of the blame when negative prejudices against them become entrenched.

The Russian American writer and philosopher Ayn Rand recognized this fact more than half a century ago:

> No man or group of men can live indefinitely under the pressure of moral injustice: they have to rebel or give in. Most of the businessmen gave in; it would have taken a philosopher to provide them with the intellectual weapons of rebellion, but they had given up any interest in philosophy. They accepted the burden of an unearned guilt; they accepted the brand of "vulgar materialists". . . . Starting as the most courageous class of men in history, the businessmen have slipped slowly into the position of men motivated by chronic fear—in all the social, political, moral, intellectual aspects of their existence. Their public policy consists of appeasing their worst enemies, placating their most contemptible attackers, trying to make terms with their own destroyers.[673]

It will never be possible to eliminate unfounded prejudices and stereotypes, whether they are directed at the rich or at other minorities.

However, experience shows that enlightenment can be the wellspring from which change flows. In many respects, we are more enlightened nowadays than were our predecessors in the early modern period. We no longer believe that witches are responsible for natural disasters. Over the past few decades, many minorities have learned that the only way to overcome prejudice is to take an active stand. As a result, attitudes toward some minorities—such as gays and lesbians—have changed greatly. However, such change has only been achieved because those minorities have taken up the fight against prejudice. In this process, scholars working in the field of prejudice and stereotypes have a valuable contribution to make.

ANNEX: THE QUESTIONNAIRE (IPSOS MORI)

SAMPLE:

1,000 adults aged 16+ in France
1,000 adults aged 16+ in Great Britain
1,000 adults aged 18–75 in the United States
(Allensbach Institute: 1,000 adults in Germany)

ASK ALL

Q1. It is sometimes said that there are certain groups of people that you have to be careful not to criticize in public. Which of these groups, if any, do you think this applies to?

Please select all that apply.

1. Unemployed people
2. Immigrants
3. Homosexual people
4. Black people
5. Muslims
6. Women
7. Disabled people

8.   People who are rich
9.   People on benefits/welfare
10. Jews
11. Christians
12. None of these
13. Refused

ASK ALL

NEW SCREEN

The following questions are about wealthy and rich people. When answering the next few questions, please think about people with assets worth at least 1 million [euros, pounds, dollars], not including the home they live in.

ASK ALL

Q2. Here is a list of things that people have said about rich people. Which, if any, of the statements on the list would you agree with?

Please think about people with assets worth at least 1 million [euros, pounds, dollars], not including the home they live in.

1.   Becoming rich primarily depends on what abilities and ideas you have.
2.   People who are rich mainly have good luck.
3.   Society as a whole benefits from the existence of rich people because many of them create jobs.
4.   Society as a whole benefits from the existence of rich people because they pay high taxes.
5.   The rich people in [INSERT COUNTRY] only became rich because there was injustice in our society.
6.   Many rich people become rich because they take more risks than others tend to.
7.   Becoming rich primarily depends on the connections and contacts you have through your parents and family.

8. Many rich people only become rich because they ruthlessly pursued their interest.
9. The state can afford to pay for our social system because the rich pay higher taxes.
10. Most rich people only become rich through inheritances.
11. Rich people are generally very industrious throughout their lives.
12. Many rich people only obtained their wealth at the expense of others.
13. Society as a whole benefits from the existence of rich people, as many of them are entrepreneurs who created new products.
14. When it comes to getting rich, the decisive factor is how good you are at establishing important connections and contacts.
15. Rich people who have succeeded through their own efforts are role models who motivate me.
16. Those who are very rich and want more and more power are to blame for many of the major problems in the world, such as financial or humanitarian issues.
17. Most rich people are tax cheats.
18. None of the above.

Q3. For some people, it is important to be rich. How important, if at all, it is for you personally to be rich?

1. Very important
2. Fairly important
3. Neither important nor unimportant
4. Not very important
5. Not at all important

Q4. Which, if any, of the following are most likely to apply to rich people?

1. Intelligent
2. Self-centered

3. Industrious
4. Greedy
5. Honest
6. Materialistic
7. Arrogant
8. Imaginative
9. Optimistic
10. Ruthless
11. Superficial
12. Bold, daring
13. Cold-hearted
14. Visionary and farsighted
15. None of the above

Q5. To what extent do you agree or disagree with the following statement: Rich people are good at earning money, but are not usually decent people.

1. Strongly agree
2. Tend to agree
3. Neither agree nor disagree
4. Tend to disagree
5. Strongly disagree

Q6. Which, if any, of the following groups of people do you personally believe deserve to be rich? Please select all that apply.

1. Lottery winners
2. Entrepreneurs
3. Self-employed people
4. Top athletes
5. Financial investors
6. Creative people and artists, such as actors or musicians
7. Senior-level managers
8. Heirs
9. Senior bankers

10. Property investors
11. None of the above

Q7. To what extent do you agree or disagree with the statement: The more the rich have, the less there is for the poor.

1. Strongly agree
2. Tend to agree
3. Neither agree nor disagree
4. Tend to disagree
5. Strongly disagree

Q8. On balance, which, if any, of the following statements do you agree with **MOST**?

A. The taxes on the rich should be high but not excessively high because they have generally worked hard to earn their wealth, and the state should not take too much away from them.
B. The rich should not only pay high taxes, but they should pay very high taxes. In this way, the state can ensure that the gap between the rich and the poor does not become too great here in our country.

1. I agree more with statement A than with statement B.
2. I agree more with statement B than with statement A.
3. Agree/disagree with both statements equally.

Q9. To what extent do you agree or disagree with this statement?
I think it would be fair to increase taxes substantially for millionaires, even if I would not benefit from it personally.

1. Strongly agree
2. Tend to agree
3. Neither agree nor disagree
4. Tend to disagree
5. Strongly disagree

Q10. Here are a few statements about the differences in earnings found between **managers who earn 100 times more than their employees**. Which of these statements would you agree with? Please select all that apply.

1. I think it is inappropriate for managers to earn so much more, as they do not work so much longer and harder than their employees.
2. As managers have a lot more responsibility, they should also earn a lot more.
3. I feel such high salaries for managers are inappropriate, as no one needs that much money.
4. It is solely up to companies to decide how much their managers earn.
5. If managers earn so much more than employees, there is less money left over for employees' salaries.
6. I feel that such high salaries are generally obscene.
7. Companies can only hire and retain the best managers if they pay salaries of this kind, otherwise these managers will go to another company that pays more or they will work for themselves.
8. I would favor drastically reducing those managers' salaries and redistributing the money more evenly among their employees, even if that would mean that they would only get a few more [pounds, dollars, euros] per month.
9. None of the above.

Q11. To what extent, if at all, do you agree or disagree with this statement?
When I hear about a millionaire who made a risky business decision and lost a lot of money because of it, I think: It serves him right.

1. Strongly agree
2. Tend to agree
3. Neither agree nor disagree
4. Tend to disagree
5. Strongly disagree

Q12. Some rich people donate a great deal of money to charitable causes. In your opinion, what is the **main** reason why people do that? Do they **primarily** donate because they want to benefit others, or **primarily** because they want to benefit themselves (e.g., for tax relief, to improve their reputation, etc.)?

1. To benefit others
2. To benefit themselves
3. To benefit both themselves and others equally

Q13. Do you know anyone that is a millionaire? This could be family members, friends, people you know through friends and that you socialize at least occasionally with.

1. I personally know one millionaire.
2. I personally know more than one millionaire.
3. I personally don't know any millionaires.

ASK Q14 AND Q16 IF SOMEONE KNOWS AT LEAST ONE MILLIONAIRE (Q13 = 1 OR 2)

Q14. Thinking about the millionaire you know best, to what extent do you say the person has a good or a bad character?

1. The person has a good character.
2. The person has neither a good nor a bad character.
3. The person has a bad character.

Q15. There are some people who are often unsure about how they should behave in everyday situations, while others are often certain. In general, which of these applies to you more?

1. I am often unsure how to behave in everyday situations.
2. I am often certain how to behave in everyday situations.

Q16. (The Allensbach Institute asked a Q16 in Germany that was not asked in the other three countries.) In Q13, you said that you know a millionaire. Thinking about the millionaire you know best, which, if any, of the following apply?

1. Intelligent
2. Self-centered
3. Industrious
4. Greedy
5. Honest
6. Materialistic
7. Arrogant
8. Imaginative
9. Optimistic
10. Ruthless
11. Superficial
12. Bold, daring
13. Cold-hearted
14. Visionary and farsighted
15. None of the above

NOTES

Preface

1. Germany, where 9 percent of interviewees said you need to be careful not to publicly criticize people who are rich, was the only country to identify a group that could be more openly criticized; only 6 percent of German interviewees said you need to be careful when criticizing Christians in public.

2. Adam Smith, "Hang the Bankers! Getting Ready to Vent in London," *Time*, March 28, 2009.

3. BBC News, "G20 Professor Suspended," March 26, 2009, http://news.bbc .co.uk/2/hi/uk/7967096.stm.

4. David Cohen, "Meet Mister Mayhem," *Evening Standard*, March 25, 2009.

5. See Friedemann Bieber's review "Gegen das oberste Prozent" in the FAZ, April 21, 2018.

6. Christian Neuhäuser, *Reichtum als moralisches Problem* (Berlin: Suhrkamp, 2018), p. 83.

7. Neuhäuser, *Reichtum als moralisches Problem*, p. 86.

8. Neuhäuser, p. 95.

9. Neuhäuser, p. 119.

10. Mary E. Kite and Bernard E. Whitley Jr., *Psychology of Prejudice and Discrimination*, 3rd ed. (New York: Routledge, 2016).

11. Johannes Hoffmann, *Stereotypen, Vorurteile, Völkerbilder in Ost und West: in Wissenschaft und Unterricht: Eine Bibliographie* (Wiesbaden: Harrassowitz, 1986).

12. See Chapter 2.

13. Stéphane Courtois, "Introduction: The Crimes of Communism," in *The Black Book of Communism: Crimes, Terror, Repression*, ed. Stéphane Courtois (Cambridge, MA: Harvard University Press, 1999), p. 8.

14. Courtois, "Crimes of Communism," p. 15.

15. Quoted in Rainer Zitelmann, *Hitler: The Policies of Seduction*, trans. Helmut Bögler (London: London House, 1999), p. 145.

16. Daniel Bultmann, *Kambodscha unter den Roten Khmer: Die Erschaffung des perfekten Sozialisten* (Paderborn: Ferdinand Schöningh, 2017), pp. 159 et seq.

17. Bultmann, *Kambodscha unter den Roten Khmer*, p. 81.

18. Bultmann, p. 98.

19. Bultmann, pp. 166–67.

20. For the causes of the financial crisis, see Rainer Zitelmann, *The Power of Capitalism* (London: LID Publishing, 2018), chap. 9.

21. See Zitelmann, *Capitalism*, chaps. 5 and 7.

CHAPTER ONE

22. Merriam-Webster, s.v. "prejudice (*n.*)," accessed December 11, 2018.

23. Gordon W. Allport, *The Nature of Prejudice* (New York: Basic Books, 1979), p. 6.

24. Allport, *Nature of Prejudice*, p. 7.

25. Allport, p. 9 (emphasis in original).

26. Earl E. Davis, *Attitude Change: A Review and Bibliography of Selected Research* (Paris: UNESCO, 1964), p. 9.

27. Heinz E. Wolf, "Soziologie der Vorurteile: Zur methodischen Problematik der Forschung und Theoriebildung," in *Handbuch der Empirischen Sozialforschung*, Band 2, ed. René König (Stuttgart: Ferdinand Enke Verlag, 1969), p. 944.

28. Bernd Estel, *Soziale Vorurteile und soziale Urteile: Kritik und wissenssoziologische Grundlegung der Vorurteilsforschung* (Opladen: Westdeutscher Verlag, 1983), p. 64.

29. Estel, *Soziale Vorurteile*, p. 17 (emphasis in original).

30. Estel, p. 17.

31. Wolf, "Soziologie der Vorurteile," p. 948 (emphasis in original).

32. Martina Thiele, *Medien und Stereotype: Konturen eines Forschungsfeldes* (Bielefeld: Transcript Verlag, 2015), p. 58.

33. Kite and Whitley, *Psychology of Prejudice*, p. 118.

34. Kite and Whitley, p. 119.

35. See Lee Jussim, *Social Perception and Social Reality: Why Accuracy Dominates Bias and Self-Fulfilling Prophecy* (Oxford: Oxford University Press, 2012), Part 6.

36. Jussim, *Social Perception*, p. 320.

37. Jussim, p. 309.

38. Psychologist Charles Stangor, quoted in Thiele, *Medien und Stereotype*, p. 59.

39. Kite and Whitley, *Psychology of Prejudice*, p. 120.

40. Rupert Brown, *Prejudice: Its Social Psychology*, 2nd ed. (Chichester, UK: Wiley-Blackwell, 2010), p. 5.

41. Brown, *Prejudice*, p. 6.

42. For more on this topic, see Thiele, *Medien und Stereotype*, p. 56.

43. Hans-Georg Gadamer, *Wahrheit und Methode, Grundzüge einer philsophischen Hermeneutik* (Tübingen: J.B.C. Mohr 1960), p. 255.

44. Juliana Degner and Dirk Wentura, "Messung von Vorurteilen," in *Stereotype, Vorurteile und soziale Diskriminierung: Theorien, Befunde und Interventionen*, ed. Lars-Eric Petersen and Bernd Six (Weinheim: Beltz Verlag, 2008), p. 150.

45. Kite and Whitley, *Psychology of Prejudice*, p. 15.

46. Kite and Whitley, p. 13.

47. Thorsten Meiser, "Illusorischen Korrelationen," in *Stereotype, Vorurteile und soziale Diskriminierung*, ed. Petersen and Six, p. 53.

48. Michael Wenzel and Sven Waldzus, "Die Theorie der Selbstkategorisierung," in *Stereotype, Vorurteile und soziale Diskriminierung*, ed. Petersen and Six, p. 234.

49. Thiele, *Medien und Stereotype*, pp. 96–97 (emphasis in original).

50. Jussim, *Social Perception*, p. 301 (emphasis in original).

51. Richard D. Ashmore and Frances K. Del Boca, quoted in Jussim, *Social Perception*, p. 302.

52. Jussim, *Social Perception*, p. 302.

53. Jussim, p. 300.

54. Alice H. Eagly and Amanda B. Diekman, "What Is the Problem? Prejudice as an Attitude-in-Context," in *On the Nature of Prejudice: Fifty Years after Allport*, ed. John F. Dovidio, Peter Glick, and Laurie A. Rudman (Malden, MA: Blackwell Publishing, 2005), p. 24.

55. Thomas F. Pettigrew and Roel W. Meertens, "Subtle and Blatant Prejudice in Western Europe," *European Journal of Psychology* 25, no. 1 (1995): 71.

56. For a comparison of direct and indirect measurement methods, see Thomas Eckes, "Messung von Stereotypen," in *Stereotype, Vorurteile und soziale Diskriminierung*, ed. Petersen and Six, pp. 98–104.

57. For more information on the three components, see Lars-Eric Petersen, "Vorurteile und Diskriminierung," in *Stereotype, Vorurteile und soziale Diskriminierung*, ed. Petersen and Six, 195.

58. Pettigrew and Meertens, "Subtle and Blatant Prejudice," p. 71.

59. Petersen, "Vorurteile und Diskriminierung," p. 195.

60. Andreas Zick and Beate Küpper, "Rassismus," in *Stereotype, Vorurteile und soziale Diskriminierung*, ed. Petersen and Six, p. 113.

61. Thiele, *Medien und Stereotype*, p. 217.

62. Pettigrew and Meertens, "Subtle and Blatant Prejudice," p. 59

63. Pettigrew and Meertens, p. 63.

64. Pettigrew and Meertens, p. 70.

65. Petersen, "Vorurteile und Diskriminierung," p. 197.

66. Allison C. Aosved, Patricia J. Long, and Emily K. Voller, "Measuring Sexism, Racism, Sexual Prejudice, Ageism, Classism, and Religious Intolerance: The Intolerant Schema Measure," *Journal of Applied Social Psychology* 39, no. 10 (2009): 2351–53.

67. Francesca M. Franco and Anne Maass, "Intentional Control over Prejudice: When the Choice of the Measure Matters," *European Journal of Social Psychology* 29, no. 4 (1999): 470.

68. Franco and Maass, "Intentional Control over Prejudice," p. 472.

Chapter Two

69. For the following, see Thiele, *Medien und Stereotype*, pp. 83–84.

70. Thiele, p. 363.

71. Bettina Spencer and Emanuele Castano, "Social Class Is Dead: Long Live Social Class! Stereotype Threat among Low Socioeconomic Status Individuals," *Social Justice Research* 20, no. 4 (2007): 421.

72. Spencer and Castano, "Social Class Is Dead," p. 428.

73. Andreas Kemper and Heike Weinbach, *Klassismus: Eine Einführung*, 2nd ed. (Münster: Unrast-Verlag 2016), p. 100.

74. Susan T. Fiske, *Envy Up, Scorn Down: How Status Divides Us* (New York: Russell Sage Foundation, 2011), p. 49.

75. Spencer and Castano, "Social Class Is Dead," p. 421.

76. Spencer and Castano, p. 421.

77. Spencer and Castano, p. 429.

78. Kemper and Weinbach, *Klassismus*, p. 47.

79. Kemper and Weinbach, p. 11.

80. Kemper and Weinbach, p. 18.

81. William Ming Liu, *Social Class and Classism in the Helping Professions: Research, Theory, and Practice* (Thousand Oaks, CA: Sage, 2011), p. 199.

82. Liu, *Social Class and Classism*, p. 200.

83. Kemper and Weinbach, *Klassismus*, p. 23.

84. Kemper and Weinbach, p. 51.

85. Kemper and Weinbach, p. 23.

86. Kemper and Weinbach, p. 105.

87. Bernice Lott, "The Social Psychology of Class and Classism," *American Psychologist* 67, no. 8 (2012): 654.

88. See Robert Frank, *Richistan: A Journey through the American Wealth Boom and the Lives of the New Rich* (New York: Random House, 2007).

89. Lott, "Social Psychology of Class and Classism," p. 654.

90. Liu, *Social Class and Classism*, p. 183.

91. Liu, p. 184.

92. Kemper and Weinbach, *Klassismus*, p. 101.

93. Bernice Lott, "Cognitive and Behavioral Distancing from the Poor," *American Psychologist* 57, no. 2 (2002): 101.

94. William Ming Liu, "Introduction to Social Class and Classism in Counseling Psychology," in *The Oxford Handbook of Social Class in Counseling*, ed. William Ming Liu (Oxford: Oxford University Press, 2013), p. 4.

95. Alexander J. Colbow et al., "Development of the Classism Attitudinal Profile (CAP)," *Journal of Counseling Psychology* 63, no. 5 (2016): 577.

96. Colbow et al., "Classism Attitudinal Profile," p. 578.

97. Colbow et al., p. 581.

98. Colbow et al., p. 574.

99. Colbow et al., p. 581.

100. Colbow et al., p. 581.

101. Diana Kendall, *Framing Class: Media Representations of Wealth and Poverty in America*, 2nd ed. (Lanham, MD: Rowman & Littlefield, 2011), p. 8 (emphasis in original).

102. Kendall, *Framing Class*, p. 22.

103. Kendall, pp. 29 et seq.

104. Kendall, pp. 32–33.

105. Kendall, p. 34.

106. Kendall, p. 41.

107. Kendall, p. 42.

108. Kendall, p. 42.

109. UBS Financial Services and PricewaterhouseCoopers, "UBS/PwC 2015 Billionaire Report: Master Architects of Great Wealth and Lasting Legacies," 2015, p. 13.

110. Kendall, *Framing Class*, pp. 46–47.

111. Kendall, p. 48.

112. Kendall, p. 47. See also Hammacher Schlemmer "Superplexus" webpage.

113. Kendall, *Framing Class*, pp. 58–59.

114. Kendall, p. 71.

115. Kendall, p. 71

116. Kendall, p. 84.

117. Kendall, p. 87.

118. Kendall, p. 87.

119. Kendall, p. 92.

120. Kendall, p. 93.

121. Kendall, p. 99.

122. Kendall, p. 117.

123. Kendall, p. 109.

124. Kendall, p. 111.

125. Heather E. Bullock, Karen Fraser Wyche, and Wendy R. Williams, "Media Images of the Poor," *Journal of Social Issues* 57, no. 2 (2001): 245.

126. Bullock, Wyche, and Williams, "Media Images," p. 240.

127. Bullock, Wyche, and Williams, p. 230.

128. Bullock, Wyche, and Williams, p. 242.

129. Bullock, Wyche, and Williams, p. 229.

130. Bullock, Wyche, and Williams, p. 234.

131. Bullock, Wyche, and Williams, p. 234.

132. Bullock, Wyche, and Williams, p. 237.

133. Liu, *Social Class and Classism*, p. 182.

134. Liu, p. 183.

135. Liu, p. 183.

136. Liu, p. 185.

137. Liu, p. 186.

138. For more details, see Barbara Jensen, *Reading Classes: On Culture and Classism in America* (Ithaca, NY: ILR Press, 2012).

139. Jensen, *Reading Classes*, p. 31 (emphasis in original).

140. Jensen, p. 31 (emphasis in original).

141. Jensen, p. 35.

142. Jensen, p. 36.

143. Jensen, p. 36.

144. Jensen, p. 39.

145. Jensen, p. 41.

146. Jensen, p. 45.

147. Jensen, p. 45.

148. Jensen, p. 46.

149. Jensen, p. 64 (emphasis in original).

150. Jensen, pp. 64–65.

151. Jensen, p. 66.

152. Jensen, p. 69.

153. Jensen, p. 76 (emphasis in original).

154. Jensen, pp. 111–12.

155. Jensen, p. 150.

156. Jensen, p. 156.

157. Jensen, p. 152.

158. Jensen, p. 161.

159. Jensen, p. 155.

Chapter Three

160. Susan T. Fiske et al., "A Model of (Often Mixed) Stereotype Content: Competence and Warmth Respectively Follow from Perceived Status and Competition," *Journal of Personality and Social Psychology* 82, no. 6 (2002): 878–902.

161. Susan T. Fiske, "Divided by Status: Upward Envy and Downward Scorn," *Proceedings of the American Philosophical Society* 157, no. 3 (2013): 1.

162. Fiske et al., "A Model of Stereotype Content," p. 879.

163. Fiske et al., p. 879.

164. Fiske et al., p. 884.

165. Fiske et al., p. 895.

166. Fiske et al., pp. 888, 893, 895.

167. Fiske et al., p. 897.

168. Fiske et al., p. 899.

169. Fiske, "Divided by Status," p. 2.

170. Fiske, p. 2.

171. Monica H. Lin et al., "Stereotype Content Model Explains Prejudice for an Envied Outgroup," *Personality and Social Psychology Bulletin* 31, no. 1 (2005): 44.

172. See Lin et al., "Stereotype Content Model," p. 37.

173. Lin et al., p. 44.

174. Lin et al., p. 35.

175. Lin et al., p. 44.

176. *Derrick,* episode 213, July 17, 1992.

177. *Derrick,* episode 218, December 11, 1992.

178. Lasana T. Harris, Mina Cikara, and Susan T. Fiske, "Envy, as Predicted by the Stereotype Content Model: A Volatile Ambivalence," in *Envy: Theory and Research*, ed. Richard H. Smith (Oxford: Oxford University Press, 2008), p. 133.

179. Harris, Cikara, and Fiske, "A Volatile Ambivalence," p. 142.

180. Harris, Cikara, and Fiske, p. 135.

181. Harris, Cikara, and Fiske, p. 136.

182. Harris, Cikara, and Fiske, p. 137.

183. For the following, see Stephen Loughnan and Nick Haslam, "Animals and Androids: Implicit Associations between Social Categories and Nonhumans," *Psychological Science* 18, no. 2 (2007): 117.

184. Loughnan and Haslam, "Animals and Androids," p. 119.

185. Nick Haslam, "Dehumanization: An Integrative Review," *Personality and Social Psychology Review* 10, no. 3 (2006): 258.

186. Susan T. Fiske, *Envy Up, Scorn Down: How Status Divides Us* (New York: Russell Sage Foundation, 2012), p. 22 (emphasis in original).

187. Harris, Cikara, and Fiske, "A Volatile Ambivalence," p. 137.

188. Fiske, *Envy Up, Scorn Down*, p. 23.

189. Harris, Cikara, and Fiske, "A Volatile Ambivalence," p. 138.

190. Harris, Cikara, and Fiske, p. 139.

191. Harris, Cikara, and Fiske, p. 143.

192. Harris, Cikara, and Fiske, p. 144.

Chapter Four

193. Elizabeth Baily Wolf and Peter Glick, "Competent but Cold: The Stereotype Content Model and Envy in Organizations," in *Envy at Work and in Organizations*, ed. Richard H. Smith, Ugo Merlone, and Michelle K. Duffy (Oxford: Oxford University Press, 2017), p. 151.

194. Gonzalo Fernández de la Mora, *Egalitarian Envy: The Political Foundations of Social Justice* (San Jose, CA: iUniverse, 2000), p. 77.

195. Mark D. Alicke and Ethan Zell, "Social Comparison and Envy," in *Envy: Theory and Research*, ed. Smith, pp. 74–75.

196. Fernández de la Mora, *Egalitarian Envy*, p. 80.

197. Alicke and Zell, "Social Comparison and Envy," p. 77.

198. Fernández de la Mora, *Egalitarian Envy*, p. 75.

199. W. Gerrod Parrott, "The Emotional Experiences of Envy and Jealousy," in *The Psychology of Jealousy and Envy*, ed. Peter Salovey (New York: Guilford Press, 1991), pp. 6–7.

200. Alicke and Zell, "Social Comparison and Envy," p. 78.

201. Alicke and Zell, pp. 342–43.

202. Christine R. Harris and Peter Salovey, "Reflections on Envy," in *Envy: Theory and Research*, ed. Smith, p. 342.

203. Harris and Salovey, "Reflections on Envy," p. 346.

204. Harris and Salovey, pp. 339–40.

205. Harris and Salovey, p. 344.

206. Alicke and Zell, "Social Comparison and Envy," p. 82.

207. Alicke and Zell, pp. 84–85.

208. Alicke and Zell, p. 85.

209. Alicke and Zell, p. 87.

210. Alicke and Zell, p. 87.

211. Alicke and Zell, p. 87.

212. Alicke and Zell, p. 87.

213. Alicke and Zell, p. 87.

214. Charles E. Hoogland, Stephen Thielke, and Richard H. Smith, "Envy as an Evolving Episode," in *Envy at Work and in Organizations*, ed. Smith, Merlone, and Duffy, p. 127.

215. Hoogland, Thielke, and Smith, "Envy as an Evolving Episode," p. 127.

216. Peter Salovey, ed. *The Psychology of Jealousy and Envy* (New York: Guilford Press, 1991), p. 93.

217. Richard H. Smith, "Envy and the Sense of Injustice," in *The Psychology of Jealousy and Envy*, ed. Salovey, p. 94.

218. Smith, "Envy and the Sense of Injustice," p. 84.

219. Smith, "Envy and the Sense of Injustice," p. 89.

220. Richard H. Smith et al., "Subjective Injustice and Inferiority as Predictors of Hostile and Depressive Feelings in Envy," *Personality and Social Psychology Bulletin* 20, no. 6 (1994): 707–8.

221. Smith et al., "Subjective Injustice," p. 710.

222. Richard H. Smith and Sung Hee Kim, "Introduction," in *Envy: Theory and Research*, ed. Smith, p. 4.

223. Smith and Kim, "Introduction," p. 5.

224. Susan T. Fiske, "Envy Up, Scorn Down: How Comparison Divides Us," *American Psychologist* 65, no. 8 (2010): 2.

225. Fiske, "How Comparison Divides Us," pp. 6–7.

226. Helmut Schoeck, *Envy: A Theory of Social Behaviour* (Indianapolis: Liberty Fund, 1966), p. 29.

227. George M. Foster, "The Anatomy of Envy: A Study in Symbolic Behavior," *University of Chicago Press Journals* 13, no. 2 (1972): 166.

228. Redzo Mujcic and Andrew J. Oswald, "Is Envy Harmful to a Society's Psychological Health and Wellbeing? A Longitudinal Study of 18,000 Adults," *Social Science & Medicine* 198 (2018): 104.

229. Mujcic and Oswald, "Is Envy Harmful?" p. 105.

230. Fernández de la Mora, *Egalitarian Envy*, p. 73.

231. Fernández de la Mora, p. 74.

232. Foster, "Anatomy of Envy," p. 166.

233. Foster, p. 184 (emphasis in original).

234. Harry Stack Sullivan, quoted in Foster, "Anatomy of Envy," p. 184.

235. Foster, "Anatomy of Envy," p. 184.

236. Schoeck, *Envy*, p. 11.

237. Schoeck, p. 25.

238. Schoeck, p. 8.

239. The German term *Missgunst* is always negative, whereas *Neid* is a general term for envy, which could also have a positive connotation (equivalent to "admiration") in colloquial language. In Russian, "black" envy is always malicious and "white" envy is always benign.

240. Jens Lange and Jan Crusius, "Dispositional Envy Revisited: Unraveling the Motivational Dynamics of Benign and Malicious Envy," *Personality and Social Psychology Bulletin* 41, no. 2 (2015): 286.

241. Lange and Crusius, "Dispositional Envy Revisited," p. 288.

242. Parrott, "Envy and Jealousy," pp. 9–10.

243. Niels van de Ven, Marcel Zeelenberg, and Rik Pieters, "Why Envy Outperforms Admiration," *Personality and Social Psychology Bulletin* 37, no. 6 (2011): 784.

244. Van de Ven, Zeelenberg, and Pieters, "Why Envy Outperforms Admiration," p. 790.

245. Mujcic and Oswald, "Is Envy Harmful?" pp. 108–9.

246. Justin D'Arms and Alison Duncan Kerr, "Envy in the Philosophical Tradition," in *Envy: Theory and Research*, ed. Smith, p. 45.

247. D'Arms and Kerr, "Envy in the Philosophical Tradition," p. 46.

248. D'Arms and Kerr, p. 47.

249. D'Arms and Kerr, p. 48.

250. D'Arms and Kerr, p. 49.

251. Harris and Salovey, "Reflections on Envy," p. 335.

252. Harris and Salovey, p. 336.

253. Yochi Cohen-Charash and Elliott Larson, "What Is the Nature of Envy?" in *Envy at Work and in Organizations*, ed. Smith, Merlone, and Duffy, p. 25.

254. Cohen-Charash and Larson, "What Is the Nature of Envy?" p. 26.

255. Caitlin A. J. Powell, Richard H. Smith, and David Ryan Schurtz, "Schadenfreude Caused by an Envied Person's Pain," in *Envy: Theory and Research*, ed. Smith, pp. 148–50.

256. Richard H. Smith et al., "Envy and Schadenfreude," *Personality and Social Psychology Bulletin* 22, no. 2 (1996): 158–68.

257. Smith et al., "Envy and Schadenfreude," p. 167.

258. Fiske, "How Comparison Divides Us," p. 7.

259. Mina Cikara and Susan T. Fiske, "Stereotypes and Schadenfreude: Affective and Physiological Markers of Pleasure at Outgroup Misfortunes," *Social Psychological and Personality Science* 3, no. 1 (2012): 69 (emphasis in original).

260. Cikara and Fiske, "Stereotypes and Schadenfreude," p. 70.

261. Powell, Smith, and Schurtz, "Schadenfreude," pp. 148–50.

262. Powell, Smith, and Schurtz, p. 151.

263. Powell, Smith, and Schurtz, p. 153.

264. Powell, Smith, and Schurtz, pp. 153–54.

265. N. T. Feather, "Attitudes towards the High Achiever: The Fall of the Tall Poppy," *Australian Journal of Psychology* 41, no. 3 (1989): 239.

266. Feather, "Fall of the Tall Poppy," p. 240.

267. Feather, p. 240.

268. Feather, p. 240.

269. Feather, p. 241.

270. Feather, pp. 241–42.

271. Feather, p. 242.

272. Feather, p. 250.

273. Feather, p. 250.

274. Feather, p. 255.

275. Feather, p. 256.

276. Feather, p. 259.

277. Feather, p. 259.

278. Feather, pp. 261 et seq.

279. Daniel Sznycer et al., "Support for Redistribution Is Shaped by Compassion, Envy, and Self-Interest, but Not a Taste of Fairness," *Proceedings of the National Academy of Sciences* 114, no. 31 (2017): 8424.

280. Sznycer et al., "Support for Redistribution," p. 8424.

281. Sznycer et al., p. 8424.

282. Sznycer et al., p. 8424.

283. Sznycer et al., p. 8424.

284. Sznycer et al., p. 8424.

285. Sznycer et al., p. 8424.

286. Sznycer et al., p. 8424.

287. Sznycer et al., pp. 8422–23.

288. Sznycer et al., p. 8422.

289. Sznycer et al., p. 8422.

290. Sznycer et al., p. 8422.

291. Fernández de la Mora, *Egalitarian Envy*, p. 93.

292. Susan T. Fiske, *Envy Up, Scorn Down: How Status Divides Us* (New York: Russell Sage Foundation, 2012), pp. 24–26.

293. Fiske, p. 24.

294. Mujcic and Oswald, "Is Envy Harmful?" p. 107.

295. Mujcic and Oswald, p. 108.

296. Schoeck, *Envy*, p. 28.

297. Schoeck, p. 125.

298. Schoeck, p. 341.

299. Hans-Peter Müller, "Soziale Ungleichheit und Ressentiment," *Merkur* 58 (2004): 885–86.

300. Müller, "Soziale Ungleichheit und Ressentiment," pp. 888–89.

301. Müller, p. 889.

302. Müller, p. 890.

303. Schoeck, *Envy*, p. 361.

304. Müller, "Soziale Ungleichheit und Ressentiment," p. 893.

Chapter Five

305. Foster, "Anatomy of Envy," p. 169 (emphasis in original).

306. Daniel V. Meegan, "Zero-Sum Bias: Perceived Competition Despite Unlimited Resources," *Frontiers in Psychology* 1, no. 191 (2010): 12.

307. Paul H. Rubin, "Folk Economics," *Southern Economic Journal* 70, no. 1 (2003): 157–58.

308. Rubin, "Folk Economics," p. 158.

309. See Rubin, p. 162.

310. Weiying Zhang, *The Logic of the Market: An Insider's View of Chinese Economic Reform* (Washington: Cato Institute, 2015), p. 286.

311. Ludwig von Mises, *Human Action: A Treatise on Economics* (Auburn, AL: The Ludwig von Mises Institute), 1949, ed. Bettina Bien Greaves 1998, p. 892.

312. Patrick Sachweh, *Deutungsmuster sozialer Ungleichheit: Wahrnehmung und Legitimation gesellschaftlicher Privilegierung und Benachteiligung* (Frankfurt: Campus Verlag, 2009), p. 151.

313. Meegan, "Zero-Sum Bias," p. 13 (emphasis in original).

314. Bertolt Brecht, "Alfabet," in *The Collected Poems of Bertolt Brecht*, trans. David Constantine and Tom Kuhn (New York: Liveright, 2018).

315. Meegan, "Zero-Sum Bias," p. 1.

316. Joanna Różycka-Tran and colleagues conducted an international study on zero-sum belief. It was these researchers that actually coined the term "belief in a zero-sum game." Unfortunately, this study has a number of significant methodological flaws and thus could not fulfill its stated purpose of measuring the differences in zero-sum beliefs in different countries, partly due to inappropriate questions, but partly because the participants were not representative of the population of these countries and one set of participants had a very high proportion of female psychology students.

Chapter Six

317. Lev. 16:8–21 (ESV).

318. Peter Glick, "Choice of Scapegoats," in *On the Nature of Prejudice: Fifty Years after Allport*, ed. John F. Dovidio, Peter Glick, and Laurie A. Rudman (Malden, MA: Blackwell, 2005), p. 244.

319. Ben Irvine, *Scapegoated Capitalism* (UK: Oldspeak Publishing, 2016), p. 12.

320. Gerd Schwerhoff, "Vom Alltagsverdacht zur Massenverfolgung: Neuere deutsche Forschung zum frühneuzeitlichen Hexenwesen," *Geschichte in Wissenschaft und Unterricht* 46 (1995): 365.

321. Irvine, *Scapegoated Capitalism*, p. 19.

322. Gordon W. Allport, *The Nature of Prejudice* (New York: Basic Books, 1979), p. 343.

323. Allport, *Nature of Prejudice*, p. 349.

324. Allport, p. 343.

325. Allport, p. 348.

326. Allport, p. 346.

327. Allport, p. 346.

328. Allport, p. 350.

329. Allport, p. 351.

330. Glick, "Choice of Scapegoats," pp. 245 et seq.

331. Glick, p. 250 (emphasis in original).

332. Glick, p. 251.

333. Glick, p. 253.

334. Glick, p. 254.

335. Glick, p. 254.

336. Glick, p. 255.

337. Susan Gniechwitz, "Antisemitismus im Licht der modernen Vorurteilsforschung: Kognitive Grundlagen latenter Vorurteile gegenüber Juden in Deutschland" (PhD diss., Universität Jena, 2006), p. 26.

338. H. Reils, contributions to the oldest history of Jews in Hamburg, quoted in Gniechwitz, "Antisemitismus im Licht der modernen Vorurteilsforschung," p. 20.

339. Édouard Drumont, *La France Juive*, p. 9, quoted in *The French Right: From de Maistre to Maurras*, ed. J. S. McLelland (London: Jonathan Cape, 1970), p. 92.

340. Adolf Hitler, quoted in Rainer Zitelmann, *Hitler: The Policies of Seduction*, trans. Helmut Bögler (London: London House, 1999), p. 265.

341. Adolf Hitler, *Mein Kampf* (London: Hurst and Blackett, 1939), p. 102.

342. Rainer Zitelmann, "Zur Begründung des 'Lebensraum'-Motivs in Hitlers Weltanschauung," in *Der Zweite Weltkrieg*, ed. Wolfgang Michalka (Munich: Seehammer, 1997).

343. Ervin Staub, *The Roots of Evil: The Origins of Genocide and Other Group Violence* (New York: Cambridge University Press, 1989), p. 40 (emphasis in original).

344. Staub, *The Roots of Evil*, pp. 234 et seq.

345. George Gilder, *Wealth and Poverty: A New Edition for the Twenty-First Century* (Washington: Regnery Publishing, 2012), p. 139.

CHAPTER SEVEN

346. Carol K. Sigelman, "Rich Man, Poor Man: Developmental Differences in Attributions and Perceptions," *Journal of Experimental Child Psychology* 113, no. 3 (2012): 416.

347. Sigelman, "Rich Man, Poor Man," p. 417.

348. Helga Dittmar, "Perceived Material Wealth and First Impressions," *British Journal of Social Psychology* 31, no. 4 (1992): 381.

349. Dittmar, "Perceived Material Wealth," p. 387.

350. Susan T. Fiske, *Envy Up, Scorn Down: How Status Divides Us* (New York: Russell Sage Foundation, 2012), p. 101.

351. Sachweh, *Deutungsmuster sozialer Ungleichheit*, pp. 165–66.

352. Sachweh, pp. 181–82.

353. Sachweh, p. 182.

354. Sachweh, pp. 182–83.

355. Sachweh, p. 171.

356. Quoted in Sachweh, p. 171.

357. Sachweh, pp. 171–72.

358. Sachweh, p. 172.

359. Thomas J. Gorman, "Cross-Class Perceptions of Social Class," *Sociological Spectrum* 20, no. 1 (2000): 107–8.

360. Gorman, "Cross-Class Perceptions," p. 104 (emphasis in original).

361. Gorman, pp. 117–18.

362. Thomas J. Gorman, *Growing Up Working Class: Hidden Injuries and the Development of Angry White Men and Women* (Cham, Switzerland: Palgrave Macmillan, 2017), pp. 116–17.

363. Gorman, *Growing Up Working Class*, p. 71.

364. Michèle Lamont, "Above 'People Above'? Status and Worth among White and Black Workers," in *The Cultural Territories of Race: Black and White Boundaries*, ed. Michèle Lamont (Chicago: University of Chicago Press, 1999), p. 127.

365. Lamont, "Status and Worth among White and Black Workers," p. 127.

366. Lamont, pp. 127–28.

367. Lamont, p. 131.

368. Lamont, p. 131.

369. Lamont, p. 131.

370. Lamont, p. 132.

371. Lamont, p. 133.

372. Lamont, p. 134.

373. Lamont, p. 141.

374. Sachweh, *Deutungsmuster sozialer Ungleichheit*, p. 48.

375. L. Richard Della Fave, "The Meek Shall Not Inherit the Earth: Self-Evaluation and the Legitimacy of Stratification," *American Sociological Review* 45, no. 6 (1980): 955–71.

376. Sachweh, *Deutungsmuster sozialer Ungleichheit*, p. 48.

377. Lamont, "Status and Worth among White and Black Workers," p. 143.

378. Lamont, p. 128.

379. Richard Sennett and Jonathan Cobb, *The Hidden Injuries of Class* (New York: W. W. Norton, 1972), pp. 250–51 (emphasis in original).

380. Sennett and Cobb, *Hidden Injuries of Class*, p. 255.

381. Lamont, "Status and Worth among White and Black Workers," p. 129.

382. Joan C. Williams, "The Class Culture Gap," in *Facing Social Class: How Societal Rank Influences Interaction*, ed. Susan T. Fiske and Hazel Rose Markus (New York: Russell Sage Foundation, 2012), p. 40.

383. Williams, "Class Culture Gap," p. 41.

384. Williams, p. 46.

385. Williams, p. 48.

386. Williams, p. 53.

387. Fiske, *How Status Divides Us*, p. 130.

388. Fiske, p. 133.

389. Fiske, p. 162.

390. Bogdan Wojciszke, Róża Bazinska, and Marcin Jaworski, "On the Dominance of Moral Categories in Impression Formation," *Personality and Social Psychology Bulletin* 24, no. 12 (1998): 1251.

391. Wojciszke, Bazinska, and Jaworski, "On the Dominance of Moral Categories," p. 1256.

392. Wojciszke, Bazinska, and Jaworski, p. 1252.

Chapter Eight

393. Michael W. Kraus, Paul K. Piff, and Dacher Keltner, "Social Class, Sense of Control, and Social Explanation," *Journal of Personality and Social Psychology* 97, no. 6 (2009): 993.

394. Kraus, Piff, and Keltner, "Social Class," p. 998.

395. Kraus, Piff, and Keltner, p. 996.

396. Kraus, Piff, and Keltner, pp. 546 et seq.

397. Kluegel and Smith, *Beliefs about Inequality*, p. 89.

398. Kluegel and Smith, p. 91.

399. Kluegel and Smith, pp. 89–90.

400. Kluegel and Smith, pp. 90–91.

401. Kluegel and Smith, p. 79.

402. Gallup News Service, "Have and Have-Nots: Perceptions of Fairness and Opportunity," July 6, 1998.

403. Gallup News Service, "Have and Have-Nots."

404. Gallup News Service.

405. Pew Research Center, American Values Survey, Question database, http://www.people-press.org/values-questions/q30e/success-in-life-determined -by-forces-outside-our-control/#total.

406. Pew Research Center, American Values Survey, Question database.

407. Wolfgang Glatzer et al., *Reichtum im Uerteil der Bevölkerung: Legitimations-probleme und Spannungspotentiale in Deutschland* (Opladen: Verlag Barbara Budrich, 2009), pp. 68–69.

408. Glatzer et al., p. 69.

409. Glatzer et al., p. 67.

410. Adrian Furnham, "Attributions for Affluence," *Personality and Individual Differences* 4, no. 1 (1983): 33.

411. Furnham, "Attributions for Affluence," p. 32.

412. Furnham, p. 39.

413. Furnham, p. 34.

414. Furnham, p. 34.

415. Karen Rowlingson and Stephen McKay, "What Do the Public Think about the Wealth Gap?" University of Birmingham, 2013.

416. Ifop, "Les Français et la richesse en France en 2017," October 2017, https://www.ifop.com/wp-content/uploads/2018/03/3904-1-study_file.pdf.

417. Ifop, "Les Français et la richesse en France en 2017."

418. Reuters, "French More Anti-Capitalist than Chinese—Poll," January 26, 2011, https://in.reuters.com/article/idINIndia-54417420110126.

419. Reuters, "Poll."

420. Ifop, "Les Français et la richesse en France en 2017."

Chapter Nine

421. Glatzer et al., *Reichtum im Urteil der Bevölkerung*, pp. 56–57.

422. Glatzer et al., p. 57.

423. Glatzer et al., p. 58, with reference to Merton.

424. Glatzer et al., pp. 60–61.

425. Glatzer et al., p. 61.

426. Kathleen Weldon, "If I Were a Rich Man: Public Attitudes about Wealth and Taxes," Roper Public Opinion Archives, February 2015.

427. Weldon, "If I Were a Rich Man."

428. These data appear in Kim Parker, "Yes, the Rich Are Different," Pew Research Center, August 2, 2012.

429. Juliet B. Schor, *Born to Buy* (New York: Scribner, 2004), pp. 150–51.

430. Schor, *Born to Buy*, pp. 150–51.

431. Schor, p. 149.

432. Jeffrey M. Jones, "Most Americans Do Not Have a Strong Desire to Be Rich," Gallup News Service, December 11, 2006.

433. David W. Moore, "Half of Young People Expect to Strike It Rich, But Expectations Fall Rapidly with Age," Gallup News Service, March 11, 2003.

434. Frank Newport, "Partisan Divide on Benefit of Having Rich People Expands," Gallup News Service, June 8, 2018.

435. Moore, "Half of Young People Expect to Strike It Rich"; Newport, "Partisan Divide."

436. Weldon, "If I Were a Rich Man."

437. The following figures are taken from Pew Research Center, American Values Survey, Question database, http://www.people-press.org/values-questions /q30f/hard-work-offers-little-guarantee-of-success/#income.

438. Pew Research Center, American Values Survey, Question database, http://www.people-press.org/values-questions/q30g/i-admire-people-who-get -rich-by-working-hard/#total.

439. Pew Research Center, American Values Survey, Question database, http://www.people-press.org/values-questions/q30g/i-admire-people-who-get -rich-by-working-hard/#income.

440. The following figures are taken from Kim Parker, "Yes, the Rich Are Different," Pew.

441. Parker, Pew.

442. Parker, Pew.

443. Allensbach Institute surveys 4218, 7013, 7059, 7082, 10018, and 10033.

444. Allensbach Institute survey 10018.

445. Allensbach Institute survey 10018.

446. Allensbach Institute survey 10018.

447. Allensbach Institute surveys 10046, 11006, and 11068.

448. Sachweh, *Deutungsmuster sozialer Ungleichheit*, p. 46.

449. Sachweh, p. 68.

450. Quoted in Sachweh, p. 236.

451. Sachweh, p. 236.

452. Sachweh, p. 45.

453. Sachweh, pp. 239–40.

454. Sachweh, p. 50.

455. Sachweh, p. 141.

456. Sachweh, p. 142.

457. Suzanne R. Horwitz and John F. Dovidio, "The Rich—Love Them or Hate Them? Divergent Implicit and Explicit Attitudes toward the Wealthy," *Group Processes & Intergroup Relations* 20, no. 1 (2017): 5.

458. Horwitz and Dovidio, p. 6.

459. Horwitz and Dovidio, p. 6.

460. Horwitz and Dovidio, p. 7.

461. Horwitz and Dovidio, p. 12.

462. Horwitz and Dovidio, p. 16.

463. Horwitz and Dovidio, pp. 17 et seq.

464. Horwitz and Dovidio, p. 24.

465. For the following, see Andrew N. Christopher et al., "Affluence Cues and First Impressions: Does It Matter How the Affluence Was Acquired?" *Journal of Economic Psychology* 26, no. 2 (2005): 198–99.

466. Christopher et al., "Affluence Cues," p. 194.

467. Christopher et al., pp. 195, 198.

468. Christopher et al., pp. 196–97.

469. Newport, "Partisan Divide," Gallup.

470. Weldon, "If I Were a Rich Man."

471. The following figures are all taken from Gallup News Service, "Taxes" webpage, http://news.gallup.com/poll/1714/taxes.aspx.

472. Gallup News Services, "Taxes (Historical Trends)."

473. Giacomo Corneo and Hans Peter Grüner, "Individual Preferences for Political Redistribution," *Journal of Public Economics* 83, no. 1 (2002): 89.

474. The following figures are all taken from Corneo and Grüner, "Individual Preferences," p. 89.

475. Corneo and Grüner, p. 89.

476. Corneo and Grüner, p. 89.

477. Corneo and Grüner, p. 89.

478. Corneo and Grüner, pp. 86 et seq.

479. Glatzer et al., *Reichtum im Urteil der Bevölkerung*, p. 73.

480. Glatzer et al., p. 73.

481. Rowlingson and McKay, "What Do the Public Think about the Wealth Gap?"

482. Rowlingson and McKay.

Chapter Ten

483. Susan T. Fiske, *Envy Up, Scorn Down: How Status Divides Us* (New York: Russell Sage Foundation, 2011), p. 2.

484. For more on this subject, see Chapter 7. Bogdan Wojciszke, Róża Bazinska, and Marcin Jaworski, "On the Dominance of Moral Categories in Impression Formation," *Personality and Social Psychology Bulletin* 24, no. 12 (1998): 1251.

485. Helmut Schoeck, *Envy: A Theory of Social Behaviour* (Indianapolis: Liberty Fund, 1966), p. 288.

486. Please note that the immigrants who participated in the Allensbach survey are largely well integrated, both because the survey was conducted in German and because well-integrated immigrants are more willing to take part in such a survey than are less well-integrated immigrants.

CHAPTER ELEVEN

487. Samuel Gregg, *Becoming Europe: Economic Decline, Culture, and How America Can Avoid a European Future* (New York: Encounter Books, 2013), pp. 10–11.

CHAPTER FOURTEEN

488. For more on the methodology used, see Chapter 10, p. 160.

489. With regard to the number of millionaires, see Knight Frank Research, "The Wealth Report 2017," p. 67.

490. The traits are listed here in numerical order, according to the number of times they were mentioned, rather than in percentages. It proved difficult to directly compare the responses in percentages because, for example, 5 percent of respondents in Germany and France selected "None of the above" or did not select any traits, compared with 26 percent in Great Britain and 14 percent in the United States. As a result, the total numbers of responses from Great Britain and from the United States are lower than those from Germany and from France. For this reason, the most appropriate comparison is the straightforward ranking presented here.

491. Wojciszke, Bazinska, and Jaworski, "On the Dominance of Moral Categories," 1251.

492. Wojciszke, Bazinska, and Jaworski, "On the Dominance of Moral Categories," 1256.

493. Melanie Böwing-Schmalenbrock, *Wege zum Reichtum: Die Bedeutung von Erbschaften, Erwerbstätigkeit und Persönlichkeit für die Entstehung von Reichtum* (Wiesbaden: Verlag für Sozialwissenschaften, 2012), p. 139.

494. Böwing-Schmalenbrock, *Wege zum Reichtum*, p. 213.

495. Böwing-Schmalenbrock, p. 187.

CHAPTER FIFTEEN

496. Silke Gronwald, "Wird die Welt immer ungerechter?" *Stern*, January 19, 2017, p. 20.

497. Ingrid Eißele and Lisa Rokahr, "Managerschreck der Woche: Markiges Klopfen," *Stern*, March 7, 2013, p. 36.

498. Hans-Ulrich Jörges, "Das letzte Gefecht," *Stern*, June 12, 2008, p. 30.

499. J. Drebes, B. Marschall, and F. Rinke, "Berlin: Streit um Deckel bei Managergehältern," *Rheinische Post*, February 9, 2017.

500. Drebes, Marschall, and Rinke, "Berlin."

501. Birgit Marschall and Eva Quadbeck, "Manager-Boni: CDU greift IG Metall an," *Rheinische Post*, February 19, 2017.

502. Marcus Krämer, "Darf's noch ein bisschen mehr sein?" ("Would You Like a Little Bit More?"), *Sächsische Zeitung*, March 22, 2012.

503. Commerzbank CEO Klaus-Peter Müller, as quoted in Georg Winters, "Kommission: Obergrenzen für Vorstandsgehälter," *Rheinische Post*, February 6, 2013.

504. "Der größte Vergütungsunfug passiert im Dunkeln," *Frankfurter Allgemeine Zeitung*, March 24, 2018.

505. "Der größte Vergütungsunfug."

506. Antje Höning, "Was dürfen Topmanager verdienen?" *Rheinische Post*, March 4, 2013.

507. Lisa Rokahr, "Die 1:12-Formel," *Stern*, November 21, 2013, p. 34.

508. David Miller, as quoted in Krämer, "Darf's noch ein bisschen mehr sein?" The original quote can be found in Ben Jackson and Paul Segal's "Why Inequality Matters," Catalyst working paper, January 2004.

509. "Wir waren vier Jungs: Wir wollten die Panzer stoppen," interview with Hans-Ulrich Wehler, *Stern*, July 10, 2014, pp. 66–72.

510. "European Auto Crisis Is an Endurance Test," interview with Volkswagen CEO Martin Winterkorn, *Spiegel Online*, February 2013.

511. Höning, "Was dürfen Topmanager verdienen?"

512. Michael Bröcker and Birgit Marschall, "All-Parteien Koalition will Managergehälter begrenzen," *Rheinische Post*, March 5, 2013.

513. Birgit Marschall, "Managergehälter den Aktionären überlassen," *Rheinische Post*, February 18, 2017.

514. Sven Siebert, "Merkel will angemessene Management-Gehälter," *Sächsische Zeitung*, March 14, 2013.

515. "VW—Erfolg zahlt sich für Vorstände aus," *Frankfurter Allgemeine Zeitung*, March 14, 2018.

516. "VW—Erfolg zahlt sich für Vorstände aus."

517. Carsten Germis, "Unter Beobachtung," *Frankfurter Allgemeine Zeitung*, March 14, 2018.

518. "VW—Erfolg zahlt sich für Vorstände aus."

519. "Managergehälter des Dax-Chefs deutlich gestiegen," *Frankfurter Allgemeine Zeitung*, March 16, 2018.

520. Nora Miethke, "Der Druck zur Mäßigung steigt" ("Calls for Moderation Intensify"), *Sächsische Zeitung*, March 5, 2013.

521. Krämer, "Darf's noch ein bisschen mehr sein?"

522. "Familienunternehmer kritisieren Managergehälter," *Sächsische Zeitung*, March 19, 2012.

523. "Familienunternehmer kritisieren Managergehälter."

524. Linda I. Reutter et al., "'Who Do They Think We Are, Anyway?' Perceptions of and Response to Poverty Stigma," *Qualitative Health Research* 19, no. 3 (2009): 306.

525. Miethke, "Der Druck zur Mäßigung steigt."

526. Georg Winters, "Managergehälter: Das Getöse der Politik," *Rheinische Post*, March 5, 2013.

527. Walter Wüllenweber, "Ist das gerecht?," *Stern*, December 8, 2016, pp. 28–36.

528. Wüllenweber, "Ist das gerecht?," pp. 28–36.

529. Frank Dohmen and Dietmar Hawranek, "Der Selbstbedienungsladen," *Der Spiegel*, February 4, 2017, pp. 70–71.

530. "Wir fordern Obergrenzen," *Der Spiegel*, February 25, 2017.

531. Max Hägler and Klaus Ott, "12 Millionen Euro—warum?" *Süddeutsche Zeitung*, February 1, 2017.

532. Gregor Le Claire, "Hohe Abfindung? Manchmal das Beste" ("Golden Handshakes? Sometimes They're for the Best"), *Nürnberger Nachrichten*, February 3, 2017.

533. For more on this topic, see Rainer Zitelmann, *The Power of Capitalism: A Journey through Recent History across Five Continents* (London: LID Publishing, 2018), Chapter 9.

534. Stefan Schmitz, "Im Inneren des Monsters," *Stern*, May 31, 2012, pp. 84–88. For original quotes, see Joris Luyendijk, "Voices of Finance: PR Officer for a Brokerage Company," *The Guardian*, September 15, 2011; Joris Luyendijk, "Voices of Finance: Employee Relations Manager at a Major Bank," *The Guardian*, November 2, 2011; and Joris Luyendijk, "Voices of Finance: Recruiter," *The Guardian*, October 13, 2011.

535. Again, for original quotes, see Luyendijk, "Voices of Finance" articles.

536. Hans-Ulrich Jörges, "Lüge in Zeiten der Gier," *Stern*, March 14, 2013, p. 22.

537. Alexander Hagelüken, "Ein Fall von Marktversagen" ("A Clear-Cut Case of Market Failure"), *Sächsische Zeitung*, March 1, 2013.

538. Martin Hesse and Christoph Pauly, "Ein Deckel für den Volkszorn" ("Putting a Lid on People's Anger"), *Der Spiegel*, March 4, 2013.

539. Meike Schreiber, "Es ist absolut sinnvoll, dass Boni zurückverlangt werden können," *Süddeutsche Zeitung Magazin*, February 2, 2018.

540. "Acht Männer reicher als die halbe Welt" ("Just Eight Men Are Richer than Half the World"), *Frankfurter Allgemeine Zeitung*, January 16, 2017.

541. "Acht Männer."

542. "Acht Männer."

543. Bastian Brinkmann, "Nein, acht Menschen besitzen nicht so viel wie die Hälfte der Welt" ("No, Eight People Do Not Own as Much as Half the World"), *Süddeutsche Zeitung,* January 16, 2017.

544. "Kluft wird immer größer" ("The Gap Is Widening All the Time"), *Nürnberger Nachrichten*, January 18, 2016.

545. "Den Reichen gehört die halbe Welt" ("Half the World Belongs to the Rich"), *Sächsische Zeitung,* January 19, 2016.

546. "Studie: 62 Reiche besitzen so viel wie die halbe Welt" ("Study: 62 Rich People Own as Much as Half the World"), *Rheinische Post,* January 18, 2016.

547. Alexandra Endres, "Soziale Ungleichheit: Wer reich ist, macht Politik," *Die Zeit,* January 22, 2018.

548. Endres, "Soziale Ungleichheit."

549. Gronwold, "Wird die Welt immer ungerechter?"

550. Thomas Piketty, *Capital in the Twenty-First Century,* trans. Arthur Goldhammer (Cambridge, MA: Belknap Press, 2014), p. 20.

551. Piketty, *Capital in the Twenty-First Century,* p. 438.

552. For more details, see Jean-Philippe Delsol, Nicolas Lecaussin, and Emmanuel Martin, eds., *Anti-Piketty: Capital for the 21st Century* (Washington: Cato Institute, 2017).

553. See Tom G. Palmer, "Foreword," in Delsol, Lecaussin, and Martin, *Anti-Piketty: Capital for the 21st Century,* p. xv.

554. Andreas Zielcke, "Spitzenkraft," *Süddeutsche Zeitung,* October 8, 2014.

555. Nils Minkmar, "Wie kann Europa wieder stark und schön werden" ("How Can Europe Ever Become Strong and Beautiful Again?"), *Frankfurter Allgemeine Zeitung,* May 8, 2014.

556. Patrick Welter, "Ein Rockstar-Ökonom erobert Amerika," *Frankfurter Allgemeine Zeitung,* May 10, 2014.

557. Norbert Höfler, "Willkommen im 18. Jahrhundert!" *Stern,* April 30, 2014, pp. 48–50.

558. "Das Kapital frisst die Zukunft" ("Capital Is Eating the Future"), interview with Thomas Piketty, *Der Spiegel,* May 5, 2014.

559. "Ins Knie geschossen," interview with Peter Bofinger, *Der Spiegel,* February 6, 2014.

560. Thomas Meyer, "Wo die jungen Wilden wohnen: Thomas Pikettys Buch über Kapital im 21. Jahrhundert wurde zu Unrecht kritisiert,"*Süddeutsche Zeitung,* June 10, 2014.

561. Rainer Zitelmann, *The Power of Capitalism* (London: LID Publishing, 2018), Chapter 1.

562. For more details, see Delsol, Lecaussin, and Martin, *Anti-Piketty,* pp. 8–9.

563. "Zuckerberg spendet," *Süddeutsche Zeitung,* December 10, 2010.

564. "Zuckerberg und Berggruen wollen Großteil ihrer Vermögen spenden," *Frankfurter Allgemeine Zeitung,* December 10, 2010.

565. Nikolaus Piper, "Ein Prozent reicht zum Leben," *Süddeutsche Zeitung,* December 11, 2010.

566. Carsten Knop, "Die großen Stifter" ("The Great Philanthropists"), *Frankfurter Allgemeine Zeitung*, August 6, 2010.

567. Sebastian Fischer, "The Giving Pledge: Der Club der Super-Spender," *Der Spiegel*, February 21, 2013.

568. Andrian Kreye, "Wohltaten mit Haken," *Süddeutsche Zeitung*, December 2, 2015.

569. Jan Rosenkranz, "Und was gebt ihr?" *Stern*, August 12, 2010, pp. 88–92. The original quote can be found in Peter Singer, *Famine, Affluence, and Morality* (Oxford: Oxford University Press, 2016), p. 67.

570. "Die Menschenfreunde hinter Gates und Buffett," *Frankfurter Allgemeine Zeitung*, August 6, 2010.

571. Thomas Moritz Koch, "Spendable Milliardäre," *Süddeutsche Zeitung*, August 5, 2010.

572. Thomas Fischermann, "Milliarden Spenden: Räuber oder Retter," *Die Zeit*, August 12, 2010. The original quote can be found on Robert Reich's blog, May 6, 2018.

573. Knut Bergmann and Heiko Geue, "Gehen den Stiftungen die Stifter aus?" ("Are Donors Turning Their Backs on Charitable Foundations?"), *Frankfurter Allgemeine Zeitung*, December 22, 2010.

574. Wolfgang Rohe, "Engere Spielräume für Stiftungen," *Frankfurter Allgemeine Zeitung*, October 28, 2010.

CHAPTER SIXTEEN

575. Bastian Obermayer and Frederick Obermaier, *The Panama Papers: Breaking the Story of How the Rich and Powerful Hide Their Money* (London: Oneworld Publications, 2016), p. 9.

576. Katrin Langhans et al., "Das Leak," *Süddeutsche Zeitung*, April 4, 2016.

577. Frederik Obermaier et al., "Der Deutsche," *Süddeutsche Zeitung*, April 4, 2016.

578. Hendrik Wieduwilt, "Panama Papers: Was bislang geschah," *Frankfurter Allgemeine Zeitung*, April 9, 2016.

579. Wieduwilt, "Panama Papers."

580. Joachim Jahn, "Auf der Empörungswelle," *Frankfurter Allgemeine Zeitung*, April 9, 2016.

581. Jahn, "Auf der Empörungswelle."

582. Jürgen Kaube, "Darf man jetzt nicht mehr moralisieren?" ("Are We Not Allowed to Moralize Anymore?"), *Frankfurter Allgemeine Zeitung*, April 12, 2016.

583. Frederik Obermaier and Bastian Obermayer, "Inseln werden romantisch verklärt," *Süddeutsche Zeitung*, April 5, 2016.

584. *Süddeutsche Zeitung*, various editions in April 2016.

585. Christoph Gieren and Alexa Olesen, "Die Prinzlinge," *Süddeutsche Zeitung*, April 7, 2016.

586. Hans Leyendecker, "Von den Reichen sparen lernen," *Süddeutsche Zeitung*, April 7, 2016.

587. Hans-Peter Kastenhuber, "In der Gier vereint: Was Despoten, Kriminelle und Reiche verbindet" ("United by Greed: What Connects Despots, Criminals and the Rich"), *Nürnberger Nachrichten*, April 5, 2016.

588. Langhans et al., "Das Leak." In their book *The Panama Papers*, Obermayer and Obermaier mention 8.2 million documents on page 255 and more than 2.6 terabytes of data on page 302. However, since the book contains continuously updated reports on the documents and data available at specific times, these figures are probably only one of many interim updates.

589. These figures are taken from Langhans et al., "Das Leak."

590. Obermayer and Obermaier, *Panama Papers*, p. 79.

591. Obermayer and Obermaier, p. 9 (emphasis in original).

592. Obermayer and Obermaier, p. 105.

593. Obermayer and Obermaier, p. 212.

594. Obermayer and Obermaier, p. 77.

595. Langhans et al., "Das Leak."

596. Obermayer and Obermaier, *Panama Papers*, p. 315.

597. Obermayer and Obermaier, p. 105.

598. Obermaier et al., "Der Deutsche."

599. Obermayer and Obermaier, *Panama Papers*, p. 124.

600. Obermayer and Obermaier, p. 23.

601. Obermayer and Obermaier, p. 75.

602. Obermayer and Obermaier, p. 75.

603. Obermayer and Obermaier, p. 33.

604. Hans Mathias Kepplinger, *Die Mechanismen der Skandalisierung: Warum man den Medien gerade dann nicht vertrauen kann, wenn es darauf ankommt*, updated and expanded edition (Reinbek, Germany: Lau Verlag, 2018), p. 28.

605. Obermayer and Obermaier, *Panama Papers*, p. 199.

606. Obermayer and Obermaier, p. 199.

607. Obermayer and Obermaier, p. 201.

608. Obermayer and Obermaier, p. 201.

609. Obermayer and Obermaier, p. 192.

610. Obermayer and Obermaier, p. 103.

611. Obermayer and Obermaier, p. 117.

612. Obermayer and Obermaier, p. 126.

613. Obermayer and Obermaier, p. 156.

614. Obermayer and Obermaier, pp. 157–58.

615. Obermayer and Obermaier, pp. 195–96.

616. Obermayer and Obermaier, p. 217.

617. Obermayer and Obermaier, pp. 255 et seq.

618. Thomas Spang, "Dollar-Paradies Miami," *Süddeutsche Zeitung*, April 7, 2016.

619. Obermayer and Obermaier, *Panama Papers*, p. 2.

620. Obermayer and Obermaier, p. 184.

621. Obermayer and Obermaier, p. 11.

622. Obermayer and Obermaier, p. 189.

623. Obermayer and Obermaier, pp. 189–90.

624. Obermayer and Obermaier, p. 5.

625. Sarah Benecke, "Halten Offshore-Firmen Immobilien in Nürnberg?" ("Do Offshore Companies Own Real Estate in Nuremberg?"), Interview with Sven Giegold from The Green Party *Nürnberger Nachrichten*, April 13, 2016.

626. Kepplinger, *Die Mechanismen der Skandalisierung*, p. 42.

627. Frederik Obermaier et al., "Verloren im Paradies" ("Lost in Paradise"), *Süddeutsche Zeitung*, April 5, 2016.

628. Langhans et al., "Das Leak." In *The Panama Papers*, Obermayer and Obermaier report finding "more than fifty billionaires from the *Forbes* list of the 500 richest people of 2015" among those mentioned in the papers (p. 185).

629. Obermayer and Obermaier, *Panama Papers*, pp. 190–91.

630. Marc Beise, "Rettet die Steuermoral" ("SOS for Tax Compliance"), *Süddeutsche Zeitung*, April 16–17, 2016.

631. Beise, "Rettet die Steuermoral."

632. Slavoh Žižek, "Finanz-Porno" ("Financial Porn"), *Der Spiegel*, April 9, 2016, pp. 108–9.

633. Martin Hesse et al., "Inseln der Anarchie" ("Islands of Anarchy"), *Der Spiegel*, April 9, 2016, p. 58.

634. Hesse et al., "Inseln der Anarchie."

635. See Kepplinger, *Die Mechanismen der Skandalisierung*, pp. 42, 61–70.

636. Interview with Peer Steinbrück in *Stern*, April 14, 2016, p. 110.

637. Elisabeth Gamperl et al., "Das nächste Leak: Die Paradise Papers bringen Politiker, Prominente, Superreiche und Konzerne in Erklärungsnot—schon wieder," *Süddeutsche Zeitung*, November 6, 2017.

638. Gamperl et al., "Das nächste Leak."

639. Gamperl et al.

640. Gamperl et al.

641. Gamperl et al.

642. Nicolas Richter, "Das Paradies der Reichen" ("Paradise of the Rich"), *Süddeutsche Zeitung*, November 6, 2017.

643. Richter, "Das Paradies der Reichen."

644. Jakob Augstein, "Zur Hölle mit den Reichen" ("To Hell with the Rich"), *Spiegel Online*, November 6, 2017.

645. Augstein, "Zur Hölle mit den Reichen."

646. Augstein.

647. Augstein.

648. Tom Wohlfarth, "Paradise Papers: Wo bleibt die Wut?" ("Where Is the Anger?"), *Zeit Online*, November 11, 2017.

649. Wohlfarth, "Paradise Papers."

650. Christian Reiermann, "Spiel der Reichen" ("The Games Rich People Play"), *Der Spiegel*, November 11, 2017.

651. Reiermann, "Spiel der Reichen."

652. Manfred Schäfers, "Fluch der Karibik," *Frankfurter Allgemeine Zeitung*, November 13, 2017.

653. Martin Benoska and Tobias Hentze, *Die Verteilung der Steuerlast in Deutschland* (Cologne: Institut der deutschen Wirtschaft, 2017), p. 109.

654. Rainer Zitelmann, "1% zahlen 22% der Einkommensteuer," *The European*, March 6, 2017, https://www.theeuropean.de/rainer-zitelmann/11897-fakten -gegen-sozialpopulismus.

655. Kepplinger, *Die Mechanismen der Skandalisierung*, p. 47.

656. Kepplinger, p. 94.

Chapter Seventeen

657. I would like to thank Dr. Alexander Knuppertz, the former head of the text department at my former company (Dr.ZitelmannPB.GmbH), and Malte Paulmann, who supported me in the analysis for this chapter.

658. Timo Nothling, "'Hart aber fair' lässt aufhorchen, Rekord für 'Morden im Norden,'" *Quotenmeter*, May 8, 2018.

659. WDR's "Netiquette für Kommentare" WDR, 2019.

660. For contributions with few reader comments (*Forbes* list, South Korea, International study, Ingvar Kamprad, Criticism of business), every comment was coded. For all other contributions, every second comment was coded.

661. Comments by Rainer Zitelmann himself have not been analyzed.

Chapter Eighteen

662. I would like to thank Anja Georgia Graw, Ansgar Graw, Dr. Alexander Knuppertz, Malte Paulmann, and Dr. Oliver Wenzlaff, all of whom provided valuable help in writing this chapter.

663. Figures for box-office revenues are taken from Nash Information Services' *The Numbers* website, https://www.the-numbers.com/box-office-records /worldwide/all-movies/cumulative/.

664. In view of its relevance to cinematic portrayals of rich people, the movie *All the Money in the World* was added to the sample. After half a year, this film had earned $7 million more than its production costs. Its box-office success, however, cannot be fully evaluated until the end of 2018 because of its belated release on December 25, 2017.

665. The film is based on a true incident, namely, the kidnapping of the grandson of oil billionaire J. Paul Getty, and thus it raises the expectation of portraying the true character of a real rich man—although, because of the family's secrecy, it remains unclear how accurately Getty in particular was portrayed. See also Olivia Truffaut-Wong, "How Accurate Is 'All the Money in the World'? Ridley Scott's New Drama Sticks to the Facts," *Bustle*, December 21, 2017.

666. Three of the films did not contain identifiable "counterpart" characters.

Conclusion

667. Walter Lippmann, *Public Opinion* (La Vergne, TN: BN Publishing, 2008).

668. Martina Thiele, *Medien und Stereotype: Konturen eines Forschungsfeldes* (Bielefeld, Germany: Transcript Verlag, 2015), p. 154.

669. Nick Haslam, "Dehumanization: An Integrative Review," *Personality and Social Psychology Review* 10, no. 3 (2006): 252–64.

670. This statistic relates to the supplementary question that was asked by the Allensbach Institute in Germany but not by Ipsos MORI in the other three countries.

671. Reutter et al., "Perceptions of and Response to Poverty Stigma," p. 306.

672. Reutter et al., p. 306.

673. Ayn Rand, *For the New Intellectual: The Philosophy of Ayn Rand* (London: Random House, 1961), p. 40.

BIBLIOGRAPHY

Alicke, Mark D., and Ethan Zell. "Social Comparison and Envy." In *Envy: Theory and Research*. Edited by Richard H. Smith. Oxford: Oxford University Press, 2008, pp. 73–93.

Allport, Gordon W. *The Nature of Prejudice*. New York: Basic Books, 1979.

Aosved, Allison C., Patricia J. Long, and Emily K. Voller. "Measuring Sexism, Racism, Sexual Prejudice, Ageism, Classism, and Religious Intolerance: The Intolerant Schema Measure." *Journal of Applied Social Psychology* 39, no. 10 (2009): 2321–54.

Arnott, Robert, William Bernstein, and Lillian Wu. "The Rich Get Poorer: The Myth of Dynastic Wealth." *Cato Journal* 35, no. 3 (2015): 447–85.

Beznoska, Martin, and Tobias Hentze. "Die Verteilung der Steuerlast in Deutschland." *IW-Trends* 1 (2017): 99–116.

Bleeker-Dohmen, Roelf. *Der öffentliche Verteilungskampf: Eine Medieninhaltsanalyse der Vermögensteuerdebatten zwischen 1995 und 2003*. Berlin: Logos Verlag, 2006.

Böwing-Schmalenbrock, Melanie. *Wege zum Reichtum: Die Bedeutung von Erbschaften, Erwerbstätigkeit und Persönlichkeit für die Entstehung von Reichtum*. Wiesbaden: Verlag für Sozialwissenschaften, 2012.

Brecht, Bertolt. "Alfabet." In *The Collected Poems of Bertolt Brecht*. Translated by David Constantine and Tom Kuhn. New York: Liveright, 2018.

Brock, Bastian, and Nick Haslam. "Psychological Essentialism and Attention Allocation: Preferences for Stereotype-Consistent Versus Stereotype-Inconsistent Information." *Journal of Social Psychology* 147, no. 5 (2007): 531–41.

Brown, Rupert, and Hanna Zagefka. "Ingroup Affiliations and Prejudice." In *On the Nature of Prejudice: Fifty Years after Allport*. Edited by John F. Dovidio, Peter Glick, and Laurie A. Rudman. Malden, MA: Blackwell Publishing, 2005, pp. 54–70.

Brown, Rupert. *Prejudice: Its Social Psychology*, 2nd ed. Chichester, UK: Wiley-Blackwell, 2010.

Bullock, Heather E., Karen Fraser Wyche, and Wendy R. Williams. "Media Images of the Poor." *Journal of Social Issues* 57, no. 2 (2001): 229–46.

Bultmann, Daniel. *Kambodscha unter den Roten Khmer: Die Erschaffung des perfekten Sozialisten*. Paderborn: Ferdinand Schöningh, 2017.

Christopher, Andrew N., Ryan D. Morgan, Pam Marek, Jordan D. Troisi, Jason R. Jones, and David F. Reinhart. "Affluence Cues and First Impressions: Does It Matter How the Affluence Was Acquired?" *Journal of Economic Psychology* 26, no. 2 (2005): 187–200.

Cikara, Mina, and Susan T. Fiske. "Stereotypes and Schadenfreude: Affective and Physiological Markers of Pleasure at Outgroup Misfortunes." *Social Psychological and Personality Science* 3, no. 1 (2012): 63–71.

Cohen-Charash, Yochi, and Elliott Larson. "What Is the Nature of Envy?" In *Envy at Work and in Organizations*. Edited by Richard H. Smith, Ugo Merlone, and Michelle K. Duffy. Oxford: Oxford University Press, 2017, pp. 1–38.

Colbow, Alexander J., Erin Cannella, Walter Vispoel, Carrie A. Morris, Charles Cederberg, Mandy Conrad, Alexander J. Rice, and William M. Liu. "Development of the Classism Attitudinal Profile (CAP)." *Journal of Counseling Psychology* 63, no. 5 (2016): 571–85.

Collange, Julie, Susan T. Fiske, and Rasyid Sanitioso. "Maintaining a Positive Self-Image by Stereotyping Others: Self-Threat and the Stereotype Content Model." *Social Cognition* 27, no. 1 (2009): 138–49.

Corneo, Giacomo, and Hans Peter Grüner. "Individual Preferences for Political Redistribution." *Journal of Public Economics* 83, no. 1 (2002): 83–107.

Courtois, Stéphane. "Introduction: The Crimes of Communism." In *The Black Book of Communism: Crimes, Terror, Repression*. Edited by Stéphane Courtois, Nicholas Werth, Jean-Louis Panné, Andrzej Paczkowski, Karel Bartosek, and Jean-Louis Margolin. Translated by Jonathan Murphy and Mark Kramer. Cambridge, MA: Harvard University Press, 1999, pp. 1–32.

Cuddy, Amy J. C., Peter Glick, and Susan T. Fiske. "The BIAS Map: Behaviors from Intergroup Affect and Stereotypes." *Journal of Personality and Social Psychology* 92, no. 4 (2007): 631–48.

Cushman, Thomas. "Intellectuals and Resentment toward Capitalism." *Society* 49, no. 3 (2012): 247–55.

D'Arms, Justin, and Alison Duncan Kerr. "Envy in the Philosophical Tradition." In *Envy: Theory and Research*. Edited by Richard H. Smith. Oxford: Oxford University Press, 2008, pp. 39–59.

Davis, Earl E. *Attitude Change: A Review and Bibliography of Selected Research*. Paris: Unesco, 1964.

Degner, Juliana, and Dirk Wentura. "Messung von Vorurteilen." In *Stereotype, Vorurteile und soziale Diskriminierung: Theorien, Befunde und Interventionen*. Edited by Lars-Eric Petersen and Bernd Six. Weinheim: Beltz Verlag, 2008, pp. 149–62.

Della Fave, L. Richard. "The Meek Shall Not Inherit the Earth: Self-Evaluation and the Legitimacy of Stratification." *American Sociological Review* 45, no. 6 (1980): 955–71.

Delsol, Jean-Philippe, Nicolas Lecaussin, and Emmanuel Martin, eds. *Anti-Piketty: Capital for the 21st Century*. Washington: Cato Institute, 2017.

Dickinson, Julie, and Nicholas Emler. "Developing Ideas about Distribution of Wealth." In *Economic Socialization: The Economic Beliefs and Behaviours of Young People*. Edited by Peter Lunt and Adrian Furnham. Cheltenham, UK; Brookfield, VT: Edward Elgar, 1996, pp. 47–68.

Dittmar, Helga. "Perceived Material Wealth and First Impressions." *British Journal of Social Psychology* 31, no. 4 (1992): 379–91.

Dovidio, John F., Peter Glick, and Laurie A. Rudman. *On the Nature of Prejudice. Fifty Years after Allport*. Malden, MA: Blackwell Publishing, 2005.

Dovidio, John F., Miles Hewstone, Peter Glick, and Victoria M. Esses. "Prejudice, Stereotyping and Discrimination: Theoretical and Empirical Overview." In *The SAGE Handbook of Prejudice, Stereotyping and Discrimination*. Edited by John F. Dovidio, Miles Hewstone, Peter Glick, and Victoria M. Esses. Los Angeles: Sage, 2010, pp. 3–28.

———, eds. *The SAGE Handbook of Prejudice, Stereotyping and Discrimination*. Los Angeles: Sage, 2010.

Drumont, Édouard. *La France Juive*. In *The French Right: From de Maistre to Maurras*. Edited by J. S. McClellan. London: Jonathan Cape, 1970.

Eagly, Alice H., and Amanda B. Diekman. "What Is the Problem? Prejudice as an Attitude-in-Context." In *On the Nature of Prejudice: Fifty Years after Allport*. Edited by John F. Dovidio, Peter Glick, and Laurie A. Rudman. Malden, MA: Blackwell Publishing, 2005, pp. 19–35.

Eckes, Thomas. "Messung von Stereotypen." In *Stereotype, Vorurteile und soziale Diskriminierung: Theorien, Befunde und Interventionen*. Edited by Lars-Eric Petersen and Bernd Six. Weinheim: Beltz Verlag, 2008, pp. 97–110.

Estel, Bernd. *Soziale Vorurteile und soziale Urteile: Kritik und wissenssoziologische Grundlegung der Vorurteilsforschung*. Opladen: Westdeutscher Verlag, 1983.

Feather, N. T. "Attitudes towards the High Achiever: The Fall of the Tall Poppy." *Australian Journal of Psychology* 41, no. 3 (1989): 239–67.

Fiske, Susan T. "Divided by Status: Upward Envy and Downward Scorn." *Proceedings of the American Philosophical Society* 157, no. 3.

———. "Envy Up, Scorn Down: How Comparison Divides Us." *American Psychologist* 65, no. 8 (2010): 698–706.

————. *Envy Up, Scorn Down: How Status Divides Us*. New York: Russell Sage Foundation, 2011.

————. "Social Cognition and the Normality of Prejudgment." In *On the Nature of Prejudice: Fifty Years after Allport*. Edited by John F. Dovidio, Peter Glick, and Laurie A. Rudman. Malden, MA: Blackwell Publishing, 2005, pp. 36–53.

Fiske, Susan T., Amy J. C. Cuddy, Peter Glick, and Jun Xu. "A Model of (Often Mixed) Stereotype Content: Competence and Warmth Respectively Follow from Perceived Status and Competition." *Journal of Personality and Social Psychology* 82, no. 6 (2002): 878–902.

Fiske, Susan T., and Hazel Rose Markus, eds. *Facing Social Class: How Societal Rank Influences Interaction*. New York: Russell Sage Foundation, 2012.

Forgas, Joseph P., Susan L. Morris, and Adrian Furnham. "Lay Explanations of Wealth: Attributions for Economic Success." *Journal of Applied Social Psychology* 12, no. 5 (1982): 381–97.

Foster, George M. "The Anatomy of Envy: A Study in Symbolic Behavior." *University of Chicago Press Journals* 13, no. 2 (1972): 165–202.

Franco, Francesca M., and Anne Maass. "Intentional Control over Prejudice: When the Choice of the Measure Matters." *European Journal of Social Psychology* 29, no. 4 (1999): 469–77.

Frank, Robert. *Richistan: Eine Reise durch die Welt der Megareichen*. Frankfurt: Fischer Taschenbuchverlag, 2009.

Furnham, Adrian. "Attributions for Affluence." *Personality and Individual Differences* 4, no. 1 (1983): 31–40.

————. *The New Psychology of Money*. London: Routledge, 2014.

Furnham, Adrian, and Michael Bond. "Hong Kong Chinese Explanations for Wealth." *Journal of Economic Psychology* 7, no. 4 (1986): 447–60.

Gaertner, Samuel, L., and John F. Dovidio. "Categorization, Recategorization, and Intergroup Bias." In *On the Nature of Prejudice: Fifty Years after Allport*. Edited by John F. Dovidio, Peter Glick, and Laurie A. Rudman. Malden, MA: Blackwell Publishing, 2005, pp. 71–88.

Gallup News Service. "Have and Have-Nots: Perceptions of Fairness and Opportunity." July 6, 1998.

Gibbons, Frederick X., Camilla Persson Benbow, and Meg Gerrard. "From Top Dog to Bottom Half: Social Comparison Strategies in Response to Poor Performance." *Journal of Personality and Social Psychology* 67, no. 4 (1994): 638–52.

Gilder, George. *Wealth and Poverty: A New Edition for the Twenty-First Century*. Washington: Regnery Publishing, 2012.

Glatzer, Wolfgang, Jens Becker, Roland Bieräugel, Geraldine Hallein-Benze, Oliver Nüchter, and Alfons Schmid. *Reichtum im Urteil der Bevölkerung: Legitimationsprobleme und Spannungspotentiale in Deutschland*. Opladen: Verlag Barbara Budrich, 2009.

Glick, Peter. "Choice of Scapegoats." In *On the Nature of Prejudice. Fifty Years after Allport.* Edited by John F. Dovidio, Peter Glick, and Laurie A. Rudman. Malden, MA: Blackwell Publishing, 2005, pp. 244–61.

Gniechwitz, Susan. "Antisemitismus im Licht der modernen Vorurteils- forschung: Kognitive Grundlagen latenter Vorurteile gegenüber Juden in Deutschland." Berlin: Wissenschaftlicher Verlag Berlin, 2006.

Gorman, Thomas J. "Cross-Class Perceptions of Social Class." *Sociological Spectrum* 20, no. 1 (2000): 93–120.

———. *Growing Up Working Class: Hidden Injuries and the Development of Angry White Men and Women.* Cham, Switz.: Palgrave Macmillan, 2017.

Gregg, Samuel. *Becoming Europe: Economic Decline, Culture, and How America Can Avoid a European Future.* New York: Encounter Books, 2013.

Harris, Christine R., and Nicole E. Henniger. "Envy, Politics, and Age." *Frontiers in Psychology* 4 (2013): 1–5.

Harris, Christine R., and Peter Salovey. "Reflections on Envy." In *Envy: Theory and Research.* Edited by Richard H. Smith. Oxford: Oxford University Press, 2008, pp. 335–56.

Harris, Lasana T., Mina Cikara, and Susan T. Fiske. "Envy, as Predicted by the Stereotype Content Model: A Volatile Ambivalence." In *Envy: Theory and Research.* Edited by Richard H. Smith. Oxford: Oxford University Press, 2008, pp. 133–47.

Haslam, Nick. "Dehumanization: An Integrative Review." *Personality and Social Psychology Review* 10, no. 3 (2006): 252–64.

Haslam, Nick, Brock Bastian, Paul Bain, and Yoshihisa Kashima. "Psycholog- ical Essentialism, Implicit Theories, and Intergroup Relations." *Group Processes & Intergroup Relations* 9, no. 1 (2006): 63–76.

Hill, Sarah E., and David M. Buss. "The Evolutionary Psychology of Envy." In *Envy: Theory and Research.* Edited by Richard H. Smith. Oxford: Oxford University Press, 2008, pp. 60–72.

Hitler, Adolf. *Mein Kampf.* London: Hurst and Blackett, 1939.

Hoffmann, Johannes. *Stereotypen, Vorurteile, Völkerbilder in Ost und West: in Wissenschaft und Unterricht: Eine Bibliographie.* Wiesbaden: Harrassowitz, 1986.

Hoogland, Charles E., Stephen Thielke, and Richard H. Smith. "Envy as an Evolving Episode." In *Envy at Work and in Organizations.* Edited by Richard H. Smith, Ugo Merlone, and Michelle K. Duffy. Oxford: Oxford University Press, 2017, pp. 57–84.

Horwitz, Suzanne R., and John F. Dovidio. "The Rich—Love Them or Hate Them? Divergent Implicit and Explicit Attitudes toward the Wealthy." *Group Processes & Intergroup Relations* 20, no. 1 (2017): 3–31.

Irvine, Ben. *Scapegoated Capitalism.* UK: Oldspeak Publishing, 2016.

Jensen, Barbara, *Reading Classes: On Culture and Classism in America*. Ithaca, NY: ILR Press, 2012.

Jones, Jeffrey M. "Most Americans Do Not Have a Strong Desire to be Rich." Gallup News Service, December 11, 2006.

Jussim, Lee. *Social Perception and Social Reality: Why Accuracy Dominates Bias and Self-Fulfilling Prophecy*. Oxford: Oxford University Press, 2012.

Kahan, Alan S. *Mind vs. Money: The War between Intellectuals and Capitalism*. New Brunswick, NJ: Transaction Publishers, 2010.

Kemper, Andreas, and Heike Weinbach. *Klassismus: Eine Einführung*. 2nd ed. Münster: Unrast-Verlag, 2016.

Kendall, Diana. *Framing Class: Media Representations of Wealth and Poverty in America*. 2nd ed. Lanham, MD: Rowman & Littlefield, 2011.

Kepplinger, Hans Mathias. *Die Mechanismen der Skandalisierung: Warum man den Medien gerade dann nicht vertrauen kann, wenn es darauf ankommt*. Updated and expanded edition. Reinbek: Lau Verlag, 2018.

Kessler, Thomas, and Nicole Syringa Harth. "Die Theorie relativer Deprivation." In *Stereotype, Vorurteile und soziale Diskriminierung: Theorien, Befunde und Interventionen*. Edited by Lars-Eric Petersen and Bernd Six. Weinheim: Beltz Verlag, 2008, pp. 249–58.

Khanna, Naveen, and Annette B. Poulsen. "Managers of Financially Distressed Firms: Villains or Scapegoats?" *Journal of Finance* 50, no. 3 (1995): 919–40.

Kite, Mary E., and Bernard E. Whitley Jr. *Psychology of Prejudice and Discrimination*. 3rd ed. New York: Routledge, 2013.

Klauer, Karl Christoph. "Soziale Kategorisierung und Stereotypisierung." In *Stereotype, Vorurteile und soziale Diskriminierung: Theorien, Befunde und Interventionen*. Edited by Lars-Eric Petersen and Bernd Six. Weinheim: Beltz Verlag, 2008, pp. 23–32.

Kluegel, James R., and Eliot R. Smith. *Beliefs about Inequality: Americans' Views of What Is and What Ought to Be*. New York: Aldine de Gruyter, 1986.

König, René, ed. *Handbuch der Empirischen Sozialforschung*. Book 2. Stuttgart: Ferdinand Enke Verlag, 1969, pp. 912–60.

Kraus, Michael W., Paul K. Piff, and Dacher Keltner. "Social Class, Sense of Control, and Social Explanation." *Journal of Personality and Social Psychology* 97, no. 6 (2009): 992–1004.

Kraus, Michael W., Paul K. Piff, Rodolfo Mendoza-Denton, Michelle L. Rheinschmidt, and Dacher Keltner. "Social Class, Solipsism, and Contextualism: How the Rich Are Different from the Poor." *Psychological Review* 119, no. 3 (2012): 546–72.

Kraus, Michael W., Michelle L. Rheinschmidt, and Paul K. Piff. "The Intersection of Resources and Rank: Signaling Social Class in Face-to-Face Encounters."

In *Facing Social Class: How Societal Rank Influences Interaction.* Edited by Susan T. Fiske and Hazel Rose Markus. New York: Russell Sage Foundation, 2012, pp. 152–71.

Lamont, Michèle. "Above 'People Above'? Status and Worth among White and Black Workers." In *The Cultural Territories of Race: Black and White Boundaries.* Edited by Michèle Lamont. Chicago: University of Chicago Press, 1999, pp. 127–51.

Lamont, Michèle, ed. *The Cultural Territories of Race: Black and White Boundaries.* Chicago: University of Chicago Press, 1999.

Lange, Jens, and Jan Crusius. "Dispositional Envy Revisited: Unraveling the Motivational Dynamics of Benign and Malicious Envy." *Personality and Social Psychology Bulletin* 41, no. 2 (2015): 284–94.

Leach, Colin Wayne. "Envy, Inferiority, and Injustice: Three Bases for Anger about Inequality." In *Envy: Theory and Research.* Edited by Richard H. Smith. Oxford: Oxford University Press, 2008, pp. 94–116.

Lin, Monica H., Virginia S. Y. Kwan, Anne Cheung, and Susan T. Fiske. "Stereotype Content Model Explains Prejudice for an Envied Outgroup: Scale of Anti-Asian American Stereotypes." *Personality and Social Psychology Bulletin* 31, no.1 (2005): 34–47.

Lippmann, Walter. *Public Opinion.* La Vergne, TN: BN Publishing, 2008.

Liu, William Ming. "Introduction to Social Class and Classism in Counseling Psychology." In *The Oxford Handbook of Social Class in Counseling.* Edited by William Ming Liu. Oxford: Oxford University Press, 2013.

———. *Social Class and Classism in the Helping Professions: Research, Theory, and Practice.* Thousand Oaks, CA: Sage, 2011.

Lott, Bernice. "Cognitive and Behavioral Distancing from the Poor." *American Psychologist* 57, no. 2 (2002): 100–110.

———. "The Social Psychology of Class and Classism." *American Psychologist* 67, no. 8 (2012): 650–58.

Loughnan, Stephen, and Nick Haslam. "Animals and Androids: Implicit Associations between Social Categories and Nonhumans." *Psychological Science* 18, no. 2 (2007): 116–21.

Ludwig, Jack. "Is America Divided into 'Haves' and 'Have-Nots'?" Gallup News Service, April 29, 2003.

Lunt, Peter, and Adrian Furnham. *Economic Socialization: The Economic Beliefs of Young People.* Cheltenham, UK; Brookfield, VT: Edward Elgar, 1996.

Meegan, Daniel V. "Zero-Sum Bias: Perceived Competition Despite Unlimited Resources." *Frontiers in Psychology* 1, no. 191 (2010).

Meiser, Thorsten. "Illusorischen Korrelationen." In *Stereotype, Vorurteile und soziale Diskriminierung: Theorien, Befunde und Interventionen.* Edited by Lars-Eric Petersen and Bernd Six. Weinheim: Beltz Verlag, 2008, pp. 53–61.

Mises, Ludwig von. *Human Action.* Indianapolis: Liberty Fund, 2007.

Moore, David W. "Half of Young People Expect to Strike It Rich: But Expectations Fall Rapidly with Age." Gallup News Service, March 11, 2003.

Mora, Gonzalo Fernández de la. *Egalitarian Envy: The Political Foundations of Social Justice.* San Jose, CA: toExcel, 2000.

Mujcic, Redzo, and Andrew J. Oswald. "Is Envy Harmful to a Society's Psychological Health and Wellbeing? A Longitudinal Study of 18,000 Adults." *Social Science & Medicine* 198 (2018): 103–11.

Müller, Hans-Peter. "Soziale Ungleichheit und Ressentiment" ("Social Inequality: The Rich Shape Our Politics"), *Merkur* 58 (2004): 885–94.

Neuhäuser, Christian. *Reichtum als moralisches Problem.* Berlin: Suhrkamp, 2018.

Newport, Frank. "More Americans See Themselves as 'Haves' than 'Have-Nots." Gallup News Service, August 19, 2015.

———. "Partisan Divide on Benefit of Having Rich People Expands." Gallup News Service, June 8, 2018.

Nozick, Robert. "Why Do Intellectuals Oppose Capitalism?" In *Socratic Puzzles.* Cambridge, MA: Harvard University Press, 1997.

Nüchter, Oliver, Roland Bieräugel, Wolfgang Glatzer, and Alfons Schmid. *Der Sozialstaat im Urteil der Bevölkerung.* Opladen: Verlag Barbara Budrich, 2010.

Obermayer, Bastian, and Frederik Obermaier. *The Panama Papers: Breaking the Story of How the Rich & Powerful Hide Their Money.* London: Oneworld Publications, 2016.

Orten, Michael, and Karen Rowlingson. *Public Attitudes to Economic Inequality.* Coventry, UK: Warwick University, 2007.

Palmer, Tom G. "Foreword." In *Anti-Piketty: Capital for the 21st-Century.* Edited by Jean-Phillipe Delsol, Nicolas Lecaussin, and Emmanuel Martin. Washington: Cato Institute, 2017, pp. xi–xvi.

Parker, Kim. "Yes, the Rich Are Different." Pew Research Center, August 2, 2012.

Parrott, W. Gerrod. "The Emotional Experiences of Envy and Jealousy." In *The Psychology of Jealousy and Envy.* Edited by Peter Salovey. New York: Guilford Press, 1991, pp. 3–30.

Parrott, W. Gerrod, and Patricia M. Rodriguez Mosquera. "On the Pleasures and Displeasures of Being Envied." In *Envy: Theory and Research.* Edited by Richard H. Smith. Oxford: Oxford University Press, 2008, pp. 117–32.

Petersen, Lars-Eric. "Vorurteile und Diskriminierung." In *Stereotype, Vorurteile und soziale Diskriminierung: Theorien, Befunde und Interventionen.* Edited by Lars-Eric Petersen and Bernd Six. Weinheim: Beltz Verlag, 2008, pp. 192–99.

Petersen, Lars-Eric, and Hartmut Blank. "Das Paradigma der minimalen Gruppen." In *Stereotype, Vorurteile und soziale Diskriminierung: Theorien, Befunde und Interventionen.* Edited by Lars-Eric Petersen and Bernd Six. Weinheim: Beltz Verlag, 2008, pp. 200–213.

Petersen, Lars-Eric, and Bernd Six, eds. *Stereotype, Vorurteile und soziale Diskriminierung: Theorien, Befunde und Interventionen.* Weinheim: Beltz Verlag, 2008.

Petersen, Thomas. *Der Fragebogen in der Sozialforschung.* Konstanz: UVK Verlagsgesellschaft, 2014.

Pettigrew, Thomas F., and Roel W. Meertens. "Subtle and Blatant Prejudice in Western Europe." *European Journal of Social Psychology* 25, no. 1 (1995): 57–75.

Piketty, Thomas. *Capital in the Twenty-First Century.* Translated by Arthur Goldhammer. Cambridge, MA: Belknap Press, 2014.

Powell, Caitlin A. J., Richard H. Smith, and David Ryan Schurtz. "Schadenfreude Caused by an Envied Person's Pain." In *Envy: Theory and Research.* Edited by Richard H. Smith. Oxford: Oxford University Press, 2008, pp. 148–66.

Rand, Ayn. *For the New Intellectual: The Philosophy of Ayn Rand.* London: Random House, 1961.

Reutter, Linda I., Miriam J. Stewart, Gerry Veenstra, Rhonda Love, Dennis Raphael, and Edward Makwarimba. "'Who Do They Think We Are, Anyway?' Perceptions of and Response to Poverty Stigma." *Qualitative Health Research* 19, no. 3 (2009): 297–311.

Rowlingson, Karen, and Stephen McKay. "What Do the Public Think about the Wealth Gap?" University of Birmingham, 2013.

Różycka-Tran, Joanna, Pawel Boski, and Bogdan Wojciszke. "Belief in a Zero-Sum Game as a Social Axiom: A 37-Nation Study." *Journal of Cross-Cultural Psychology* 46, no. 4 (2015): 525–48.

Różycka-Tran, Joanna, Pawel Jurek, Michal Olech, Jaroslaw Piotrowski, and Magdalena Żemojtel-Piotrowska. "Measurement Invariance of the Belief in a Zero-Sum Game Scale across 36 Countries." *International Journal of Psychology* 54, no. 3 (2017): 406–13.

Rubin, Paul H. "Folk Economics." *Southern Economic Journal* 70, no. 1 (2003): 157–71.

Sachweh, Patrick. *Deutungsmuster sozialer Ungleichheit: Wahrnehmung und Legitimation gesellschaftlicher Privilegierung und Benachteiligung.* Frankfurt: Campus Verlag, 2009.

Salovey, Peter, ed. *The Psychology of Jealousy and Envy.* New York: Guilford Press, 1991.

Schoeck, Helmut. *Envy: A Theory of Social Behavior.* Indianapolis: Liberty Fund, 1966.

Schor, Juliet B. *Born to Buy.* New York: Scribner, 2004.

Schwerhoff, Gerd. "Vom Alltagsverdacht zur Massenverfolgung: Neuere deutsche Forschung zum frühneuzeitlichen Hexenwesen." *Geschichte in Wissenschaft und Unterricht* 46 (1995): 359–80.

Sennett, Richard, and Jonathan Cobb. *The Hidden Injuries of Class.* New York: W. W. Norton, 1972.

Sigelman, Carol K. "Rich Man, Poor Man: Developmental Differences in Attributions and Perceptions." *Journal of Experimental Child Psychology* 113, no. 3 (2012): 415–29.

Singer, Peter. *Famine, Affluence and Morality.* Oxford: Oxford University Press, 2016.

Six-Materna, Iris. "Sexismus." In *Stereotype, Vorurteile und soziale Diskriminierung: Theorien, Befunde und Interventionen.* Edited by Lars-Eric Petersen and Bernd Six. Weinheim: Beltz Verlag, 2008, pp. 121–30.

Smith, Richard H. "Envy and the Sense of Injustice." In *The Psychology of Jealousy and Envy.* Edited by Peter Salovey. New York: Guilford Press, 1991, pp. 79–102.

———, ed. *Envy: Theory and Research.* Oxford: Oxford University Press, 2008.

Smith, Richard H., and Sung Hee Kim. "Introduction." In *Envy: Theory and Research.* Edited by Richard H. Smith. Oxford: Oxford University Press, 2008, pp. 3–14.

Smith, Richard H., Ugo Merlone, and Michelle K. Duffy, eds. *Envy at Work and in Organizations.* Oxford: Oxford University Press, 2017.

Smith, Richard H., W. Gerrod Parrott, Daniel Ozer, and Andrew Moniz. "Subjective Injustice and Inferiority as Predictors of Hostile and Depressive Feelings in Envy." *Personality and Social Psychology Bulletin* 20, no. 6 (1994): 705–11.

Smith, Richard H., Terence J. Turner, Ron Garonzik, Colin W. Leach, Vanessa Urch-Druskat, and Christine M. Weston. "Envy and Schadenfreude." *Personality and Social Psychology Bulletin* 22, no. 2 (1996): 158–68.

Spencer, Bettina, and Emanuele Castano. "Social Class Is Dead: Long Live Social Class! Stereotype Threat among Low Socioeconomic Status Individuals." *Social Justice Research* 20, no. 4 (2007): 418–32.

Staub, Ervin. *The Roots of Evil: The Origins of Genocide and Other Group Violence.* New York: Cambridge University Press, 1989.

Staud, Wieland. *Making Money: 51 Irrtümer, die Sie vermeiden sollten.* Munich: Herbig, 2011.

Steed, Lyndall, and Maxine Symes. "The Role of Perceived Wealth Competence, Wealth Values, and Internal Wealth Locus of Control in Predicting Wealth Creation Behavior." *Journal of Applied Social Psychology* 39, no. 10 (2009): 2525–40.

Sterling, Christopher M., Niels van de Ven, and Richard H. Smith. "The Two Faces of Envy: Studying Benign and Malicious Envy in the Workplace." In *Envy at Work and in Organizations.* Edited by Richard H. Smith, Ugo Merlone, and Michelle K. Duffy. Oxford: Oxford University Press, 2017, pp. 57–84.

Stonecash, Jeffrey M. "Inequality and the American Public: Results of the Fourth Annual Maxwell School Survey Conducted September 2007." Campbell Public Affairs Institute, Syracuse University, New York.

Sznycer, Daniel, Maria Florencia Lopez Seal, Aaron Sell, Julian Lim, Roni Porat, Shaul Shalvi, Eran Halperin, Leda Cosmides, and John Tooby. "Support for Redistribution Is Shaped by Compassion, Envy, and Self-Interest, but Not a Taste of Fairness." *Proceedings of the National Academy of Sciences* 114, no. 31 (2017): 8420–25.

Tesser, Abraham. "Toward a Self-Evaluation Maintenance Model of Social Behavior." *Advances in Experimental Social Psychology* 21 (1988): 181–227.

Thiele, Martina. *Medien und Stereotype: Konturen eines Forschungsfeldes.* Bielefeld: Transcript Verlag, 2015.

Thomas, Tanja. *Deutschstunden: Zur Konstruktion nationaler Identität im Fernsehtalk.* Frankfurt: Campus Verlag, 2003.

UBS/PwC (PricewaterhouseCoopers). "Billionaires: Master Architects of Great Wealth and Lasting Legacies." Billionaires Report, December 2015.

Ven, Niels van de, Marcel Zeelenberg, and Rik Pieters. "Why Envy Outperforms Admiration." *Personality and Social Psychology Bulletin* 37, no. 6 (2011): 784–95.

Weldon, Kathleen. "If I Were a Rich Man: Public Attitudes about Wealth and Taxes." Roper Center Public Opinion Archives, February 2015.

Wenzel, Michael, and Sven Waldzus. "Die Theorie der Selbstkategorisierung." In *Stereotype, Vorurteile und soziale Diskriminierung: Theorien, Befunde und Interventionen.* Edited by Lars-Eric Petersen and Bernd Six. Weinheim: Beltz Verlag, 2008, pp. 231–39.

Wilcox, Clifton W. *Scapegoat: Targeted for Blame.* Denver, CO: Outskirts Press, 2010.

Williams, Joan C. "The Class Culture Gap." In *Facing Social Class: How Societal Rank Influences Interaction.* Edited by Susan T. Fiske and Hazel Rose Markus. New York: Russell Sage Foundation, 2012, pp. 39–57.

Wojciszke, Bogdan, Róża Bazinska, and Marcin Jaworski. "On the Dominance of Moral Categories in Impression Formation." *Personality and Social Psychology Bulletin* 24, no. 12 (1998): 1251–63.

Wolf, Elizabeth Baily, and Peter Glick. "Competent but Cold: The Stereotype Content Model and Envy in Organizations." In *Envy at Work and in Organizations.* Edited by Richard H. Smith, Ugo Merlone, and Michelle K. Duffy. Oxford: Oxford University Press 2017, pp. 143–64.

Wolf, Heinz E. "Soziologie der Vorurteile: Zur methodischen Problematik der Forschung und Theoriebildung." In *Handbuch der Empirischen Sozialforschung.* Band 2. Edited by René König. Stuttgart: Ferdinand Enke Verlag, 1969, pp. 912–60.

Zhang, Weying. *The Logic of the Market: An Insider's View of Chinese Economic Reform.* Washington: Cato Institute, 2015.

Zhou, Fan, and Dengfeng Wang. "Dissociation between Implicit and Explicit Attitudes towards the Rich in a Developing Country: The Case of China." *Social Behavior and Personality* 35, no. 3 (2007): 295–302.

Zick, Andreas, and Beate Küpper. "Rassismus." In *Stereotype, Vorurteile und soziale Diskriminierung: Theorien, Befunde und Interventionen*. Edited by Lars-Eric Petersen and Bernd Six. Weinheim: Beltz Verlag, 2008, pp. 111–20.

Zitelmann, Rainer. *Dare to Be Different and Grow Rich!* London: LID Publishing, 2020.

———. *Hitler: The Policies of Seduction*. Translated by Helmut Bögler. London: London House, 1999.

———. *The Power of Capitalism*. London: LID Publishing, 2018.

———. *Reich werden und bleiben: Ihr Wegweiser zur finanziellen Freiheit*. Munich: Finanzbuch Verlag, 2015.

———. *The Wealth Elite: A Groundbreaking Study of the Psychology of the Super Rich*. London: LID Publishing, 2018.

———. "Zur Begründung des 'Lebensraum'-Motivs in Hitlers Weltanschauung." In *Der Zweite Weltkrieg*. Edited by Wolfgang Michalka. Munich: Seehammer, 1997.

Zizzo, Daniel John. "The Cognitive and Behavioral Economics of Envy." In *Envy: Theory and Research*. Edited by Richard H. Smith. Oxford: Oxford University Press 2008, pp. 190–210.

INDEX

Note: Page numbers followed by "f" or "t" indicate figures and tables, respectively. Page numbers with "n" or "nn" indicate notes.

ability and intelligence
  attitudes about rich people and,
    132–33ff, 132–37, 134f
  British perceptions of rich people,
    242f, 247t, 250t, 255
  French perceptions of rich people, 217t
  German perceptions of rich people,
    153–56, 154f, 156f, 166–68, 166f,
    168–69ff
  U.S. perceptions of rich people, 200t,
    204t, 210t, 212
Adams, Michael, 304
admiration frame, 29
Adorno, Theodor, 6
affirmative action, 16
African Americans
  criticism of wealth by, 98–99
  stereotypes about, 8
ageist prejudice, 18
age and attitudes toward wealth and
    rich people
  British wealth research, 249–51, 250f,
    250t, 267–69, 390
  expectations about wealth and,
    128–29, 128–29tt
  French wealth research, 232–38,
    233–35ff, 237f, 267

German envy research, 171–72,
  179–81, 180f
international comparisons in
  envy research, 266–70, 266f,
  390–91
self-made rich as role models, 215–16,
  266, 267f
U.S. envy research, 203–9, 204t,
  205–9ff
aggression, envy as, 63–67
agreeableness, attitudes on wealth
  and, 139
Alicke, Mark, 56
Allensbach Institute, ix, 132–36, 149–51,
  156, 175–79
Allport, Gordon, 5, 86, 88, 171
All the Money in the World (film), 375–77,
  449nn664–65
ambivalence about wealth
  British research, 240–44
  French research, 218–22, 223–24ff
  international comparisons of social
    envy, 260–64
  United States, 140–46
American Psychological Association
  (APA), 22–23
angry white men, 97

anti-capitalism
    anti-Semitism and, 89
    in France, 118–19
    television talk show comments about,
        353
anti-Semitism, xiii, 16, 85–92
antistatus ethic, in working-class
    culture, 39
Aosved, Allison, 17–18
APA. See American Psychological
    Association (APA)
Ashmore, Richard, 13
Asian Americans, in stereotype content
    model, 46–47
asset levels, in Germany, 121–22
assimilation, 39–41
attitudes in survey research
    implicit associations and, 137–39
    about rich people, 121, 131–37, 132f
    socioeconomic status and, 107
    talk show commentary on rich and
        superrich, 345–55
    about wealth, 123–31
attribution theory, scapegoating and, 86–87
Augstein, Jakob, 339–40
authoritarian personality, 6
avarice frame, 295

bad-apple frame, 31–32
bankers' bonuses, media coverage of,
    308–10, 309f, 396
Basic Instinct (film), 379
Bazinska, Róża, 103, 153–56, 278
Beckmann, Markus, 307
benign envy, 63–67
bias, in classism research, 29–31
blatant prejudice, 15–20
Bloomberg, Michael, 318
blue-collar workers, 24–28
The Bodyguard (film), 379
Bofinger, Peter, 316–17
Brecht, Bertolt, 82–83
Britain. See United Kingdom
Brown, Rupert, 9
Buffett, Warren, 311, 318, 319–20
Bullock, Heather E., 34–36

Capital in the Twenty-First Century (Le capital
    au XXIème siècle) (Piketty), 314–18
capitalist system
    online reader comments about, 359–62
    Panama Papers' framing of, 332

Piketty's analysis of, 314–18
poverty and, 32–36
Casino Royale (film), 378
Castano, Emanuele, 22–23
Center for Public Integrity, 326
charitable donations
    French attitudes about, 221–22, 222f
    German attitudes about, 157–58, 158f,
        188–89, 189f
    media framing of, 318–22
    self-interest as linked to, 169–70, 170f
    U.S. attitudes about, 199–200
children, attitudes about wealth and
    income, 123–26, 123–26ff
Christopher, Andrew N., 138–39
Cikara, Mina, 49, 68
class culture gap, 101
classism research
    compensation theory, 94–104
    downward and upward classism,
        22–28, 385–86
    ethnicity and class prejudices, 22–23
    Germany, 149–51, 150f
    ideology class, 34–36
    media framing of class, 28–36
    as perpetuation of middle-class
        values, 36–41
    United States, 304–5, 395–96
Cobb, Jonathan, 99–100, 104
cognitive distancing, 400
Cohen-Charash, Yochi, 66–67
Colbow, Alexander J., 27
cold and calculating rich stereotype,
    on television, 47–49
collectivist values, envy research and,
    69–72
compensation theory, 93–104
    French envy research, 219–22,
        223–24ff, 231–32
    German envy research, 164
    international comparisons in envy
        research, 268–70, 268t, 272–75
    need to feel superior to the rich, 387–88
    U.S. envy research, 196–97, 196f
competence traits. See also ability and
    intelligence
    in film, 380–83
    in high-status groups, 51–52
    in stereotype content model, 43–47,
        385–86
    wealth as linked to, 93–94, 153–56,
        154f, 156f, 166–68, 166f, 168–69ff

conscientiousness, and attitudes on wealth, 135, 139, 301–2
consensus frame, 29
constructivism, prejudice, stereotypes, and, 10
contextualism, and social outcomes, 107–13
Corneo, Giacomo, 142–46
correlation analysis, and perceptions of wealth, 122
Crusius, Jan, 63–64
cultural classism, 38–41, 53–57, 60–63

Daimler, 300–301, 305–6, 358
Dallas (television show), 31
D'Arms, Justin, 65–67
Davis, Earl E., 5–6
dehumanization, in classism, 50–52
Del Boca, Frances, 13
Della Fave, L. Richard, 99
Deng Xiaoping, 81
Derrick (German television show), 47–49
Der Spiegel (magazine)
    coverage of wealth and rich people in, 290–94, 320
    on Oxfam reports, 310
    Panama Papers coverage in, 332–33
    Paradise Papers coverage in, 340–41
    Piketty's book covered in, 316–17
Deutsche Post, 297
Deutsche Presse-Agentur (DPA), 312
Deutsche Schutzvereinigung für Wertpapierbesitz (DSW), 303–4
Die Another Day (film), 380
Diekman, Amanda B., 15
distributive justice, and economics, 81–82
Dittmar, Helga, 93–94
Doctor Strange (film), 383
domain relevance, in envy research, 54–55
donations. *See* charitable donations
Dovidio, John F., 137–39
downward classism, 23–28, 385–86
DPA. *See* Deutsche Presse-Agentur (DPA)
Drumont, Édouard, 88–89
DSW. *See* Deutsche Schutzvereinigung für Wertpapierbesitz (DSW)

Eagly, Alice H., 15
earnings gap, 295–308, 310–18, 354, 392
economics
    anti-Semitism linked to, 88–92
    distributive justice and, 81–82

envy research and, 400–401
    folk, 79–81
education levels and attitudes towards rich people, 171–72, 182–84, 272–75, 273–75tt, 391
effort
    debate over wealth and success as linked to, 32–41
    international comparisons in envy research, 280–85, 392
    online reader comments about wealth and, 360–62
    public attitudes about, 128–33, 128f, 132–33ff, 165–66ff, 165–69, 168–69ff
    role in poverty, 110–11, 111f
egalitarian values, in envy research, 61–63, 69–72
emotion, envy as, 60–63
employee mindset
    Germany, 156–57
    international comparisons, 280–85
    United Kingdom, 241–44, 244f, 248
    United States, 199–200, 199f, 284, 285f
emulation frame, 29–30
entrepreneurs
    in British envy research, 245–47, 253–55
    distancing from bankers and managers by, 202–3, 304–5
    in French envy research, 236–38
    in German envy research, 132–33, 133f, 146, 153–56, 154f, 165, 166f, 167, 181
    international comparisons in envy research, 275–76, 276t, 279–85, 392
    media criticism of, 305
    personality traits of, 46–49, 139
    in U.S. envy research, 208–9, 284, 284f, 394–95
Envy: A Theory of Social Behaviour (Schoeck), 60–63
envy research, 53–77. *See also* Social Envy Scale
    collectivist values, 69–72
    compensation theory and, 102–4
    denial of, 60–63
    equality and reduction of, 75–77
    in France, 217–22, 223–25ff, 390, 393–94

in Germany, 158, 160–74, 160f,
    163–66ff, 168–70ff, 175f, 176f
of high-status groups, 49–52
injustice perceptions, 57–60
international comparisons in, 259–85
positive aspects of envy, 63–67
schadenfreude, 67–72
social comparison research on envy,
    53–57
tall poppy syndrome, 69–72
television talk show comments about
    envy, 355
in United Kingdom, 239–57, 240f
in United States, 191–213, 193–94ff
wealth redistribution advocacy,
    72–75
zero-sum beliefs and envy, 79–83,
    172–75, 388–89
episodic framing, 35–36
equality
    classism research and, 37–41
    envy research, 61–63, 75–77
    French belief in, 393–94
    interpretive models of, 82–83
    public attitudes about, 136–37, 355
Estel, Bernd, 6–7
ethnicity, prejudice based on, 22–23
evolutionary biology, compensation
    theory perspective, 103–4
executive pay. See managers' salaries
expectations of wealth, 123–31
external circumstances vs. individual
    ability, 105–19. See also structural
    advantage

fairness, and wealth redistribution,
    73–75, 144, 144t
fair pay concept, 36
FAZ. See Frankfurter Allgemeine
    Zeitung (FAZ)
fear, envy's relationship to, 61–63
Feather, Norman T., 69–72
Federation of Family Businesses
    (Germany), 303–4
Fernández de la Mora, Gonzalo, 61–63
Fifty Shades of Grey (film), 379
Fillon, François, 118
film, wealth and rich people in, 363–84.
    See also specific films by name
    characterizations, 380–83, 381–83ff
    competence and moral traits, 380–83
    framing, 377–80, 397–98

gender distribution and professions of
    rich people, 383–84, 384f
greed portrayals, 378
humanity of the rich, 379–80
limits of wealth, 378
list of movies analyzed, 365t
ruthlessness of the rich, 377–78
Fiske, Susan T., 43, 46, 49, 51, 60, 68,
    74–75, 102
folk economics, 79–81
Fonseca, Mossack, 325, 330–31
Foster, George M., 60–63, 79
Framing Class: Media Representations
    of Wealth and Poverty in America
    (Kendall), 28–36
framing the rich. See also media
    representations of wealth
    categories of, 28–36, 294–95, 308–10
    in film, 377–80, 397–98
    media use of, 289–95, 291t, 293t,
        308–10, 309f, 318–22, 394–95
France, viewing the rich from, 215–38
    age-related research, 232–38,
        233–35ff, 237f, 267
    education levels and envy in, 272–75,
        391
    envy levels and perspectives, 217–24,
        220–22ff, 223–25ff, 228t, 390,
        393–94
    gender differences in envy research,
        272
    income levels and views of the rich,
        228–32, 229f
    international comparisons of social
        envy, 259–85
    scapegoating in, 236–38, 238f
    self-made rich as role models, 215–16
    tax policies and wealth in, 228–31,
        229f
    traits linked to rich people, 216–17,
        217t, 220–21ff, 220–22
    wealth attitudes generally, 117–19, 118f
    youth perceptions of the rich, 232–38
    zero-sum beliefs, 222–28, 225–27ff,
        235–38, 235f
Franco, Francesca M., 19–20
Frank, Robert, 25
Frankfurter Allgemeine Zeitung (FAZ), 290,
    299, 302–03, 311, 315–16, 319–21,
    323–24, 333, 341, 423n5
French Antisemitic League, 88
Furnham, Adrian, 115–17

Gadamer, Hans-Georg, 12
Gallup News Service
  benefits of wealth surveys by, 140–46
  poverty surveys, 110–13
  wealth expectation surveys, 126–31,
    127f
  wealth perception surveys, 122
Gates, Bill, xi–xii, 311, 318
gender
  class and, 22–23
  expectations about wealth and,
    127–28, 127f, 128t
  in film portrayals of rich people,
    383–84
  in German envy research, 171–72,
    181–82, 271
  international comparisons in envy
    research and, 271–72, 271t
  opinions on poverty and, 110–13
genocide, and scapegoating, 89–92
Germany, viewing the rich from,
    149–90
  age-related research, 179–81, 180f,
    267, 390
  on charitable donations by the rich,
    157–58, 158f, 188–89, 189f
  education levels and envy in, 171–72,
    182–84
  entrepreneurs admired in, 132–33,
    133–34ff
  on entrepreneurs and executives,
    132–36, 133–34ff
  envy levels and perspectives, 158,
    160–74, 160f, 163–66ff, 168–70ff,
    175f, 176f, 390, 392–93
  on fairness and wealth, 144, 144t
  gender differences in envy research,
    181–82, 271
  immigrant perceptions of the rich in,
    188–90, 440n486
  importance of wealth in, 179–81, 180f
  income levels and social envy, 121–22,
    177–79
  international comparisons of social
    envy, 259–85
  manager salaries and severance
    payments attitudes in, 155–60,
    156f, 165–67, 175–77, 176f, 260–61,
    295–308
  media coverage of wealth and rich
    people, 289–94, 290t, 325–29,
    394–95

politics and envy, 171–72, 184–88,
    185f, 187–89ff, 392–93
post-reunification differences in
    wealth attitudes, 152–53
prejudice in, 113–15, 114t, 149–51,
    150f
reader comments on online media
    outlets, 356–62
scapegoating in, 175–77, 177t, 264–66,
    265f, 388–89
schadenfreude about rich people,
    156–57, 186–88, 187f, 260–61
tax policies and wealth in, 178–79,
    185–88, 186f
television talk show discussions of
    rich people, 345–55
wealth redistribution attitudes,
    113–15, 142–43
zero-sum beliefs, 172–75, 175f, 188f
Getty, J. Paul, 375–77
Getty, John Paul III, 376–77
Gilder, George, 91–92
Giving Pledge campaign, 318–22,
    396–97
Glatzer, Wolfgang, 113
Glick, Peter, 53, 85–88, 90–91
Goebel, Lutz, 304
Goodwin, Sir Fred, x–xi
Göring-Eckardt, Katrin, 301
Gorman, Thomas J., 96–97, 100–101
Great Britain. *See* United Kingdom
The Great Gatsby (film), 379
greed
  attitudes about rich people and,
    132–37
  in film, 378–79
  of managerial elites, 155–57
greedy banker frame, 308–10, 309f
Groener, Christoph, 346
groups who deserve to be rich
  creative people such as actors, artists,
    or musicians, 154, 165, 236, 251,
    254, 275, 276t, 391
  entrepreneurs, 154–55, 165, 178, 181,
    183, 219, 236, 251, 276t
  financial investors, 154–55, 219, 251,
    276t
  heirs, 154, 183, 251, 255, 276t
  lottery winners, 154–55, 165, 178,
    183, 251, 254, 276t
  property investors, 154–55, 181, 219,
    236, 251, 276t

self-employed people, 154, 165, 181,
    183, 236, 251, 255, 276t
senior bankers, 154–55. 219, 236, 251
senior-level managers, 154–55, 219,
    251, 254, 276t
top athletes, 154–55, 181, 219, 236,
    251, 276t
Growing Up Working Class: Hidden Injuries
    and the Development of Angry White
    Men and Women (Gorman), 97
Grüner, Hans Peter, 142–46

halo effect, in comparison theory, 102
Hannibal (film), 380
Hans Böckler Foundation, 297
hard work. See effort
Harrington, Brooke, 338
Harris, Christine, 55, 66–67
Harris, Lasana T., 49, 52
Hart aber fair (Hard but Fair) (German
    television show), 345–46
Hartmann, Michael, 346
Haslam, Nick, 50–52
Hayek, F. A., 107
"hidden injuries" thesis, 100, 104
The Hidden Injuries of Class (Sennett and
    Cobb), 99–100
Hitler, Adolf, xiv, 89–90
Hofreiter, Anton, 303
Hohmann-Dennhardt, Christine, 305–7
Hollande, François, 224–28
Hollywood film industry. See film,
    wealth and rich people in
Holzmann, 358
Hoogland, Charles E., 57–60
Horwitz, Suzanne R., 137–39
Hume, David, 107

Iceland, Panama Papers' effect in, 328
ICIJ. See International Consortium of
    Investigative Journalists (ICIJ)
Ifop survey, 117–19
immigrants
    German perceptions of the rich,
        188–90, 440n486
    prejudice concerning, 17, 149, 150
    implicit associations, 137–39
implicit measurement techniques, social
    desirability bias, 18–20
income levels
    British envy and, 251–55, 254t
    in classism research, 37–41

expectations about wealth linked to,
    128–31
French attitudes about the rich and,
    228–32, 229f
in Germany, 121–22, 177–79
inequality and envy, 58–60, 72–77,
    399–400
international comparisons on envy,
    282–84, 283t
managers' salaries and severance and,
    295–308
perceptions of wealth and, 121–22
self-made role models and, 215–16
tax attitudes and, 140–46
U.S. envy and, 142–43, 142t, 210–12,
    210t, 211f
An Indecent Proposal (film), 370–71, 378,
    383
indignation, envy and, 57–58
individualist explanations for wealth,
    106–17, 108f, 111–13ff, 114t
industriousness. See effort
inequality
    in classism research, 37–41
    envy and, 58–63, 72–77, 399–400
    interpretive models of, 82–83
    media frame using, 295
    Oxfam reports on, 310–14
    Piketty's analysis of, 314–18
    television talk show comments about,
        353–54
    U.S. attitudes about, 142–43, 142t
inferiority beliefs, and envy, 59–60
in-groups, warmth and competence
    ratings for, 44–47
injustice
    envy and perceptions of, 57–60, 65–67
    in French wealth research, 218–22
    in U.S. envy research, 192–94
Institute of Economic Affairs, 311
international comparisons, social envy,
    259–85
    age of survey subjects, 266–70, 266f
    compensation theory, 268–70, 268t,
        272–75
    education levels of survey subjects,
        272–75, 273–74tt, 391
    gender differences, 271–72, 271t
    income levels, 282–84, 283t
    managers' salaries, 260–64, 261t, 269,
        280–85, 282f
    non-enviers vs. enviers, 279–80

personal connections to millionaires, 261–64, 263f, 392, 394–95
role models, 215–16, 267, 267f
scapegoating susceptibility, 264–66, 265f, 389
schadenfreude, 259–61, 274–75, 275t
social envy coefficient, 259–60, 260f, 388–89
Social Envy Scale in, 259–62, 262f, 269–70, 389–90
tax policies, 260–64, 260t
traits and talents of rich people, 276–77tt, 276–78, 277f, 279–80tt
zero-sum beliefs, 268–70, 270t, 273–75
International Consortium of Investigative Journalists (ICIJ), 326, 336–37
intolerance, measurements of, 17–18
The Intouchables (film), 364
Ipsos MORI poll on wealth, 9, 116–19, 147, 191, 215, 403–10
Iron Man (film), 379, 383
Irvine, Ben, 85
Islamophobic stereotypes, 16–17

Jaworski, Marcin, 103, 153–56, 278
Jensen, Barbara, 26, 37–41
Jews, in stereotype content model, 43–47
Jörges, Hans-Ulrich, 297, 309–10
Jussim, Lee, 8, 13–14
justice. *See also* injustice
APA advocacy for, 22–23
envy and perceptions of, 57–60, 65–67
in French wealth research, 218–22
managers' salaries and severance pay and, 298
in U.S. envy research, 192–94

Kant, Immanuel, 65
Keltner, Dacher, 106
Kemper, Andreas, 23
Kendall, Diana, 28–36
Kepplinger, Hans Mathias, 326, 329–30, 335–36, 341–42
kernel of truth theory, 10
Kerr, Alison Duncan, 65–67
Khmer Rouge, xiv
Kim, Sung Hee, 57
Kingsman: The Secret Service (film), 378
The King's Speech (film), 364
Kistler, Marco, 299–300

Kite, Mary E., 12
Kluegel, James R., 107–13
Knight, Chris, x–xi
knowledge, prejudice and, 4
Knuppertz, Alexander, 345
Krämer, Peter, 320
Kraus, Michael W., 106
Kühnert, Kevin, 346

Lamont, Michèle, 97–101
Lange, Jens, 63–64
language
prejudicial and stereotypical, 10–12
in working-class culture, 39–41
Larson, Elliott, 66–67
lateral classism, 24
Laumann, Karl-Josef, 298
Lehman Brothers, 308
letterbox companies, references in Panama Papers coverage, 333–36, 334t
liability laws, and managers' salaries and severance, 301–2
life satisfaction, and upward classism, 27–28
Lin, Monica H., 46
Lippmann, Walter, 21, 385
Littlewood, Mark, 311
Liu, William Ming, 23–26, 36–41
Long, Patricia, 17–18
Lott, Bernice, 25–26
lottery winners, 155, 159–60, 165–66, 183–84, 307–8
Loughnan, Stephen, 50
Lucas, George, 318
luck, as success component, 105, 114t, 116, 155. *See also* lottery winners

Maass, Anne, 19–20
Macron, Emmanuel, 118
malicious envy, 63–67
managers' salaries, attitudes about
age-related differences, 181–82
education levels and, 183–84
in France, 228–30
fraud and errors separated from facts, 302–3
in Germany, 155–57, 156f, 165–67, 166f, 175–77, 176f, 260–61
greedy banker frame and, 308–10, 309f
international comparisons of social envy and, 260–64, 261t, 269, 280–85, 282f, 394
media coverage of, 295–308, 296f

online reader comments about, 358–62
television talk show comments about,
    354
in United Kingdom, 241–44
in United States, 202–3, 304–5
Marxist ideology, 37, 107
The Mask of Zorro (film), 377
media representations of wealth,
    289–322. *See also* film, wealth and
    rich people in; online coverage of
    rich people; Panama Papers
classism in, 28–36
cold and calculating rich stereotype,
    47–49
criticism of entrepreneurs and
    investors, 305
framing categories, 28–32
framing negative behavior, 31–36
in Germany, 289–94, 290t, 325–29,
    394–95
Giving Pledge coverage, 319–22, 396–97
greedy banker frame, 308–10, 309f,
    396
on managers' salaries and severance,
    295–308, 296f
Oxfam reports on wealth, 310–14
Paradise Papers, 290–94, 336–43, 397
Piketty's book coverage and, 314–18
television talk show comments about,
    345–55
Medienagentur content analysis
excessive executive pay and severance
    packages, 295–308
German media framing of rich people,
    289–95, 394–95
Giving Pledge coverage, 319–22,
    396–97
Panama Papers coverage, 333–36
Paradise Papers and, 337–43
Piketty's work and, 314–18
Meegan, Daniel V., 79, 83
Meertens, Roel W., 15–17
Mein Kampf (Hitler), 89–90
Mélenchon, Jean-Luc, 119
Merkel, Angela, 303
middle-class values, classism's
    perpetuation of, 36–41
Miller, David, 300
millionaires, international comparisons
    in envy research, 263–64, 263t
minorities, scapegoating of, 87–92,
    175–77, 236–38, 238f

moral traits
    in classism, 94, 153–56, 154f, 360–62
    in film, 380–83
    socioeconomic status and, 99–104
Mossack, Erhard, 326
movies. *See* film, wealth and rich people in
Müller, Hans-Peter, 76–77

National Socialism (Nazism), 89–91
naturalistic perspective, in classism
    research, 37
The Nature of Prejudice (Allport), 4, 86
negative behavior
    class-based stereotypes and, 26–28
    media framing of, 31–36
Neuhäuser, Christian, xi–xii
non-enviers in research surveys
    British, 239–44
    French, 218–22, 226–28
    German, 162
    international comparisons, 260–64,
        279–80, 280t
    U.S., 192–94
nonnormative science, stereotypes and
    prejudice in, 13
Notting Hill (film), 378
Nuix software, 325

Obermaier, Frederik, 325–29
Obermayer, Bastian, 325–29
objectivity, relationship to prejudice, 4–5
occupation-based stereotypes, 21–22
Ocean's Thirteen (film), 378
October Revolution, xiv
offshore companies, in Paradise Papers
    coverage, 337–43, 337t
Once Upon a Time in the West (film),
    366, 377
online coverage of rich people, 345–62
    categories and subcategories, 347–49tt
    comment analysis, 349f
    comment categories and subcategories,
        350–52ff
    reader comments on articles, 356–57tt,
        356–62, 361t, 362f
    television talk show commentary,
        345–55
openness to experience, and attitudes
    on wealth, 139
out-groups, judging, 43–52
    cold and calculating characteristic of
        the rich, 47–49

envy factor, 49–52
  moral traits and, 103–4
  warmth and competence ratings for,
    43–47, 385–86
Oxfam reports on wealth, 310–14

Panama Papers, 323–43
  framing of wealth and rich people by,
    290–94, 323–24, 342–43
  generalizations in, 397
  investigative research behind, 325–29,
    446n588
  legal and illegal activities in, 335–36,
    335f
  Medienagentur content analysis of,
    333–36
  shadiness frame in, 333–34, 334f
  tax avoidance frame in coverage of,
    329–36
The Panama Papers: Breaking the Story of
  How the Rich and Powerful Hide Their
  Money (Obermayer and Obermaier),
  325–29, 446n588
Paradise Papers, 290–94, 336–43, 397
Parrott, W. Gerrod, 54, 57, 64
Paulmann, Malte, 345
perceptions of wealth, 122. See also
  attitudes in survey research
personal connections to millionaires
  British envy research, 243–44, 248
  French envy research, 223, 228, 232
  German opinions and influence of,
    159–60, 160f, 170–74, 184, 189
  international comparisons in
    envy research, 261–64, 263f,
    392, 394–95
  media framing in place of, xiii, 289
  U.S. envy research, 211–13
personal liability, managers' salaries and
  severance, 301–2
Personal Responsibility and Work
  Opportunity Reconciliation Act
  (PRWORA Act), 35–36
Petersen, Lars-Eric, 17
Pettigrew, Thomas F., 15–17
Pew Research Center, 112–13, 113f,
  122–23
philanthropy, 320. See also charitable
  donations
Piëch, Ferdinand, 329
Pieters, Rik, 64–67
Piff, Paul K., 106

Piketty, Thomas, 227, 314–18
politics, attitudes about the rich and
  in France, 224–28
  generally, 58–60, 116–19, 131–37
  in Germany, 171–72, 184–88, 185f,
    187–89ff, 392–93
  influence of the rich in politics, 353
  managers' salaries and severance issue,
    304–5
  online reader comments about, 362
  in United Kingdom, 244–49, 245–47ff,
    247t, 392–93
polling methodology, ix–x
Porsche family, 329
positive thinking, role in success, 33–36
poverty
  Gallup survey on, 110–13
  individualistic explanations for, 110
  invisibility in research, 24–28
  media framing of, 32–33
  middle-class values in research on,
    36–41
  stereotypes of, 34–36
  structural explanations for, 32–36, 110,
    111f
Poverty and Wealth Report (Germany),
  144–46
Powell, Caitlin A. J., 68–69
power of wealth
  film images of, 380
  in Panama Papers, 325–29
  research on, 317–18, 346
The Power of Capitalism (Zitelmann),
  317–18
prejudice
  accuracy of research on, 8–12
  blatant vs. subtle, 15–20
  classism and, 20, 23–28, 423n1
  criteria for, 6–7
  definitions of, 3–8
  in Germany, 113–15, 114t, 149–51, 150f
  history of, xii–xv, 4–8, 21–22, 386–87
  against immigrants, 17, 149, 150
  scapegoating theory and, 86–92
  sexism, 18, 21–22
  toward out-groups, 44–47
  value-free definitions of, 12–15
Pretty Woman (film), 368–70, 379, 383
price-tag frame, 30
professions, in film portrayals of rich
  people, 383–84
Protocols of the Elders of Zion, 89

PRWORA Act. *See* Personal
    Responsibility and Work
    Opportunity Reconciliation Act
    (PRWORA Act)
public opinion. *See* attitudes in survey
    research
Public Opinion (Lippmann), 21, 385
public values effect, of wealth
    redistribution attitudes, 143–44

Quandt, Silvia, 329
Quandt family, 305
Quantum of Solace (film), 378

racial or ethnic prejudice, 16, 18, 21–23
RAF. *See* Red Army Faction (RAF)
Rand, Ayn, 401–2
Rawls, John, 298
*Reading Classes: On Culture and Classism
    in America* (Jensen), 37
Red Army Faction (RAF), 92
redemption of rich people, film
    representations of, 379–80
redistribution of wealth
    British attitudes, 145–46, 145f
    envy as impetus for, 72–75
    French attitudes, 217–22
    German attitudes, 113–15
    television talk show comments
        about, 353
    U.S. attitudes, 141–46, 141t, 144t
*Reichtum als moralisches Problem (Wealth as an
    Ethical Problem)* (Neuhäuser), xi–xii
Reithofer, Norbert, 305
religious intolerance, 18
Richistan (Frank), 25
rich people. *See also* groups who deserve
    to be rich; traits and talents of rich
    people; *individual countries studied*
    acceptability of prejudice against,
        20, 423n1
    in classism research, 24–28
    definitions of, 10–11, 121–23
    history of targeting, 49–52
    implicit associations about, 137–39
    warmth and competence ratings
        for, 43–47
risk-taking, attitudes toward rich
    people's, 169–70
role models, the rich as, 215–16, 267, 267f
*The Roots of Evil: The Origins of Genocide
    and Other Group Violence* (Staub), 91

Rosberg, Nico, 323–24
Rubin, Paul H., 79–81

Sachweh, Patrick, 82, 95–96, 99,
    100–101, 135–37
Salovey, Peter, 55–60, 66–67
scapegoating, 85–92
    in French attitude toward minorities,
        236–38, 238f
    German envy and, 175–77, 177t,
        264–66, 388–89
    international comparisons in envy
        research, 264–66, 265f
    U.S. envy and, 193–94
schadenfreude
    envy and, 67–72
    in Germany, 156–57, 186–88, 187f,
        260–61
    international comparisons of social
        envy and, 259–61, 274–75, 275t
    in United Kingdom, 253–55, 254t
    in United States, 192–94, 211–12, 211f
Schindler's List (film), 379
Schoeck, Helmut, 60–67, 75–76
Schor, Juliet B., 123–26
Schurtz, David Ryan, 68–69
secondary control mechanisms, in
    regulating envy, 56–57
self-categorization theory, 13
self-employment, wealth as linked to,
    181, 275–76
self-esteem, and compensation theory,
    93–104, 387–88
self-interest, charitable donations as
    linked to, 169–70, 170f, 188–89,
    199–200, 221–22
Sennett, Richard, 99–100, 104
SES. *See* socioeconomic status (SES)
severance packages, media framing of,
    295–308, 296f
sexism, 18, 21–22
sexual orientation, 17, 86–87
shadiness frame, 333–34, 334f,
    337–43, 338f
Siemens, 358
Sigelman, Carol K., 93
Simmel, Georg, 77
Singer, Peter, 320–21
slant in media coverage
    bankers' bonuses and, 308–10, 309f
    in framing of wealth and rich people,
        291–94, 292–94tt, 394–95

on manager salaries and severance
payments, 295–308, 296f
Sleeping with the Enemy (film), 379
Smith, Eliot R., 107–13
Smith, Richard H., 57–60, 65–66, 67–69
social comparison research, 53–57
social connections, French success as
linked to, 215–16
social desirability bias, 18–20
social envy coefficient, 259–64, 260f
Social Envy Scale
age-related comparisons using,
259–62, 269–70
British attitudes toward wealth,
239–44, 242f
French envy research, 218–24, 220f, 222f
German envy research, 162–72, 163f
international comparisons using,
259–62, 262f, 269–70, 389–90
U.S. envy research, 191–213, 195f
zero-sum beliefs and, 172–75
social justice. *See* justice
Social Perception and Social Reality (Jussim), 8
socioeconomic status (SES)
attitudes about rich people and, 131–37
class and, 99, 106–13
in comparison research, 94
downward and upward classism, 24–28
in German social envy research, 177–79
implicit associations, 138–39
moral component, 99–104
social outcomes and, 106–13
targeting of, 49–52
wealth perceptions based on, 121–22
Solms, Hermann Otto, 346
sour-grapes frame, 30–31
Spencer, Bettina, 22–23
Spiegel Online, 339
Spinoza, Baruch, 67
Stalin, Joseph, xiv
Staub, Ervin, 91
stereotype content model, 43–47, 385–86
stereotypes
accuracy of research on, 8–12
classism and, 22–28
definitions, 3, 12–15
history of research on, xii–xv, 21–22,
386–87
scapegoating and, 87–92
Stern (German news and current affairs
magazine), 290–94, 297, 299–300,
305, 308, 316, 336

structural advantage
classism based on, 24
as explanation for wealth, 109–10, 109f,
111f, 113–17
poverty due to lack of, 32–36, 110, 111f
wealth acquisition and, 151–52
subjective injustice beliefs, envy and,
59–60
subtle prejudice, 15–20
success, theoretical perspectives, 105–19,
112f
superrich
Giving Pledge and, 318–22
Panama Papers' effect on, 328–31
in Paradise Papers coverage, 338–43
research on, 30
supply and demand, managers' salaries
and severance due to, 307–8
Switzerland, managers' salaries and
severance payments in, 297, 299–300
symbolic racism, 16

"tall poppy syndrome," 69–72
tax avoidance frame
managers' salaries and severance
and, 305
in media representations of wealth,
294–95
in Panama Papers coverage, 329–36
in Paradise Papers coverage, 339–43
television talk show comments about,
353, 355
tax policies
benefits to rich in, 140–46
British envy and, 241, 244, 253,
254t, 255
French envy and, 217–22, 224–31, 229f
German envy and, 178–79, 185–88,
186f
international comparisons of attitudes,
260–64, 260t
U.S. attitudes about wealth and, 201–2
wealth redistribution and, 72–75,
141–46
technology, threat to jobs from, 80–81
Telekom, 358
Telepolis (online medium), 356–62, 357t
television
cold and calculating rich stereotype
on, 47–49
representations of rich people on,
345–55, 397–98

thematic framing, 35–36
Thiele, Martina, 13
Thielke, Stephen, 57–60
Tichys Einblick (online medium),
    356–62, 357t
Titanic (film), 371–73, 379
The Towering Inferno (film), 366–67, 377
traits and talents of rich people
    American perceptions about, 130–32,
        132f
    attitudes in surveys, 138–39
    in British envy, 239–44, 242f
    in film, 377–80
    in French envy, 216–17, 217t,
        220–21ff, 220–22
    in German envy, 155–60, 160f,
        167–68, 168–69ff, 179–81, 184–88
    human nature and, 50–52
    international comparison of survey
        responses, 276–77tt, 276–78, 277f,
        279–80tt, 388–89, 441n490
    moral traits, 94, 99–104, 153–56, 154f,
        360–62, 380–83
    online comments about, 358
    success as linked to, 32–36, 105–19, 112f
    television talk show comments about,
        354–55
    in U.S. envy, 194–96, 195–96ff, 204t,
        210t, 211–12
    wealth acquisition and, 151–52
Trump, Donald, 102

Ungleichland—Wie aus Reichtum Macht
    wird (Land of Inequality—How Wealth
    Becomes Power) (documentary), 346
United Kingdom, viewing the rich from,
    239–57
    age-related research in, 249–51, 250f,
        250t, 267–69, 390
    critique of Furnham's study, 115–17
    education levels and envy in, 391
    employee mindset, 241–44, 244f, 248
    envy levels and perspectives, 239–41,
        240f, 242–44ff, 390, 391
    gender differences in envy, 272
    income levels and envy, 251–55, 254t
    international comparisons of social
        envy, 259–85
    politics and envy in, 244–49, 245–47ff,
        247t, 392–93
    regression analysis of envy in, 243t
    schadenfreude in, 253–55, 254t

tax policies and wealth, 241, 244, 253,
    254t, 255
traits linked to rich people, 239–44,
    242f
U.S. attitudes about wealth compared
    to, 239–44
wealth redistribution attitudes,
    145–46, 145f
zero-sum beliefs, 241–49, 243f, 245f,
    255–57, 256–57ff
United States, viewing the rich from,
    191–213
    age-related research in, 203–9, 204t,
        205–9ff, 267–69
    attitudes about attaining wealth in,
        123–31, 127f
    British attitudes about wealth
        compared to, 239–44
    education levels and envy in, 272–75,
        391
    employee mindset, 199–200, 199f,
        284, 285f
    entrepreneurs in, 208–9, 284,
        284–85ff, 394–95
    envy levels and perspectives, 191–200,
        193–94ff, 203–9, 267–69, 390
    gender differences in envy, 272
    income levels and attitudes about rich
        people, 177–79, 210–12, 210t, 211f
    injustice and wealth, 192–94
    international comparisons of social
        envy, 259–85
    positive attitudes toward the rich,
        212–13
    scapegoating of wealthy in, 193–94
    schadenfreude in, 211–12, 211f
    social class and outcomes research in,
        106–13, 108–9ff, 111–13ff
    tax policies and wealth, 140–46
    traits and talents linked to wealth in,
        194–96, 195–96ff, 204t, 210t
    wealth perception in general, 122–23
    wealth redistribution attitudes,
        141–46, 141t, 144t
    zero-sum beliefs, 197–203, 197f, 200t,
        202–3ff, 207f

valence, in media framing of wealth and
    rich people, 291–94, 291t, 293t,
    333–43, 394–95
value-free definitions, of prejudice and
    stereotypes, 12–15

van de Ven, Niels, 64–67
Volkswagen, 297–98, 300, 302–3, 305–7
Voller, Emily, 17–18
von Mises, Ludwig, 81–82

Wall Street (film), 367–68, 378
Walter-Borjans, Norbert, 301
warmth
    in high-status groups, 49–52
    in stereotype content model, 43–47,
        385–86
wealth. *See* redistribution of wealth; rich
    people
Wealth and Poverty (Gilder), 91–92
Weber, Max, 99
Wehler, Hans-Ulrich, 300
Weiguny, Bettina, 346
Weinbach, Heike, 23
welfare recipients, media images of, 34–36
Whitley, Bernard E., 12
Williams, Joan C., 101–2
Williams, Wendy R., 34–36
willpower, contribution to success, 33–36
Winfrey, Oprah, 30
Winterkorn, Martin, 300
Wojciszke, Bogdan, 103, 153–56, 278
Wolf, Elizabeth Baily, 53
Wolf, Heinz E., 6, 7

The Wolf of Wall Street (film), 373–75, 378
working-class culture, 38–41, 95–104, 388
workload. *See* effort
The World Is Not Enough (film), 378
Wyche, Karen Fraser, 34–36

Zeelenberg, Marcel, 64–67
Zeit Online, 340
Zell, Ethan, 56
zero-sum beliefs, 79–83
    in British envy, 241–49, 243f, 245f,
        255–57, 256–57ff
    in envy research, 55, 79–83, 172–77,
        388–89, 434n316
    in French envy, 222–28, 225–27ff,
        235–38, 235f
    in German envy, 172–75, 175f
    German political affiliation and,
        186–88
    international comparisons in envy
        research, 268–70, 270t, 273–75
    U.S. income levels and, 178–79
    in U.S. envy, 197–203, 197f, 200t,
        202–3ff, 207f
Zetsche, Dieter, 300–301
Ziegler, Jean, 327
Zitelmann, Rainer, 356–62
Zuckerberg, Mark, 318

ABOUT THE AUTHOR

Rainer Zitelmann was born in Frankfurt, Germany, in 1957. He studied history and political science from 1978 to 1983 and was awarded his first doctorate summa cum laude in 1986 with his dissertation *Hitler: The Policies of Seduction.*

In the late 1980s and early 1990s, Zitelmann worked at the Central Institute for Social Science Research at the Free University of Berlin. He became editor in chief of Ullstein-Propyläen-Verlag, at the time Germany's third-largest book publishing group. From 1992 to 2000, he headed various departments at one of Germany's leading premium daily newspapers, *Die Welt.* In 2000, Zitelmann started his own company, Dr. ZitelmannPB GmbH, which is the leading public relations firm for real estate companies in Germany. He sold the company in 2016.

In 2016, Zitelmann received a doctorate in sociology under the mentorship of the wealth researcher Professor Wolfgang Lauterbach at the University of Potsdam. Zitelmann's second dissertation was published as *The Wealth Elite: A Groundbreaking Study of the Psychology of the Super Rich.*

To date, Zitelmann has written and edited 23 books, which have been published worldwide in numerous languages. He writes for prestigious European media such as *Neue Zürcher Zeitung* (Switzerland); *Die Welt, Focus,* and *Frankfurter Allgemeine Zeitung* (Germany); and *The Daily Telegraph* and *City AM* (London). Every Monday, he publishes a column on *Forbes.com.*

Read more about the author at www.rainer-zitelmann.com.

CATO INSTITUTE

Founded in 1977, the Cato Institute is a public policy research foundation dedicated to broadening the parameters of policy debate to allow
consideration of more options that are consistent with the principles of
limited government, individual liberty, and peace. To that end, the Institute strives to achieve greater involvement of the intelligent, concerned
lay public in questions of policy and the proper role of government.

The Institute is named for *Cato's Letters*, libertarian pamphlets that
were widely read in the American Colonies in the early 18th century
and played a major role in laying the philosophical foundation for the
American Revolution.

Despite the achievement of the nation's Founders, today virtually no
aspect of life is free from government encroachment. A pervasive intolerance for individual rights is shown by government's arbitrary intrusions
into private economic transactions and its disregard for civil liberties.
And while freedom around the globe has notably increased in the past
several decades, many countries have moved in the opposite direction,
and most governments still do not respect or safeguard the wide range of
civil and economic liberties.

To address those issues, the Cato Institute undertakes an extensive publications program on the complete spectrum of policy issues.
Books, monographs, and shorter studies are commissioned to examine

the federal budget, Social Security, regulation, military spending, international trade, and myriad other issues. Major policy conferences are held throughout the year, from which papers are published thrice yearly in the *Cato Journal*. The Institute also publishes the quarterly magazine *Regulation*.

In order to maintain its independence, the Cato Institute accepts no government funding. Contributions are received from foundations, corporations, and individuals, and other revenue is generated from the sale of publications. The Institute is a nonprofit, tax-exempt, educational foundation under Section 501(c)3 of the Internal Revenue Code.

CATO INSTITUTE
1000 Massachusetts Avenue NW
Washington, DC 20001
www.cato.org